MAO

7

Story and Art by
Rumiko Takahashi

Characters

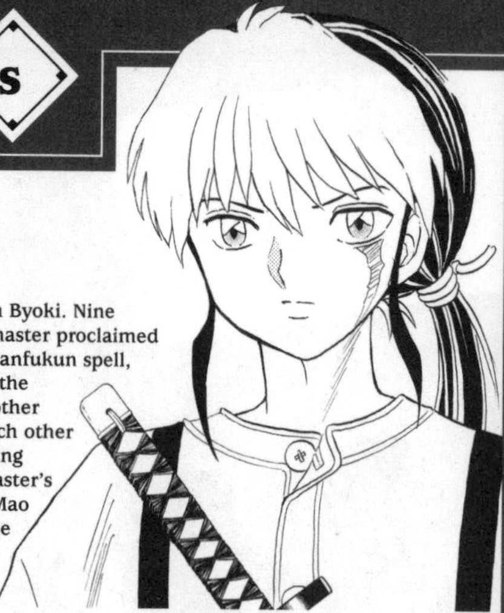

TAISHO ERA

MAO

An exorcist cursed by the cat demon Byoki. Nine hundred years ago, Mao's onmyoji master proclaimed Mao his successor to inherit the Taizanfukun spell, which controls life spans. In reality, the master's intention was to goad the other five trainees into killing Mao and each other until only one survived. In the ensuing melee, Mao might have killed his master's daughter, Sana. For nine centuries, Mao has searched for Byoki to uncover the truth and purge his curse.

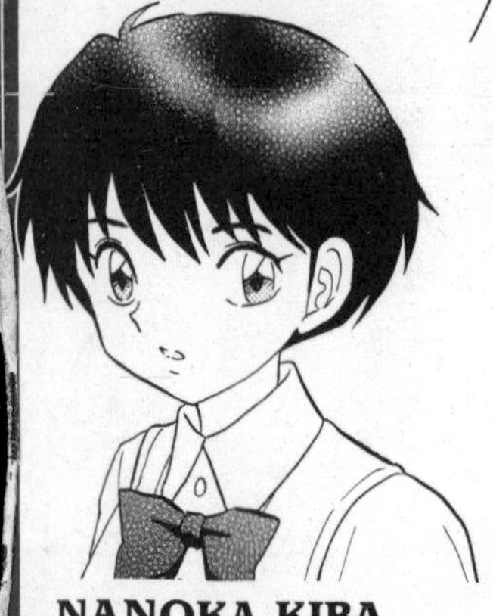

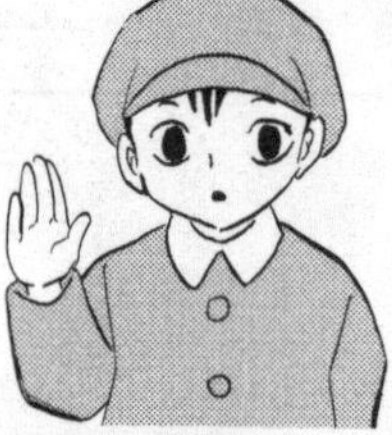

OTOYA

Mao's hard-working shikigami.

NANOKA KIBA

A third-year middle school student living in the present day. As a child, she was involved in a car accident that killed her parents and temporarily thrust her into the Taisho era. There, her body was cursed by Byoki. Nanoka's body, like Mao's, is a potential vessel that Byoki seeks to inhabit.

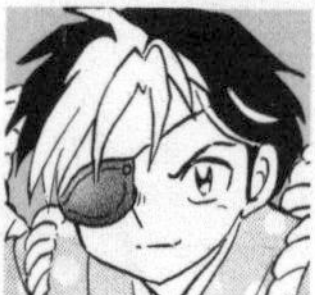

HYAKKA

Mao's senior student apprentice. Wields fire spells.

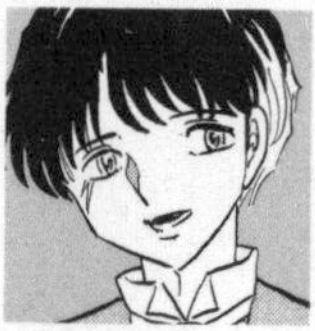

KAMON (KUCHINAWA)

Mao's senior student apprentice. Wields tree spells.

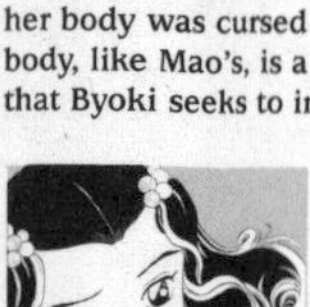

YURAKO

Her true identity might be Sana, the master's daughter. Works for Shiranui.

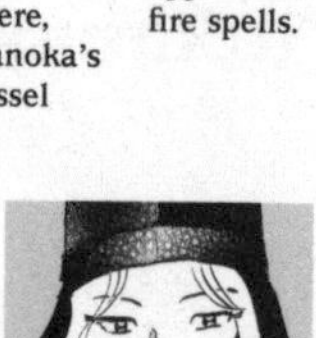

SHIRANUI

Mao's senior student apprentice. Wields water spells. Seeks vengeance on Mao.

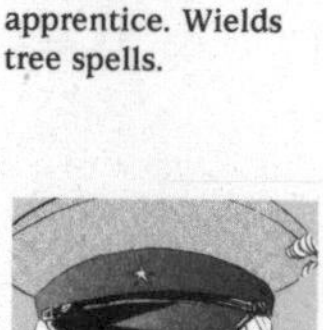

HAKUBI

Mao's senior student apprentice. Wields metal spells. Works for Shiranui.

HEIAN PERIOD

HOUSE OF GOKO

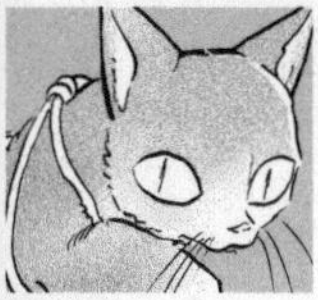

HAIMARU

Sana's beloved cat. Only liked her and Mao.

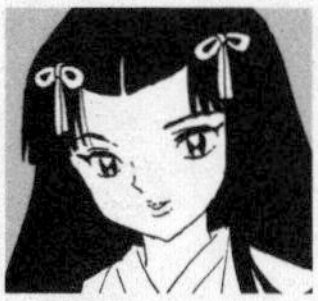

SANA

The master's daughter. Betrothed to Mao by her father. Murdered, possibly by Mao.

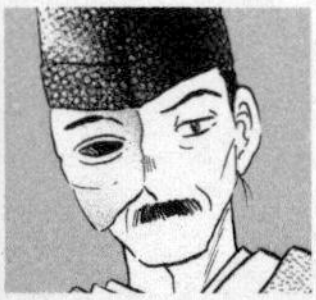

MASTER

The head of the Goko clan and Mao's former master. Wields forbidden spells and attempted to sacrifice Mao for his own ends.

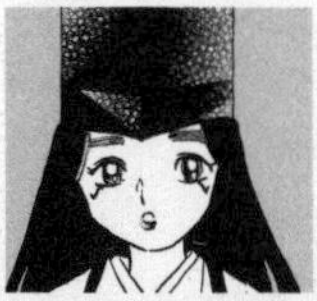

MASAGO

A Goku clan onymoji. The most powerful wielder of water spells.

PRESENT DAY

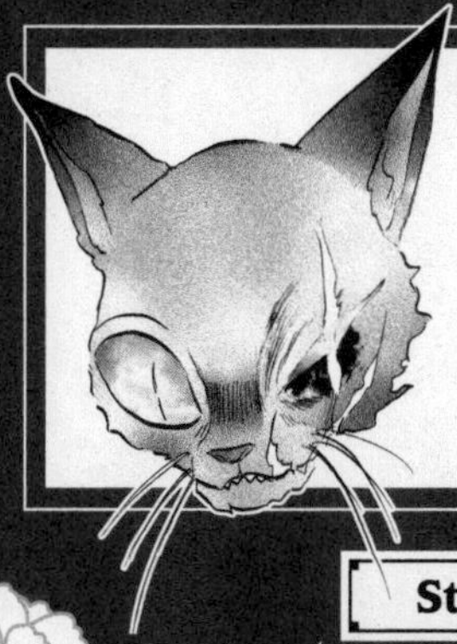

BYOKI

The kodoku cat who cursed Mao and Nanoka. Survives by possessing human bodies. After eating the forbidden scroll containing the Taizanfukun spell, he gained the ability to use it to control life spans.

Story thus far...

When Nanoka Kiba was seven years old, she was orphaned in a violent accident. Now she is a third-year student in middle school. One day she passes the spot where the accident occurred and is miraculously transported to the Taisho era. There she meets an exorcist named Mao. When they realize they have both been cursed by Byoki, a cat demon, they join forces to find him and free themselves. Centuries ago, Mao's master told five of Mao's senior apprentices that he had chosen Mao as his successor. However, they could win the honor for themselves if they killed Mao. None of the five knew who the others were. Now Mao and Nanoka are on a quest to identify these apprentices and find Sana, the woman Mao once loved. Thus far, they've located four of the five apprentices and someone who looks like Sana. When Mao learns that people are spontaneously transforming into dust, a hint from the past leads him to suspect that an exorcist with the power to wield earth spells is behind the murders...

CONTENTS

Chapter 1:
Home for Foundlings

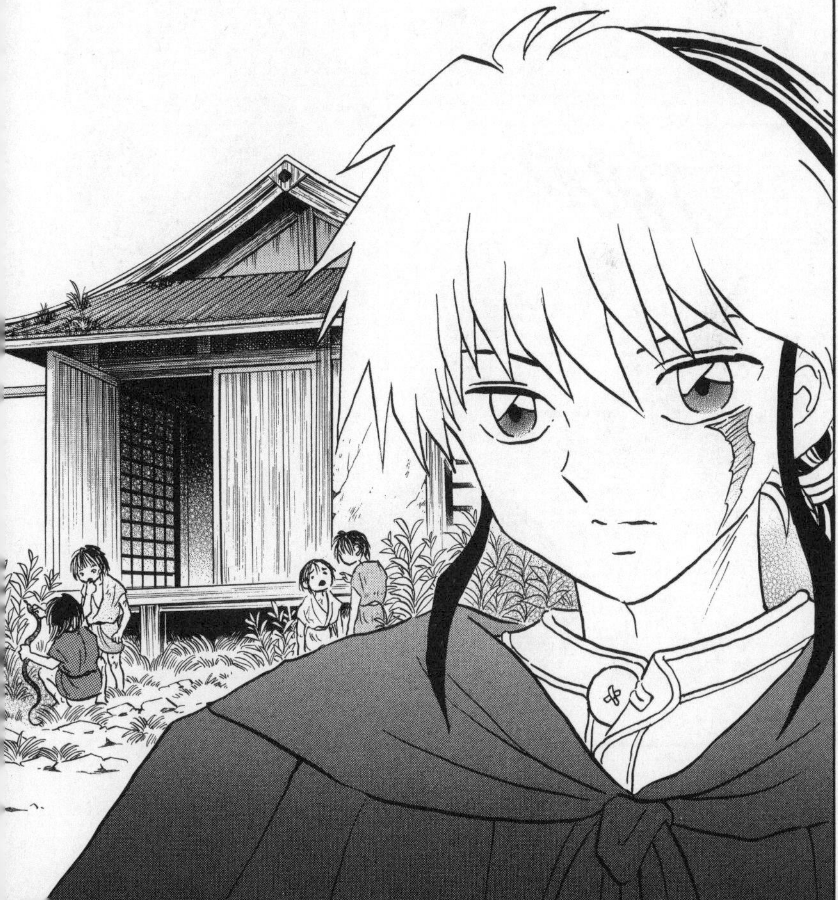

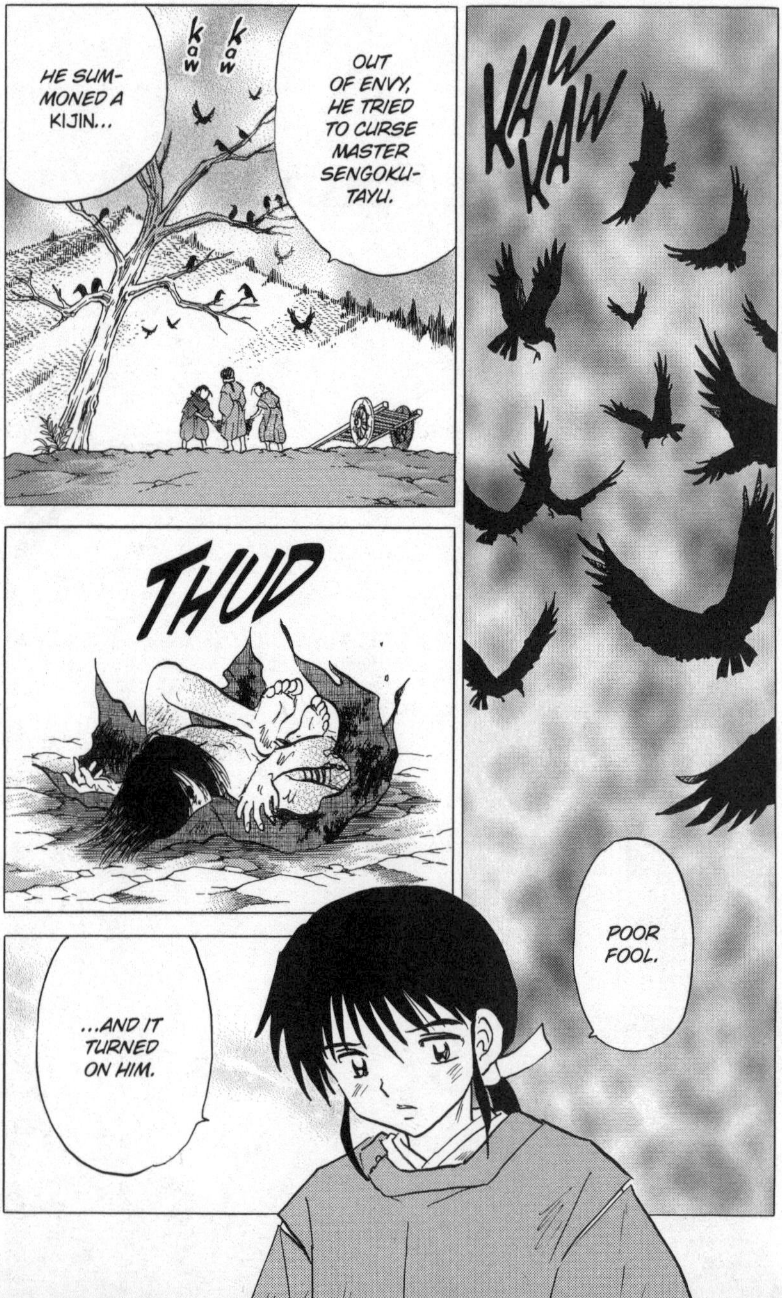
KAW KAW
KAW KAW
POOR FOOL.
OUT OF ENVY, HE TRIED TO CURSE MASTER SENGOKU-TAYU.
kaw kaw
HE SUM-MONED A KIJIN...
THUD
...AND IT TURNED ON HIM.

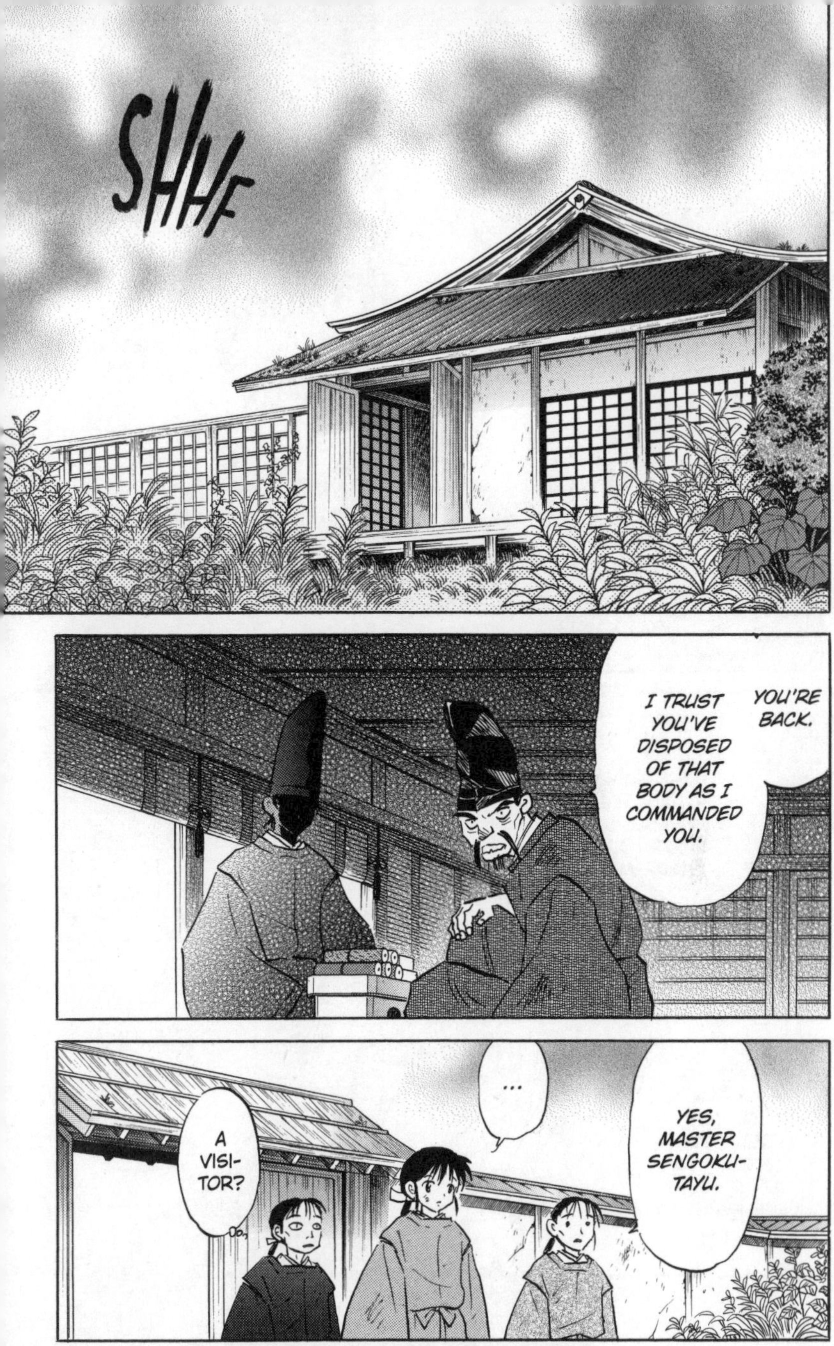
SHHF
YOU'RE BACK.
I TRUST YOU'VE DISPOSED OF THAT BODY AS I COMMANDED YOU.
YES, MASTER SENGOKU-TAYU.
...
A VISI-TOR?

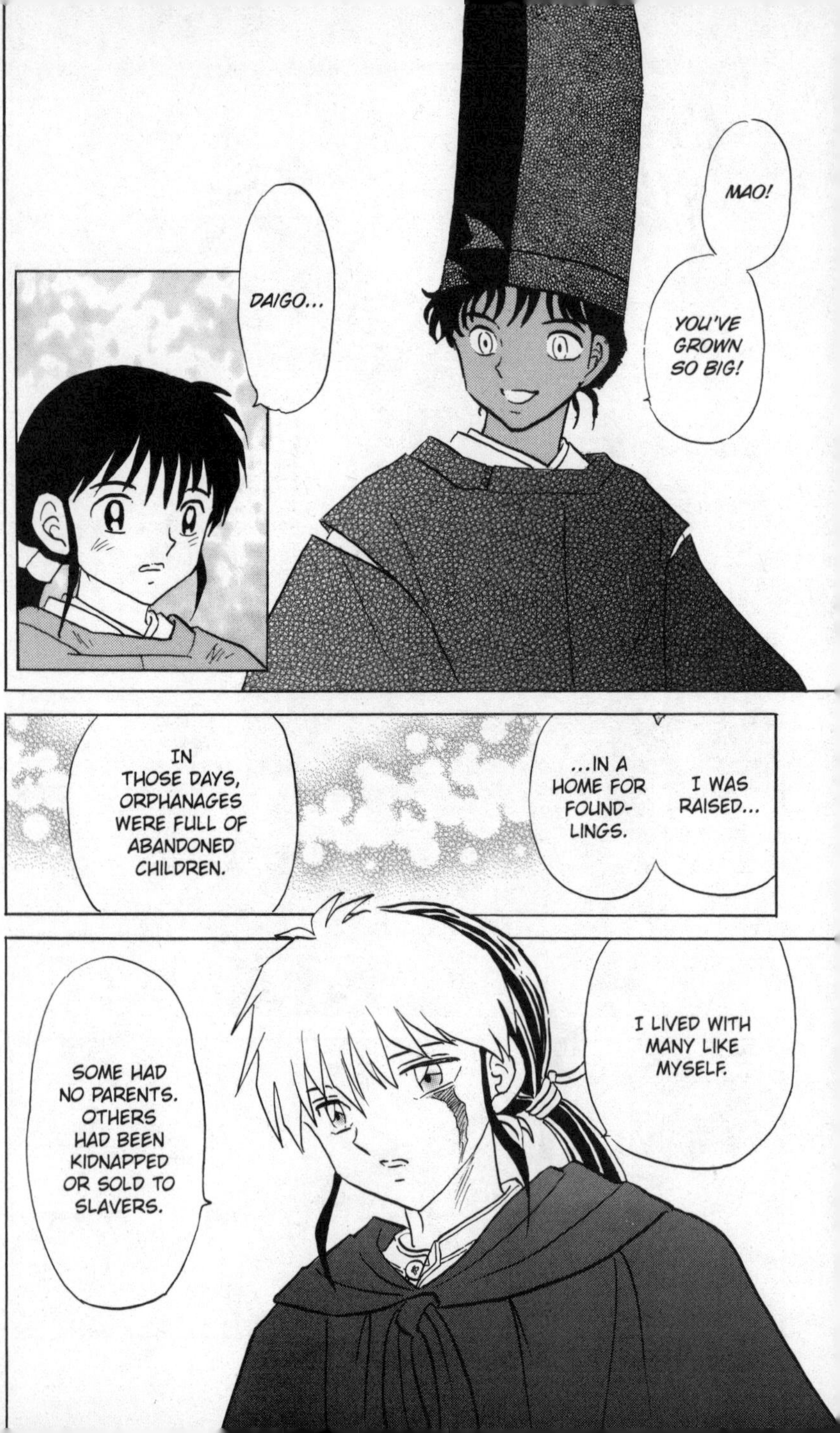
MAO!
YOU'VE GROWN SO BIG!
DAIGO...
I WAS RAISED...
...IN A HOME FOR FOUND-LINGS.
IN THOSE DAYS, ORPHANAGES WERE FULL OF ABANDONED CHILDREN.
I LIVED WITH MANY LIKE MYSELF.
SOME HAD NO PARENTS. OTHERS HAD BEEN KIDNAPPED OR SOLD TO SLAVERS.

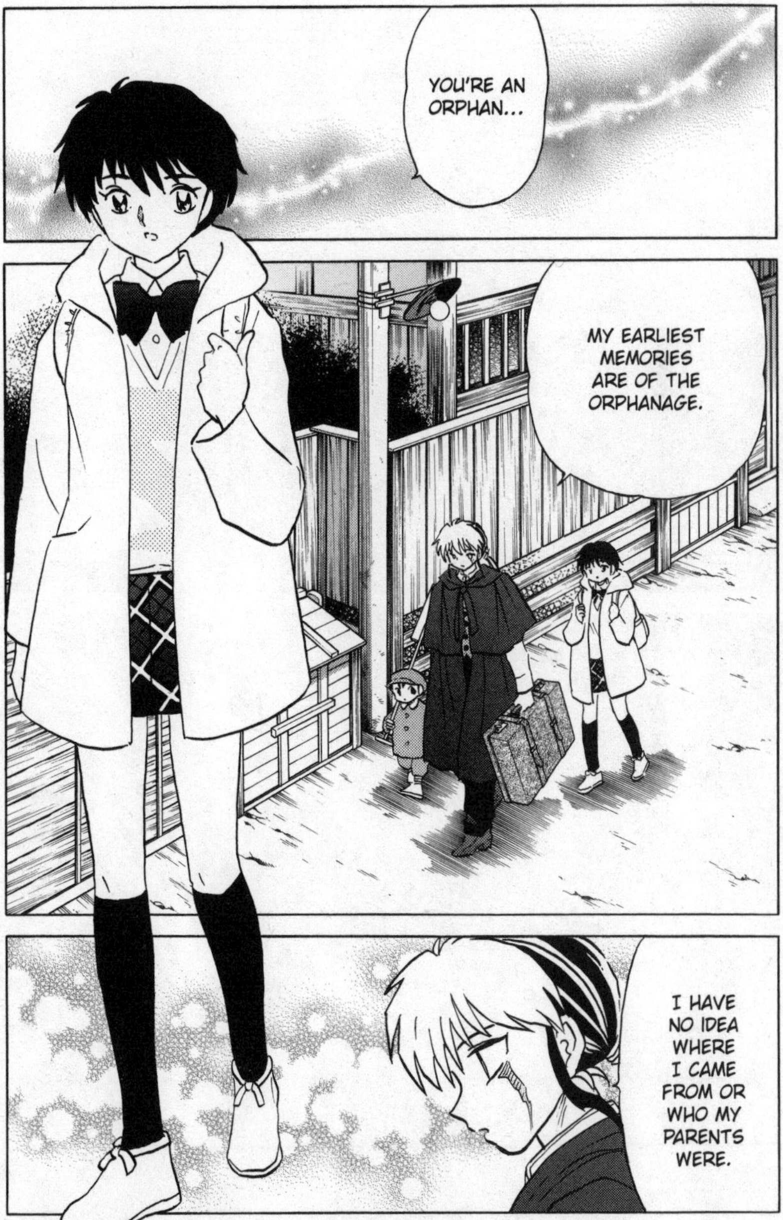
YOU'RE AN ORPHAN...
MY EARLIEST MEMORIES ARE OF THE ORPHANAGE.
I HAVE NO IDEA WHERE I CAME FROM OR WHO MY PARENTS WERE.

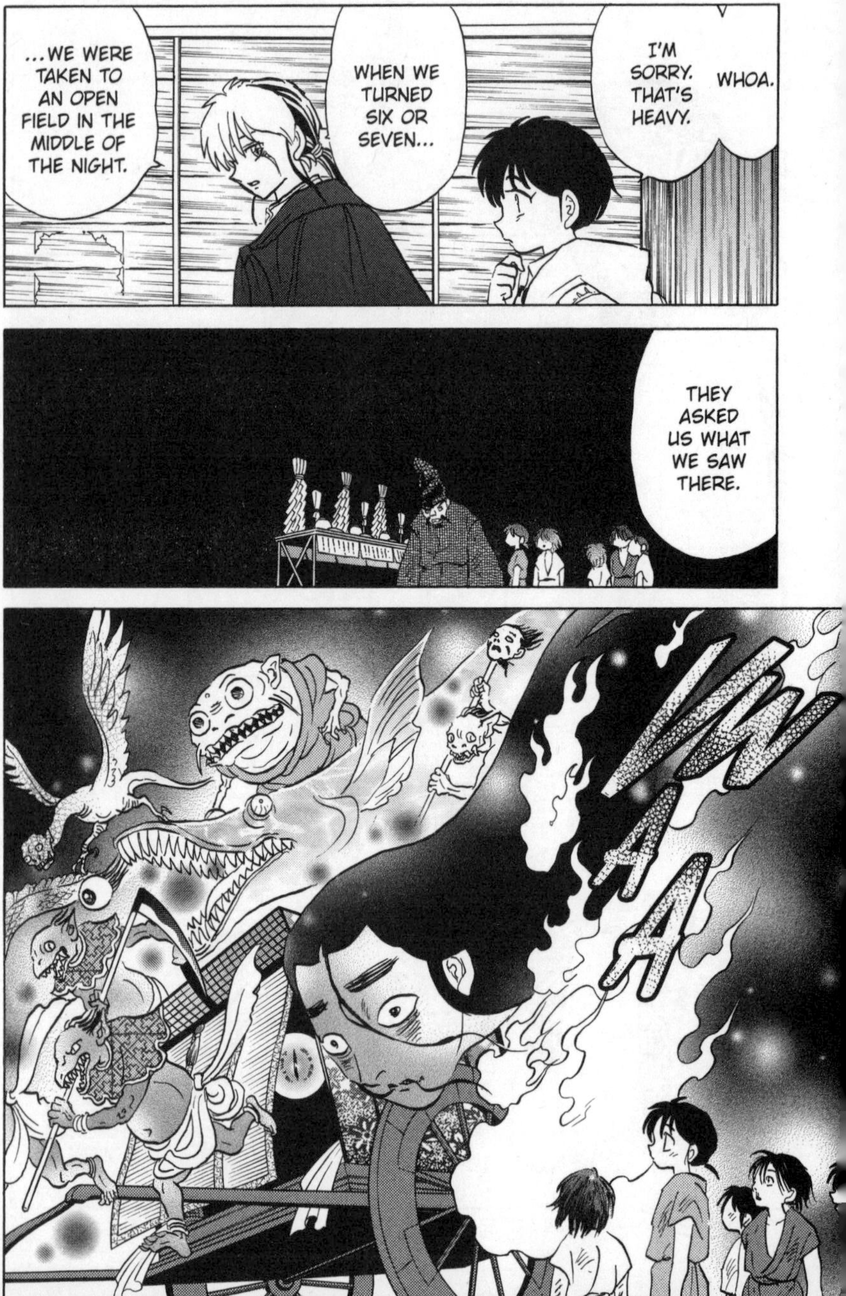
WHOA.
I'M SORRY. THAT'S HEAVY.
WHEN WE TURNED SIX OR SEVEN...
...WE WERE TAKEN TO AN OPEN FIELD IN THE MIDDLE OF THE NIGHT.
THEY ASKED US WHAT WE SAW THERE.
WAAA

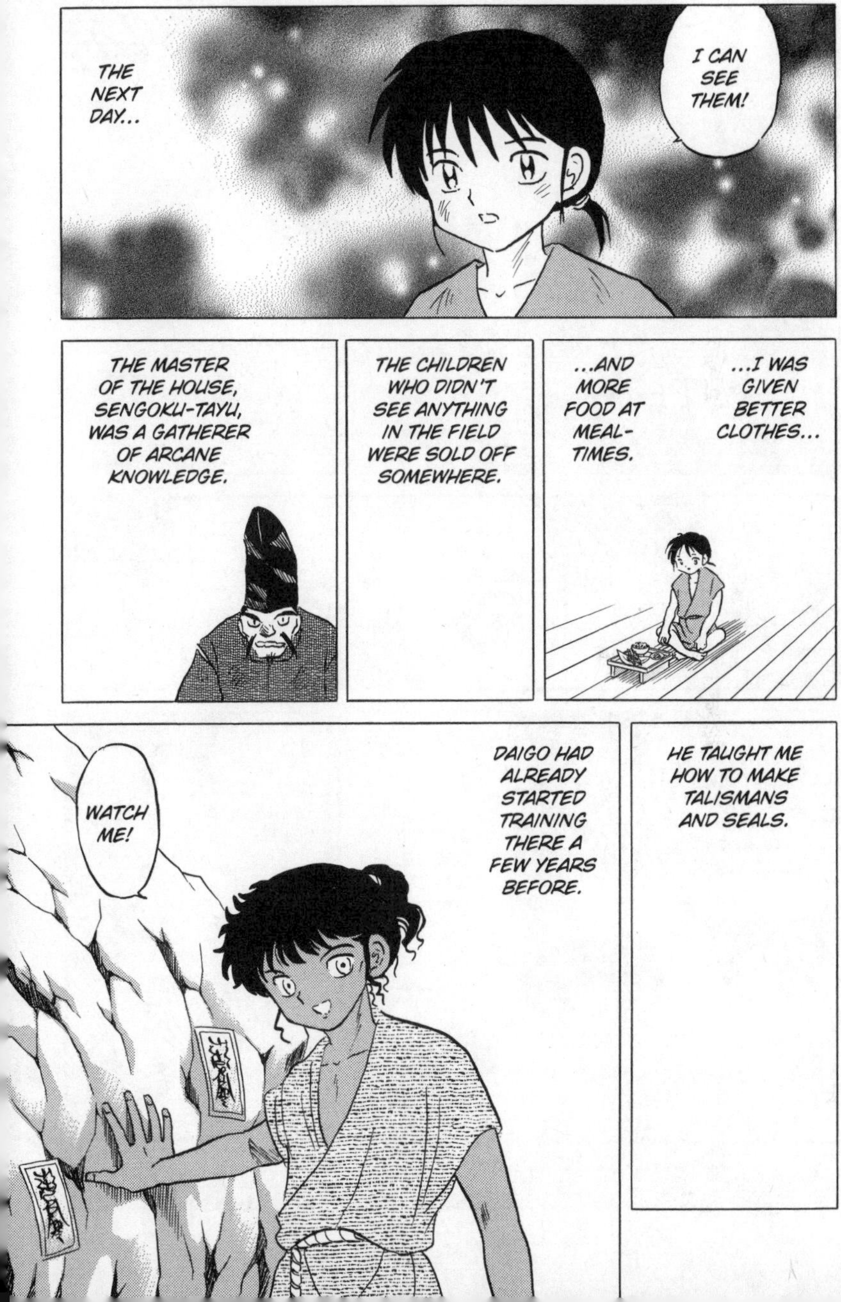
I CAN SEE THEM!
THE NEXT DAY...
...I WAS GIVEN BETTER CLOTHES...
...AND MORE FOOD AT MEAL-TIMES.
THE CHILDREN WHO DIDN'T SEE ANYTHING IN THE FIELD WERE SOLD OFF SOMEWHERE.
THE MASTER OF THE HOUSE, SENGOKU-TAYU, WAS A GATHERER OF ARCANE KNOWLEDGE.
HE TAUGHT ME HOW TO MAKE TALISMANS AND SEALS.
DAIGO HAD ALREADY STARTED TRAINING THERE A FEW YEARS BEFORE.
WATCH ME!

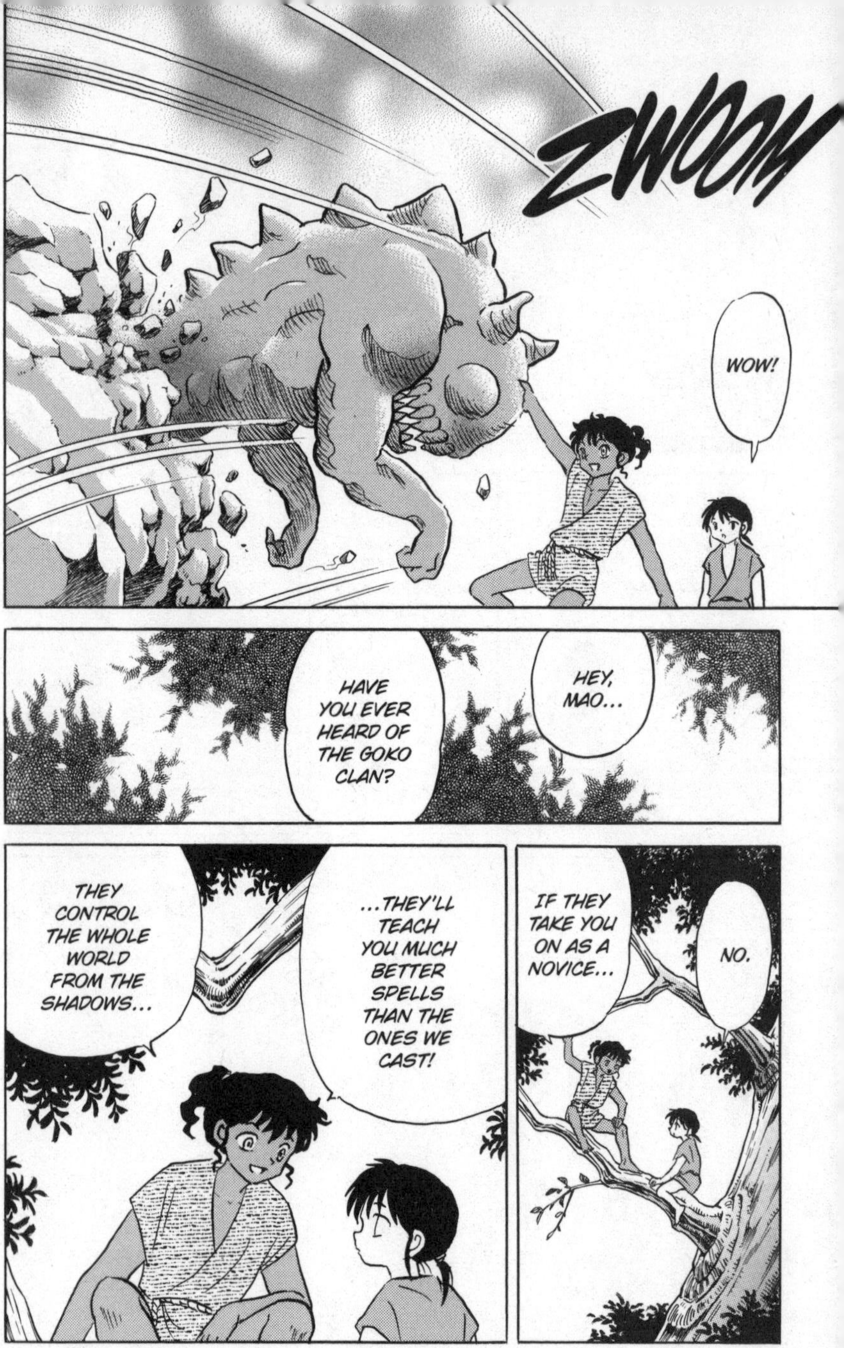
ZWOOM
WOW!
HEY, MAO...
HAVE YOU EVER HEARD OF THE GOKO CLAN?
NO.
IF THEY TAKE YOU ON AS A NOVICE...
...THEY'LL TEACH YOU MUCH BETTER SPELLS THAN THE ONES WE CAST!
THEY CONTROL THE WHOLE WORLD FROM THE SHADOWS...

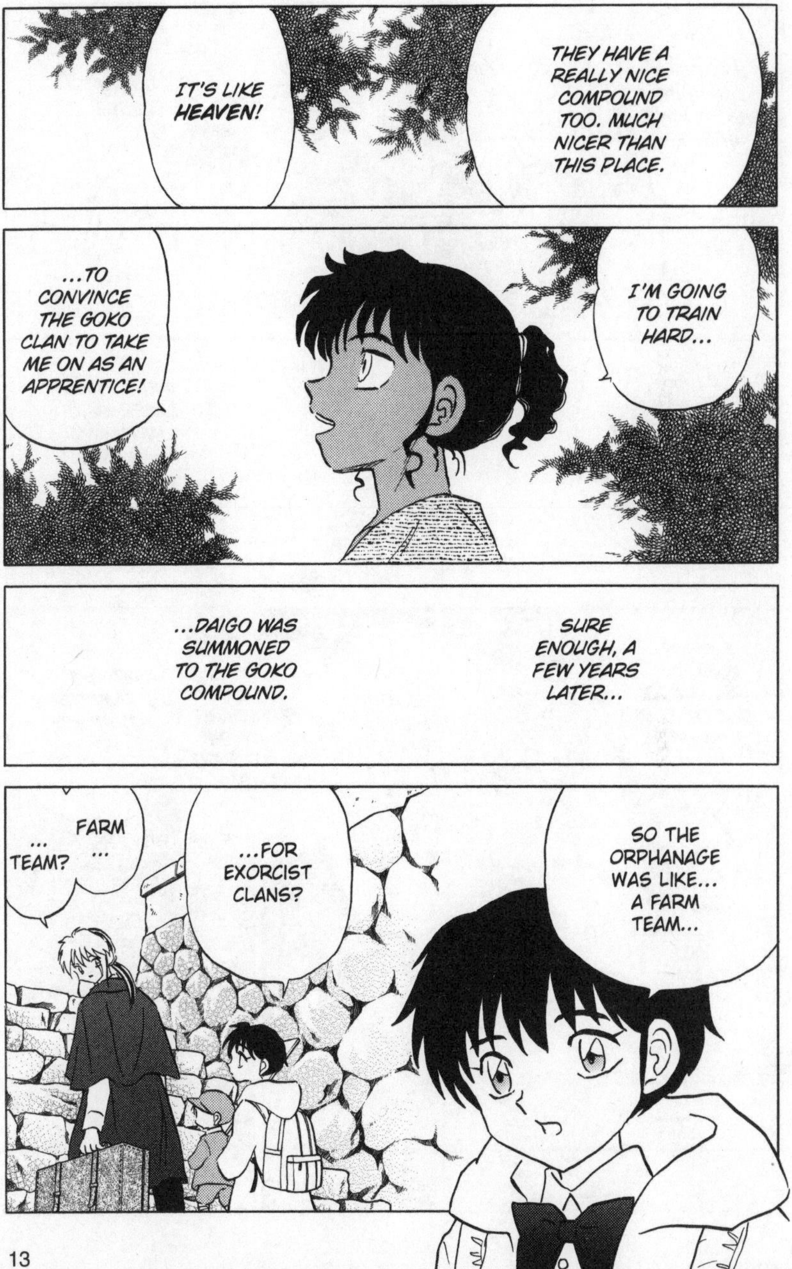
THEY HAVE A REALLY NICE COMPOUND TOO. MUCH NICER THAN THIS PLACE.
IT'S LIKE HEAVEN!
I'M GOING TO TRAIN HARD...
...TO CONVINCE THE GOKO CLAN TO TAKE ME ON AS AN APPRENTICE!
SURE ENOUGH, A FEW YEARS LATER...
...DAIGO WAS SUMMONED TO THE GOKO COMPOUND.
SO THE ORPHANAGE WAS LIKE... A FARM TEAM...
...FOR EXORCIST CLANS?
FARM ...
... TEAM?

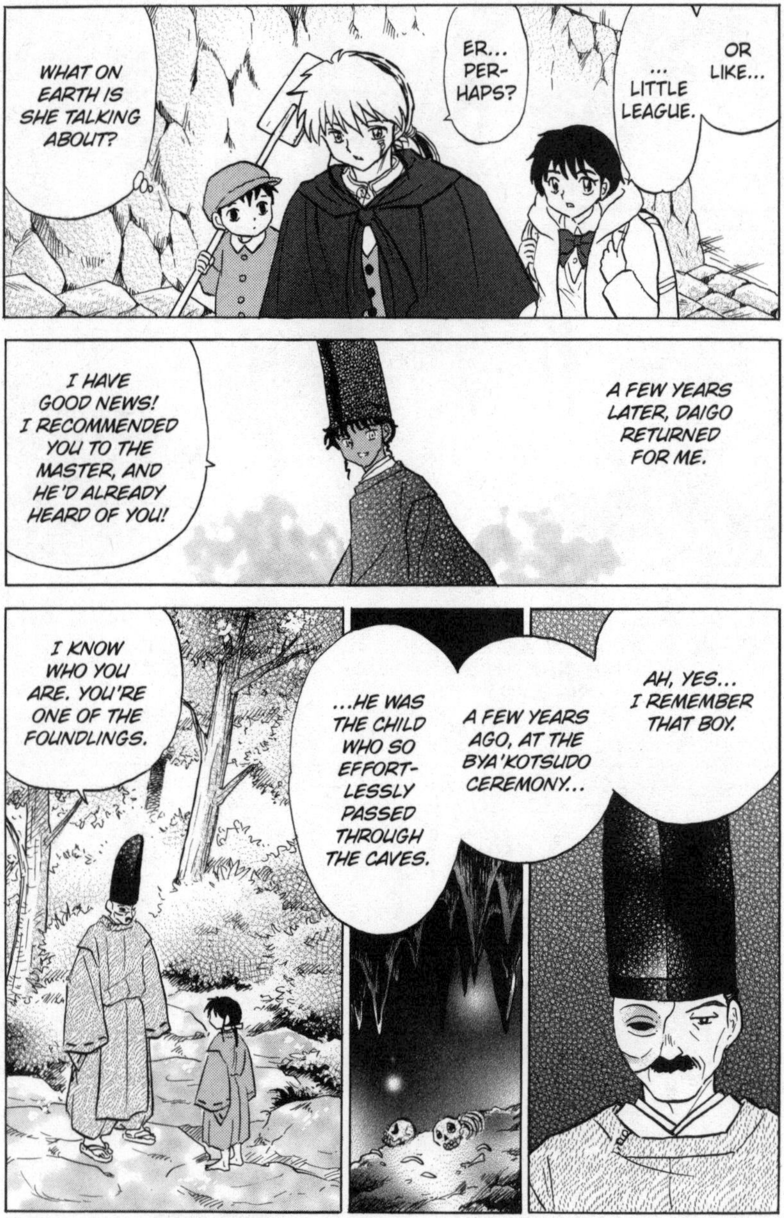
OR LIKE...
... LITTLE LEAGUE.
ER... PER-HAPS?
WHAT ON EARTH IS SHE TALKING ABOUT?
A FEW YEARS LATER, DAIGO RETURNED FOR ME.
I HAVE GOOD NEWS! I RECOMMENDED YOU TO THE MASTER, AND HE'D ALREADY HEARD OF YOU!
AH, YES... I REMEMBER THAT BOY.
A FEW YEARS AGO, AT THE BYA'KOTSUDO CEREMONY...
...HE WAS THE CHILD WHO SO EFFORT-LESSLY PASSED THROUGH THE CAVES.
I KNOW WHO YOU ARE. YOU'RE ONE OF THE FOUNDLINGS.

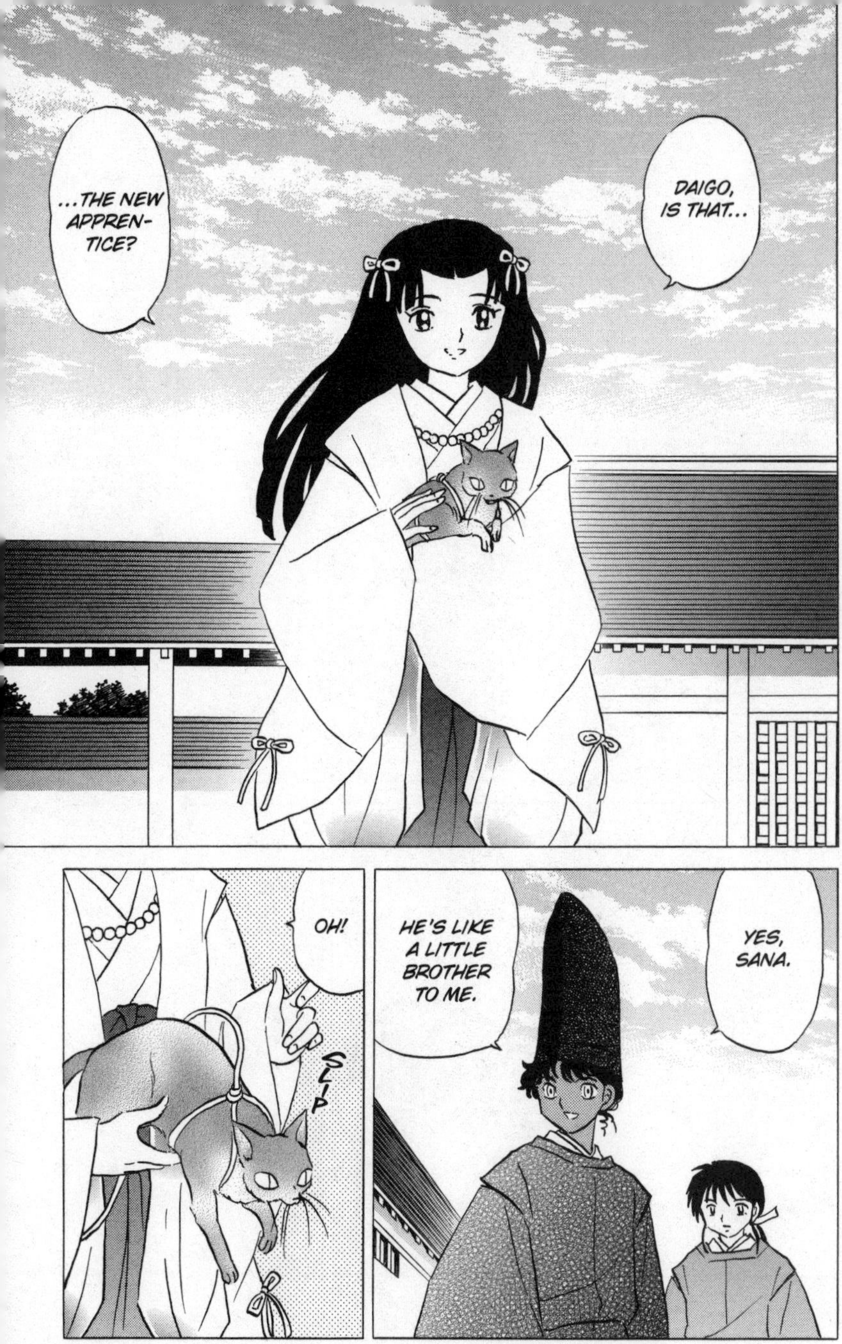
DAIGO, IS THAT...
...THE NEW APPREN-TICE?
YES, SANA.
HE'S LIKE A LITTLE BROTHER TO ME.
OH!
SLIP

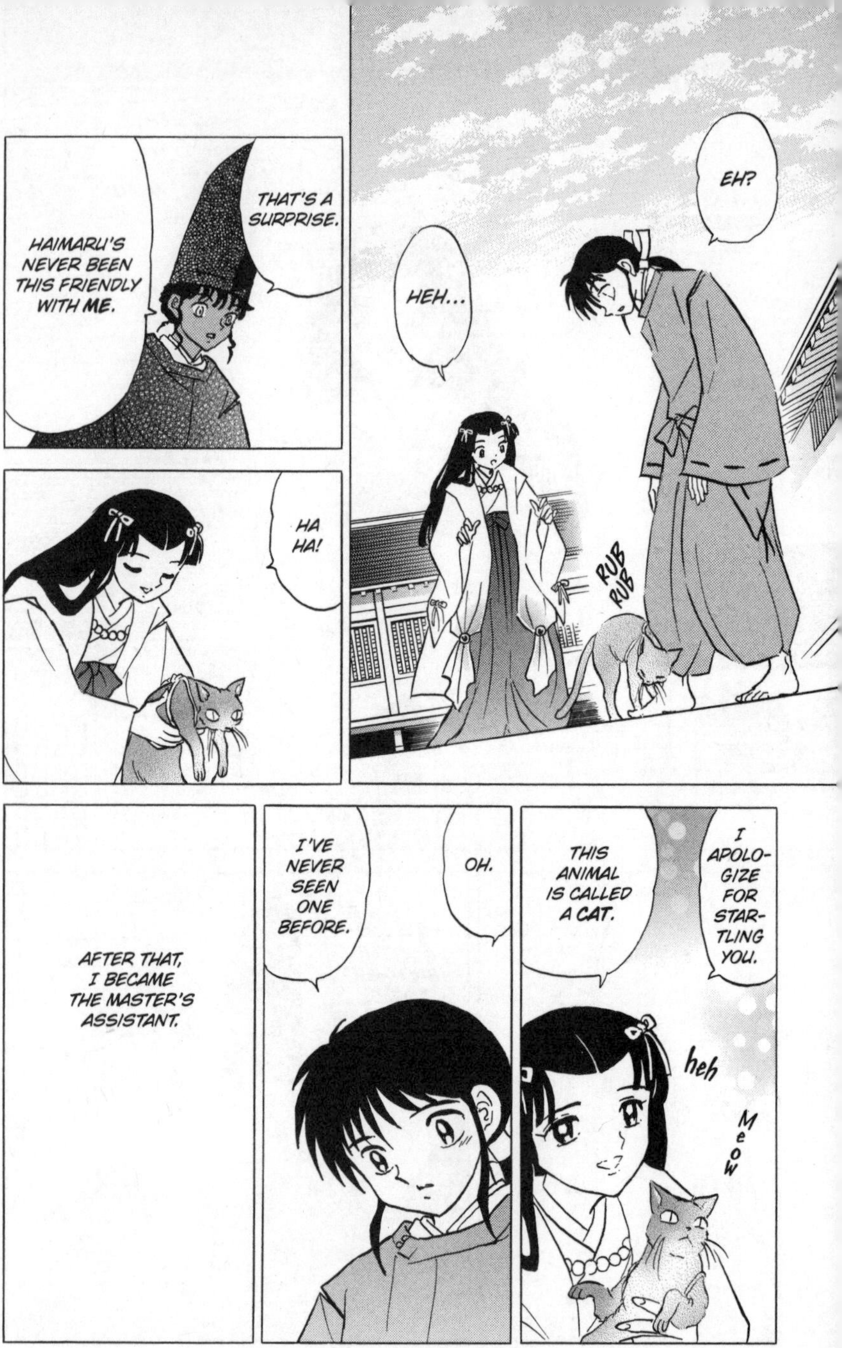
EH?
HEH...
RUB RUB
THAT'S A SURPRISE.
HAIMARU'S NEVER BEEN THIS FRIENDLY WITH ME.
HA HA!
I APOLOGIZE FOR STARTLING YOU.
THIS ANIMAL IS CALLED A CAT.
heh
Meow
OH.
I'VE NEVER SEEN ONE BEFORE.
AFTER THAT, I BECAME THE MASTER'S ASSISTANT.

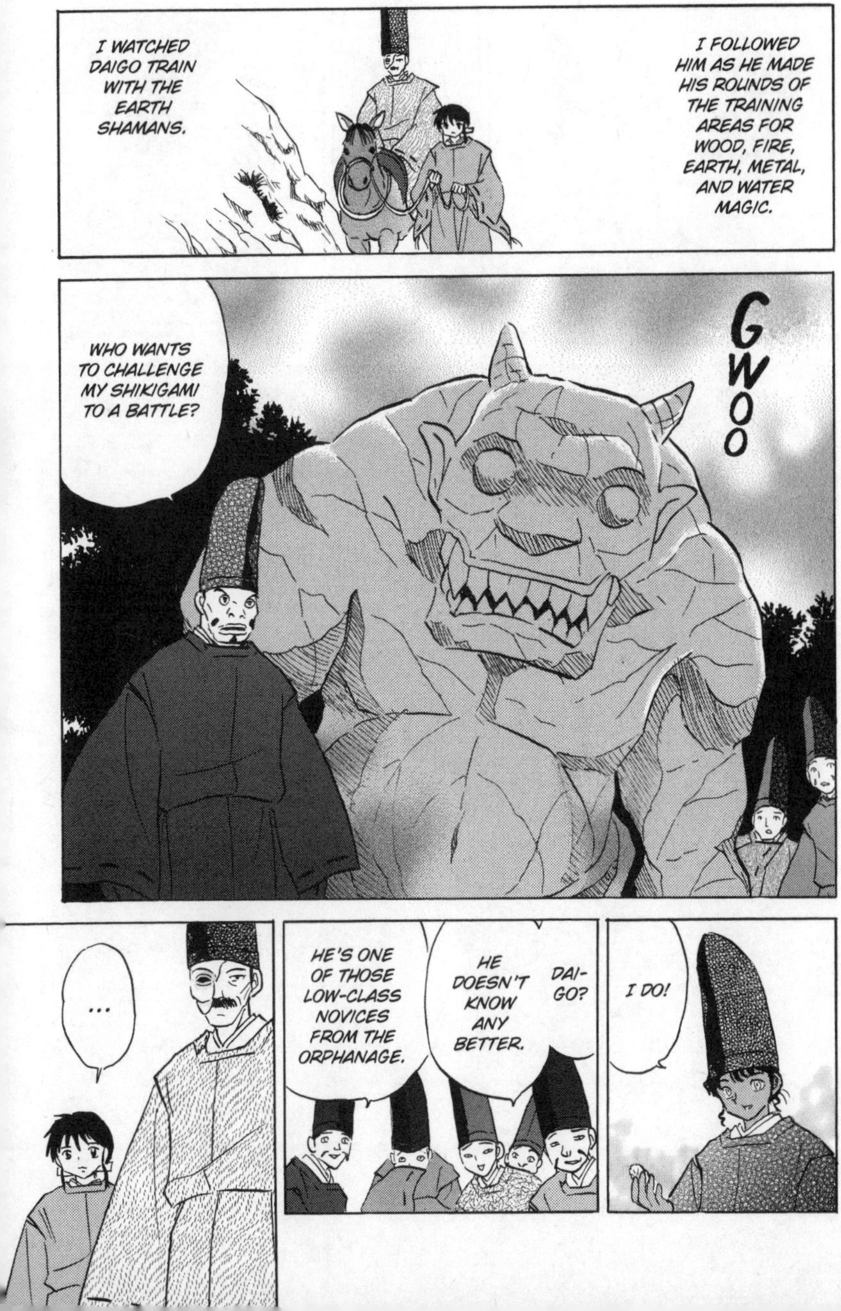
I FOLLOWED HIM AS HE MADE HIS ROUNDS OF THE TRAINING AREAS FOR WOOD, FIRE, EARTH, METAL, AND WATER MAGIC.
I WATCHED DAIGO TRAIN WITH THE EARTH SHAMANS.
GWOO
WHO WANTS TO CHALLENGE MY SHIKIGAMI TO A BATTLE?
I DO!
DAI-GO?
HE DOESN'T KNOW ANY BETTER.
HE'S ONE OF THOSE LOW-CLASS NOVICES FROM THE ORPHANAGE.
...

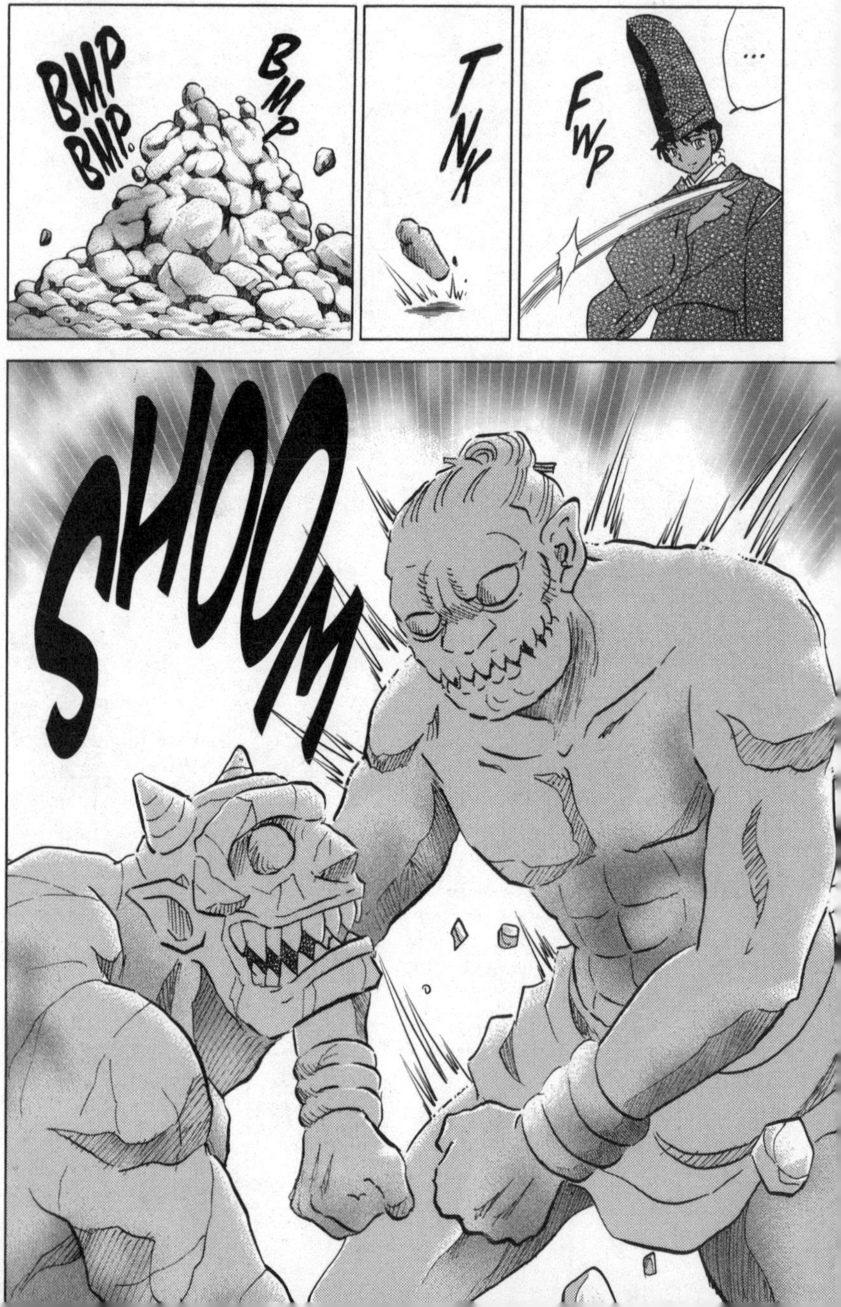
...
FWP
TNK
BMP BMP
BMP
SHOOM

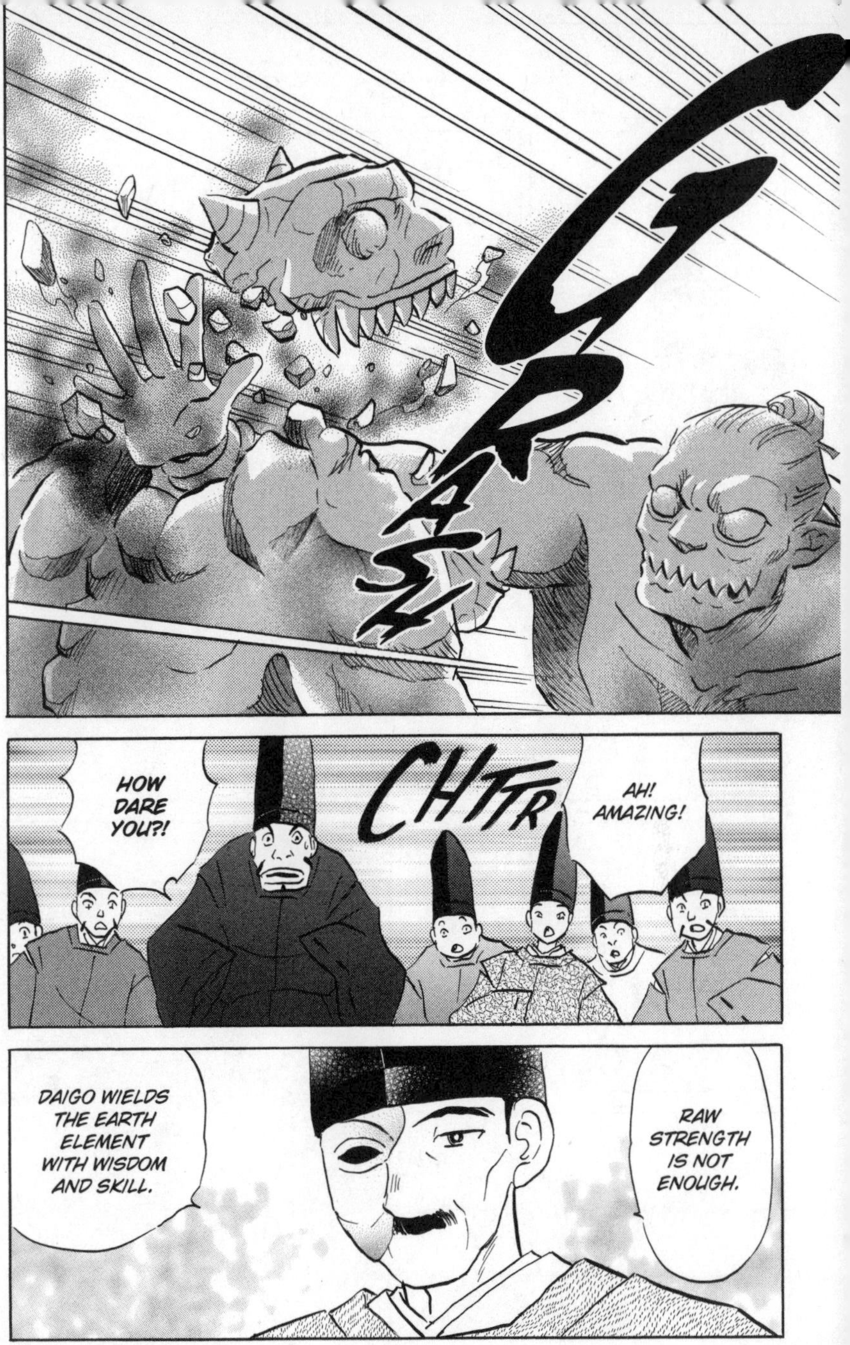
CRASH
AH! AMAZING!
CHITTR
HOW DARE YOU?!
RAW STRENGTH IS NOT ENOUGH.
DAIGO WIELDS THE EARTH ELEMENT WITH WISDOM AND SKILL.

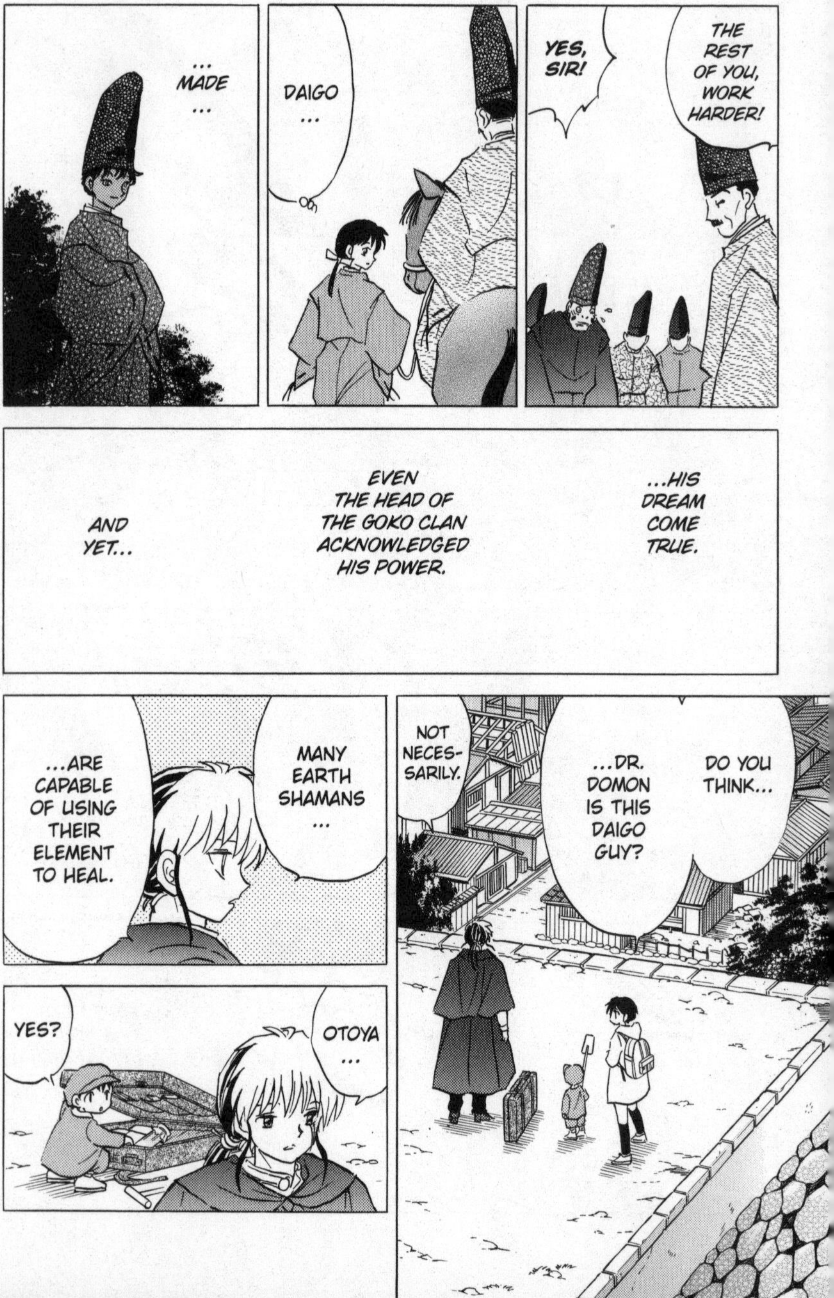
THE REST OF YOU, WORK HARDER!
YES, SIR!
DAIGO ...
... MADE ...
...HIS DREAM COME TRUE.
EVEN THE HEAD OF THE GOKO CLAN ACKNOWLEDGED HIS POWER.
AND YET...
DO YOU THINK...
...DR. DOMON IS THIS DAIGO GUY?
NOT NECES-SARILY.
MANY EARTH SHAMANS ...
...ARE CAPABLE OF USING THEIR ELEMENT TO HEAL.
OTOYA ...
YES?

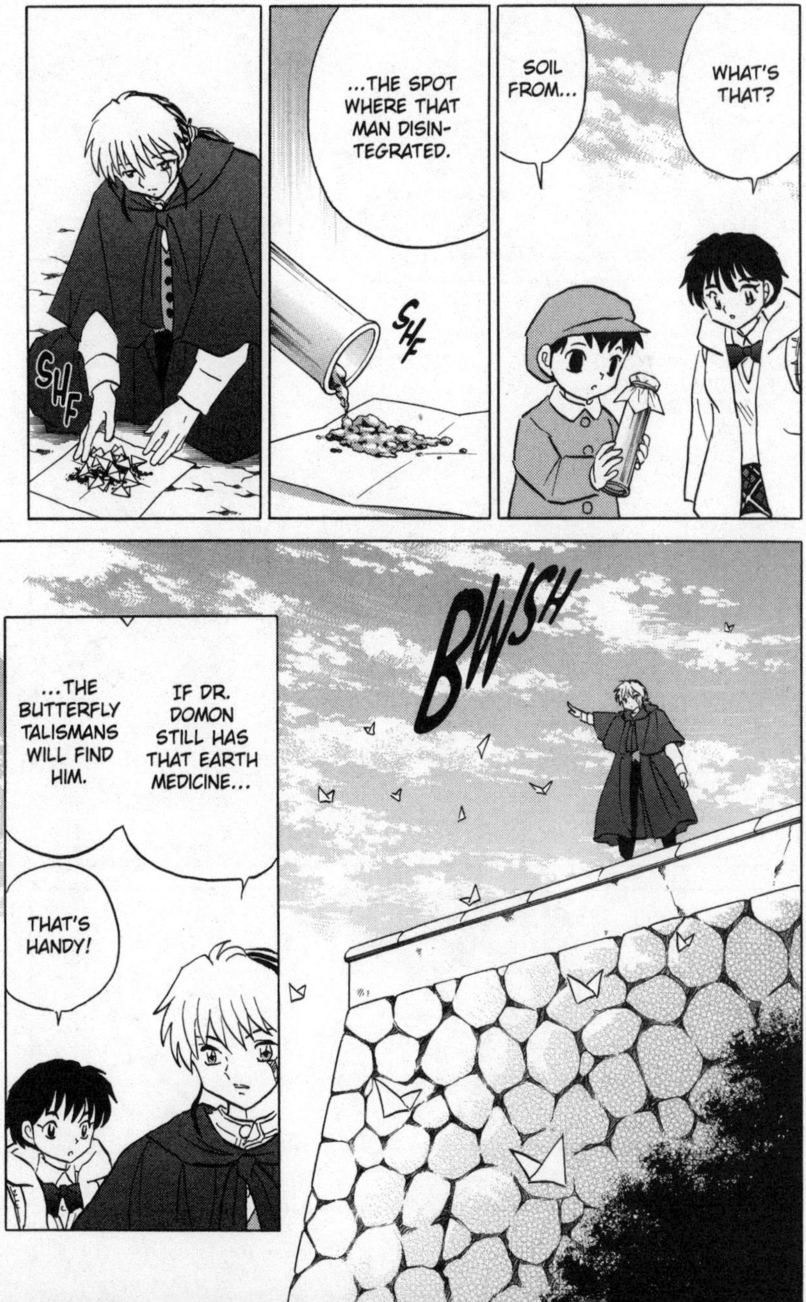
WHAT'S THAT?
SOIL FROM...
...THE SPOT WHERE THAT MAN DISINTEGRATED.
SHF
SHF
BWSH
IF DR. DOMON STILL HAS THAT EARTH MEDICINE...
...THE BUTTERFLY TALISMANS WILL FIND HIM.
THAT'S HANDY!

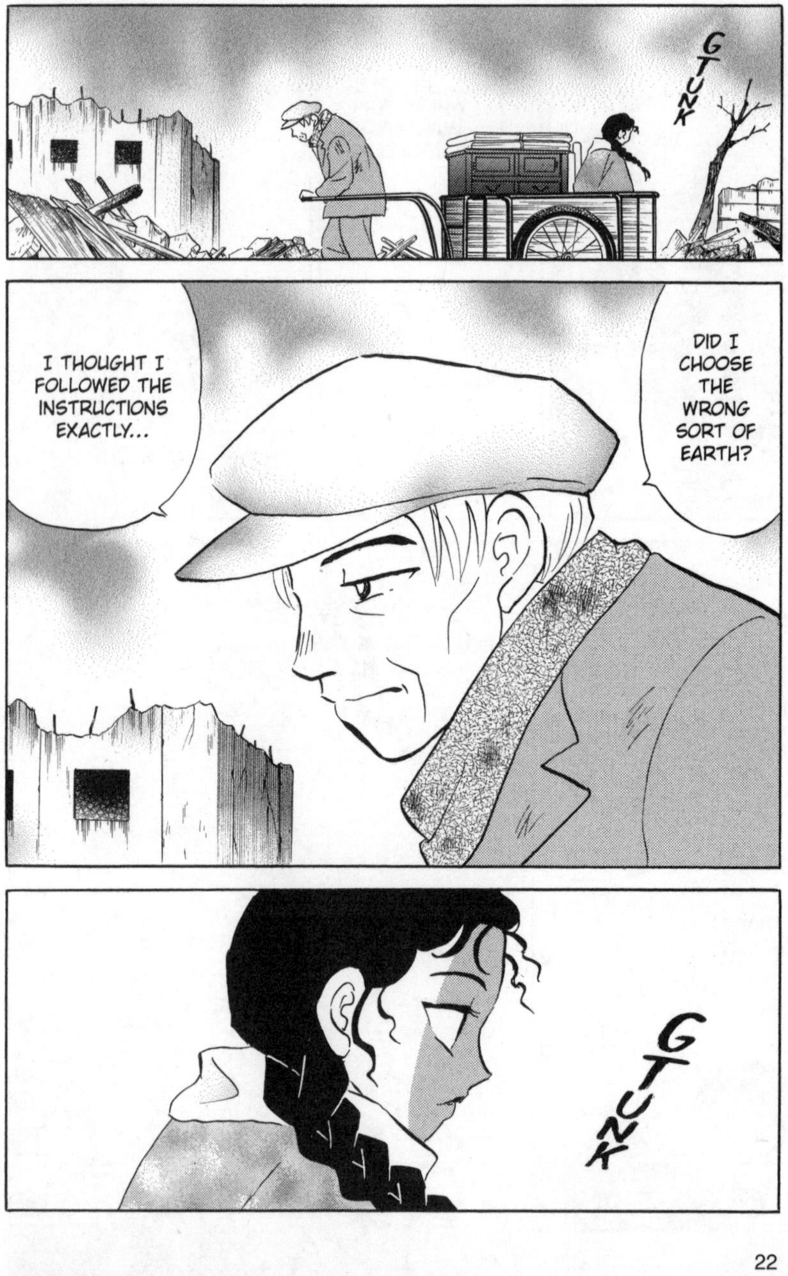
GTUNK
DID I CHOOSE THE WRONG SORT OF EARTH?
I THOUGHT I FOLLOWED THE INSTRUCTIONS EXACTLY...
GTUNK

Chapter 2:
Earth Medicine

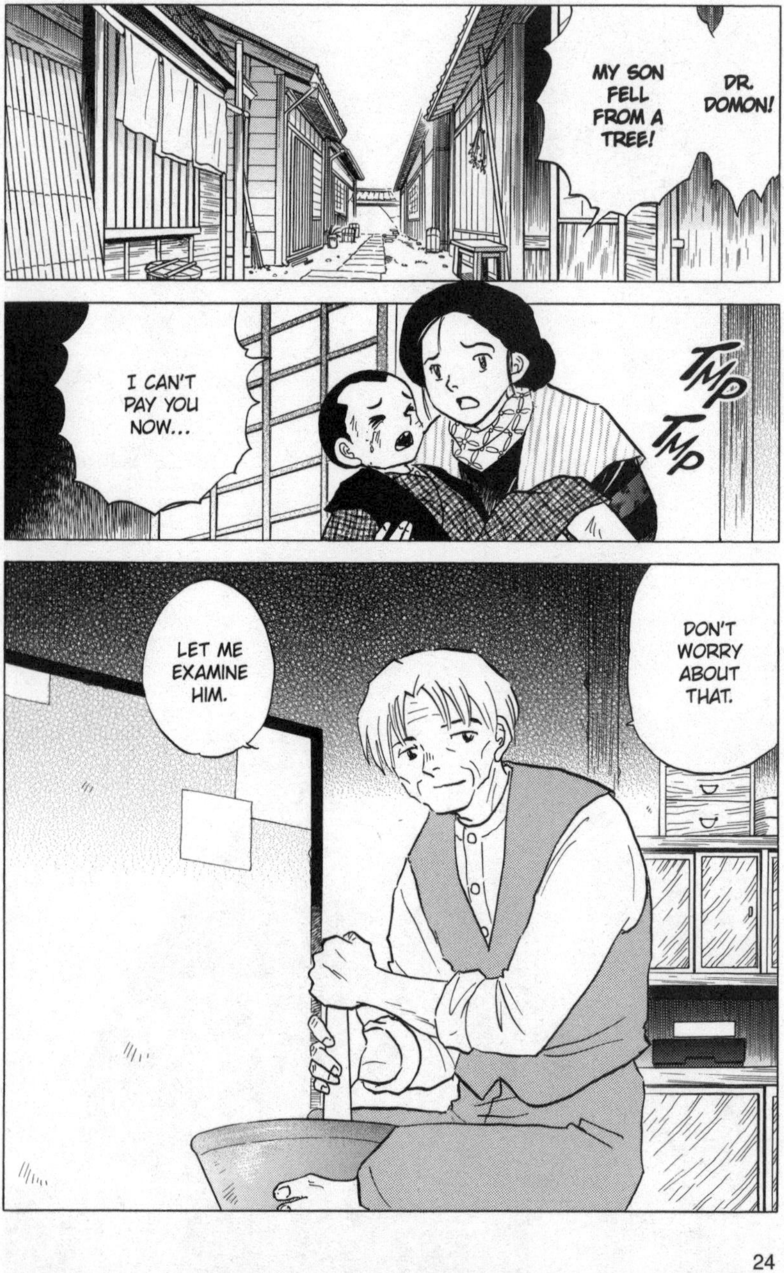
DR. DOMON!
MY SON FELL FROM A TREE!
TMP TMP
I CAN'T PAY YOU NOW...
DON'T WORRY ABOUT THAT.
LET ME EXAMINE HIM.

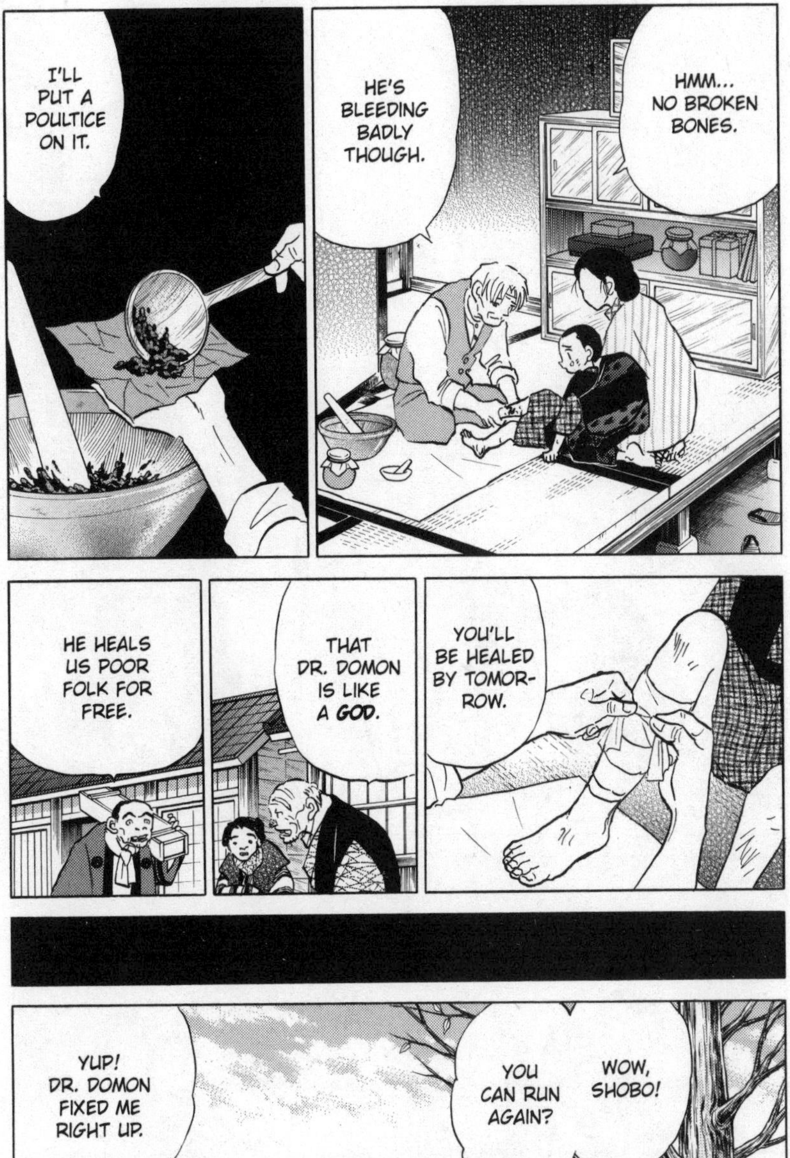
HMM... NO BROKEN BONES.
HE'S BLEEDING BADLY THOUGH.
I'LL PUT A POULTICE ON IT.
YOU'LL BE HEALED BY TOMOR-ROW.
THAT DR. DOMON IS LIKE A **GOD**.
HE HEALS US POOR FOLK FOR FREE.
WOW, SHOBO!
YOU CAN RUN AGAIN?
YUP! DR. DOMON FIXED ME RIGHT UP.

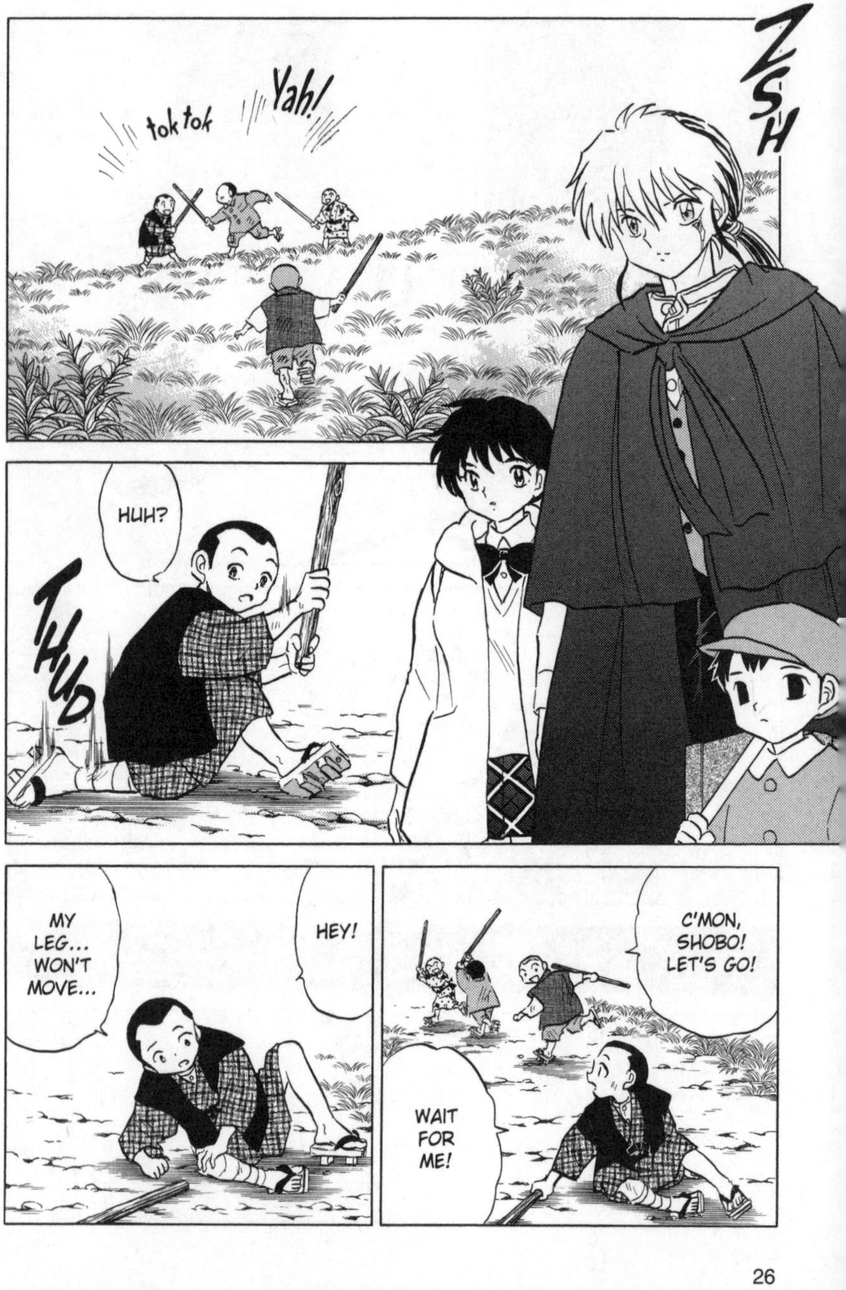
ZSH
Yah!
tok tok
HUH?
THUD
C'MON, SHOBO! LET'S GO!
WAIT FOR ME!
HEY!
MY LEG... WON'T MOVE...

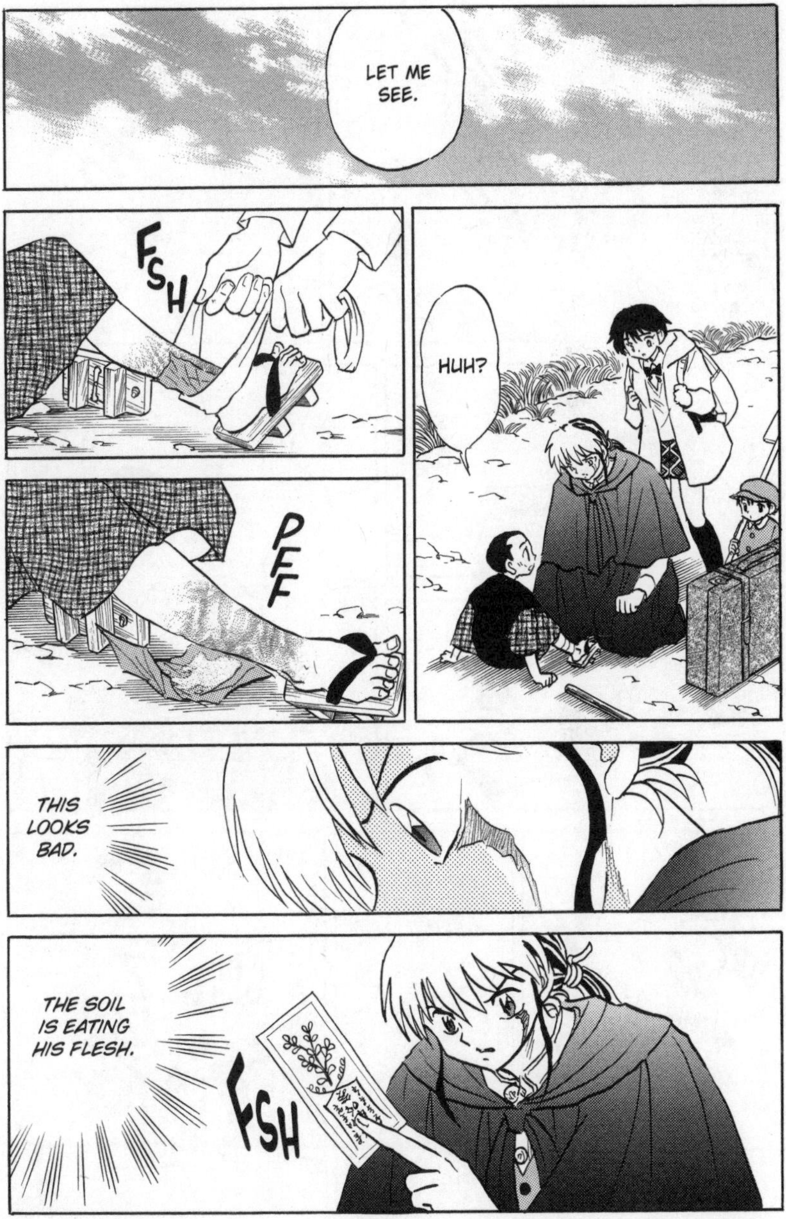
LET ME SEE.
HUH?
FSH
PFF
THIS LOOKS BAD.
THE SOIL IS EATING HIS FLESH.
FSH

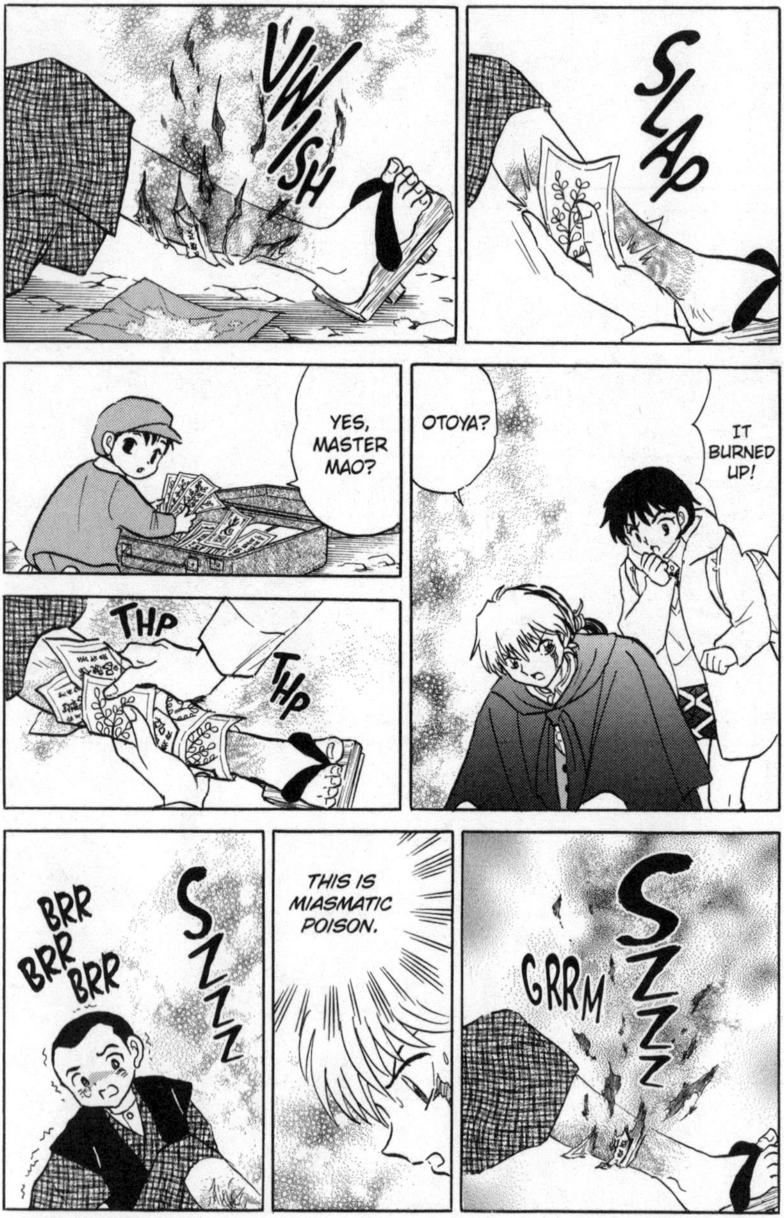
SLAP
VWISH
IT BURNED UP!
OTOYA?
YES, MASTER MAO?
THP
THP
SZZZ
GRRM
THIS IS MIASMATIC POISON.
SZZZ
BRR BRR BRR

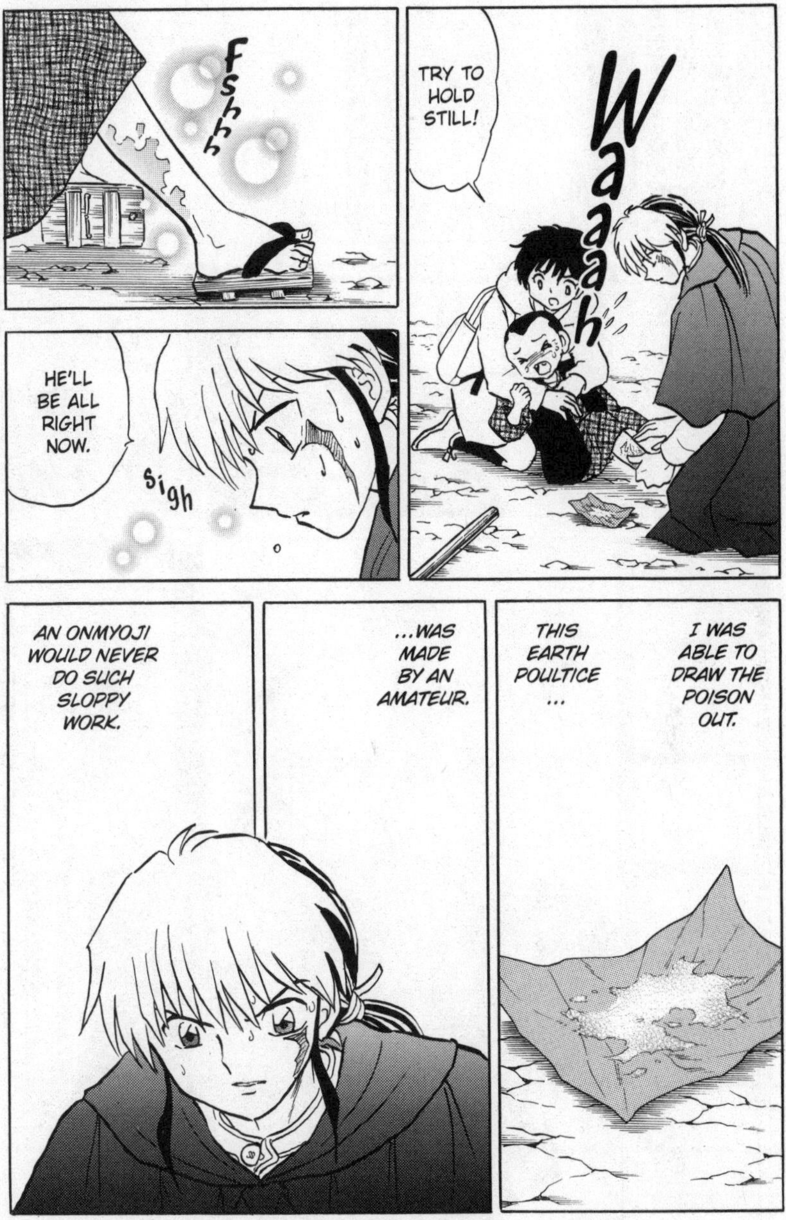
TRY TO HOLD STILL!
Waaaah
fshhh
HE'LL BE ALL RIGHT NOW.
sigh
I WAS ABLE TO DRAW THE POISON OUT.
THIS EARTH POULTICE ...
...WAS MADE BY AN AMATEUR.
AN ONMYOJI WOULD NEVER DO SUCH SLOPPY WORK.

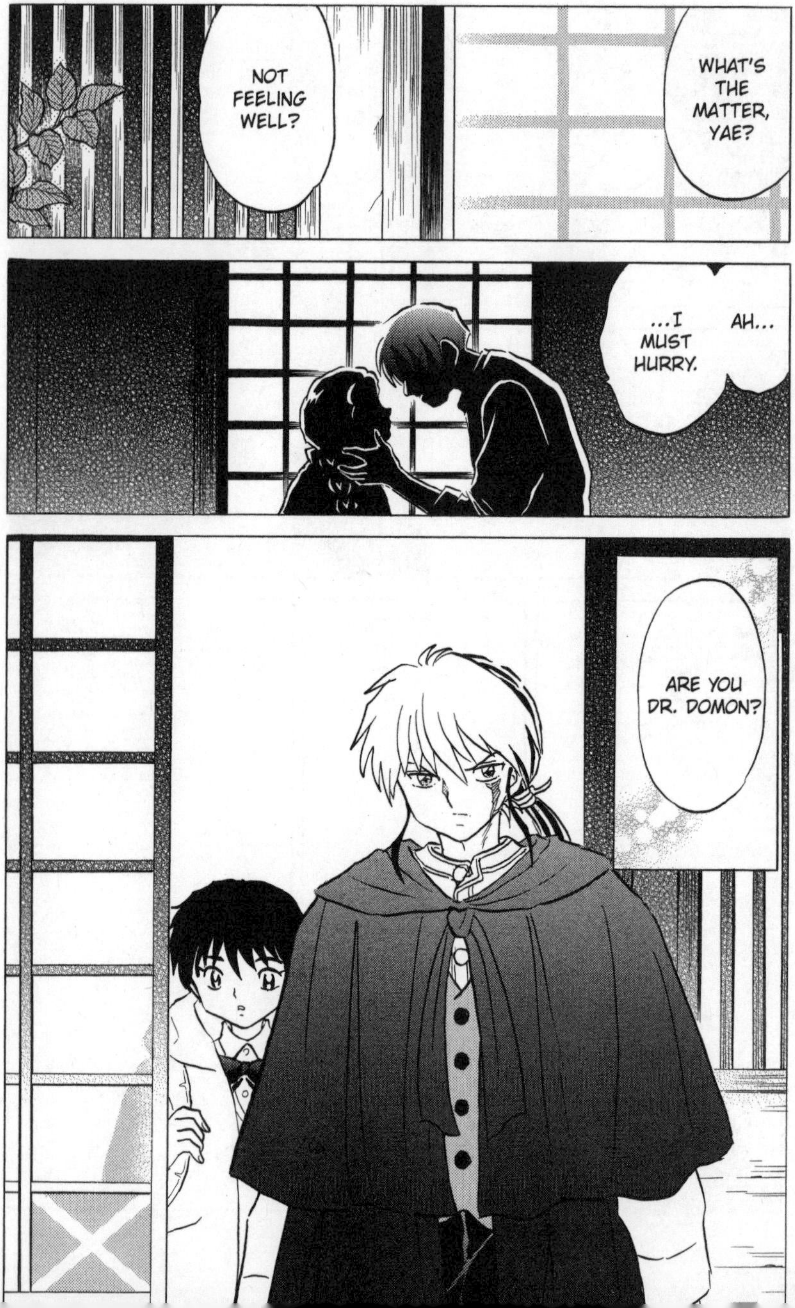
WHAT'S THE MATTER, YAE?
NOT FEELING WELL?
AH...
...I MUST HURRY.
ARE YOU DR. DOMON?

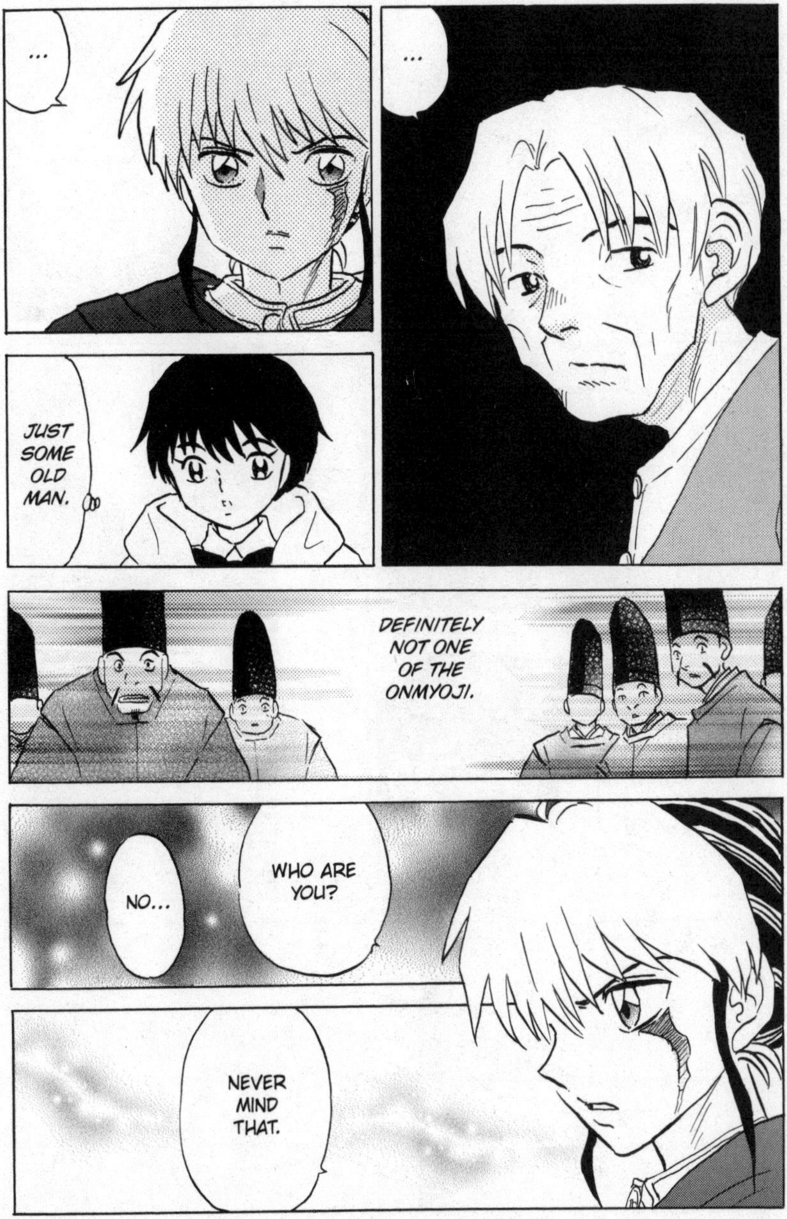
...
...
JUST SOME OLD MAN.
DEFINITELY NOT ONE OF THE ONMYOJI.
WHO ARE YOU?
NO...
NEVER MIND THAT.

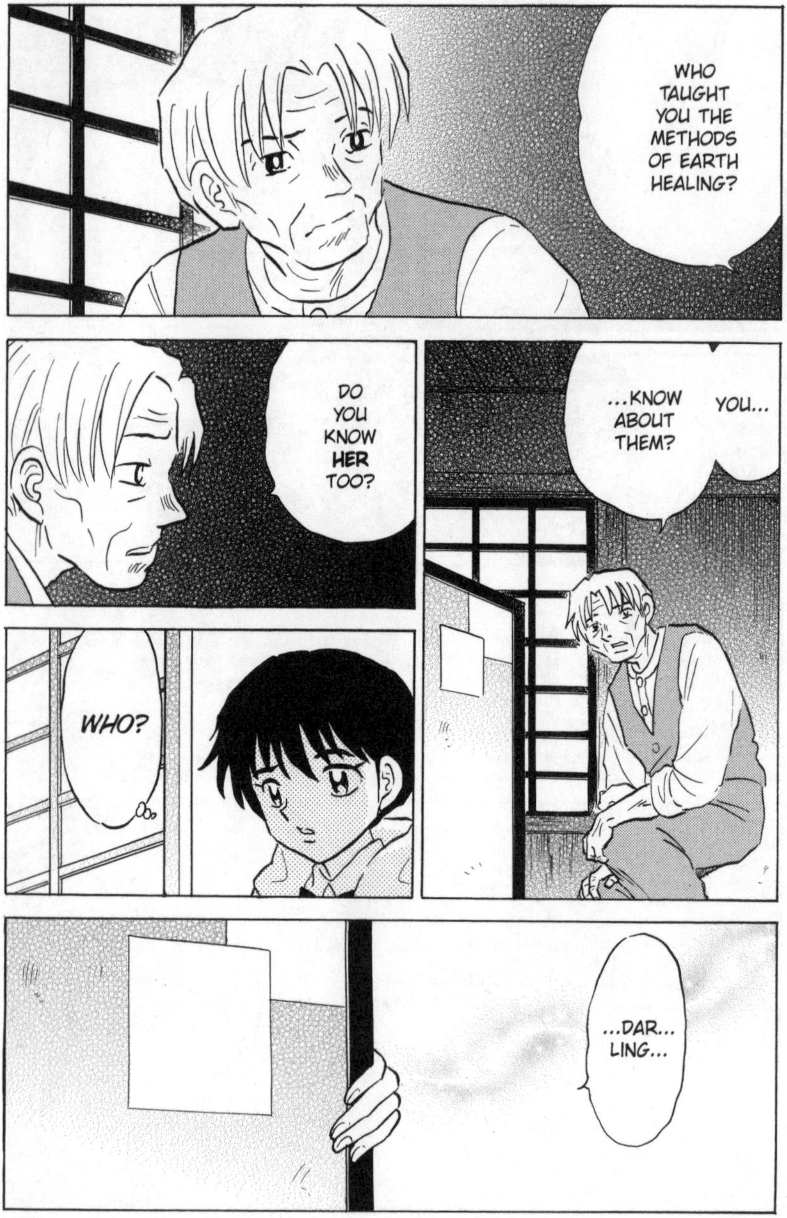
WHO TAUGHT YOU THE METHODS OF EARTH HEALING?
YOU...
...KNOW ABOUT THEM?
DO YOU KNOW HER TOO?
WHO?
...DAR... LING...

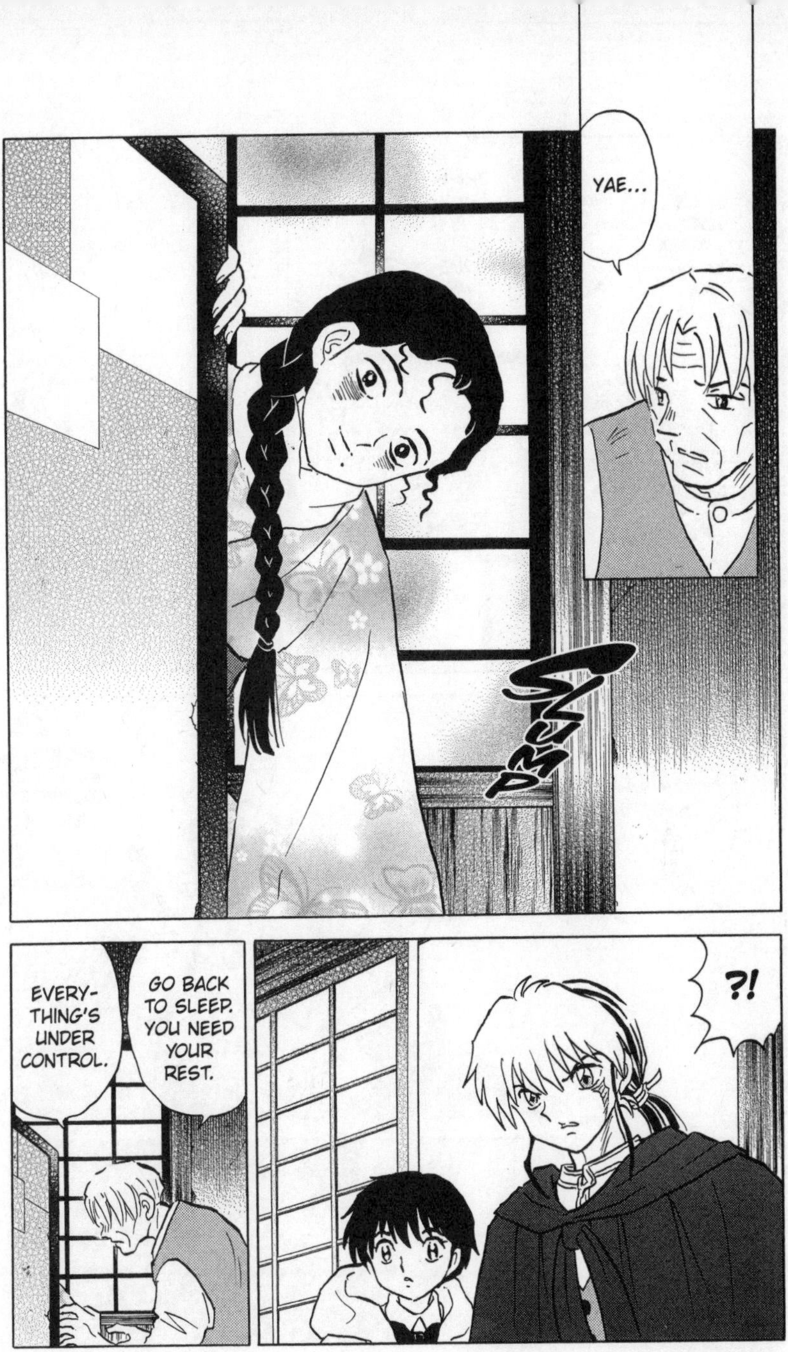
YAE...
SLUMP
?!
GO BACK TO SLEEP. YOU NEED YOUR REST.
EVERY-THING'S UNDER CONTROL.

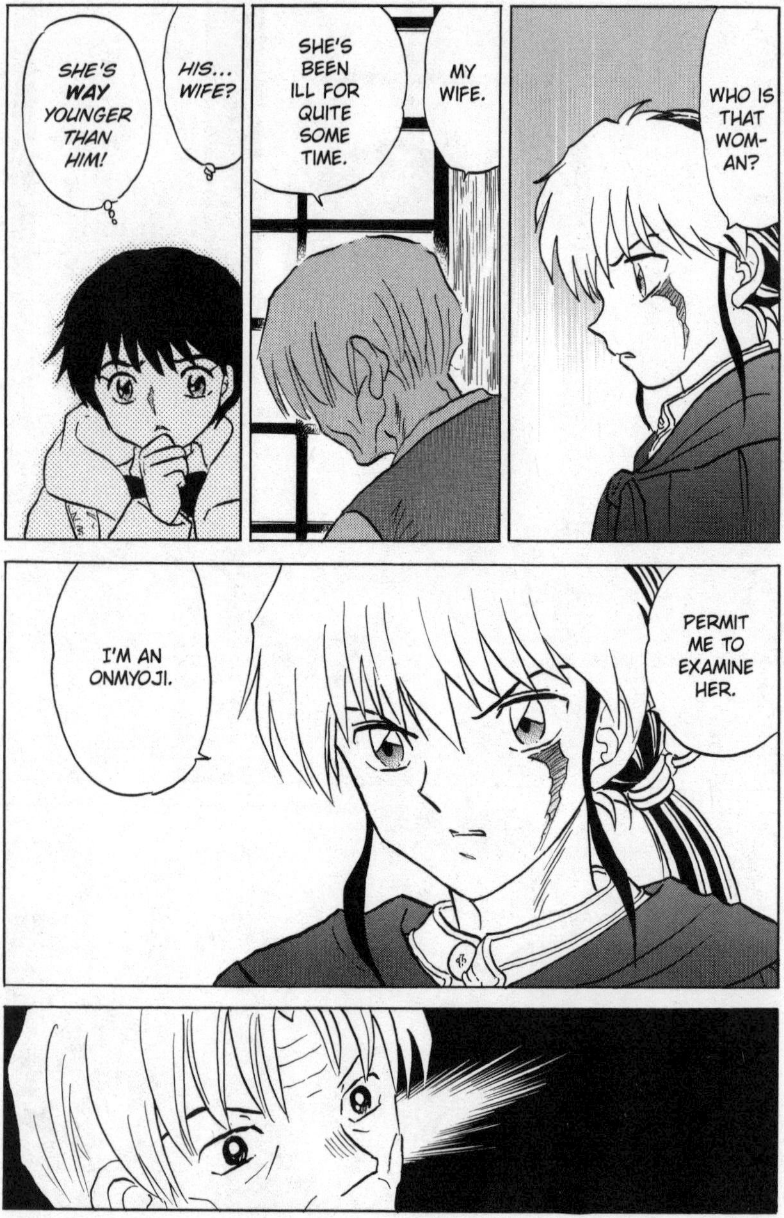
WHO IS THAT WOM-AN?
MY WIFE.
SHE'S BEEN ILL FOR QUITE SOME TIME.
HIS... WIFE?
SHE'S **WAY** YOUNGER THAN HIM!
PERMIT ME TO EXAMINE HER.
I'M AN ONMYOJI.

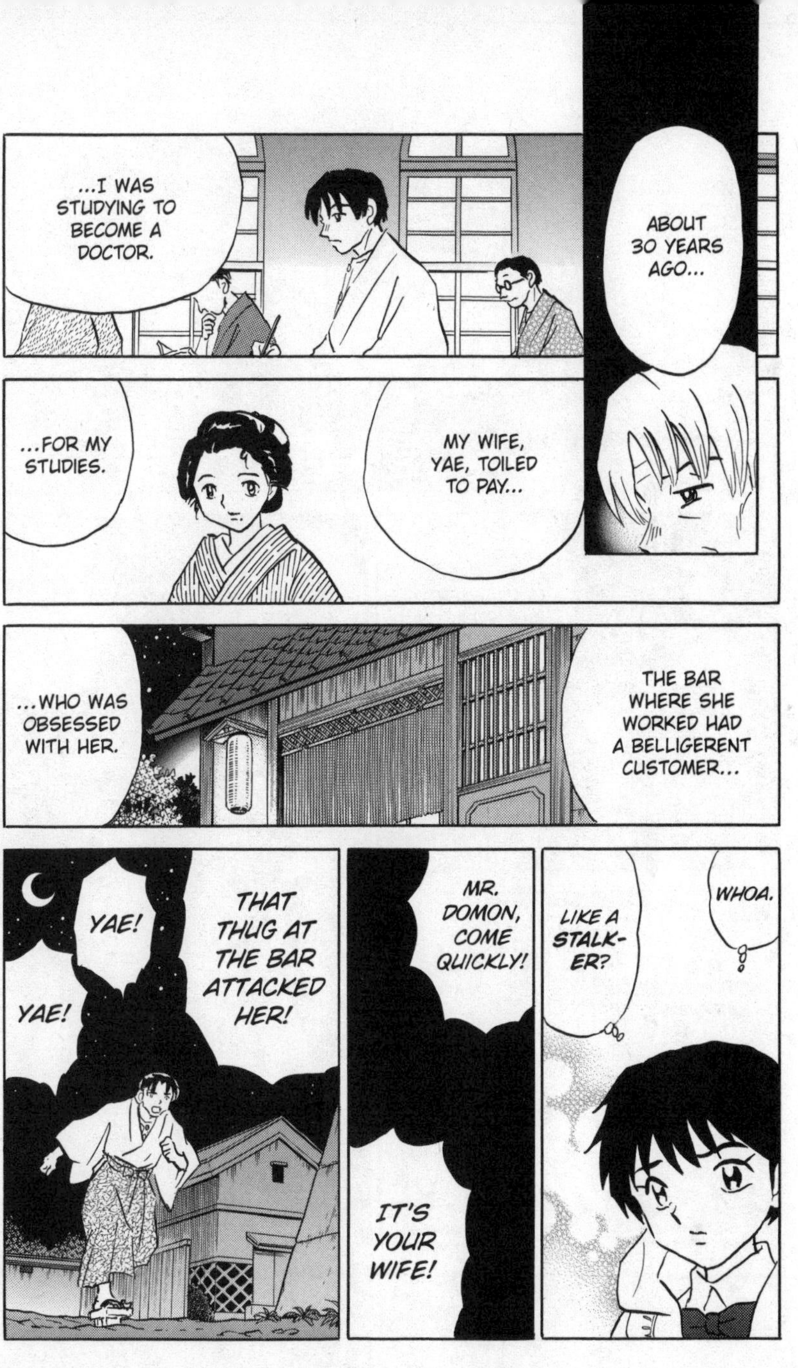
ABOUT 30 YEARS AGO...
...I WAS STUDYING TO BECOME A DOCTOR.
MY WIFE, YAE, TOILED TO PAY...
...FOR MY STUDIES.
THE BAR WHERE SHE WORKED HAD A BELLIGERENT CUSTOMER...
...WHO WAS OBSESSED WITH HER.
WHOA.
LIKE A STALKER?
MR. DOMON, COME QUICKLY!
IT'S YOUR WIFE!
THAT THUG AT THE BAR ATTACKED HER!
YAE!
YAE!

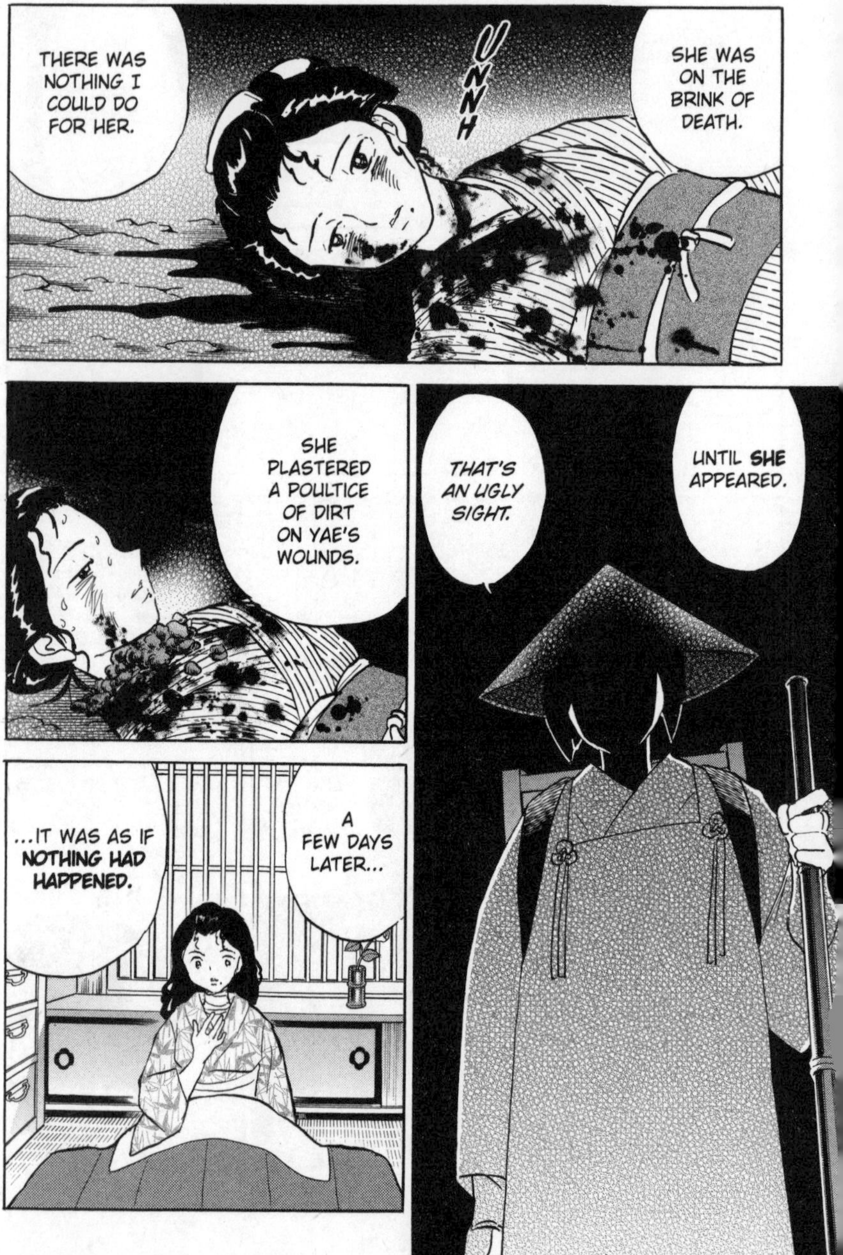
SHE WAS ON THE BRINK OF DEATH.
UNNH
THERE WAS NOTHING I COULD DO FOR HER.
UNTIL SHE APPEARED.
THAT'S AN UGLY SIGHT.
SHE PLASTERED A POULTICE OF DIRT ON YAE'S WOUNDS.
A FEW DAYS LATER...
...IT WAS AS IF NOTHING HAD HAPPENED.

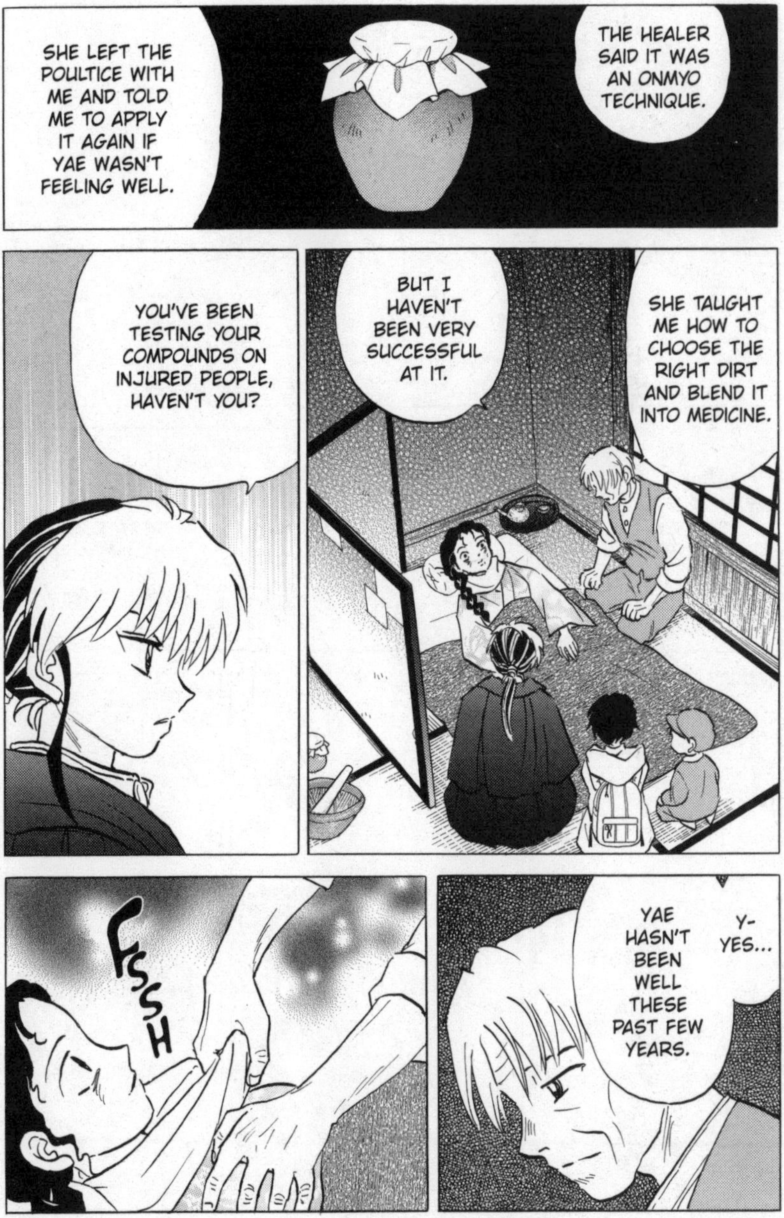
THE HEALER SAID IT WAS AN ONMYO TECHNIQUE.
SHE LEFT THE POULTICE WITH ME AND TOLD ME TO APPLY IT AGAIN IF YAE WASN'T FEELING WELL.
SHE TAUGHT ME HOW TO CHOOSE THE RIGHT DIRT AND BLEND IT INTO MEDICINE.
BUT I HAVEN'T BEEN VERY SUCCESSFUL AT IT.
YOU'VE BEEN TESTING YOUR COMPOUNDS ON INJURED PEOPLE, HAVEN'T YOU?
Y-YES...
YAE HASN'T BEEN WELL THESE PAST FEW YEARS.
FSSH

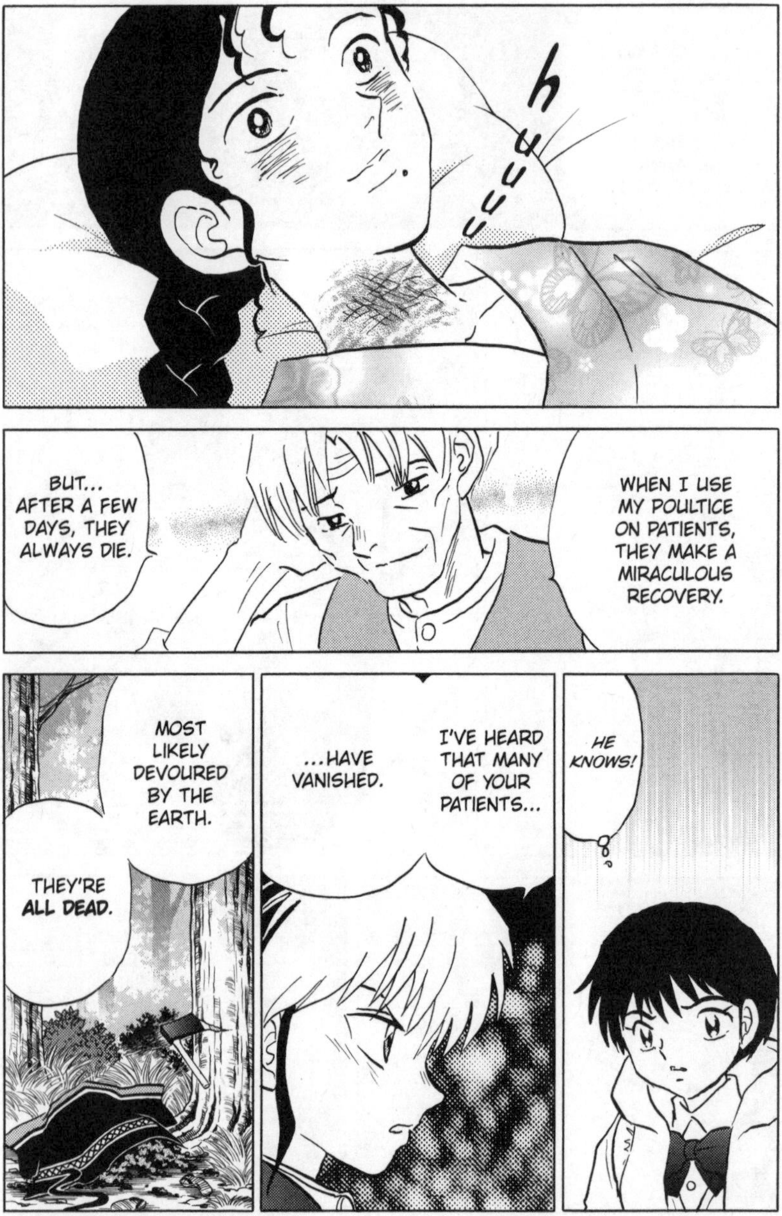
huuuuu
WHEN I USE MY POULTICE ON PATIENTS, THEY MAKE A MIRACULOUS RECOVERY.
BUT... AFTER A FEW DAYS, THEY ALWAYS DIE.
HE KNOWS!
I'VE HEARD THAT MANY OF YOUR PATIENTS...
...HAVE VANISHED.
MOST LIKELY DEVOURED BY THE EARTH.
THEY'RE **ALL DEAD.**

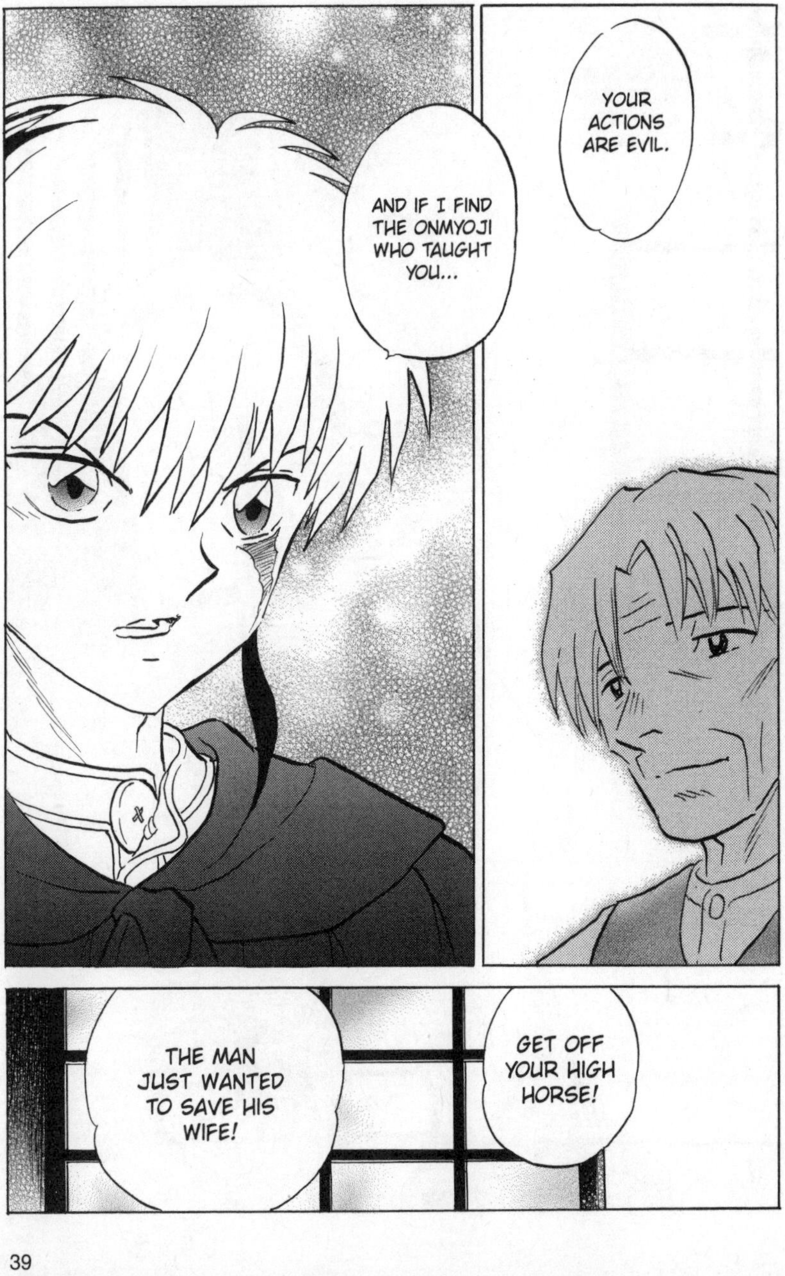
YOUR ACTIONS ARE EVIL.
AND IF I FIND THE ONMYOJI WHO TAUGHT YOU...
GET OFF YOUR HIGH HORSE!
THE MAN JUST WANTED TO SAVE HIS WIFE!

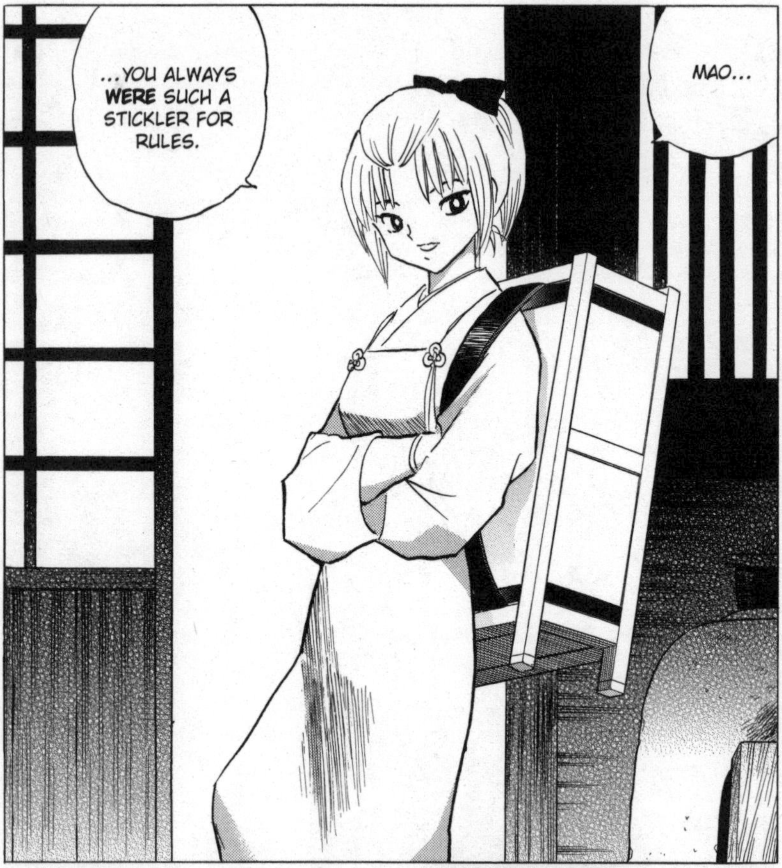
MAO...
...YOU ALWAYS **WERE** SUCH A STICKLER FOR RULES.
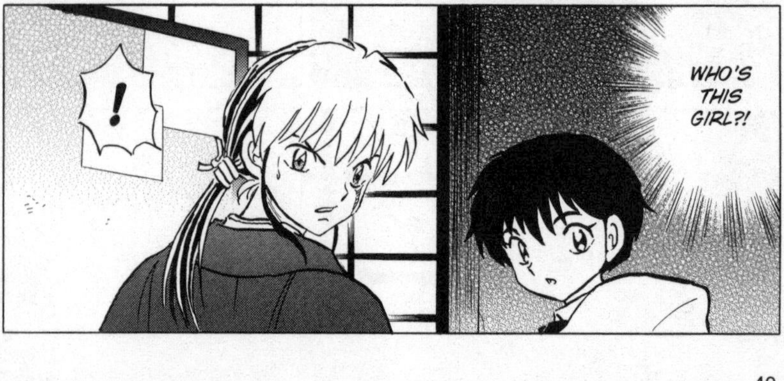
WHO'S THIS GIRL?!
!

Chapter 3: Natsuno

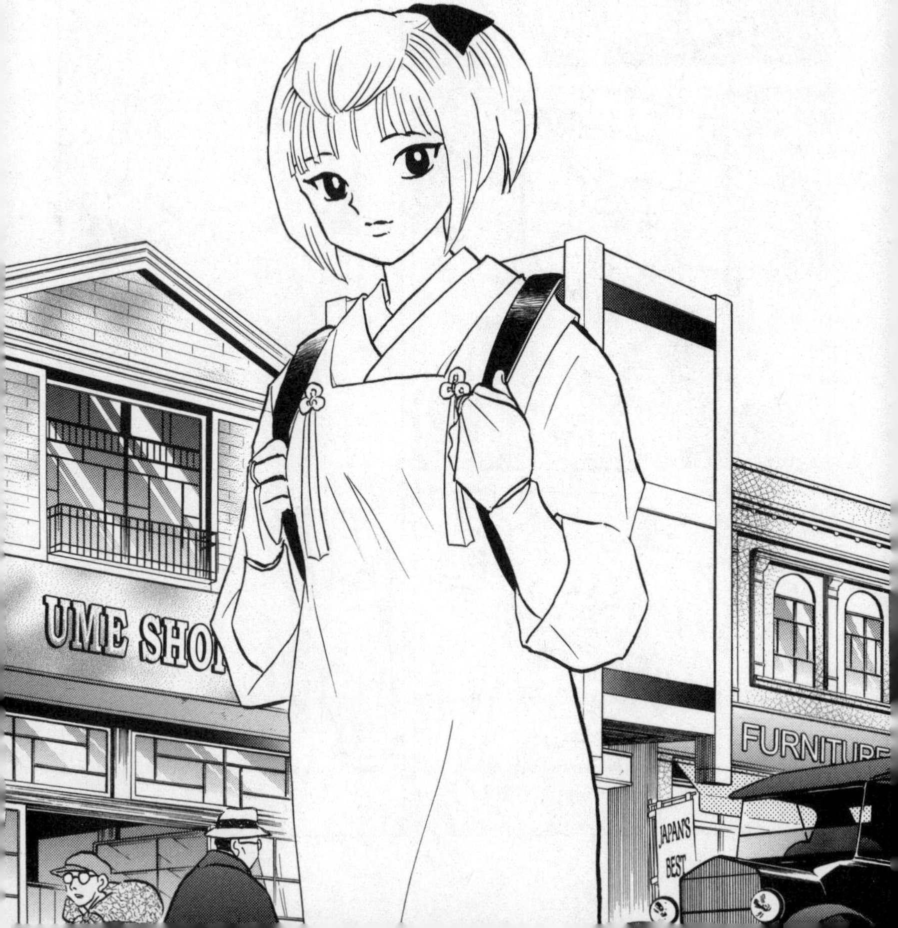
UME SHOP
FURNITURE
JAPAN'S BEST

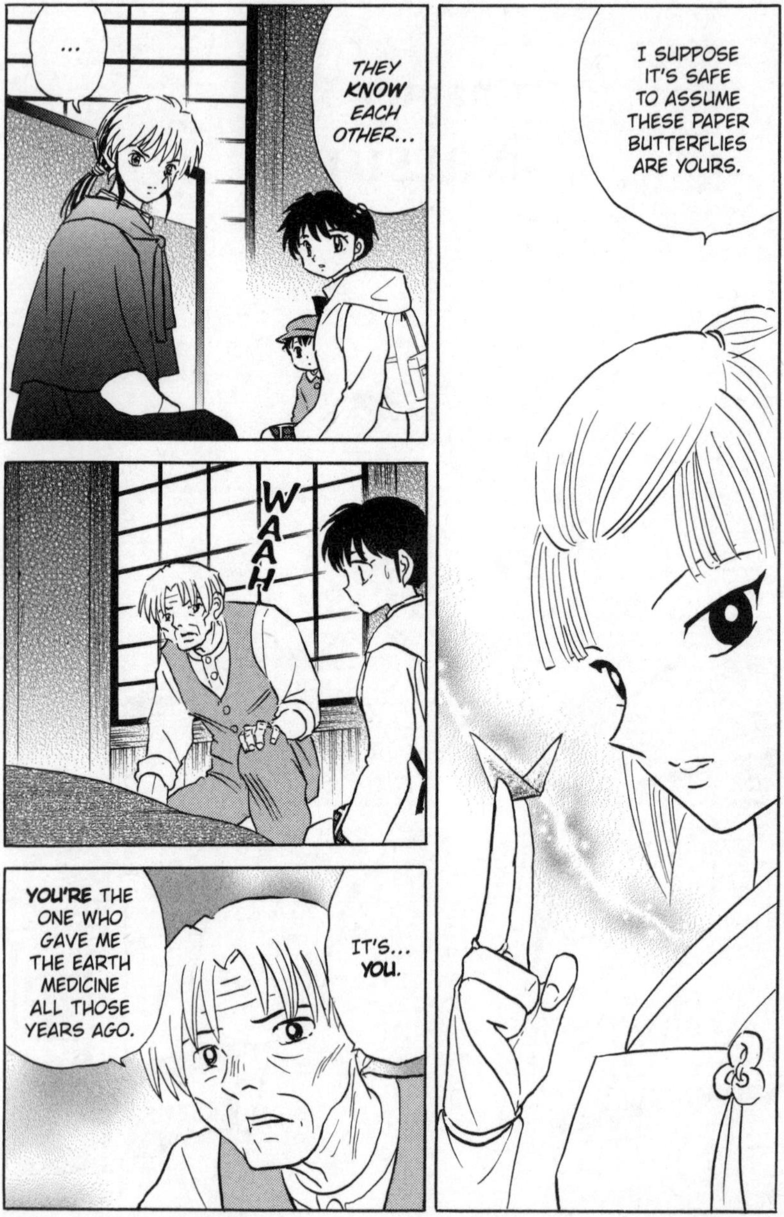
I SUPPOSE IT'S SAFE TO ASSUME THESE PAPER BUTTERFLIES ARE YOURS.
THEY **KNOW** EACH OTHER...
...
WAAH
IT'S... **YOU.**
YOU'RE THE ONE WHO GAVE ME THE EARTH MEDICINE ALL THOSE YEARS AGO.

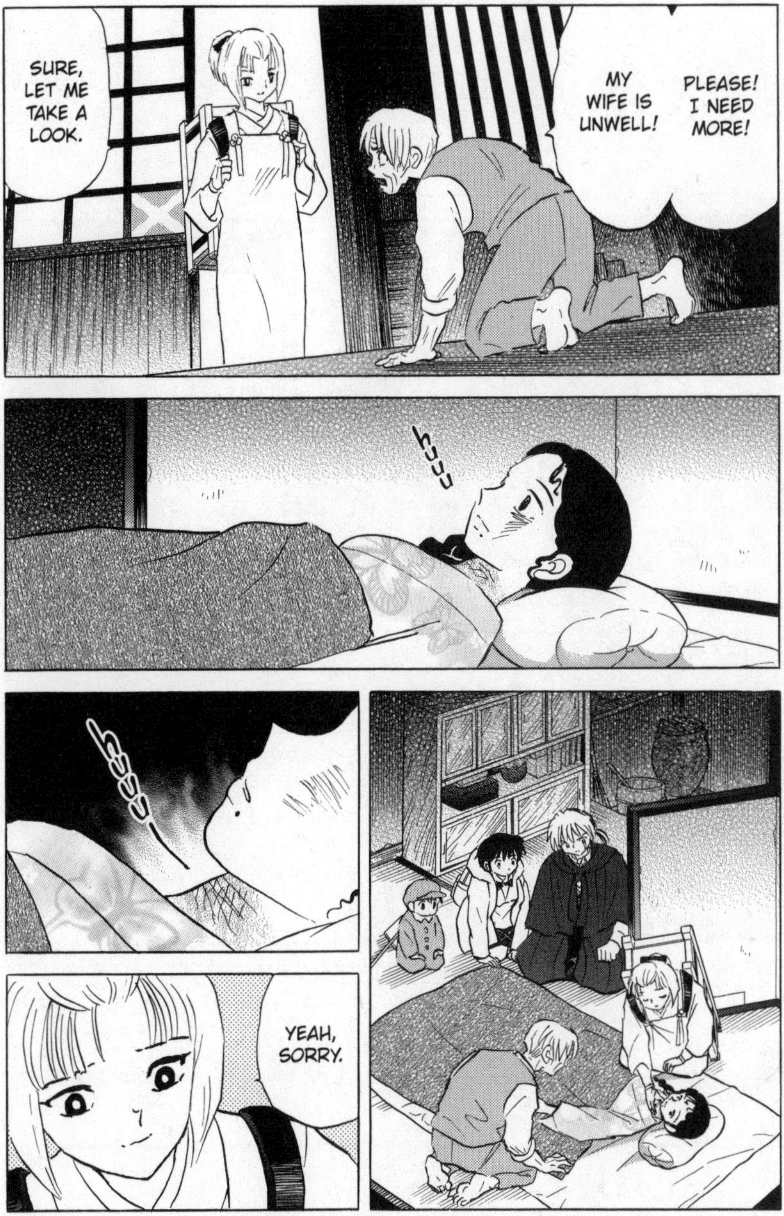
PLEASE! I NEED MORE!
MY WIFE IS UNWELL!
SURE, LET ME TAKE A LOOK.
huuu
huuu
YEAH, SORRY.

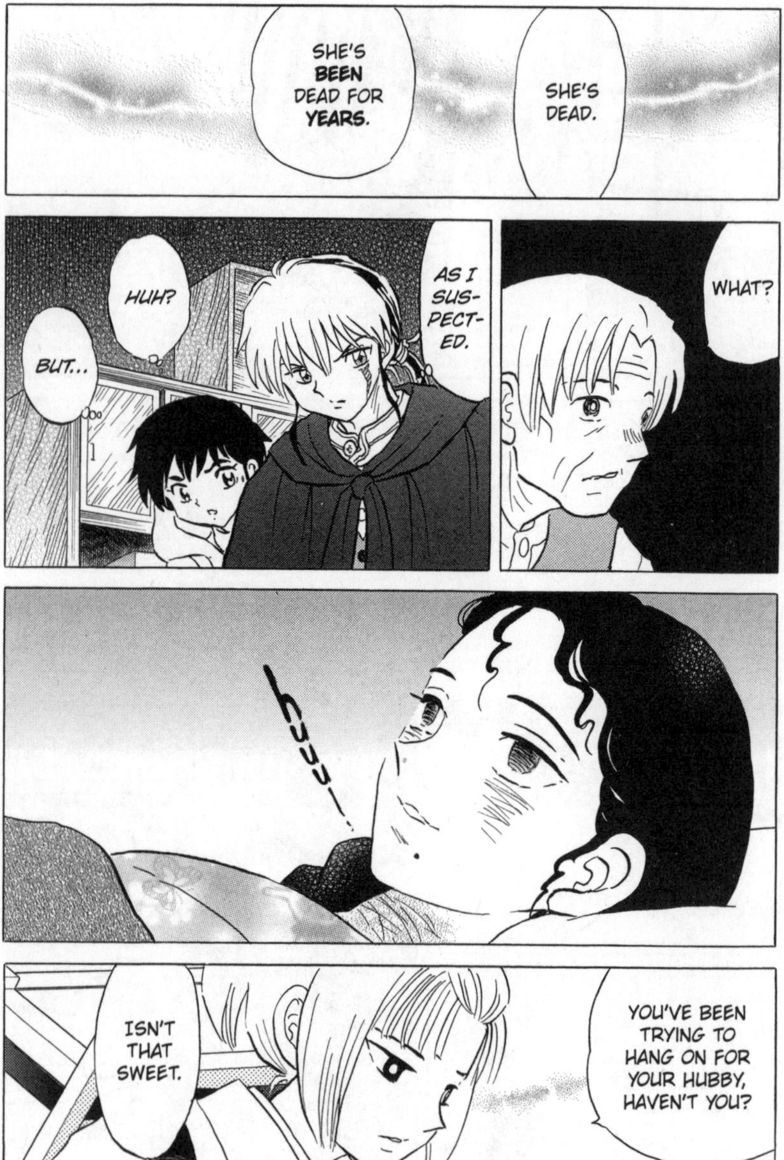
SHE'S DEAD.
SHE'S BEEN DEAD FOR YEARS.
WHAT?
AS I SUS-PECT-ED.
HUH?
BUT...
YOU'VE BEEN TRYING TO HANG ON FOR YOUR HUBBY, HAVEN'T YOU?
ISN'T THAT SWEET.

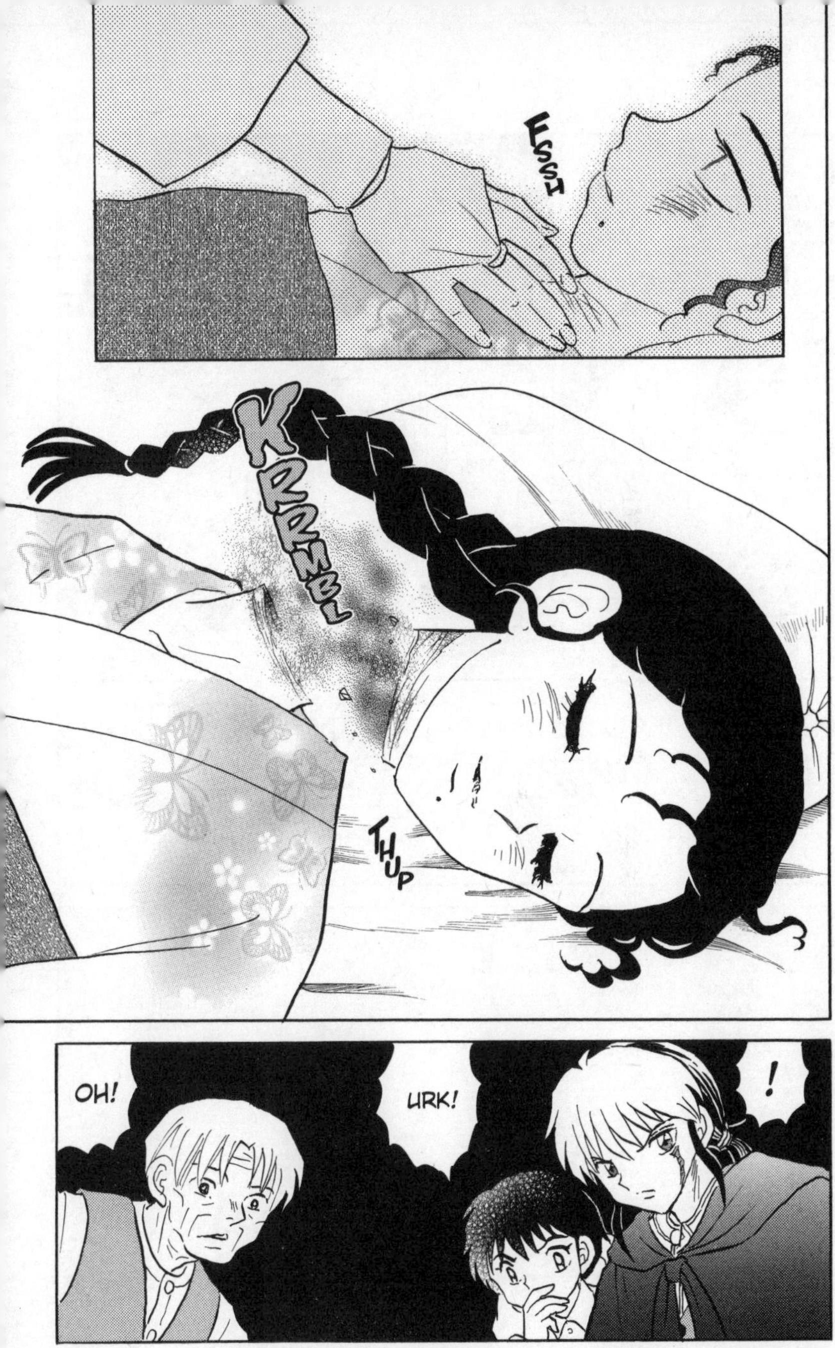
FSSH
KRRMBL
THUP
!
URK!
OH!

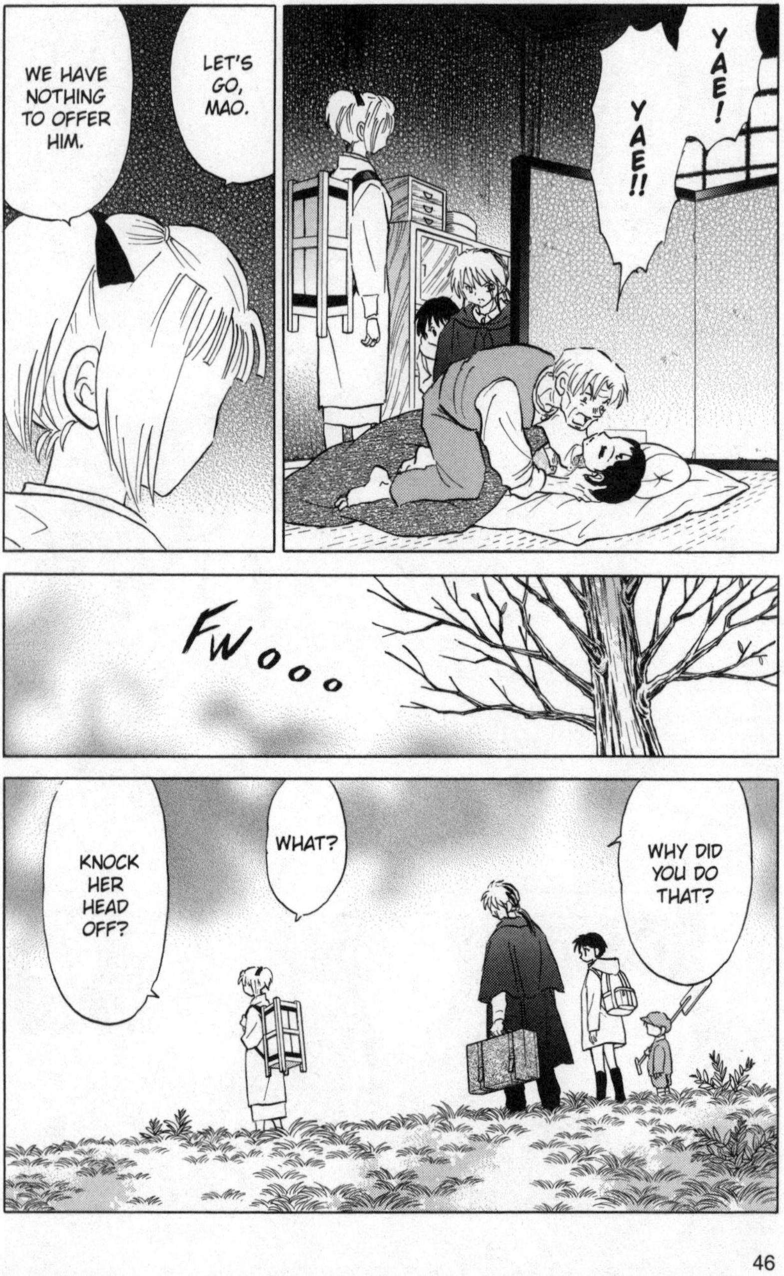
YAE!
YAE!!
LET'S GO, MAO.
WE HAVE NOTHING TO OFFER HIM.
FWOOO
WHY DID YOU DO THAT?
WHAT?
KNOCK HER HEAD OFF?

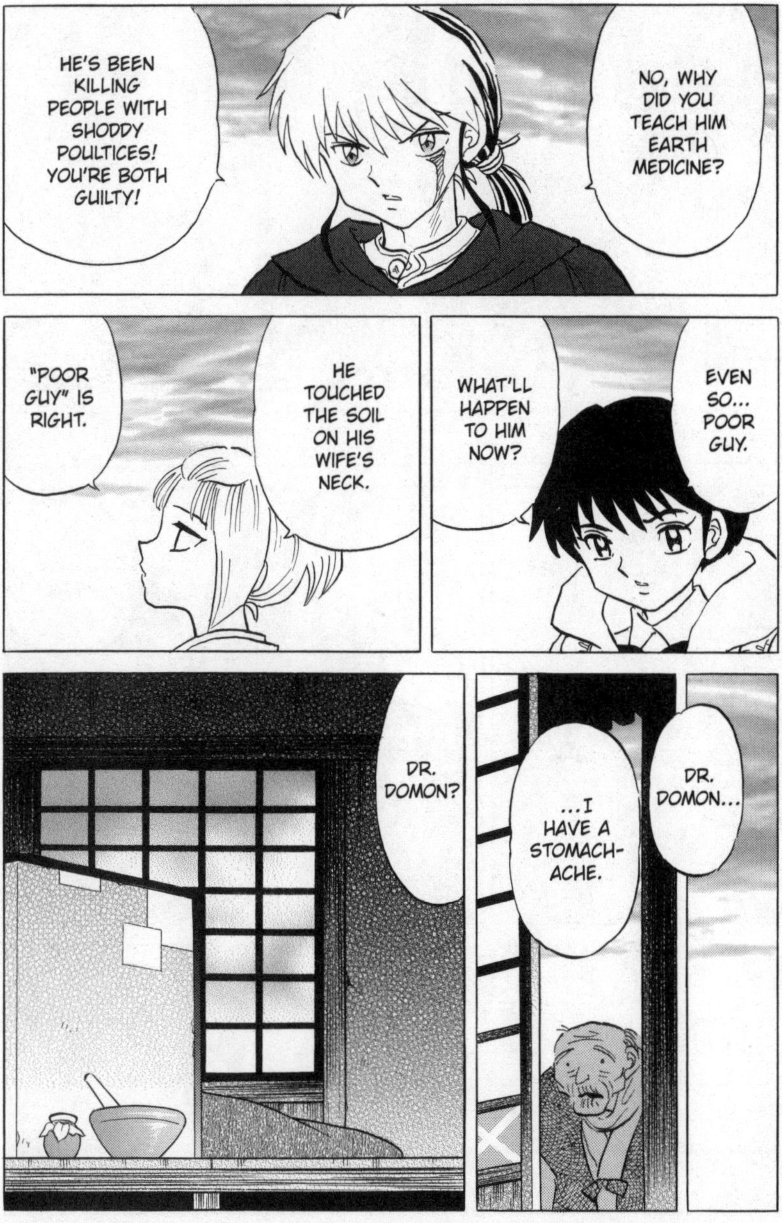

NO, WHY DID YOU TEACH HIM EARTH MEDICINE?
HE'S BEEN KILLING PEOPLE WITH SHODDY POULTICES! YOU'RE BOTH GUILTY!
EVEN SO... POOR GUY.
WHAT'LL HAPPEN TO HIM NOW?
HE TOUCHED THE SOIL ON HIS WIFE'S NECK.
"POOR GUY" IS RIGHT.
DR. DOMON...
...I HAVE A STOMACH-ACHE.
DR. DOMON?

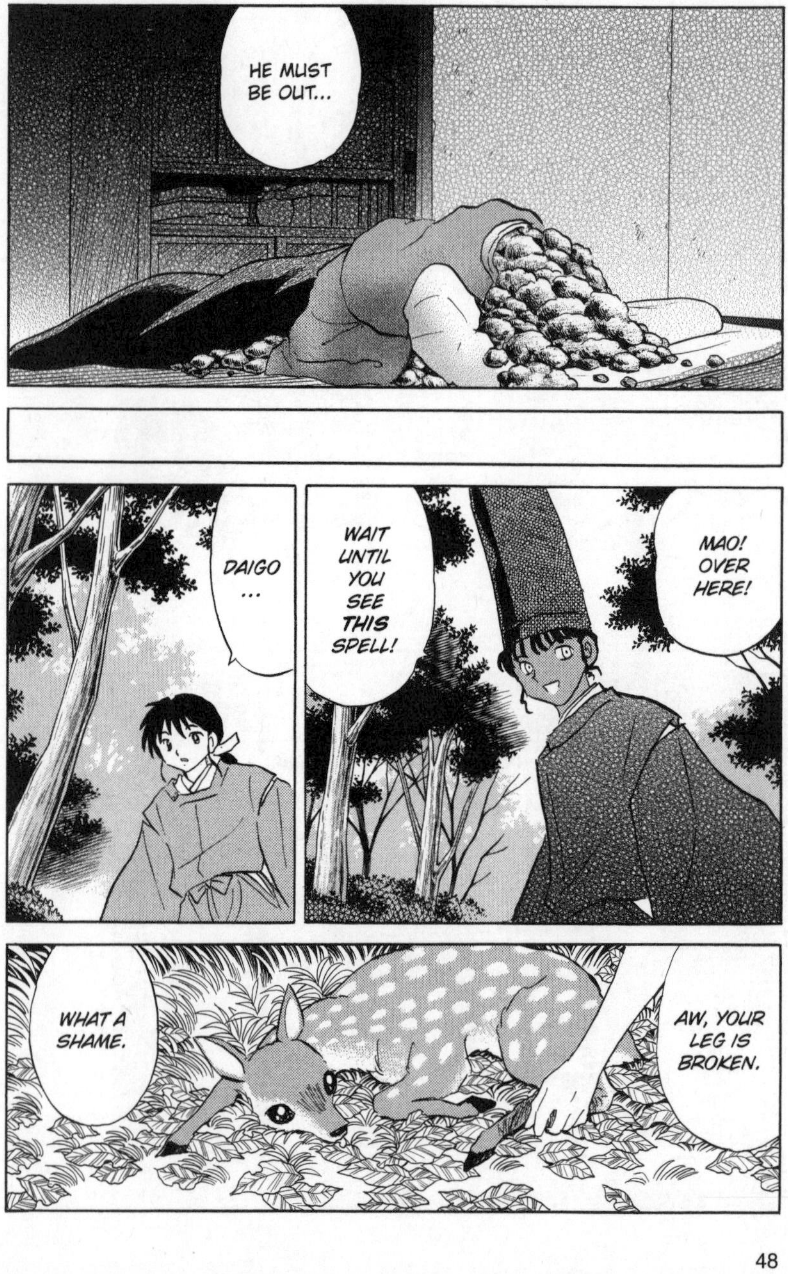
HE MUST BE OUT...
MAO! OVER HERE!
WAIT UNTIL YOU SEE THIS SPELL!
DAIGO ...
AW, YOUR LEG IS BROKEN.
WHAT A SHAME.

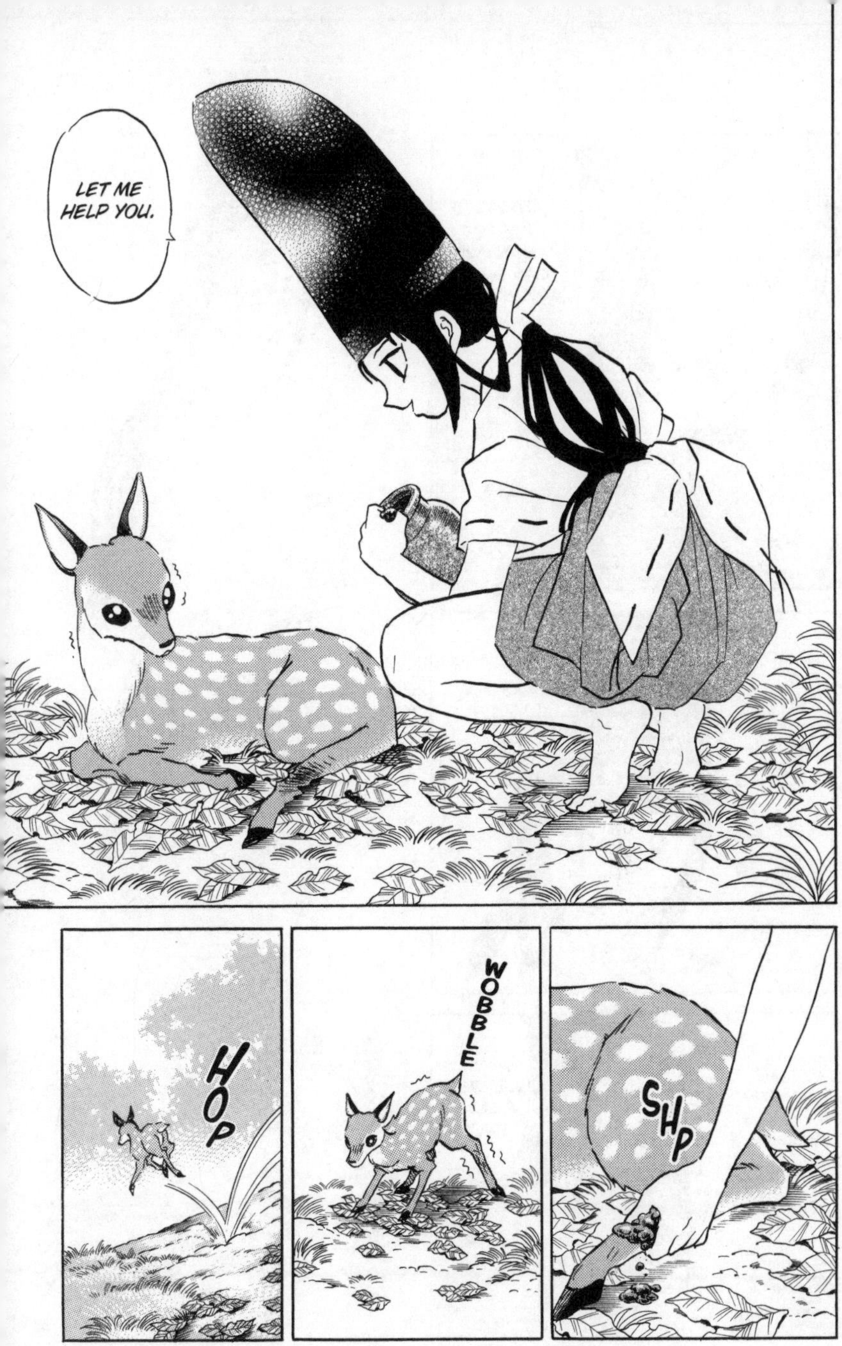
LET ME HELP YOU.
SHP
WOBBLE
HOP

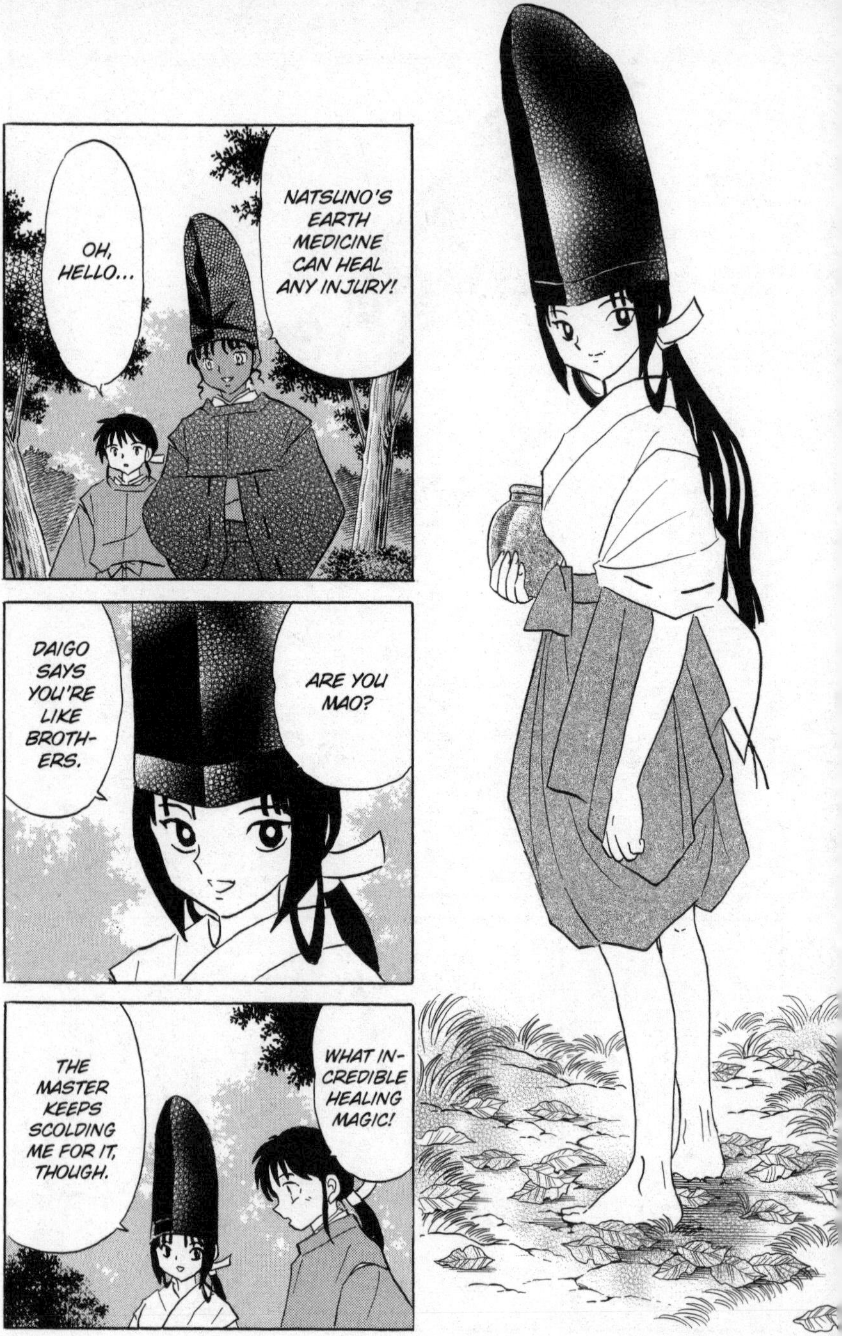
NATSUNO'S EARTH MEDICINE CAN HEAL ANY INJURY!
OH, HELLO...
ARE YOU MAO?
DAIGO SAYS YOU'RE LIKE BROTHERS.
WHAT INCREDIBLE HEALING MAGIC!
THE MASTER KEEPS SCOLDING ME FOR IT, THOUGH.

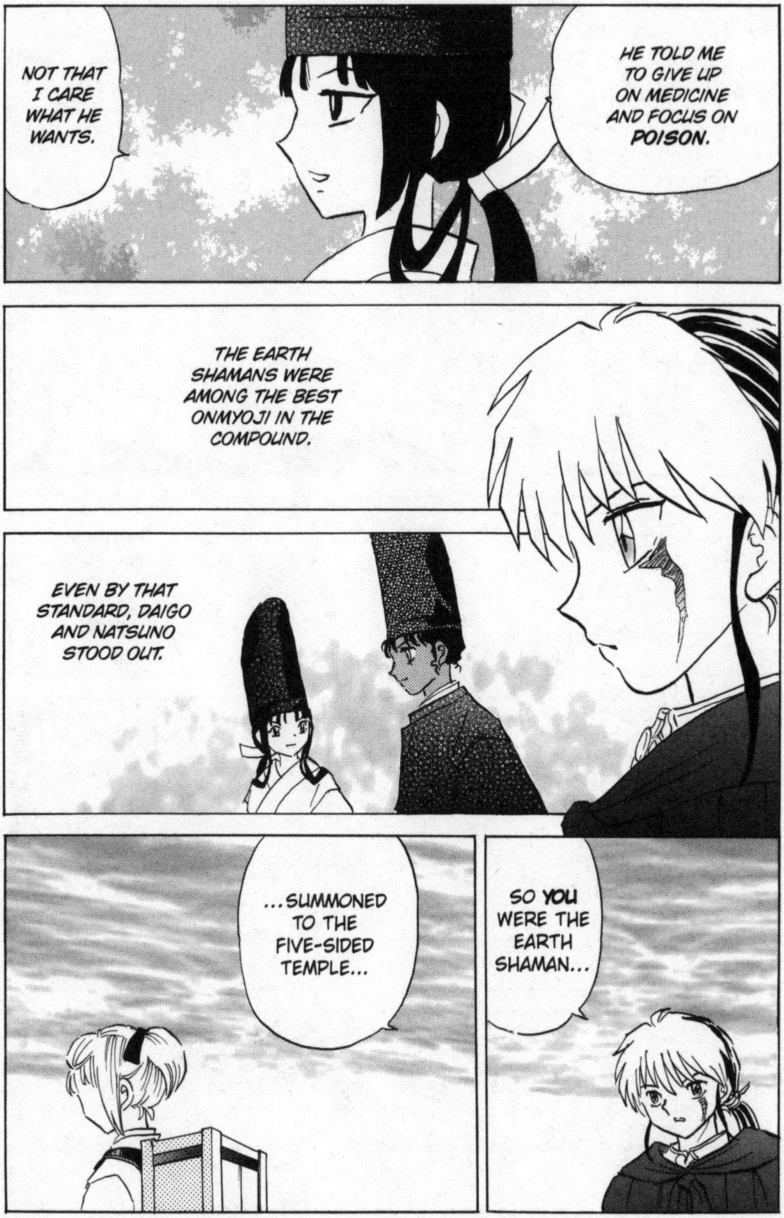
HE TOLD ME TO GIVE UP ON MEDICINE AND FOCUS ON **POISON**.
NOT THAT I CARE WHAT HE WANTS.
THE EARTH SHAMANS WERE AMONG THE BEST ONMYOJI IN THE COMPOUND.
EVEN BY THAT STANDARD, DAIGO AND NATSUNO STOOD OUT.
SO **YOU** WERE THE EARTH SHAMAN...
...SUMMONED TO THE FIVE-SIDED TEMPLE...

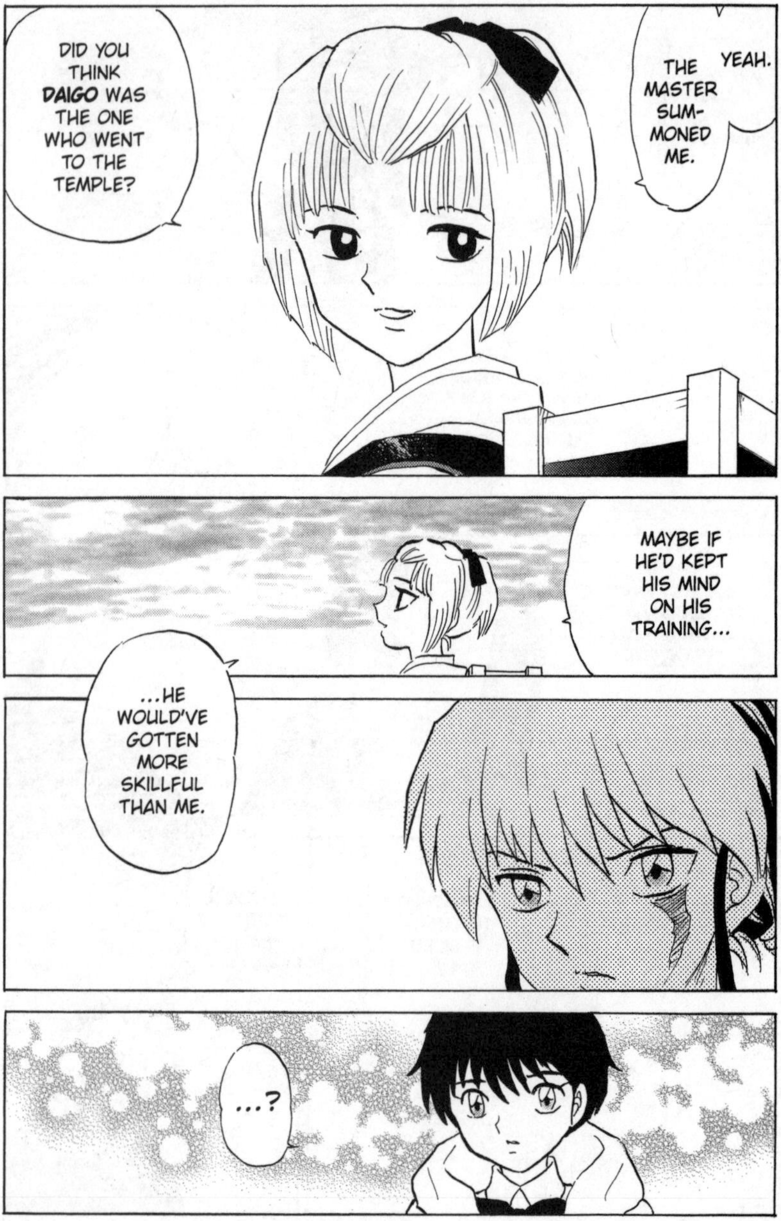
YEAH.
THE MASTER SUMMONED ME.
DID YOU THINK DAIGO WAS THE ONE WHO WENT TO THE TEMPLE?
MAYBE IF HE'D KEPT HIS MIND ON HIS TRAINING...
...HE WOULD'VE GOTTEN MORE SKILLFUL THAN ME.
...?

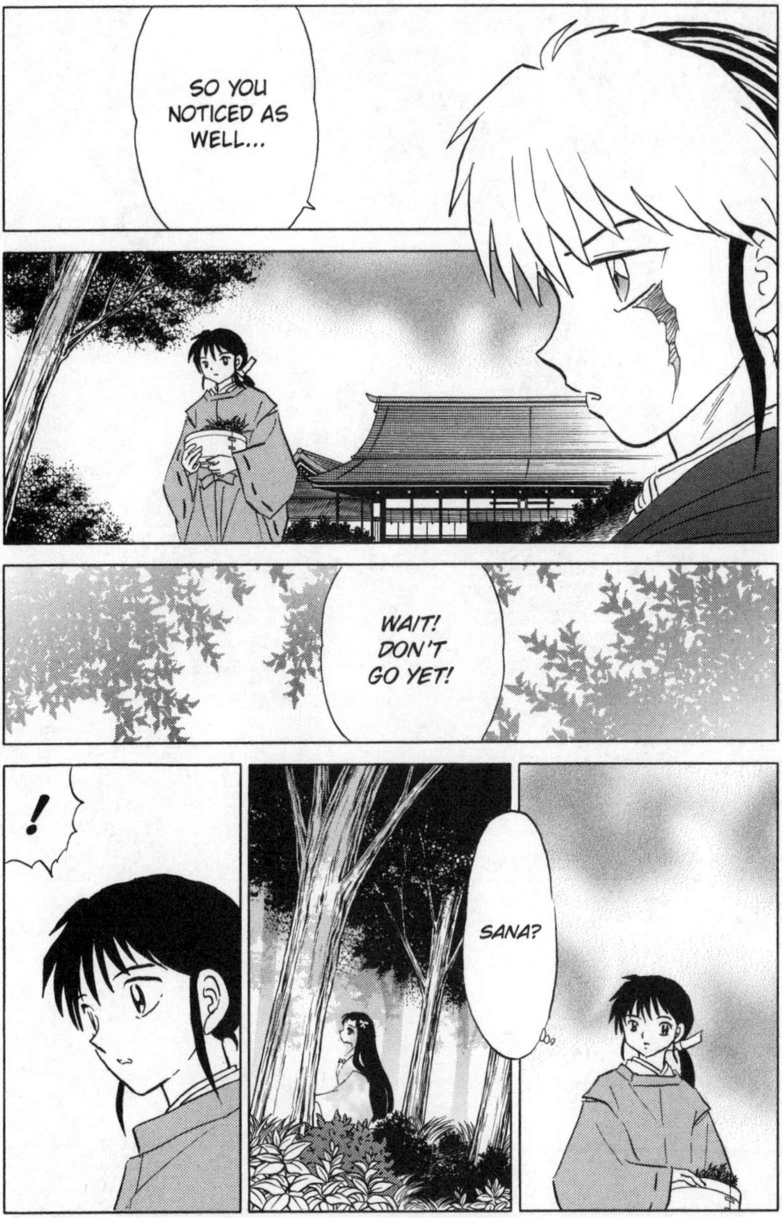
SO YOU NOTICED AS WELL...
WAIT! DON'T GO YET!
SANA?
!

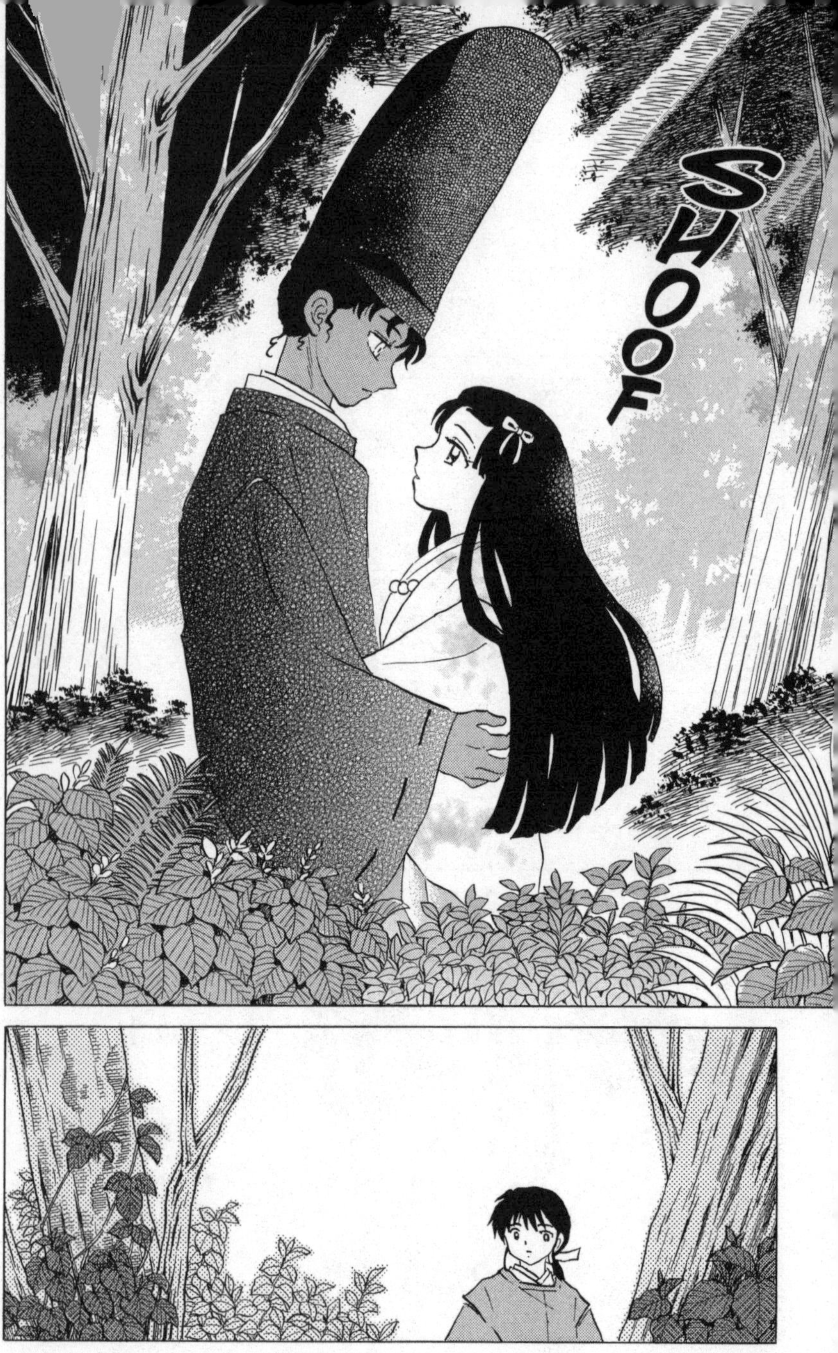
SHOOOF

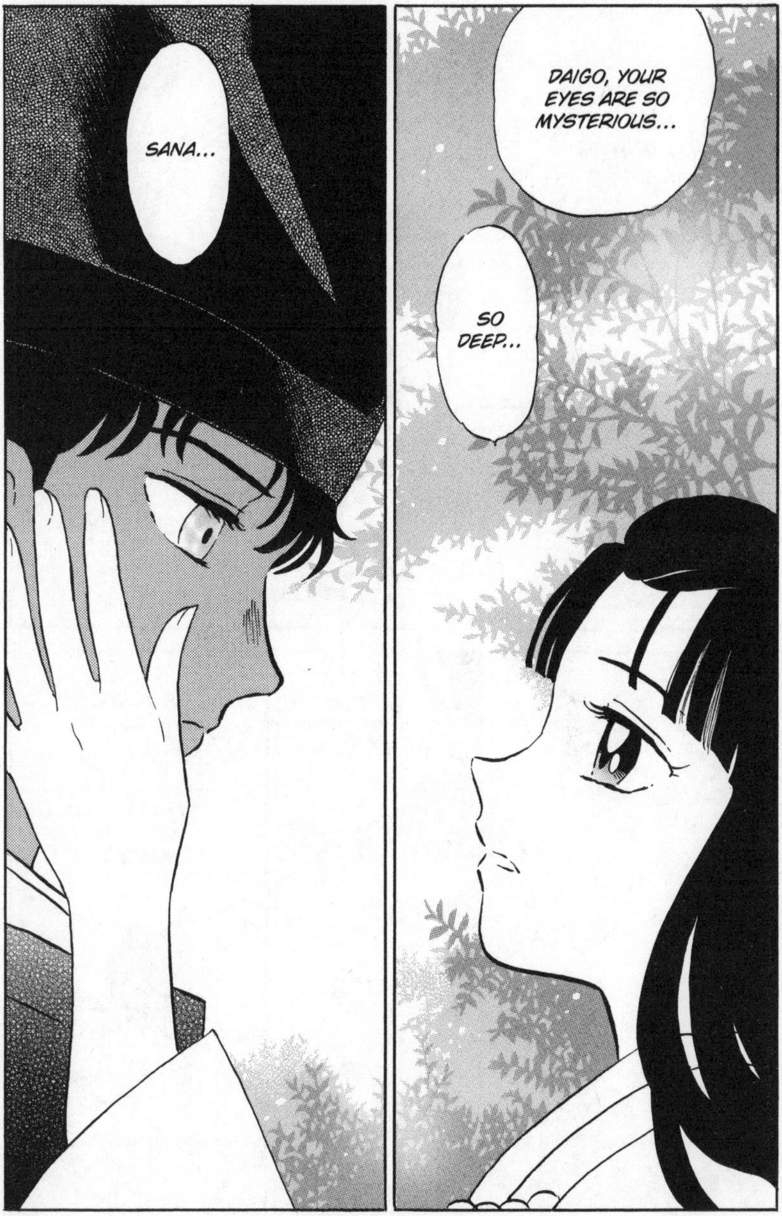
DAIGO, YOUR EYES ARE SO MYSTERIOUS...
SO DEEP...
SANA...

HUH?
SANA WAS IN LOVE WITH DAIGO?
THEY TRIED TO KEEP THEIR TRYSTS SECRET...
...BUT SOME OF US NOTICED.
IF ANYONE WERE JEALOUS OF DAIGO, IT WOULD'VE BEEN AWFULLY TEMPTING TO TELL THE MASTER.
THAT REMINDS ME, MAO...
YOU WERE IN LOVE WITH SANA, WEREN'T YOU?
!

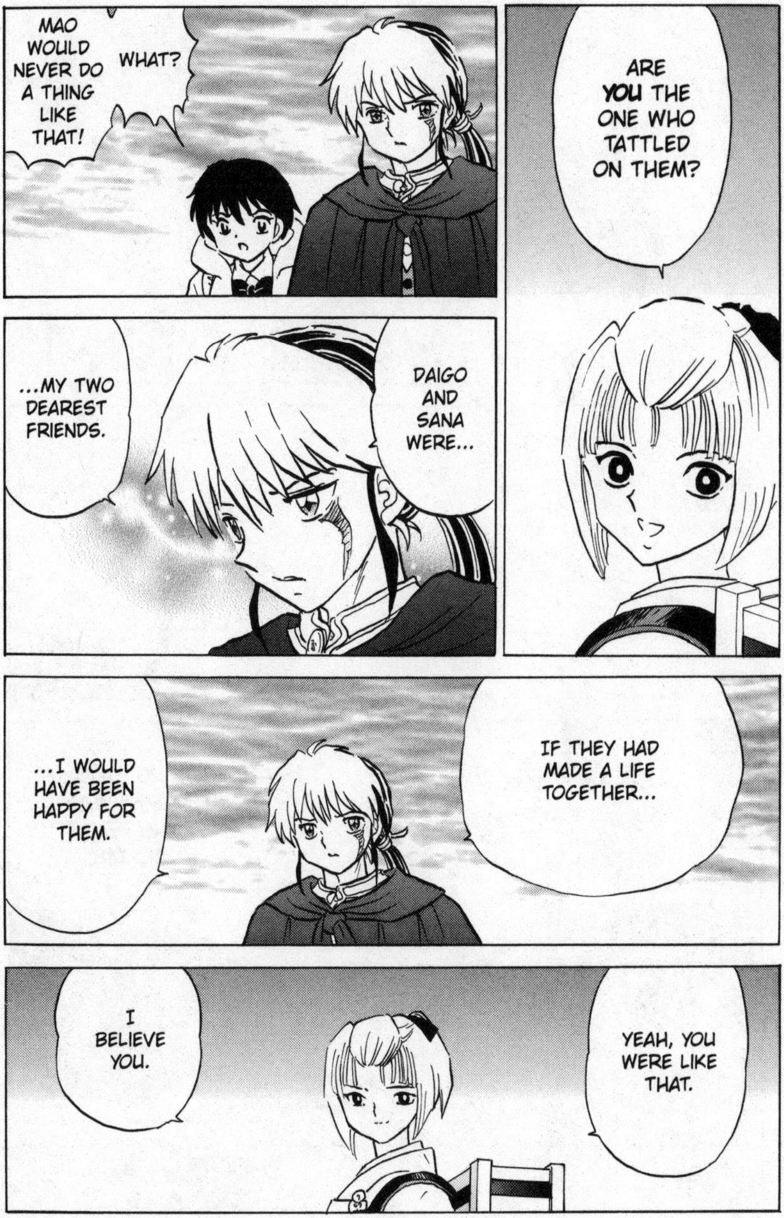
ARE **YOU** THE ONE WHO TATTLED ON THEM?
WHAT?
MAO WOULD NEVER DO A THING LIKE THAT!
DAIGO AND SANA WERE...
...MY TWO DEAREST FRIENDS.
IF THEY HAD MADE A LIFE TOGETHER...
...I WOULD HAVE BEEN HAPPY FOR THEM.
YEAH, YOU WERE LIKE THAT.
I BELIEVE YOU.

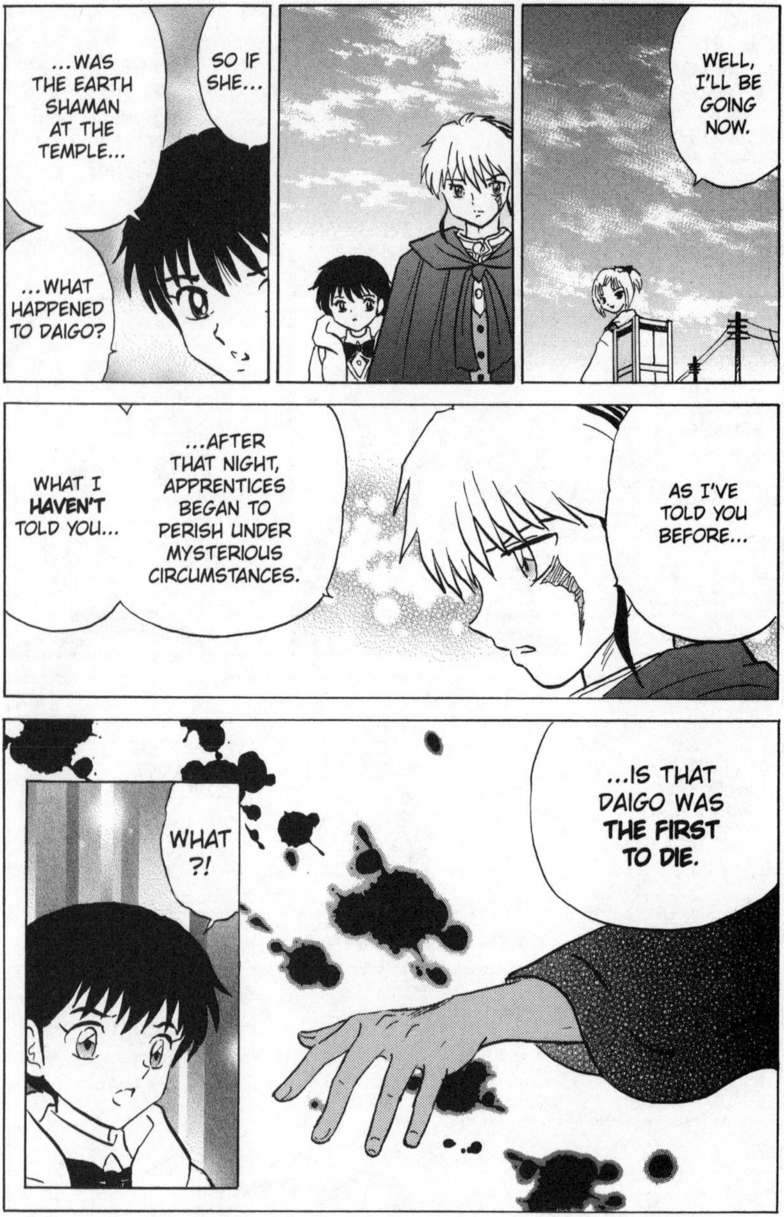
WELL, I'LL BE GOING NOW.
SO IF SHE...
...WAS THE EARTH SHAMAN AT THE TEMPLE...
...WHAT HAPPENED TO DAIGO?
AS I'VE TOLD YOU BEFORE...
...AFTER THAT NIGHT, APPRENTICES BEGAN TO PERISH UNDER MYSTERIOUS CIRCUMSTANCES.
WHAT I **HAVEN'T** TOLD YOU...
...IS THAT DAIGO WAS **THE FIRST TO DIE.**
WHAT?!

Chapter 4: Daigo's Death

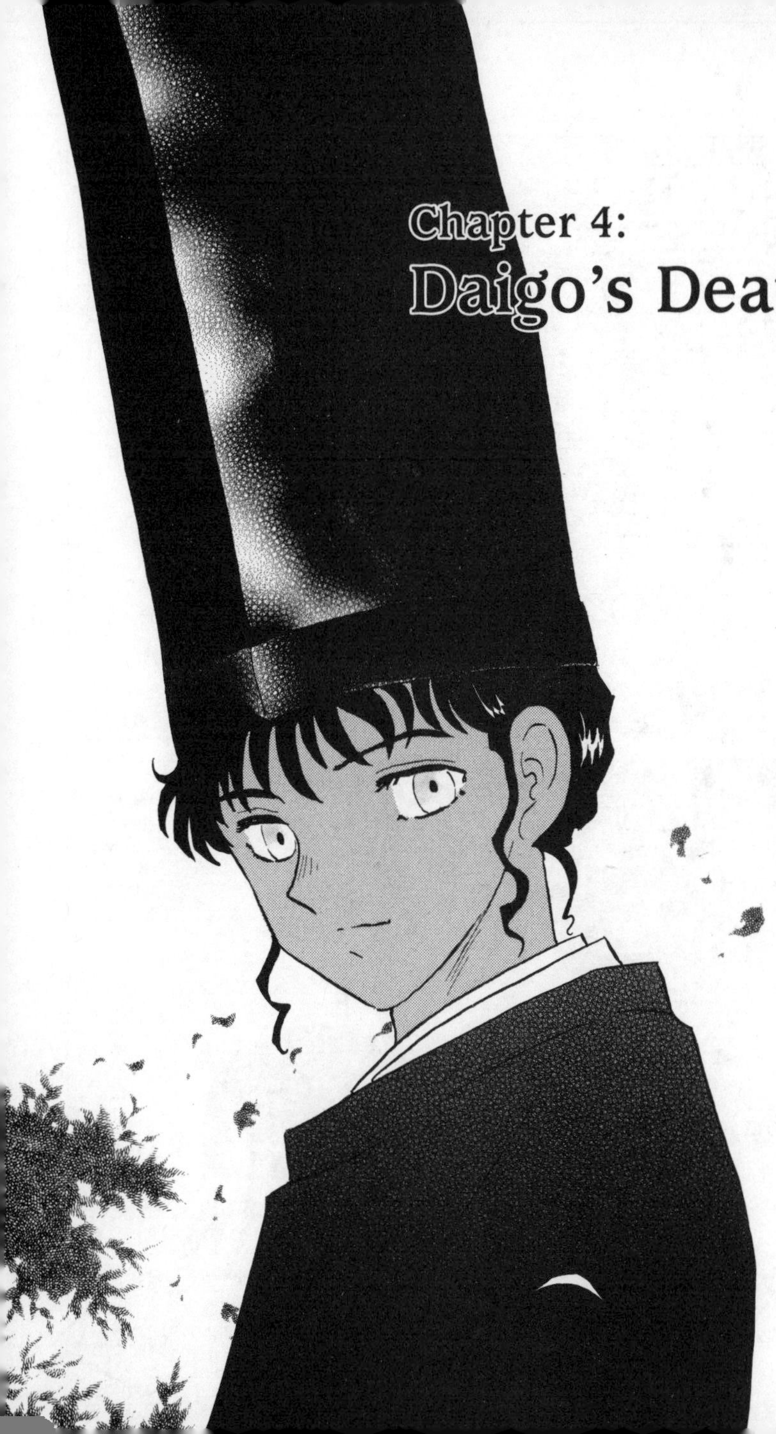

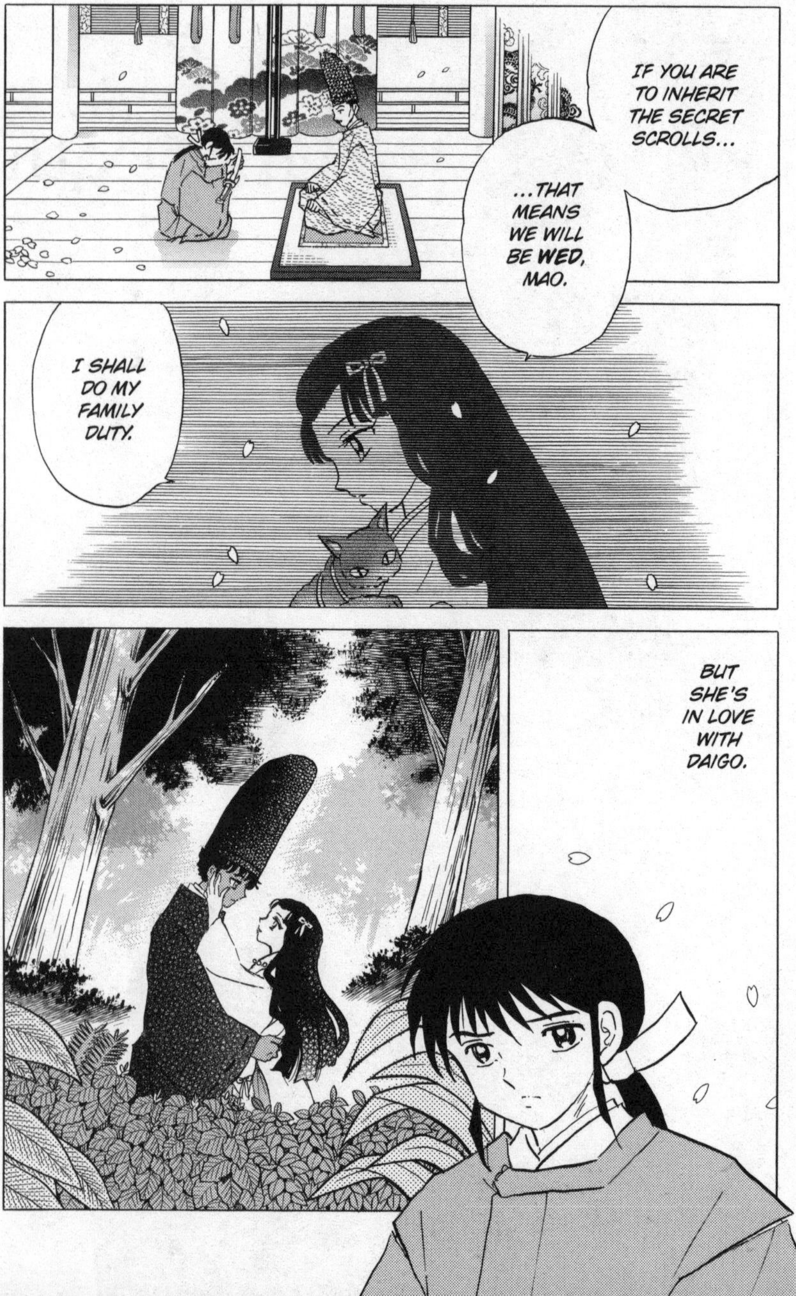
IF YOU ARE TO INHERIT THE SECRET SCROLLS...
...THAT MEANS WE WILL BE WED, MAO.
I SHALL DO MY FAMILY DUTY.
BUT SHE'S IN LOVE WITH DAIGO.

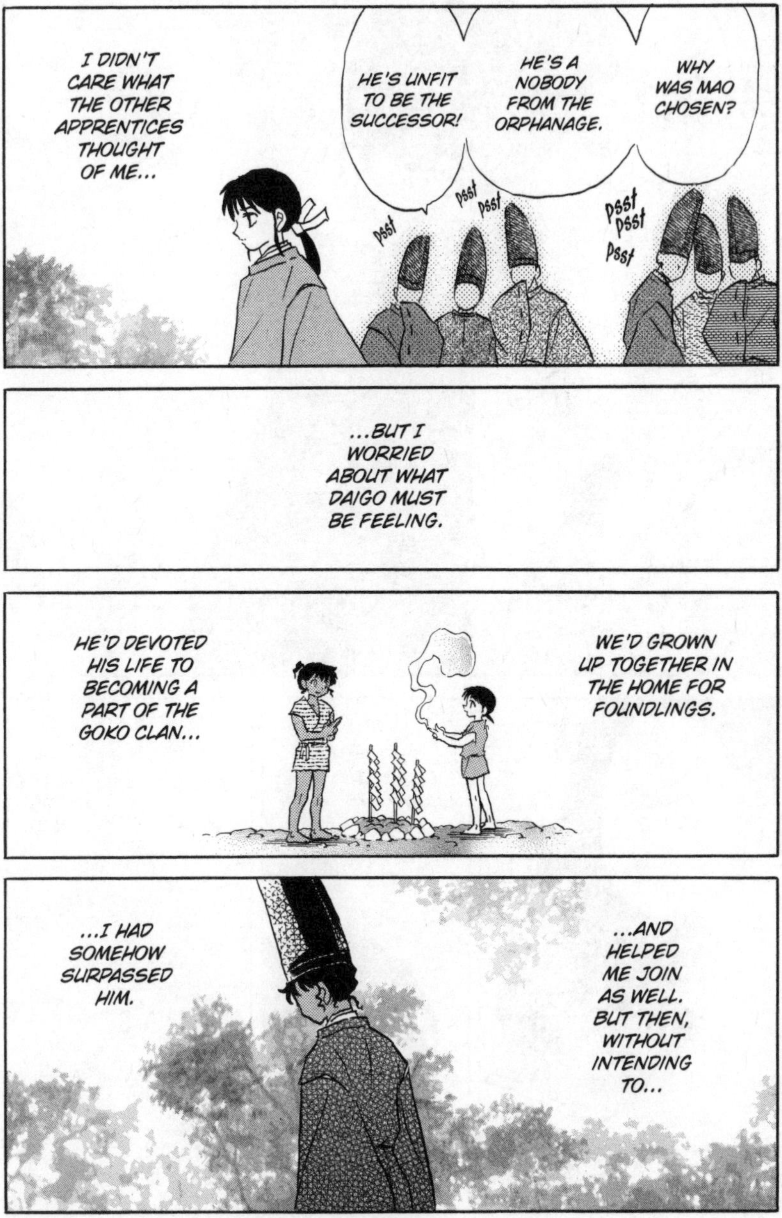
WHY WAS MAO CHOSEN?
HE'S A NOBODY FROM THE ORPHANAGE.
HE'S UNFIT TO BE THE SUCCESSOR!
pssst pssst pssst
pssst pssst
I DIDN'T CARE WHAT THE OTHER APPRENTICES THOUGHT OF ME...
...BUT I WORRIED ABOUT WHAT DAIGO MUST BE FEELING.
WE'D GROWN UP TOGETHER IN THE HOME FOR FOUNDLINGS.
HE'D DEVOTED HIS LIFE TO BECOMING A PART OF THE GOKO CLAN...
...AND HELPED ME JOIN AS WELL. BUT THEN, WITHOUT INTENDING TO...
...I HAD SOMEHOW SURPASSED HIM.

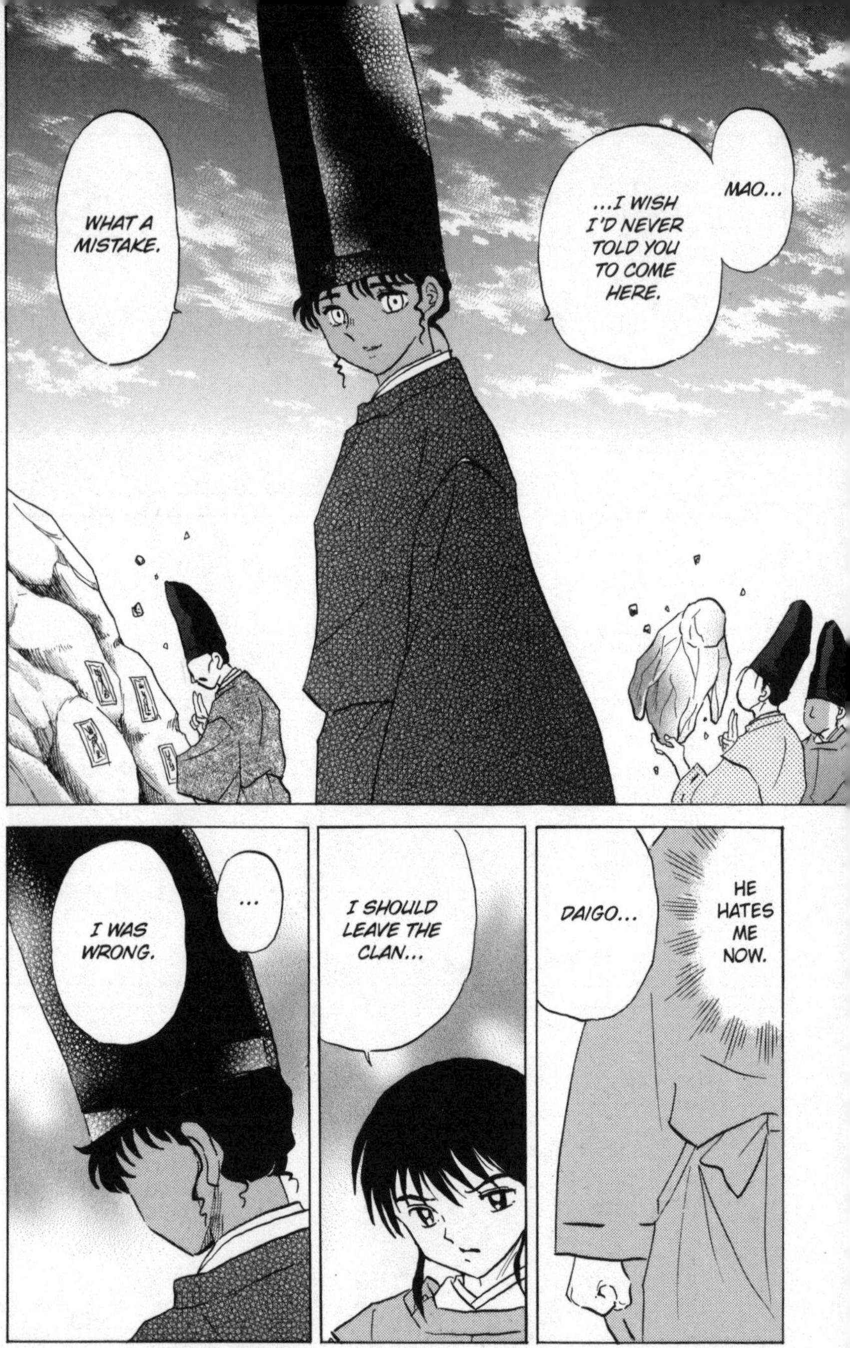
MAO...
...I WISH I'D NEVER TOLD YOU TO COME HERE.
WHAT A MISTAKE.
HE HATES ME NOW.
DAIGO...
I SHOULD LEAVE THE CLAN...
...
I WAS WRONG.

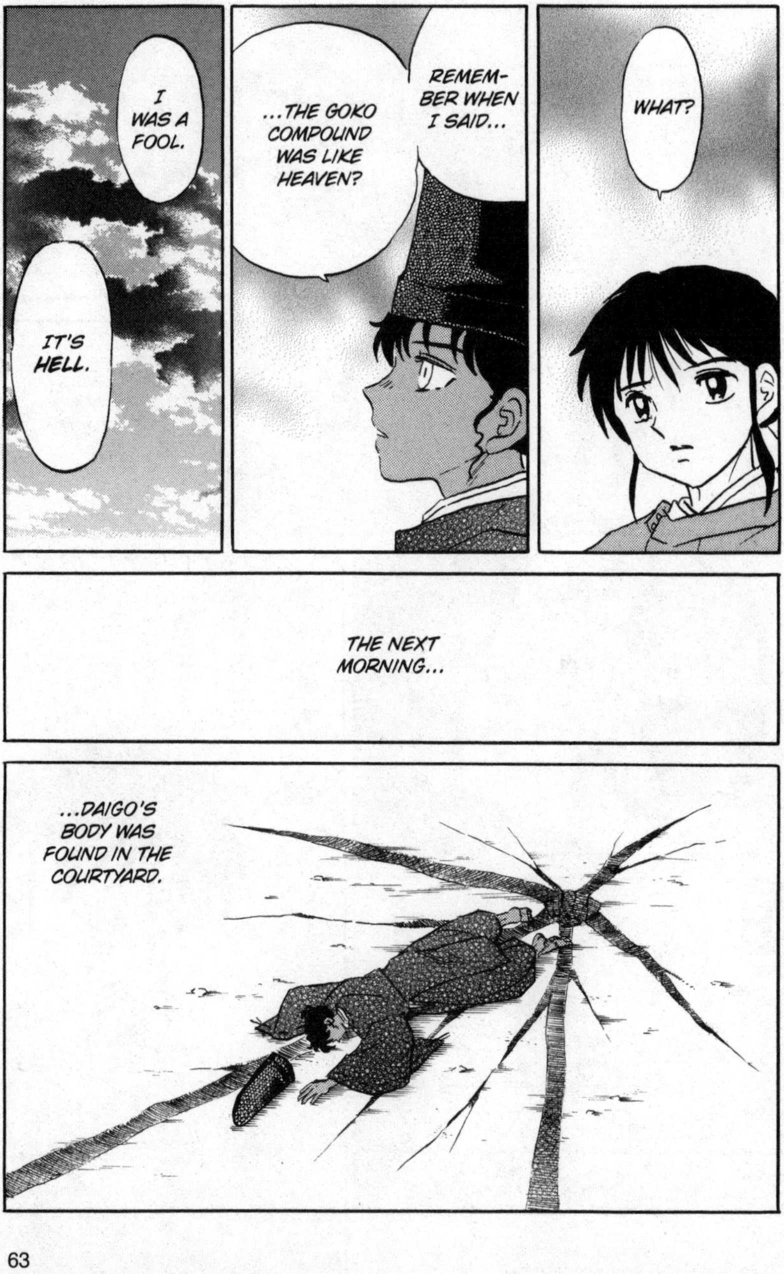
WHAT?
REMEMBER WHEN I SAID...
...THE GOKO COMPOUND WAS LIKE HEAVEN?
I WAS A FOOL.
IT'S HELL.
THE NEXT MORNING...
...DAIGO'S BODY WAS FOUND IN THE COURTYARD.

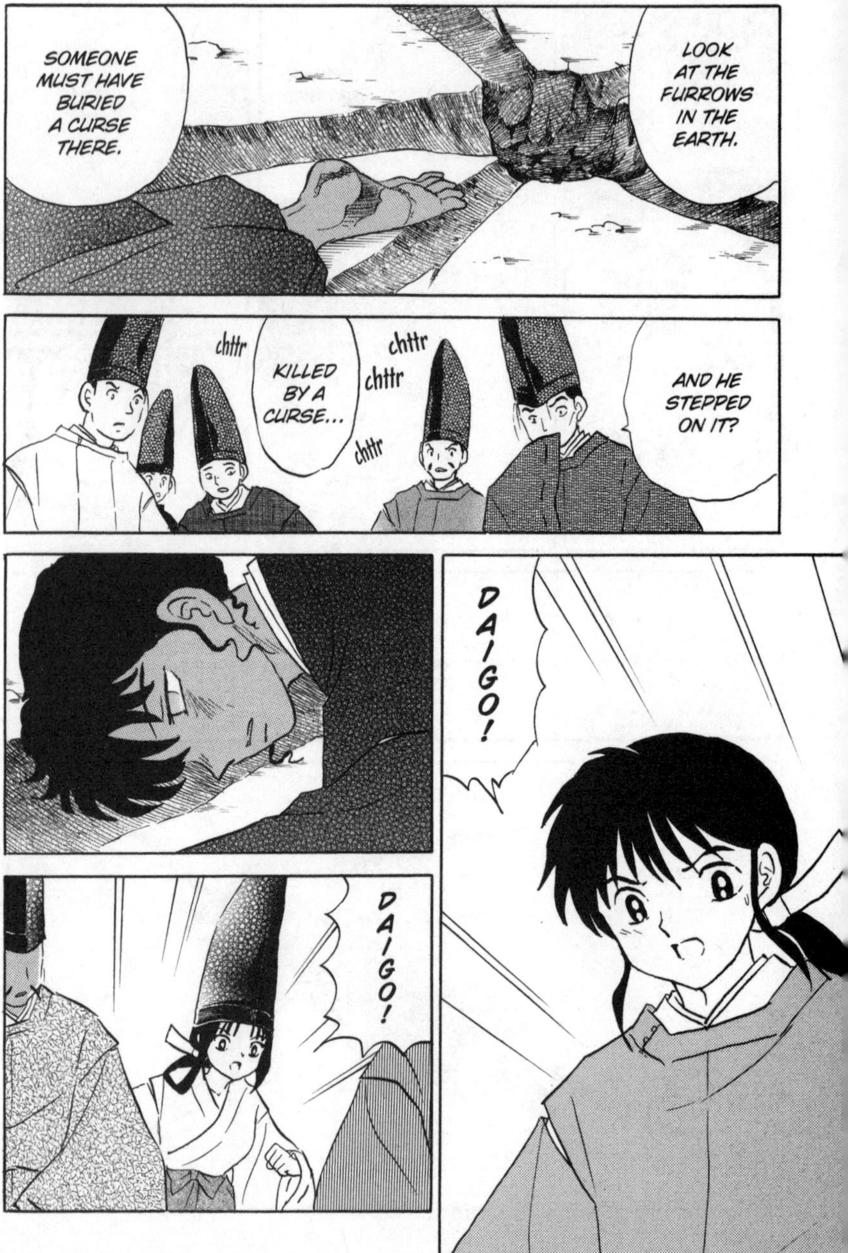
LOOK AT THE FURROWS IN THE EARTH.
SOMEONE MUST HAVE BURIED A CURSE THERE.
AND HE STEPPED ON IT?
chttr
chttr
KILLED BY A CURSE...
chttr
chttr
DAIGO!
DAIGO!

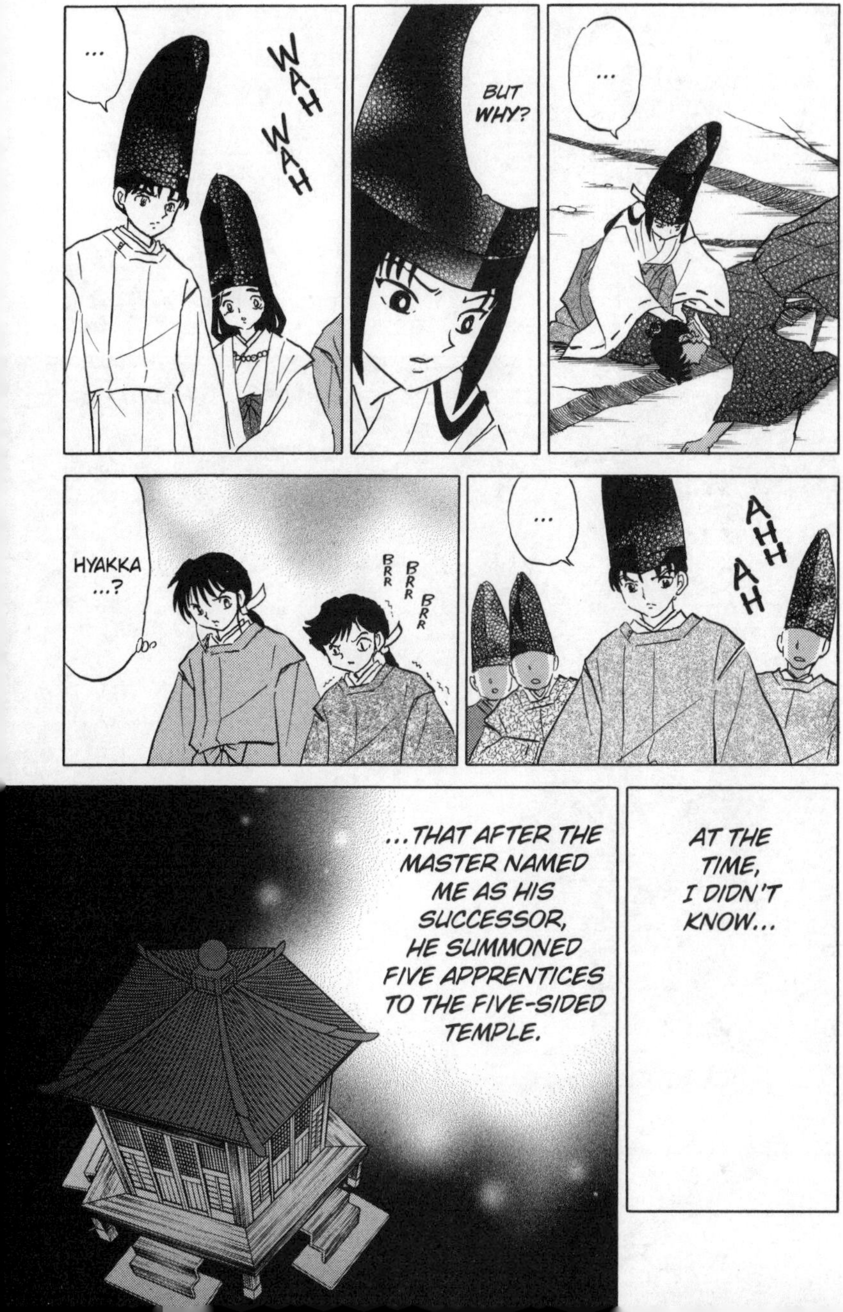
...
BUT WHY?
WAH WAH
...
AHH AH
...
BRR BRR BRR
HYAKKA ...?
AT THE TIME, I DIDN'T KNOW...
...THAT AFTER THE MASTER NAMED ME AS HIS SUCCESSOR, HE SUMMONED FIVE APPRENTICES TO THE FIVE-SIDED TEMPLE.

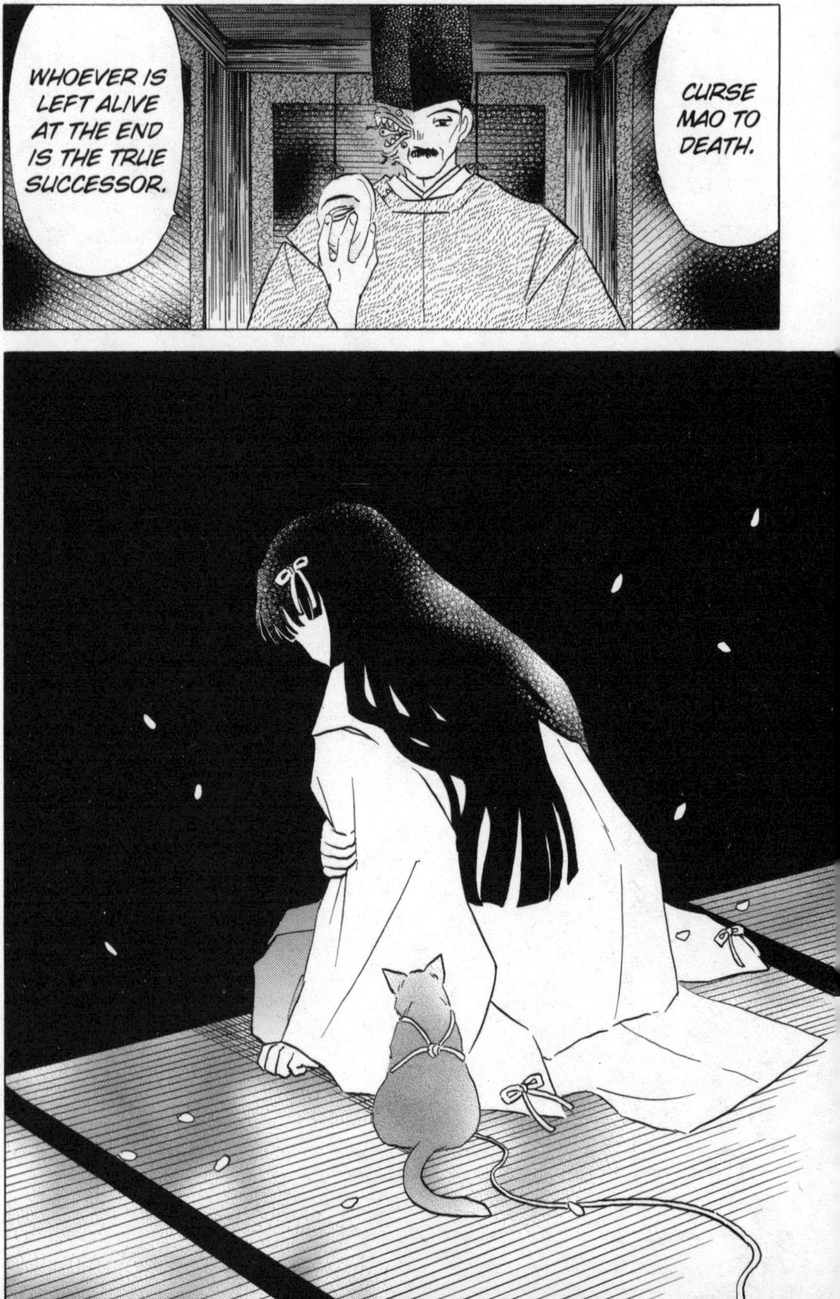
CURSE MAO TO DEATH.
WHOEVER IS LEFT ALIVE AT THE END IS THE TRUE SUCCESSOR.

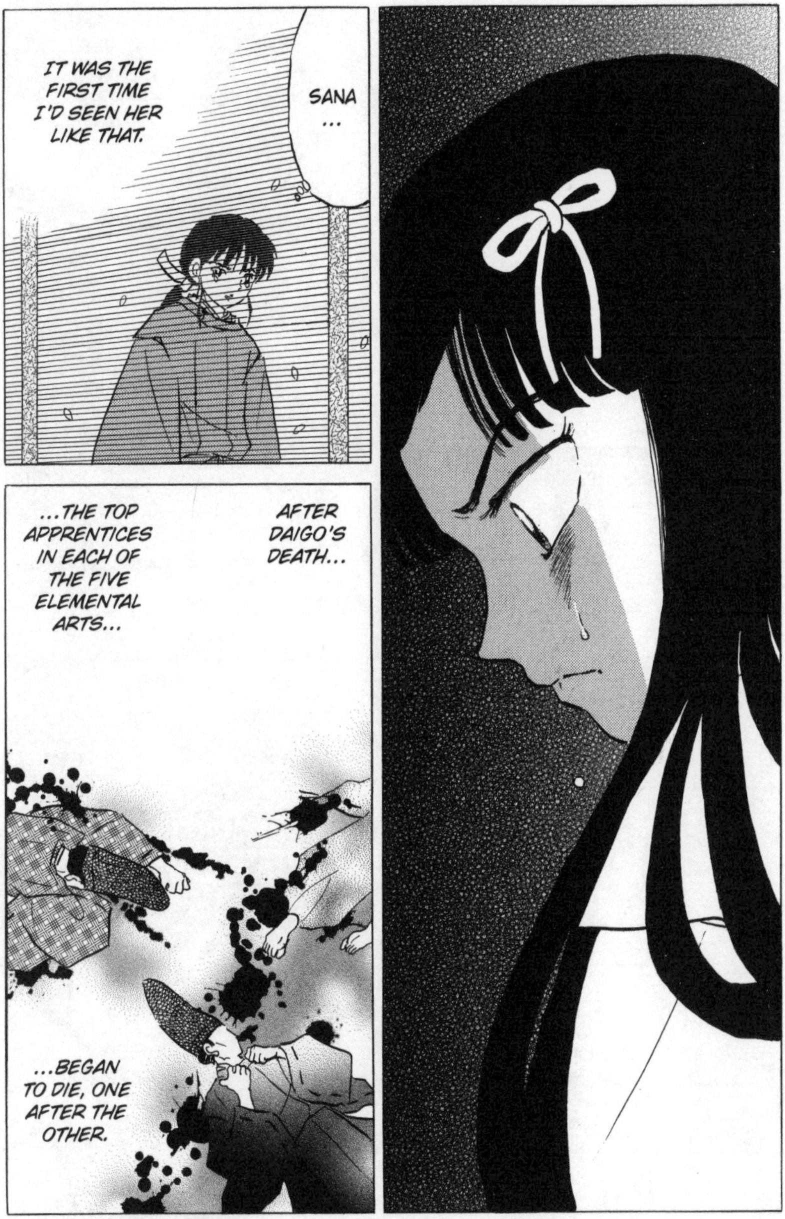
SANA ...
IT WAS THE FIRST TIME I'D SEEN HER LIKE THAT.
AFTER DAIGO'S DEATH...
...THE TOP APPRENTICES IN EACH OF THE FIVE ELEMENTAL ARTS...
...BEGAN TO DIE, ONE AFTER THE OTHER.

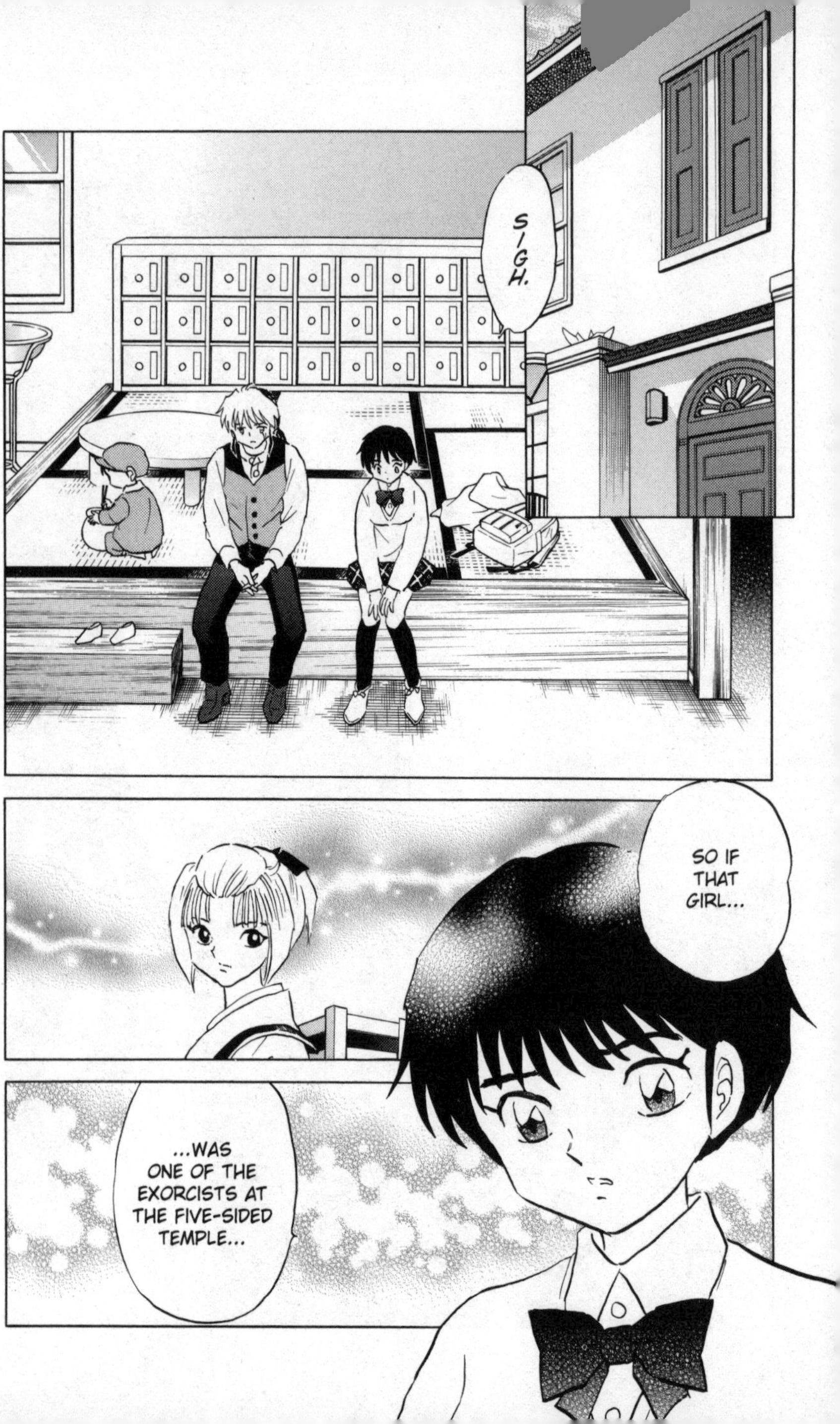
SIGH.
SO IF THAT GIRL...
...WAS ONE OF THE EXORCISTS AT THE FIVE-SIDED TEMPLE...

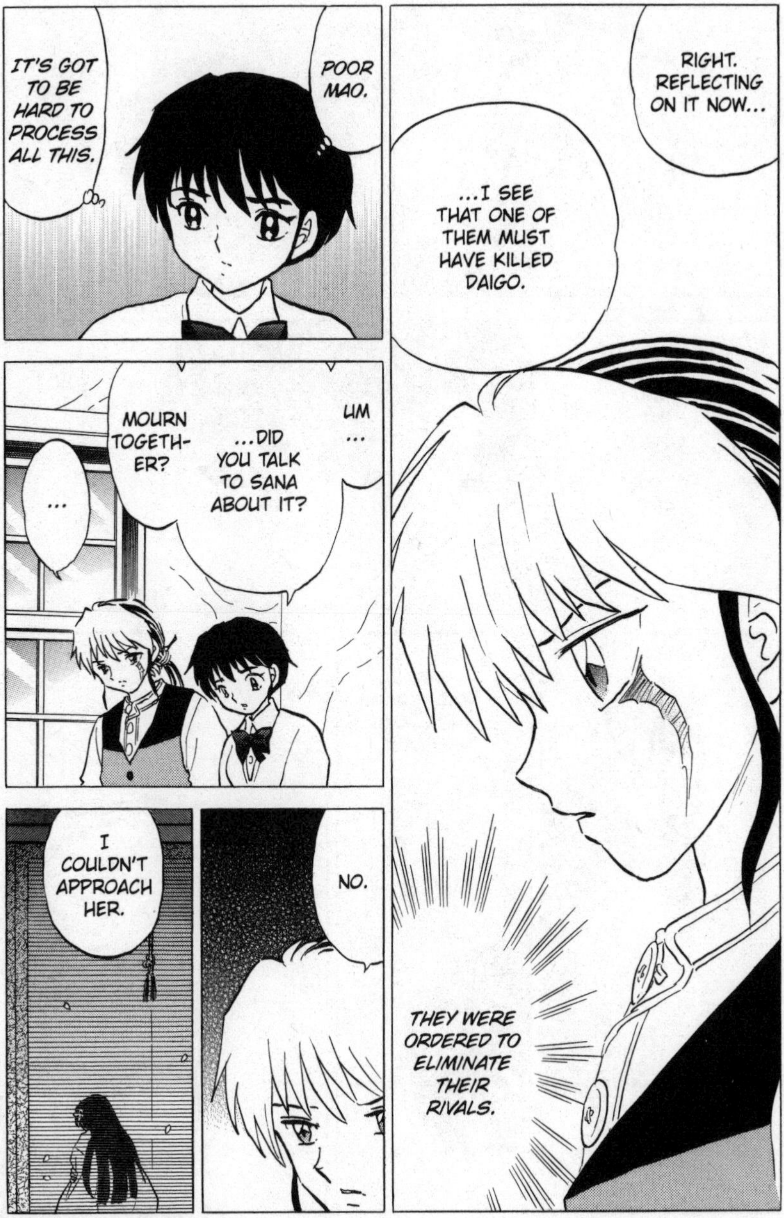
RIGHT. REFLECTING ON IT NOW...
...I SEE THAT ONE OF THEM MUST HAVE KILLED DAIGO.
THEY WERE ORDERED TO ELIMINATE THEIR RIVALS.
POOR MAO.
IT'S GOT TO BE HARD TO PROCESS ALL THIS.
UM ...
...DID YOU TALK TO SANA ABOUT IT?
MOURN TOGETH-ER?
...
NO.
I COULDN'T APPROACH HER.

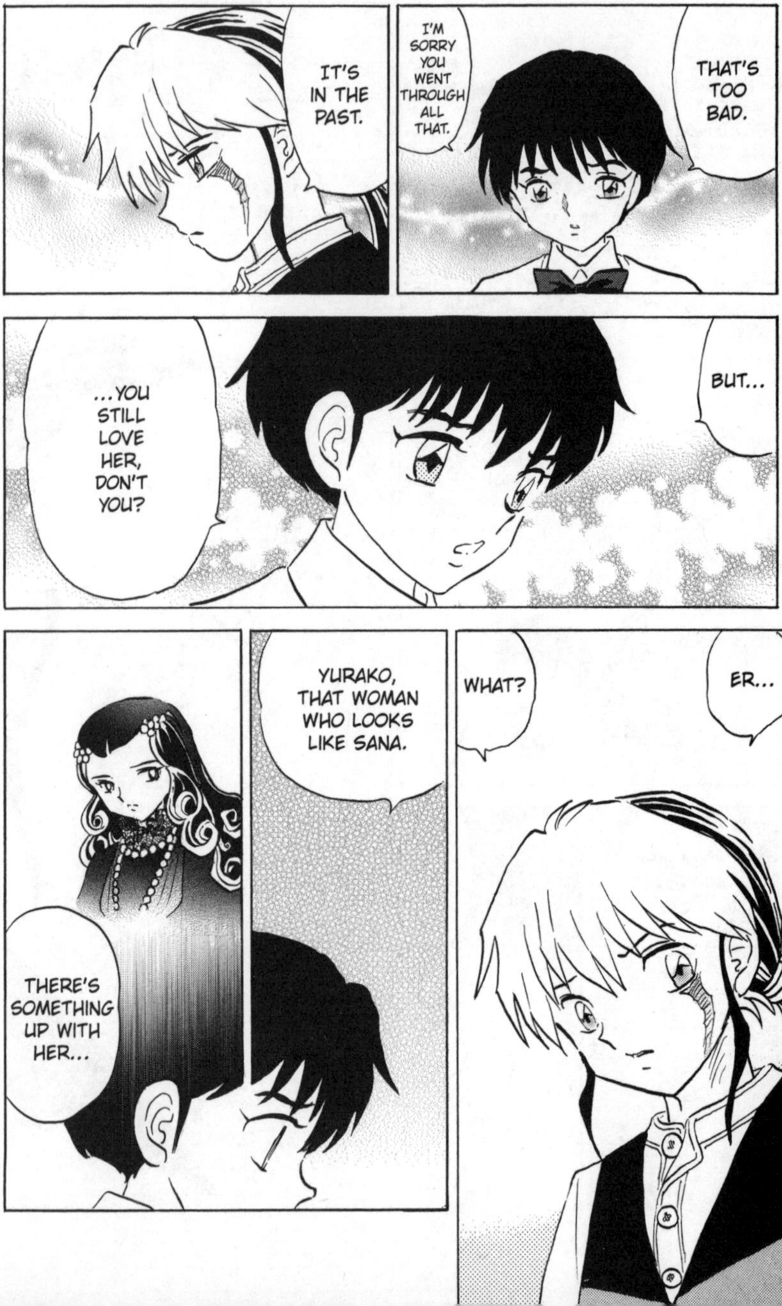
THAT'S TOO BAD.
I'M SORRY YOU WENT THROUGH ALL THAT.
IT'S IN THE PAST.
BUT...
...YOU STILL LOVE HER, DON'T YOU?
ER...
WHAT?
YURAKO, THAT WOMAN WHO LOOKS LIKE SANA.
THERE'S SOMETHING UP WITH HER...

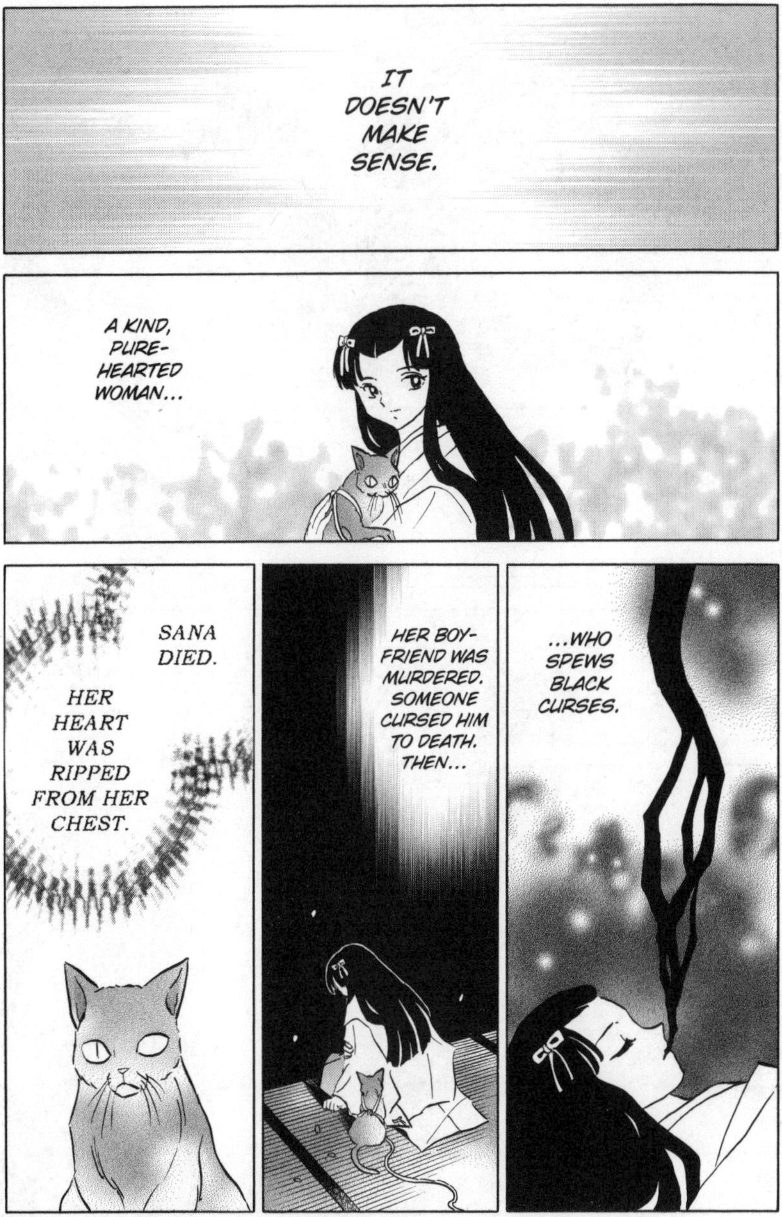
IT DOESN'T MAKE SENSE.
A KIND, PURE-HEARTED WOMAN...
...WHO SPEWS BLACK CURSES.
HER BOY-FRIEND WAS MURDERED. SOMEONE CURSED HIM TO DEATH. THEN...
SANA DIED.
HER HEART WAS RIPPED FROM HER CHEST.

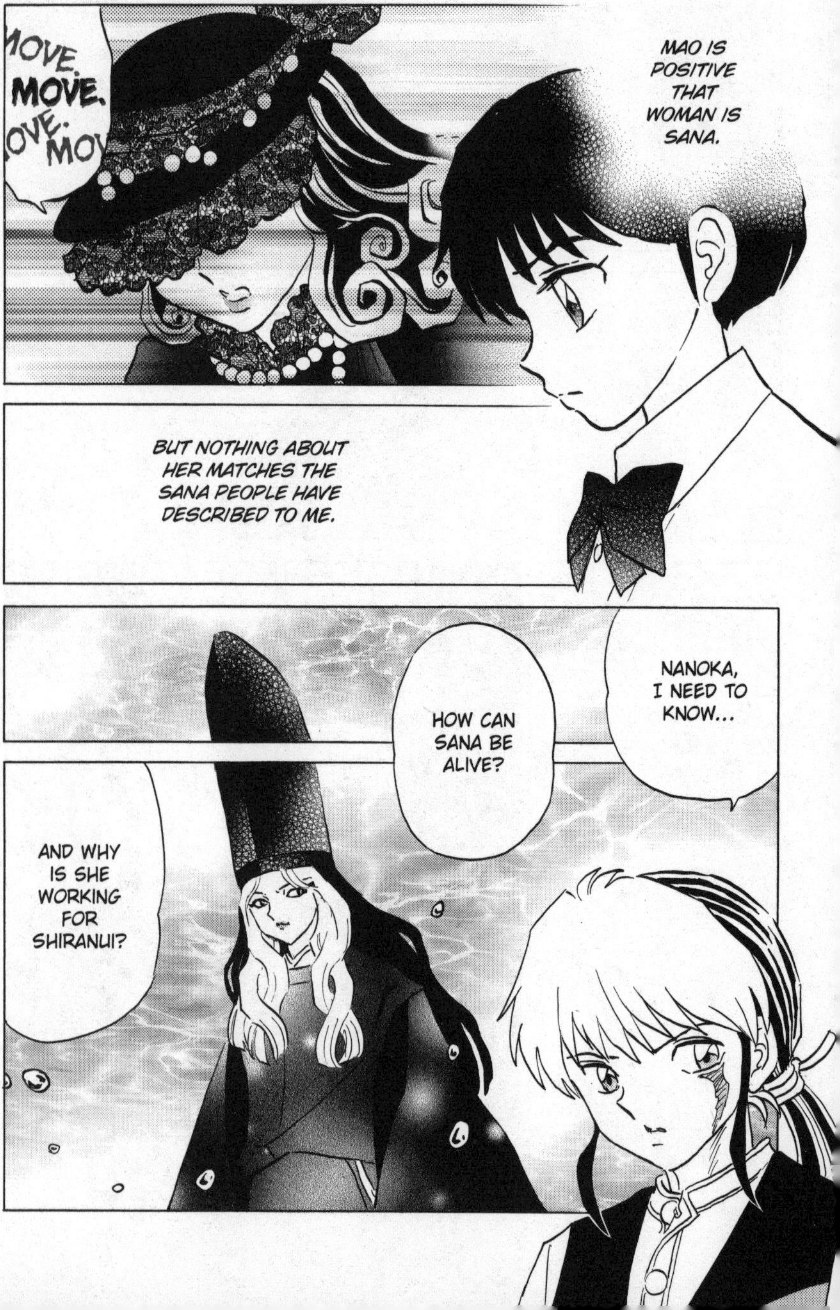
MAO IS POSITIVE THAT WOMAN IS SANA.
MOVE.
BUT NOTHING ABOUT HER MATCHES THE SANA PEOPLE HAVE DESCRIBED TO ME.
NANOKA, I NEED TO KNOW...
HOW CAN SANA BE ALIVE?
AND WHY IS SHE WORKING FOR SHIRANUI?

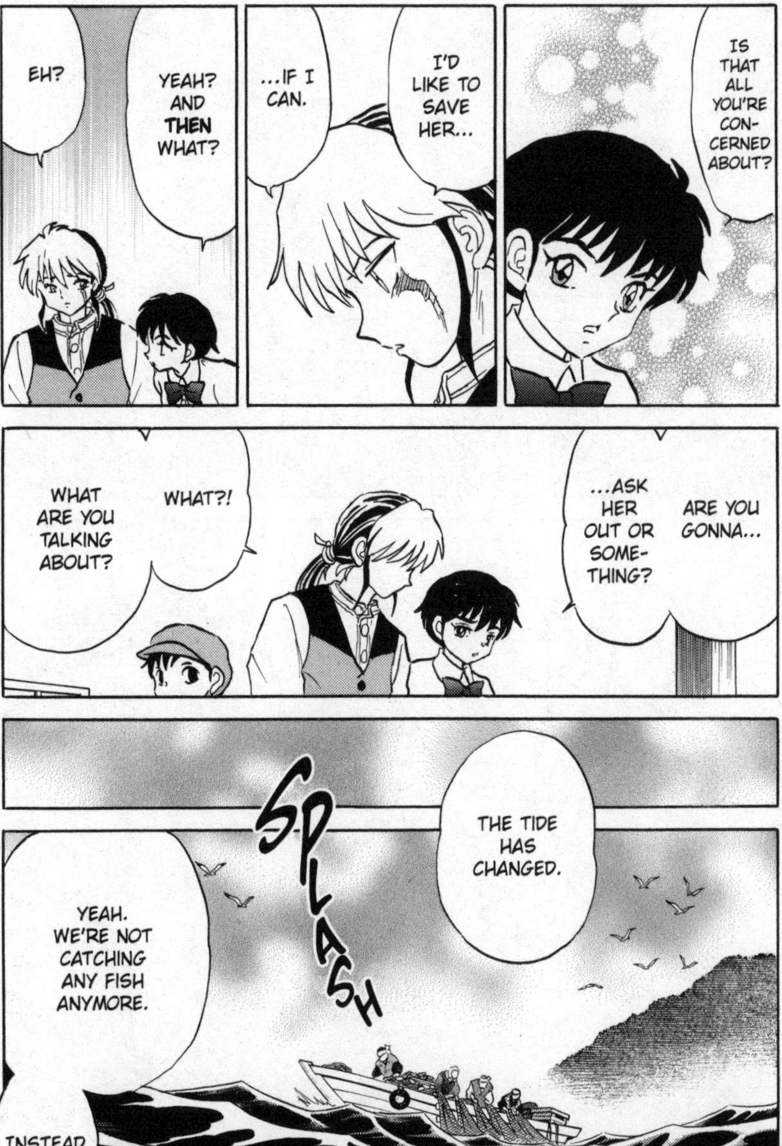
IS THAT ALL YOU'RE CON-CERNED ABOUT?
I'D LIKE TO SAVE HER...
...IF I CAN.
YEAH? AND **THEN** WHAT?
EH?
ARE YOU GONNA...
...ASK HER OUT OR SOME-THING?
WHAT?!
WHAT ARE YOU TALKING ABOUT?
THE TIDE HAS CHANGED.
SPLASH
YEAH. WE'RE NOT CATCHING ANY FISH ANYMORE.
INSTEAD ...

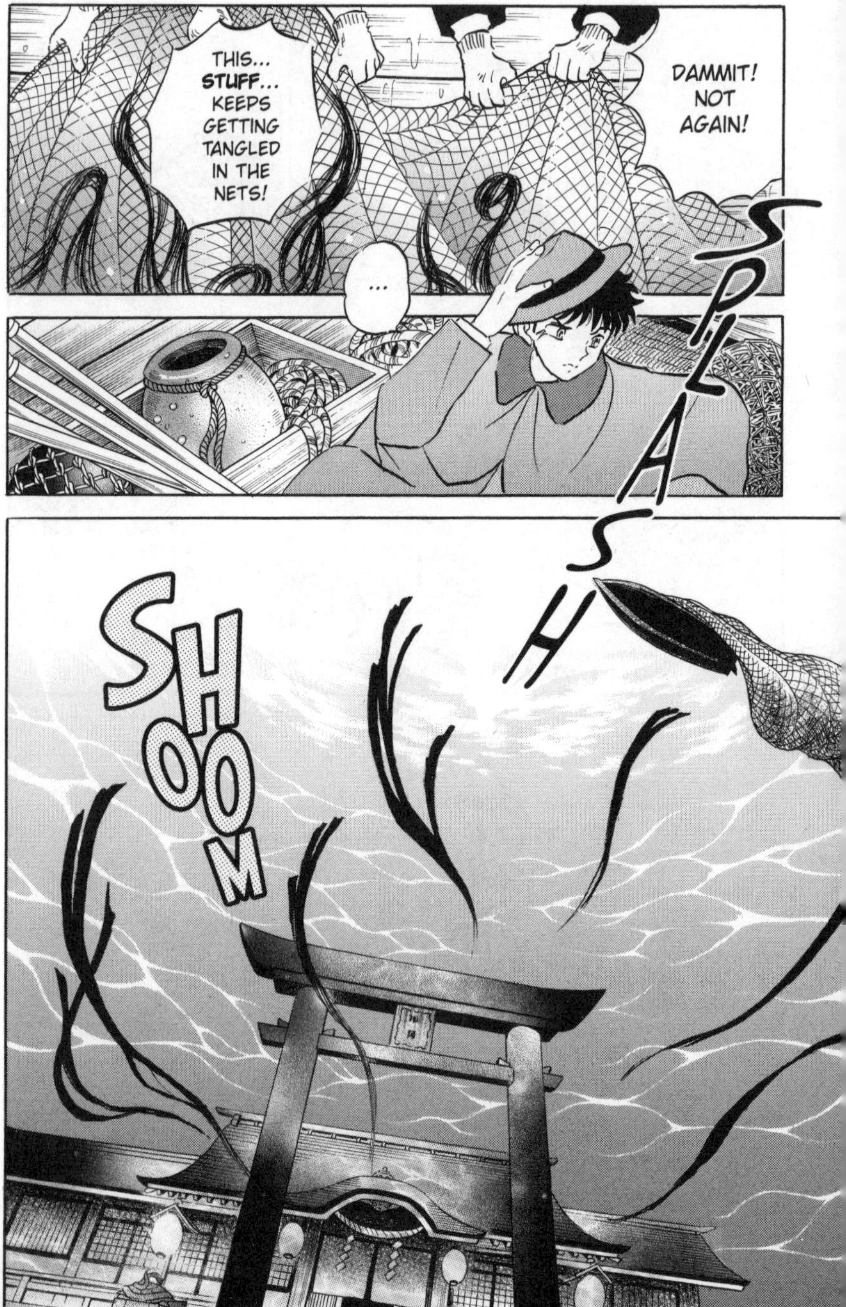
DAMMIT! NOT AGAIN!
THIS... STUFF... KEEPS GETTING TANGLED IN THE NETS!
...
SPLASH
SHOOM

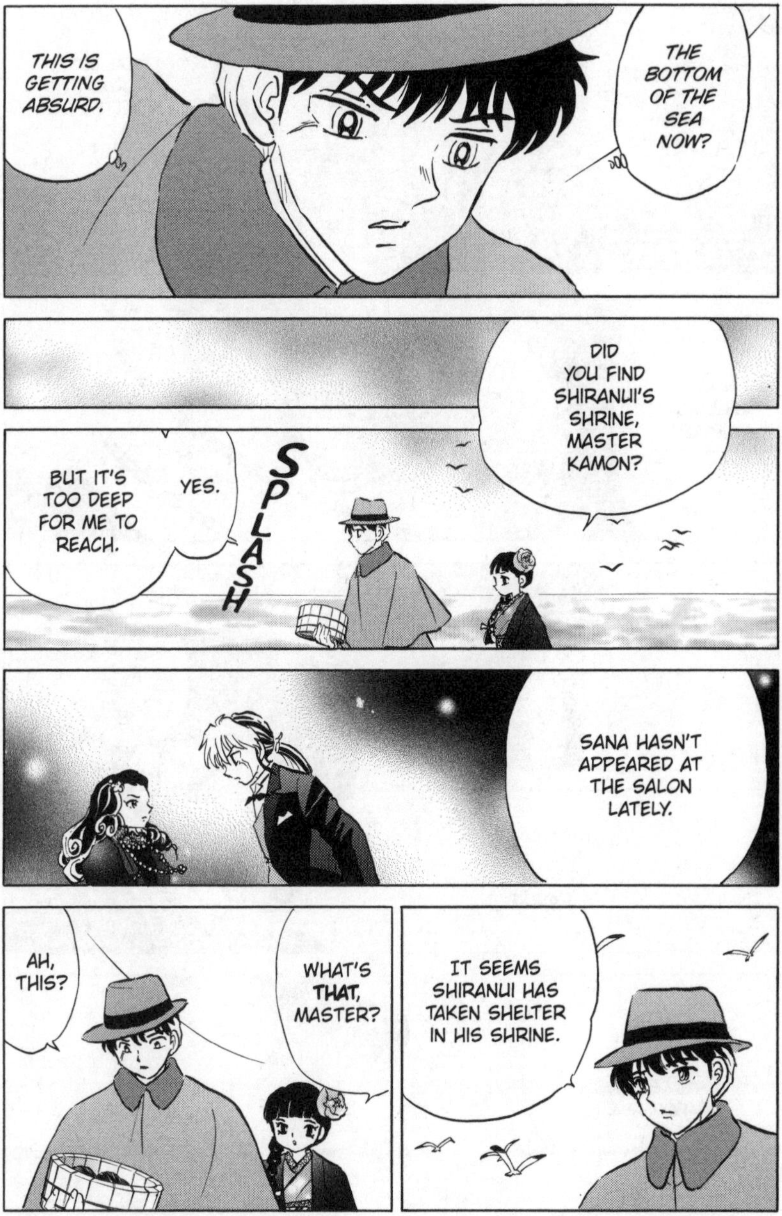
THE BOTTOM OF THE SEA NOW?
THIS IS GETTING ABSURD.
DID YOU FIND SHIRANUI'S SHRINE, MASTER KAMON?
SPLASH
YES.
BUT IT'S TOO DEEP FOR ME TO REACH.
SANA HASN'T APPEARED AT THE SALON LATELY.
IT SEEMS SHIRANUI HAS TAKEN SHELTER IN HIS SHRINE.
WHAT'S THAT, MASTER?
AH, THIS?

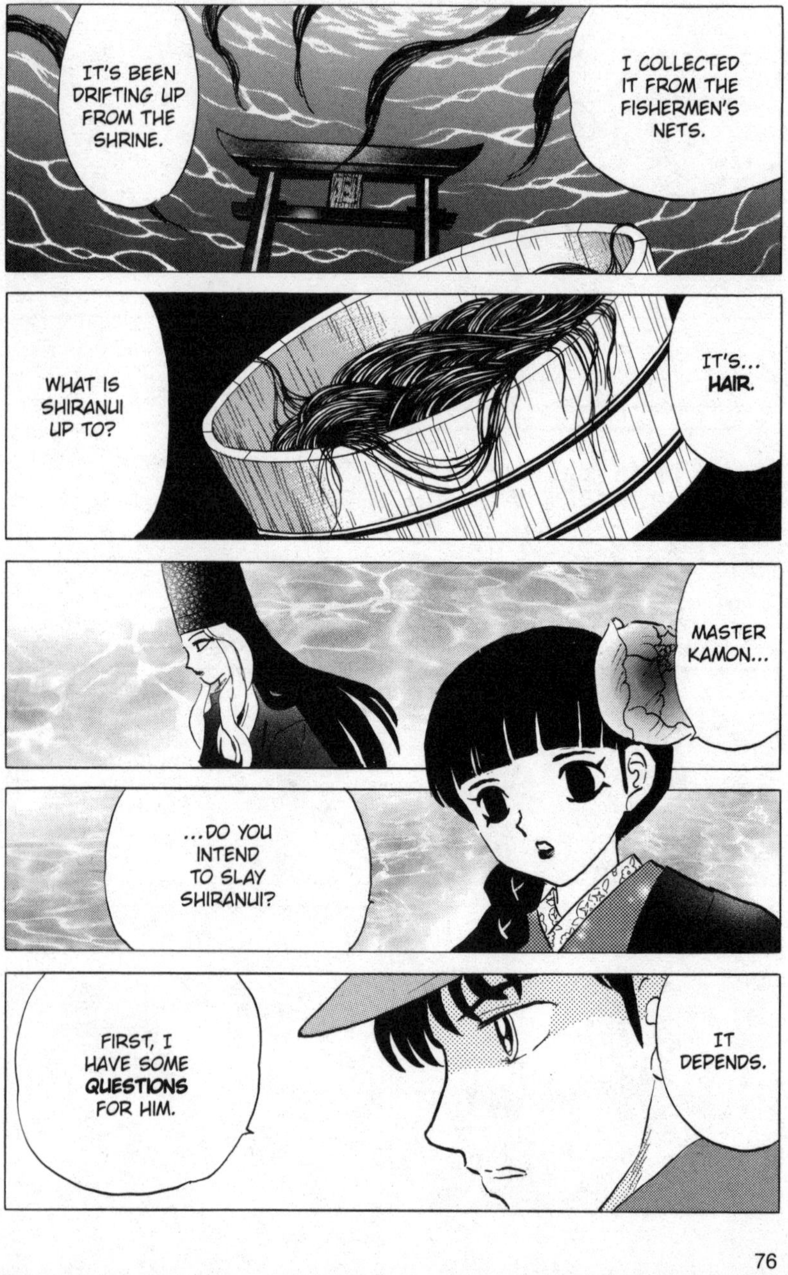
I COLLECTED IT FROM THE FISHERMEN'S NETS.
IT'S BEEN DRIFTING UP FROM THE SHRINE.
IT'S... **HAIR.**
WHAT IS SHIRANUI UP TO?
MASTER KAMON...
...DO YOU INTEND TO SLAY SHIRANUI?
IT DEPENDS.
FIRST, I HAVE SOME **QUESTIONS** FOR HIM.

Chapter 5:
The Seance

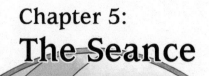

MAO

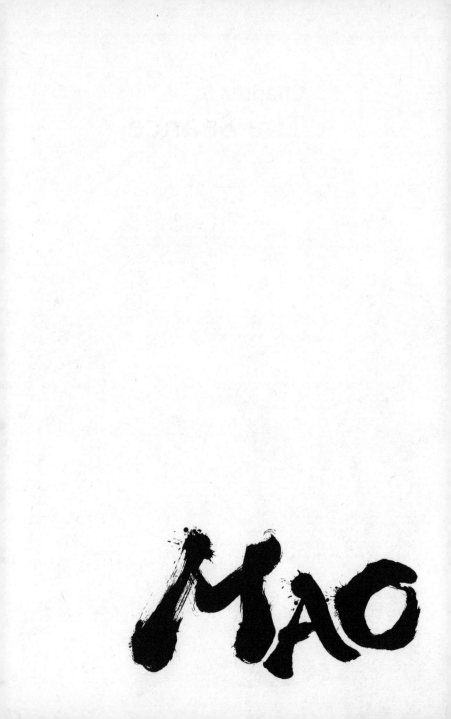

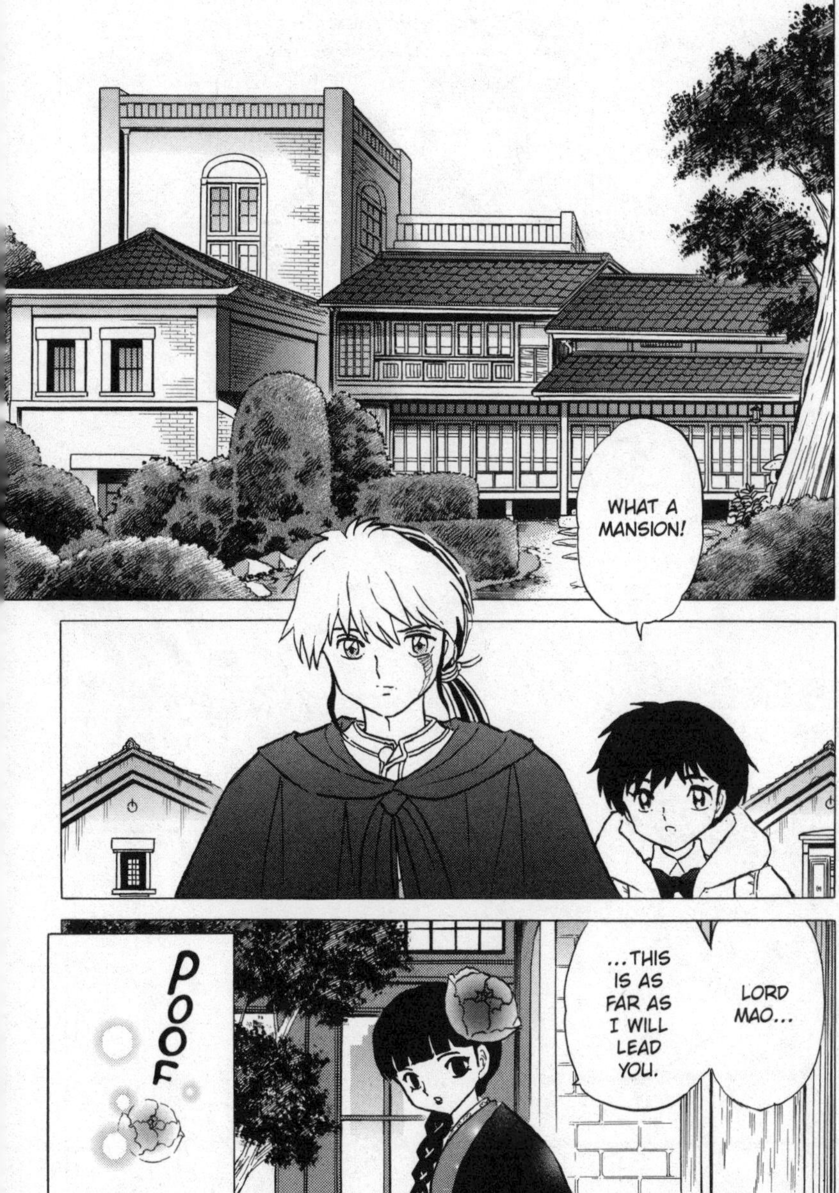
WHAT A MANSION!
LORD MAO...
...THIS IS AS FAR AS I WILL LEAD YOU.
POOF

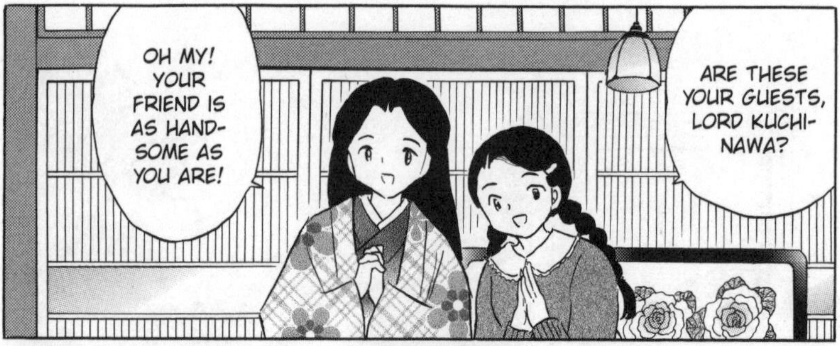
ARE THESE YOUR GUESTS, LORD KUCHI-NAWA?
OH MY! YOUR FRIEND IS AS HAND-SOME AS YOU ARE!

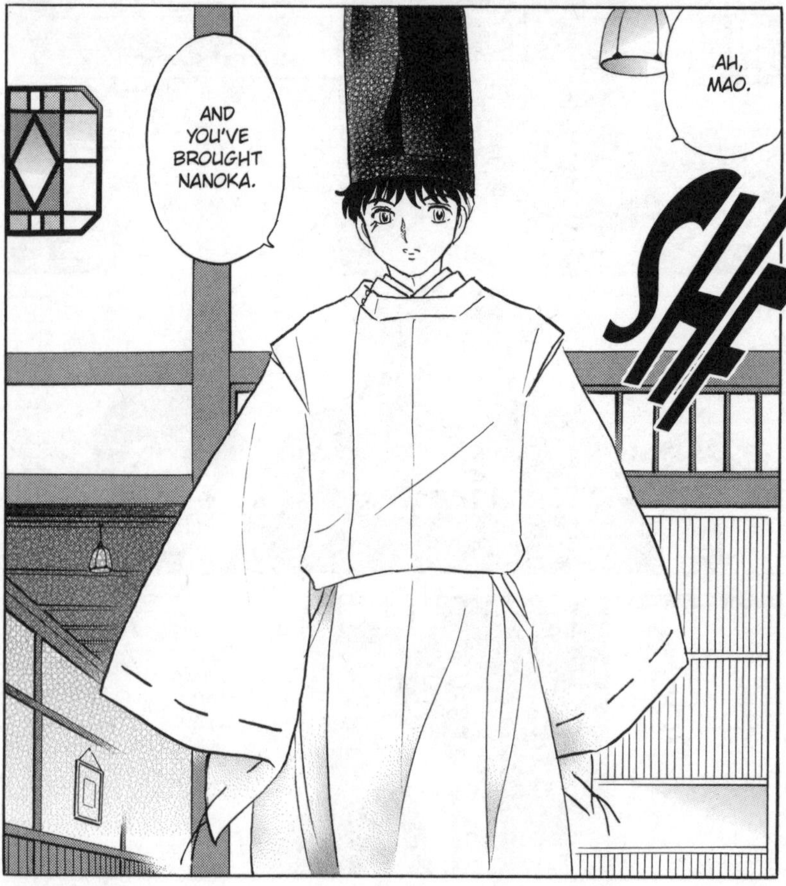
AH, MAO.
SHF
AND YOU'VE BROUGHT NANOKA.

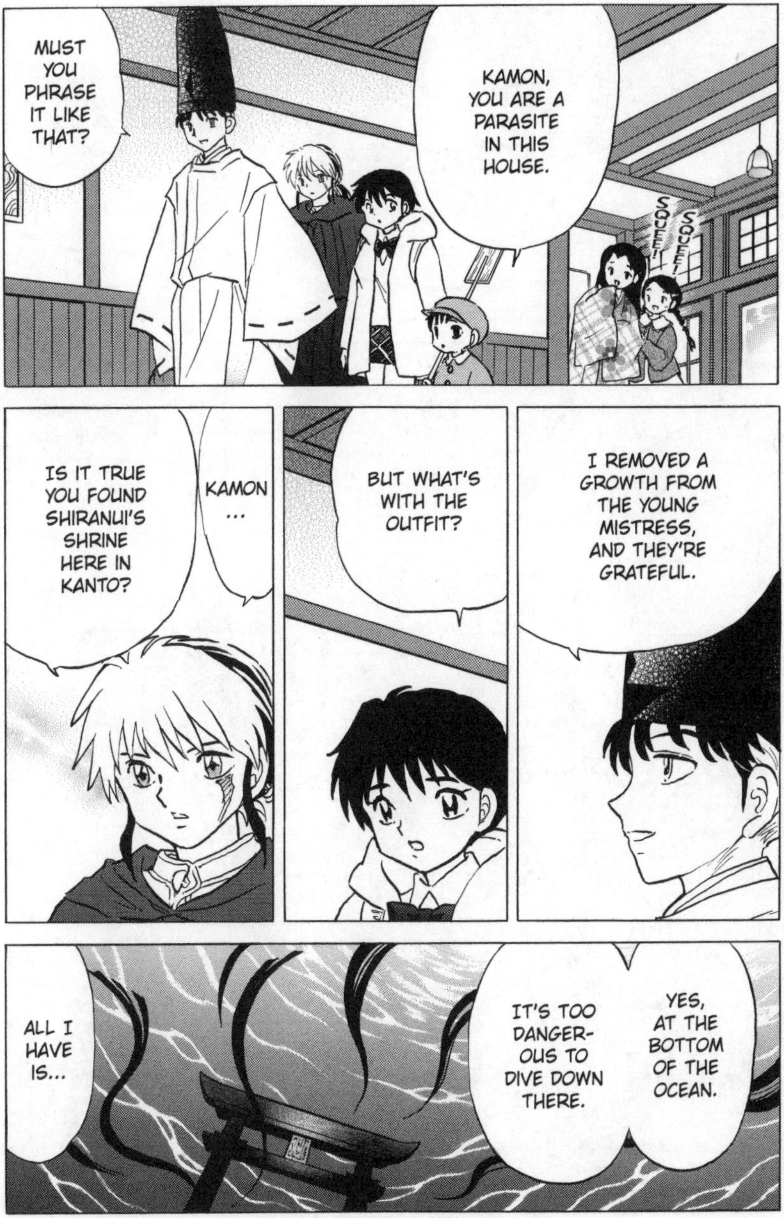
KAMON, YOU ARE A PARASITE IN THIS HOUSE.
SQUEE! SQUEE!
MUST YOU PHRASE IT LIKE THAT?
I REMOVED A GROWTH FROM THE YOUNG MISTRESS, AND THEY'RE GRATEFUL.
BUT WHAT'S WITH THE OUTFIT?
KAMON ...
IS IT TRUE YOU FOUND SHIRANUI'S SHRINE HERE IN KANTO?
YES, AT THE BOTTOM OF THE OCEAN.
IT'S TOO DANGER-OUS TO DIVE DOWN THERE.
ALL I HAVE IS...

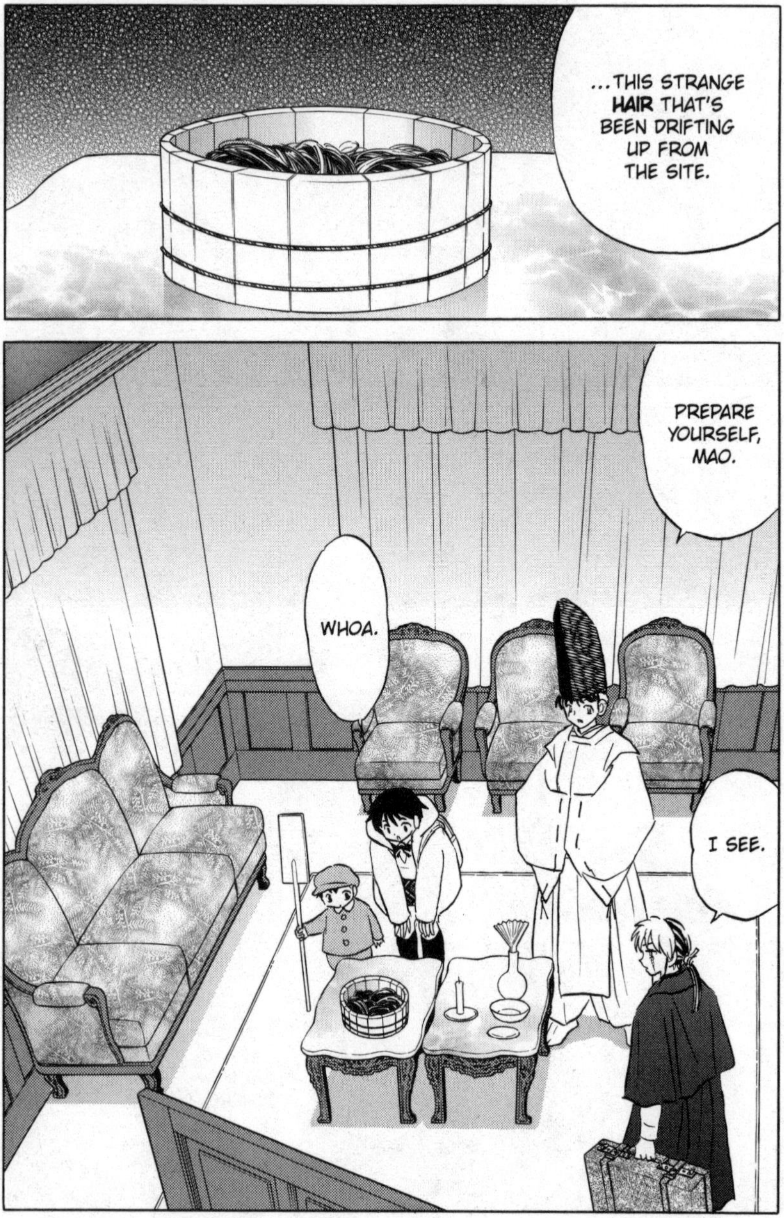
...THIS STRANGE **HAIR** THAT'S BEEN DRIFTING UP FROM THE SITE.
PREPARE YOURSELF, MAO.
WHOA.
I SEE.

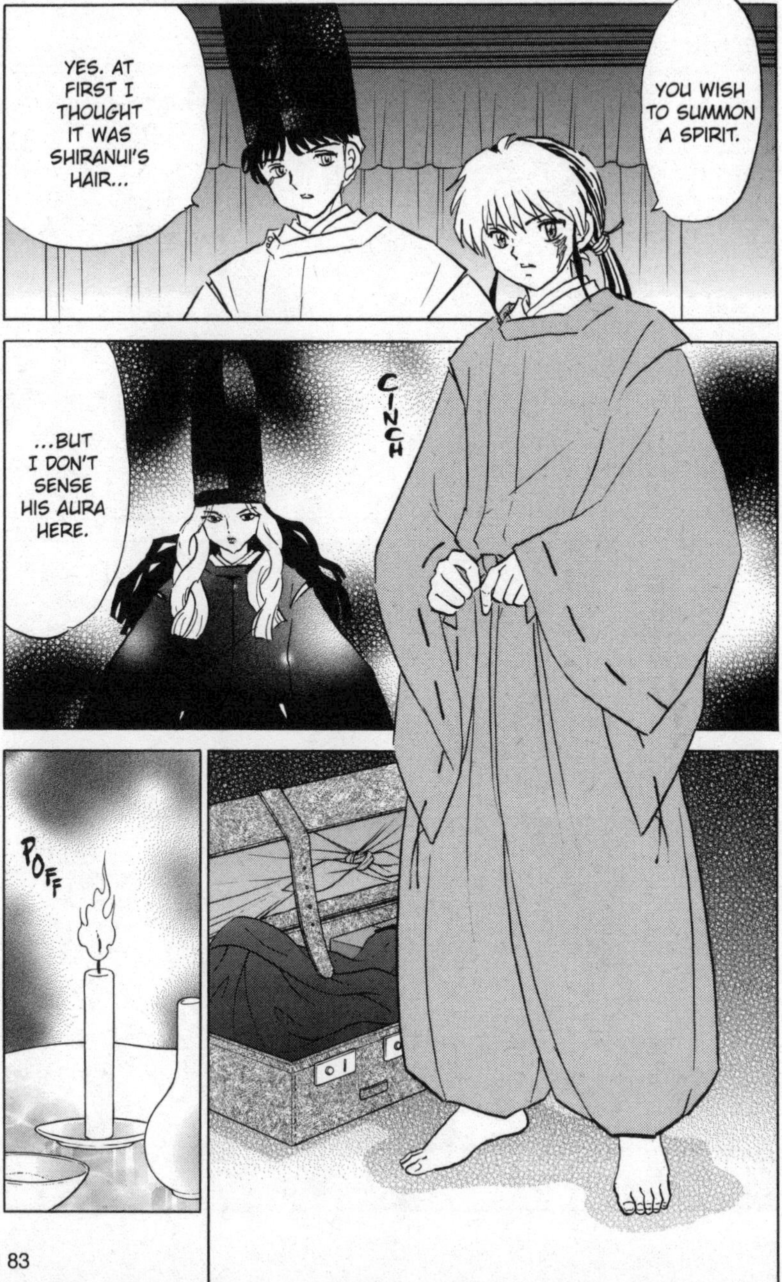
YOU WISH TO SUMMON A SPIRIT.
YES. AT FIRST I THOUGHT IT WAS SHIRANUI'S HAIR...
CINCH
...BUT I DON'T SENSE HIS AURA HERE.
POFF

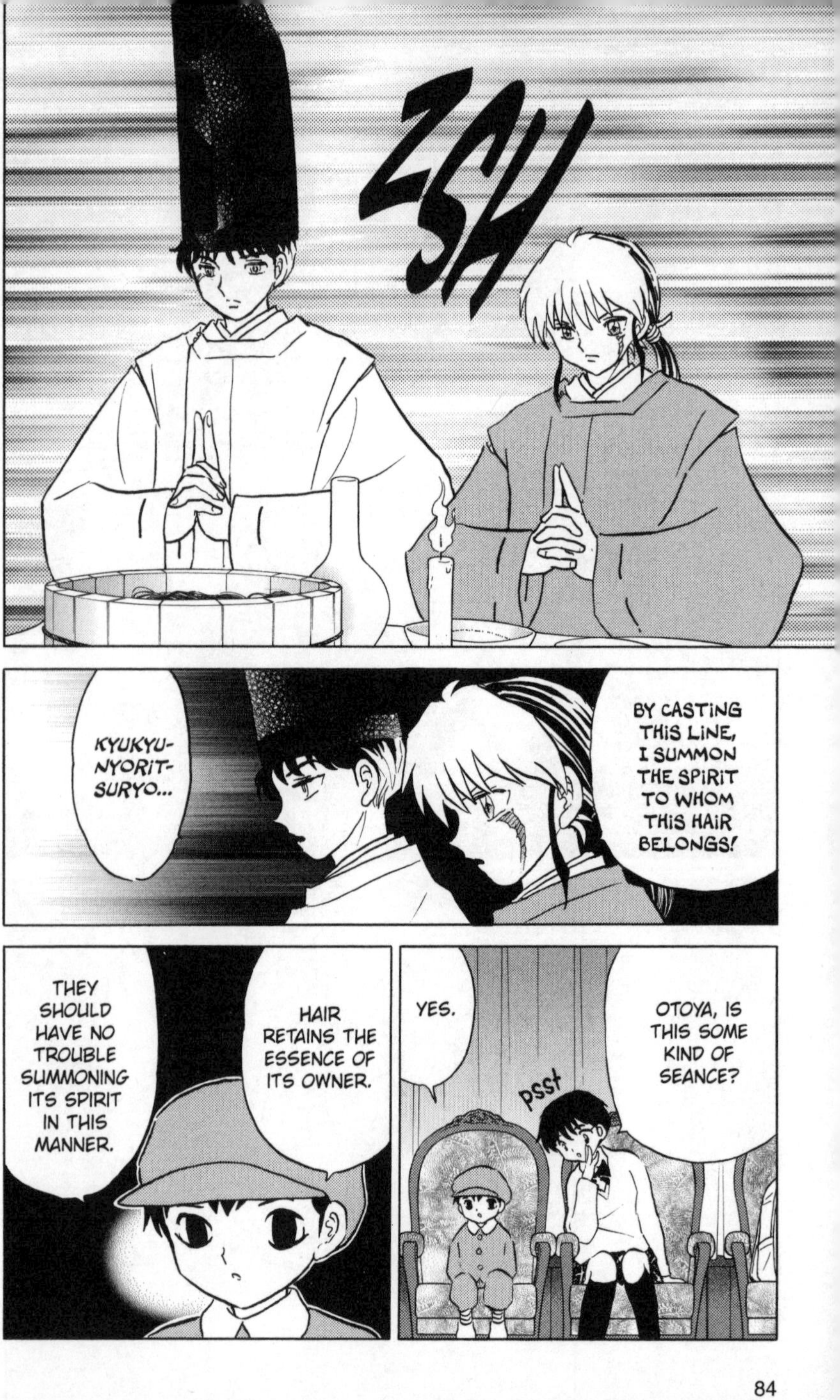
ZSH
BY CASTING THIS LINE, I SUMMON THE SPIRIT TO WHOM THIS HAIR BELONGS!
KYUKYU-NYORIT-SURYO...
OTOYA, IS THIS SOME KIND OF SEANCE?
psst
YES.
HAIR RETAINS THE ESSENCE OF ITS OWNER.
THEY SHOULD HAVE NO TROUBLE SUMMONING ITS SPIRIT IN THIS MANNER.

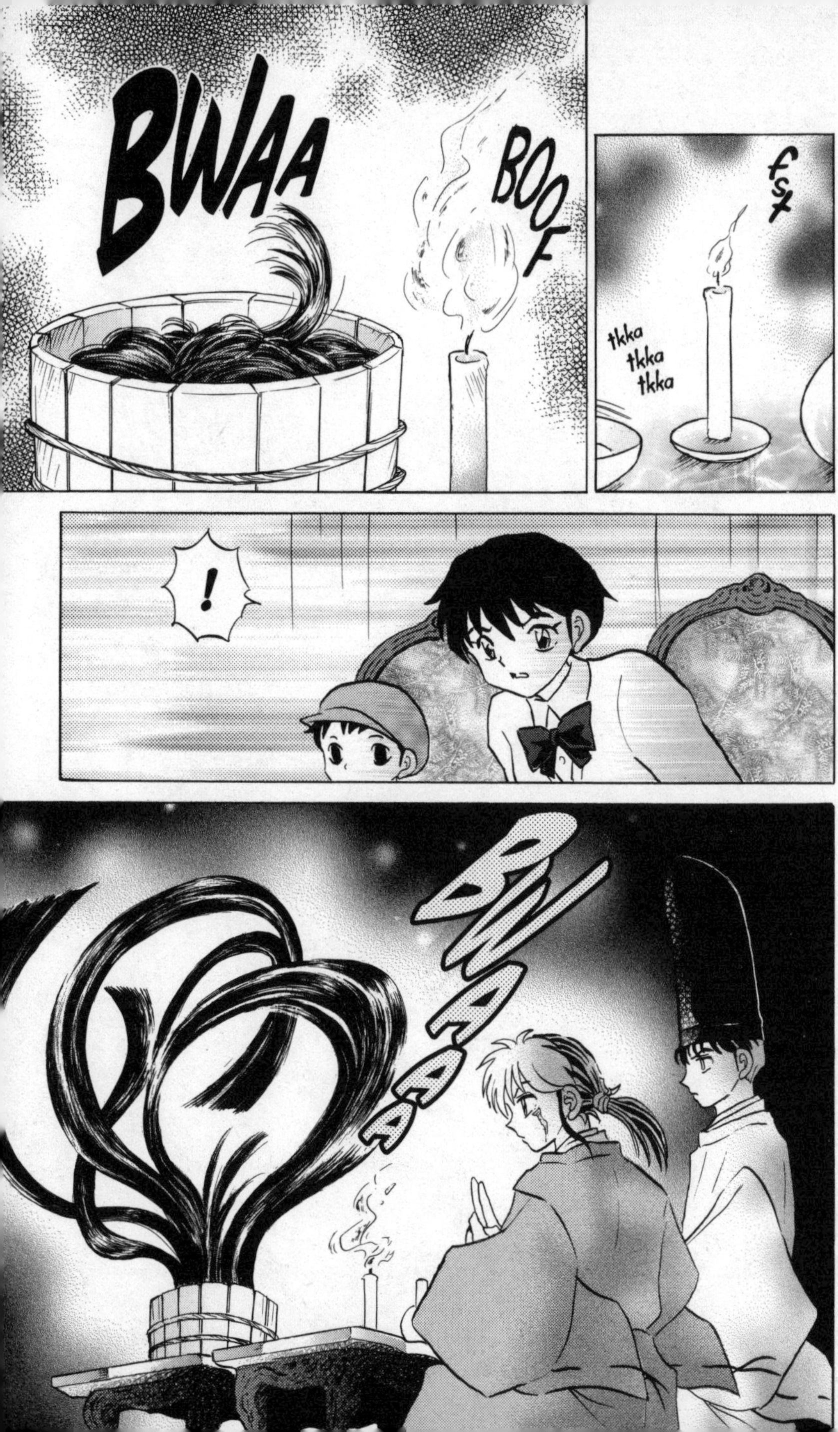
fst
tkka tkka tkka
BOOF
BWAA
!
BWAAAAA

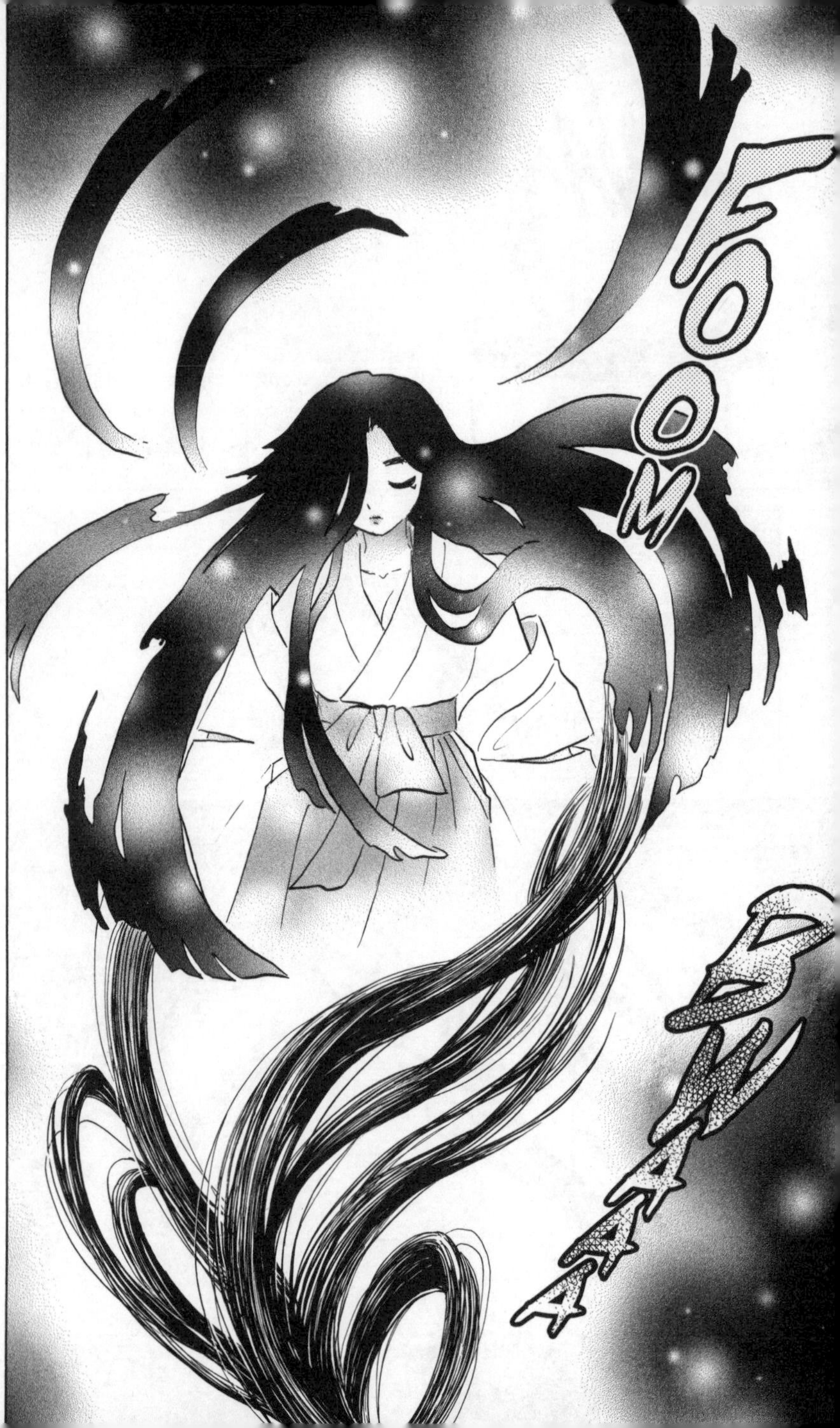
FOOM
BWAAA

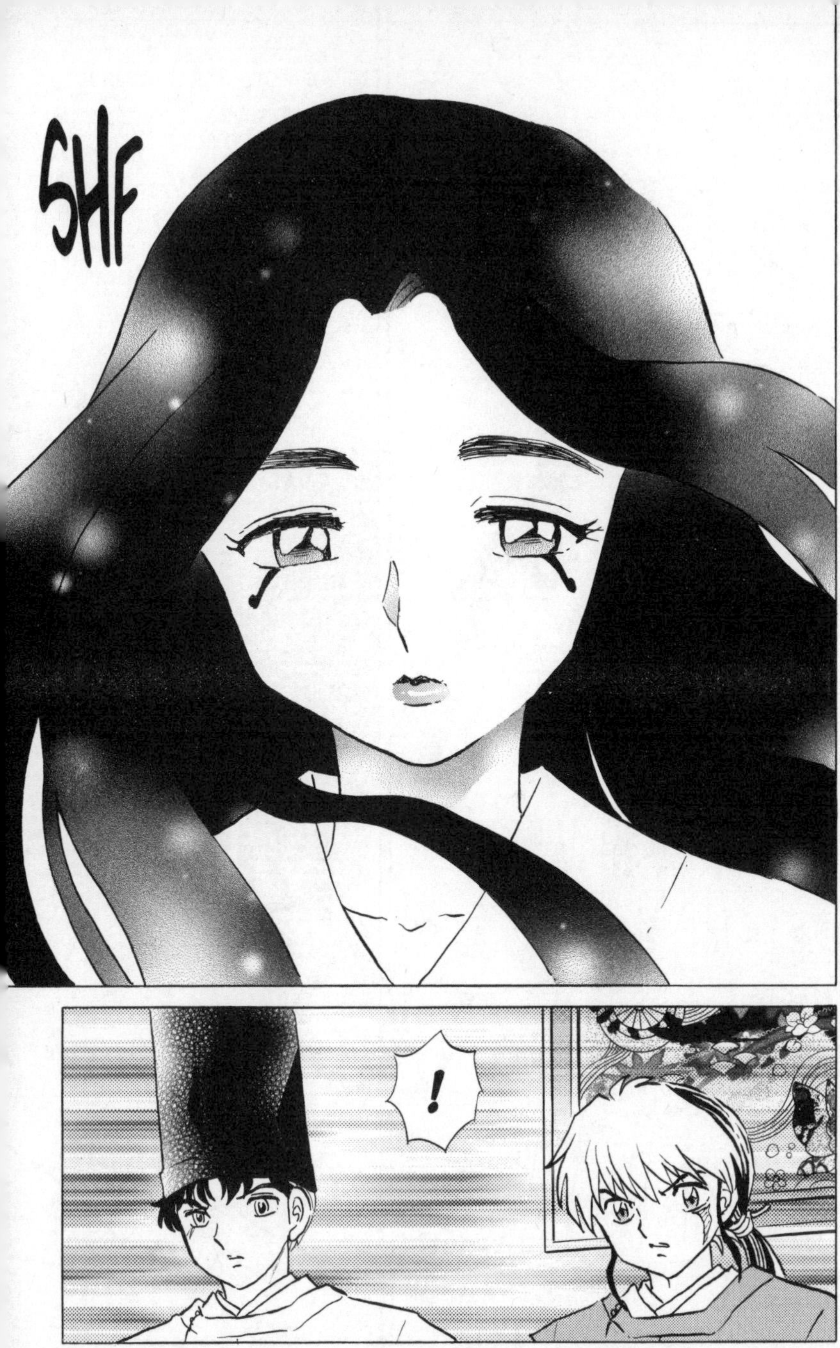
SHF
!

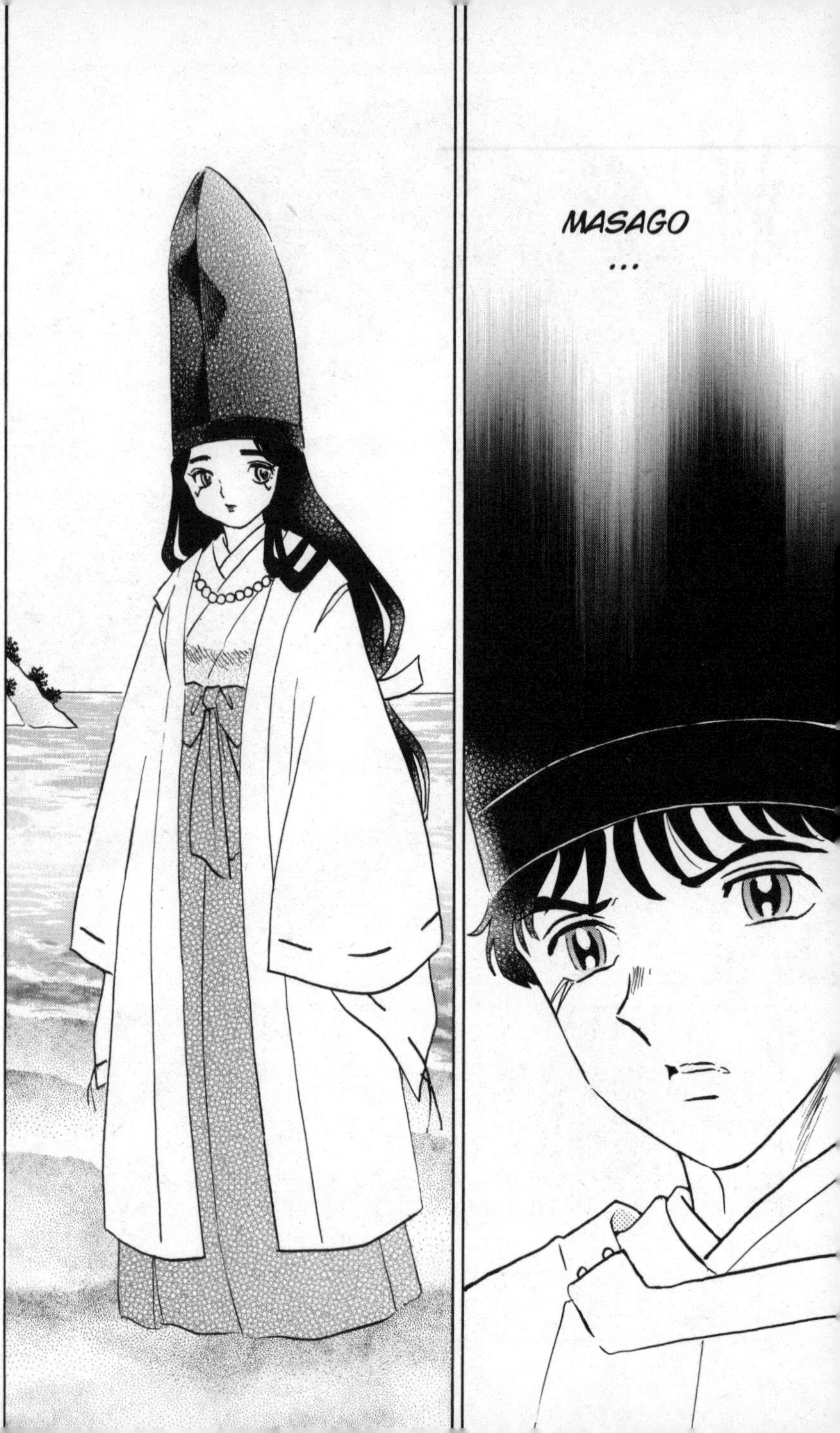
MASAGO
...

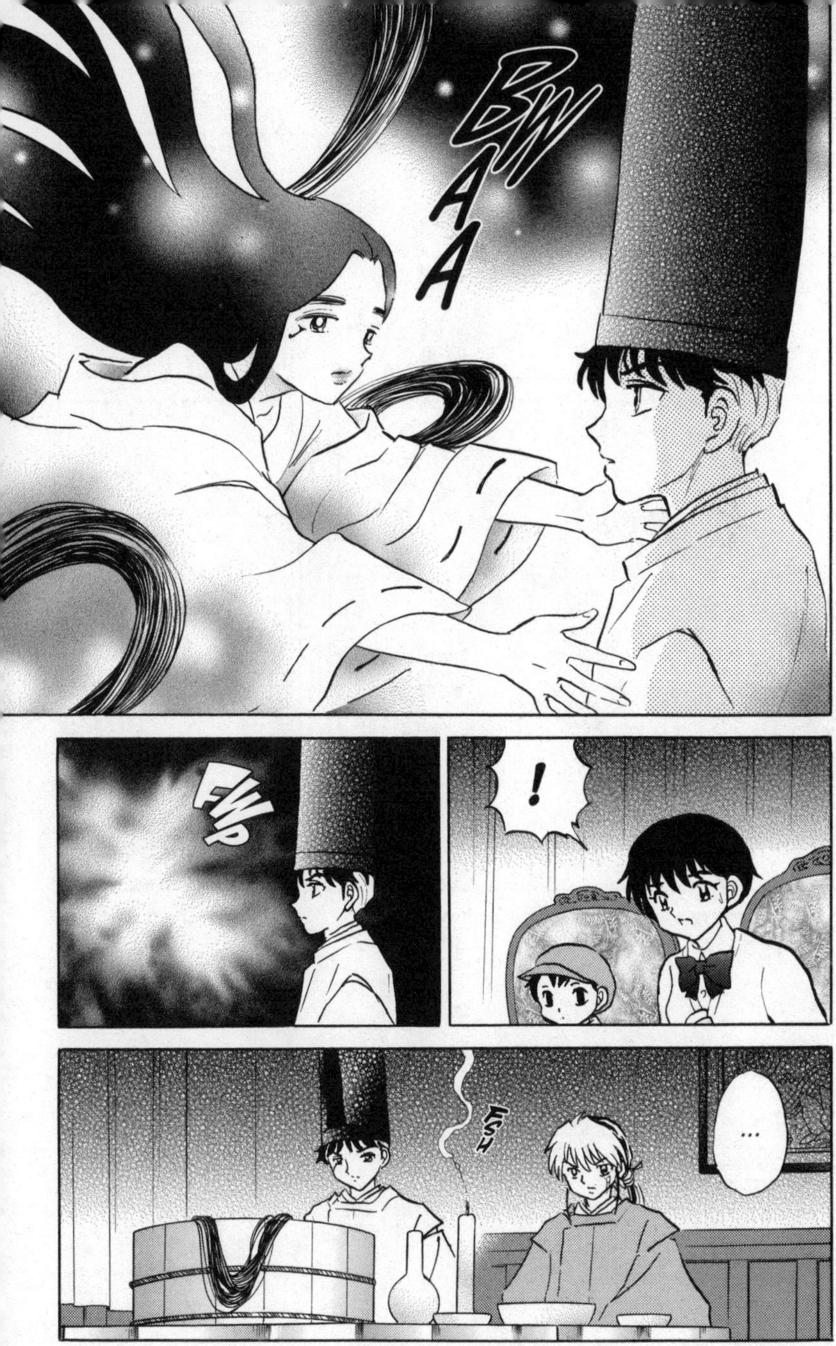
BWAAA
!
FWP
...
FSSH

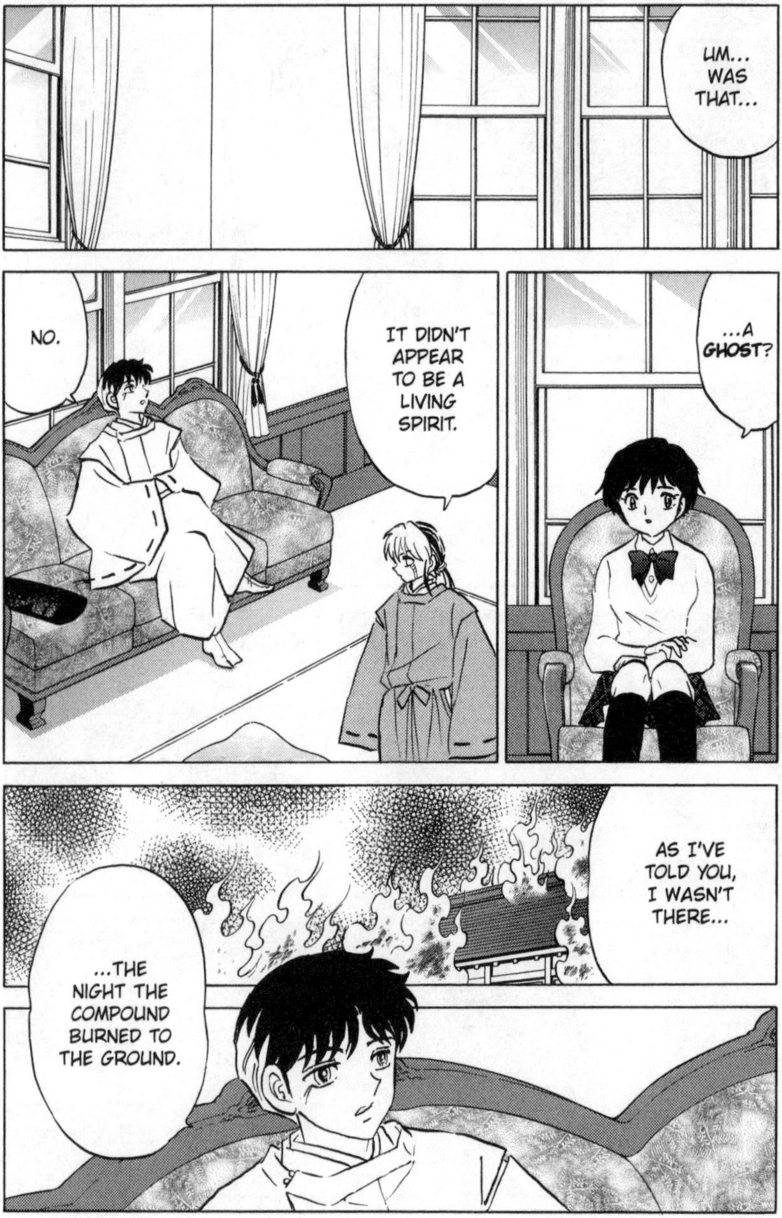
UM... WAS THAT...
...A GHOST?
IT DIDN'T APPEAR TO BE A LIVING SPIRIT.
NO.
AS I'VE TOLD YOU, I WASN'T THERE...
...THE NIGHT THE COMPOUND BURNED TO THE GROUND.

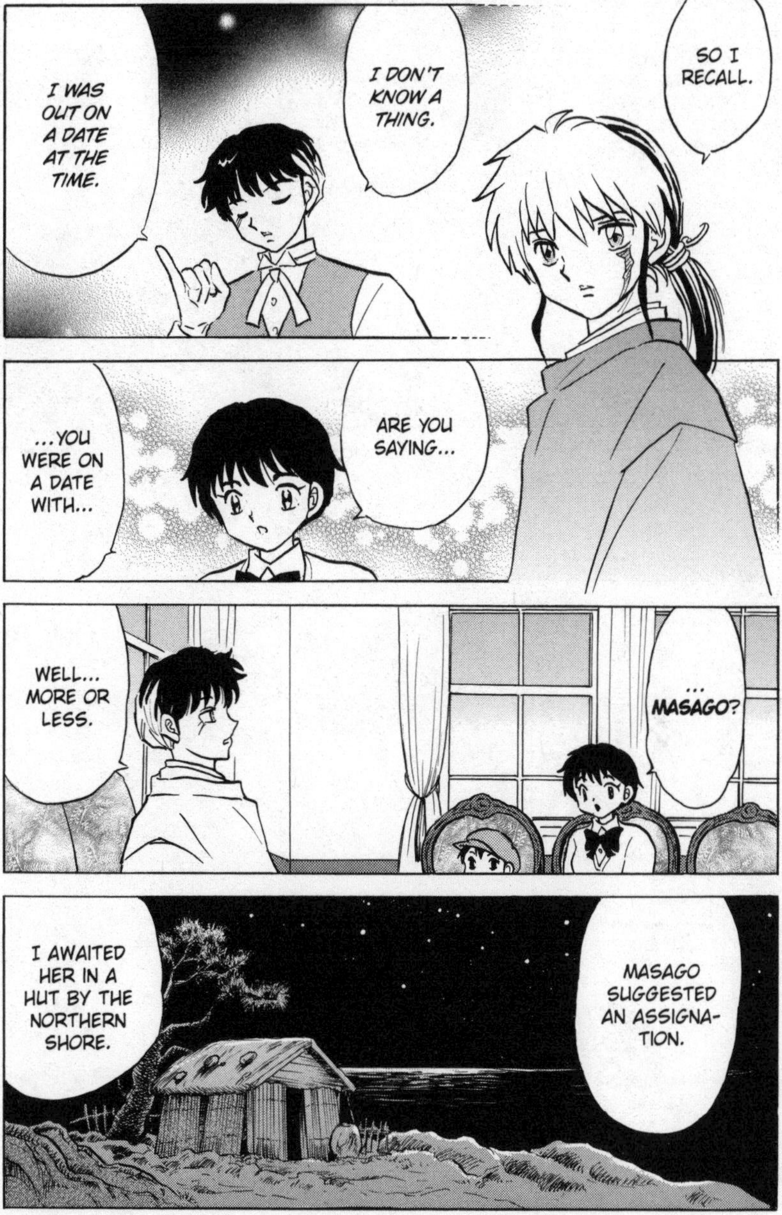
SO I RECALL.
I DON'T KNOW A THING.
I WAS OUT ON A DATE AT THE TIME.
ARE YOU SAYING...
...YOU WERE ON A DATE WITH...
...MASAGO?
WELL... MORE OR LESS.
MASAGO SUGGESTED AN ASSIGNATION.
I AWAITED HER IN A HUT BY THE NORTHERN SHORE.

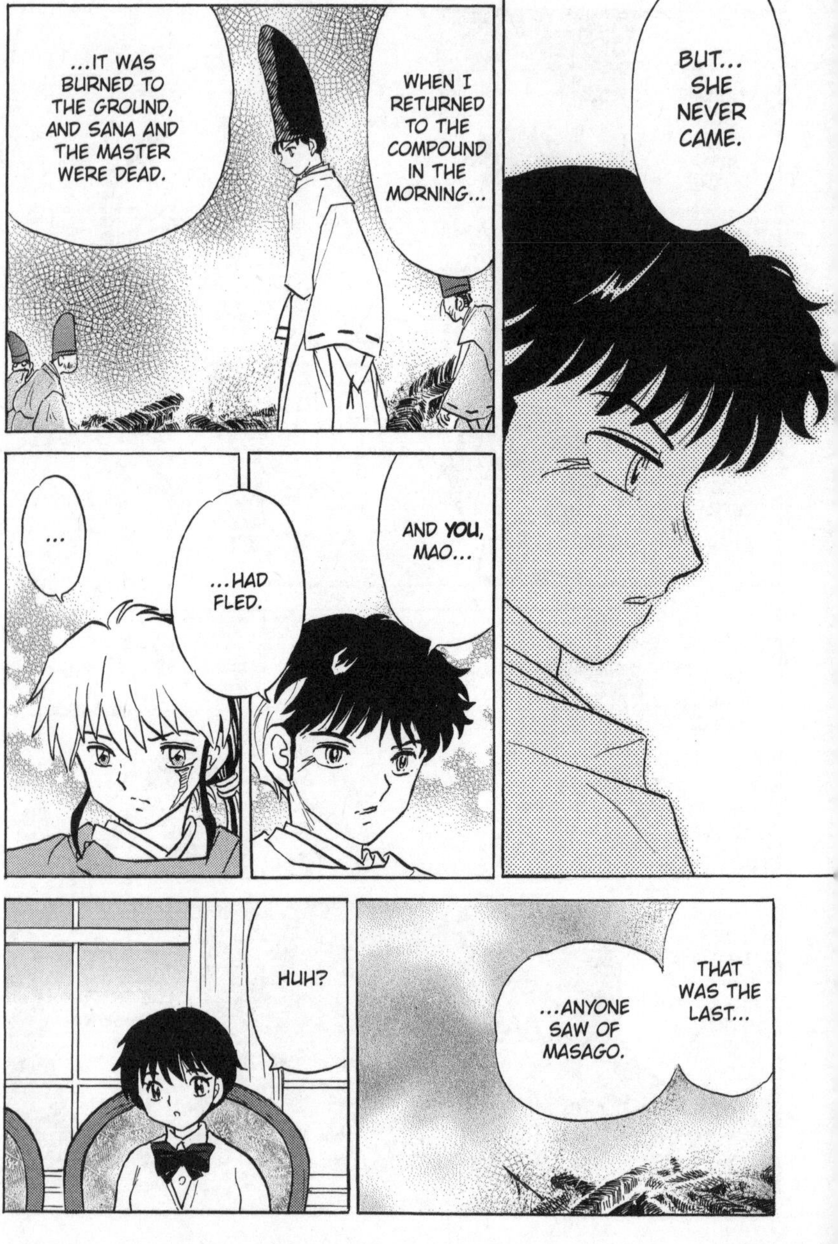
BUT... SHE NEVER CAME.
WHEN I RETURNED TO THE COMPOUND IN THE MORNING...
...IT WAS BURNED TO THE GROUND, AND SANA AND THE MASTER WERE DEAD.
AND **YOU**, MAO...
...HAD FLED.
...
THAT WAS THE LAST...
...ANYONE SAW OF MASAGO.
HUH?

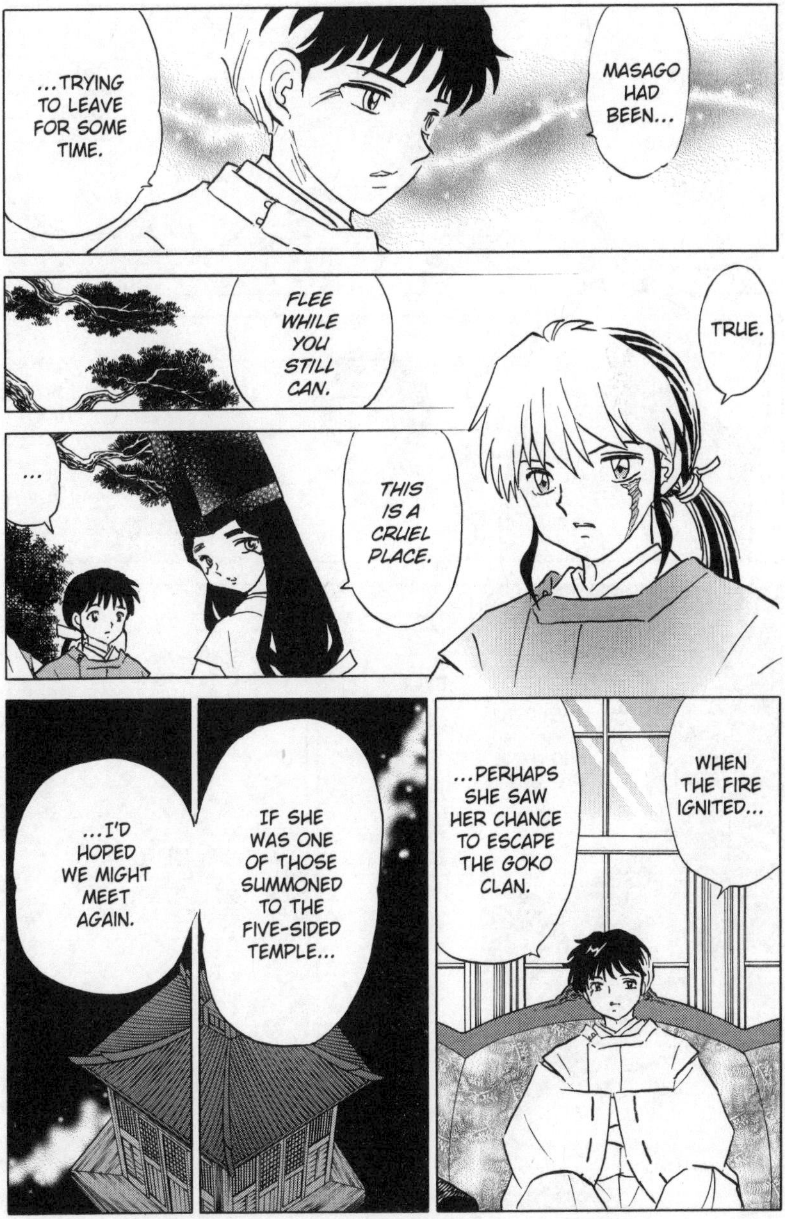
MASAGO HAD BEEN…
…TRYING TO LEAVE FOR SOME TIME.
TRUE.
THIS IS A CRUEL PLACE.
FLEE WHILE YOU STILL CAN.
…
WHEN THE FIRE IGNITED…
…PERHAPS SHE SAW HER CHANCE TO ESCAPE THE GOKO CLAN.
IF SHE WAS ONE OF THOSE SUMMONED TO THE FIVE-SIDED TEMPLE…
…I'D HOPED WE MIGHT MEET AGAIN.

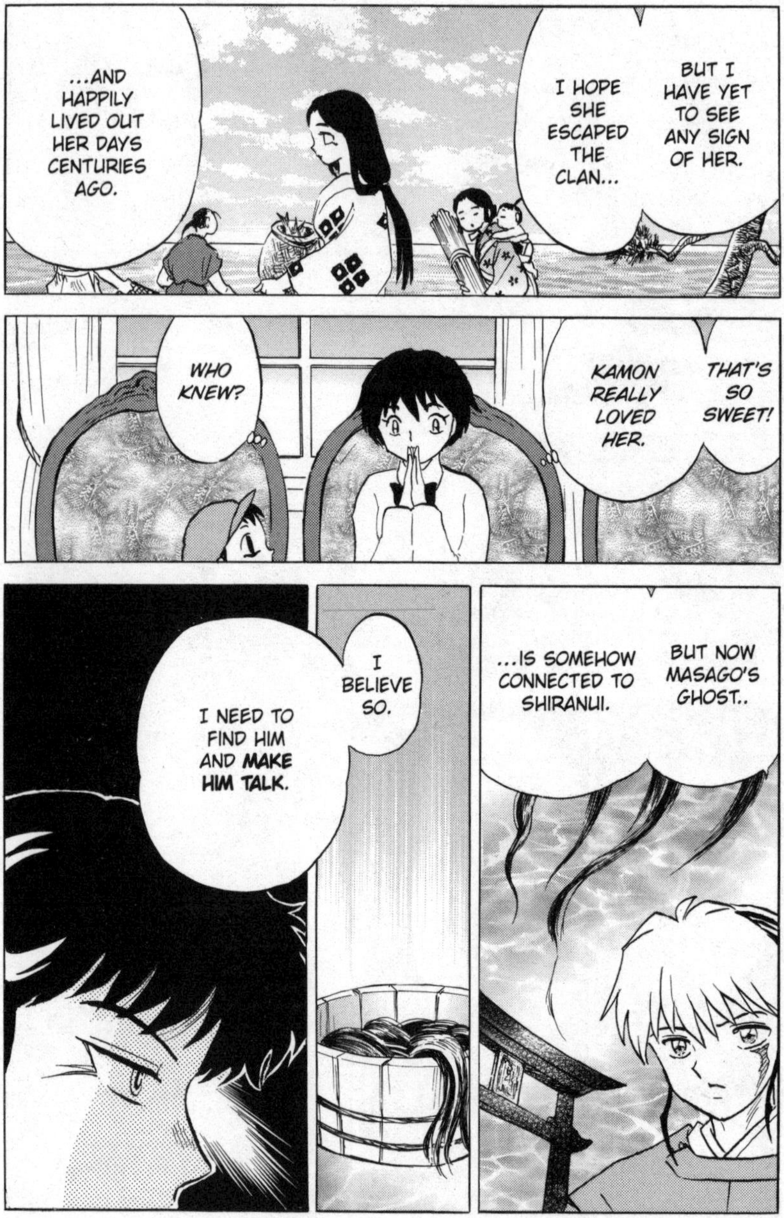
BUT I HAVE YET TO SEE ANY SIGN OF HER.
I HOPE SHE ESCAPED THE CLAN...
...AND HAPPILY LIVED OUT HER DAYS CENTURIES AGO.
THAT'S SO SWEET!
KAMON REALLY LOVED HER.
WHO KNEW?
BUT NOW MASAGO'S GHOST..
...IS SOMEHOW CONNECTED TO SHIRANUI.
I BELIEVE SO.
I NEED TO FIND HIM AND **MAKE HIM TALK.**

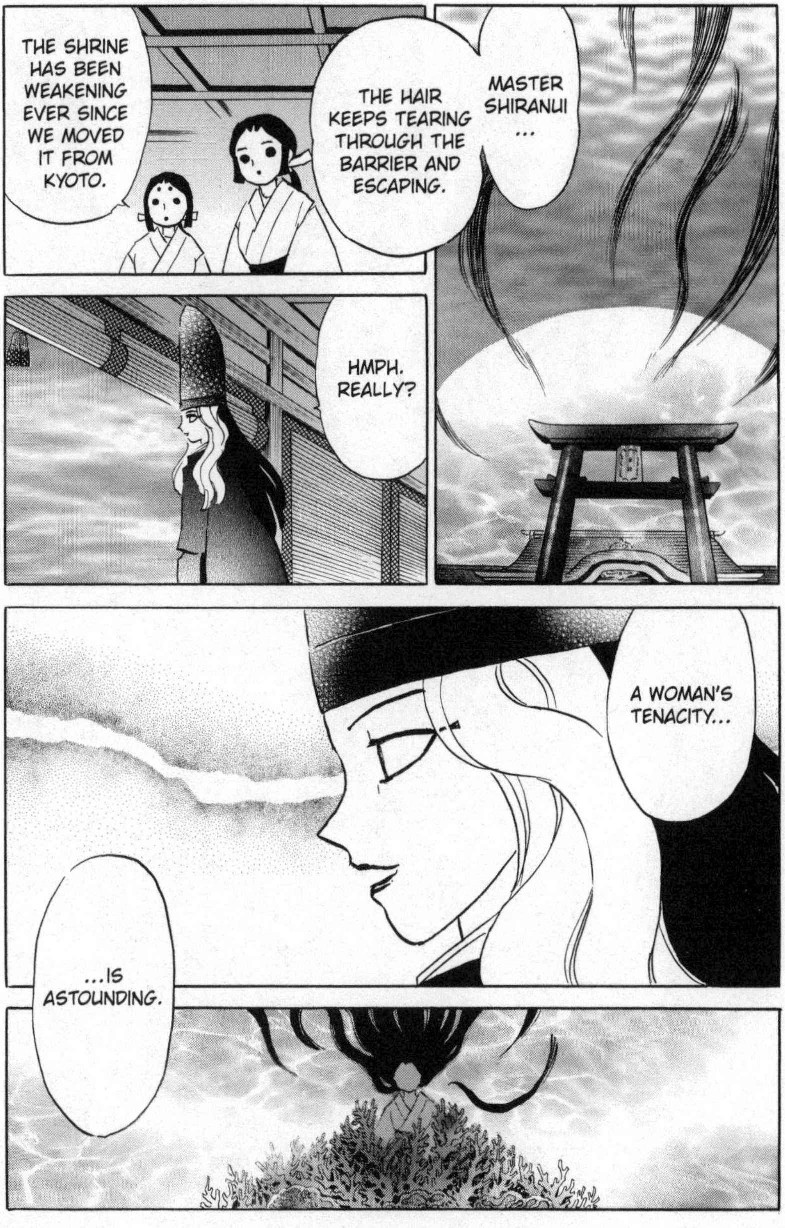
MASTER SHIRANUI ...
THE HAIR KEEPS TEARING THROUGH THE BARRIER AND ESCAPING.
THE SHRINE HAS BEEN WEAKENING EVER SINCE WE MOVED IT FROM KYOTO.
HMPH. REALLY?
A WOMAN'S TENACITY...
...IS ASTOUNDING.

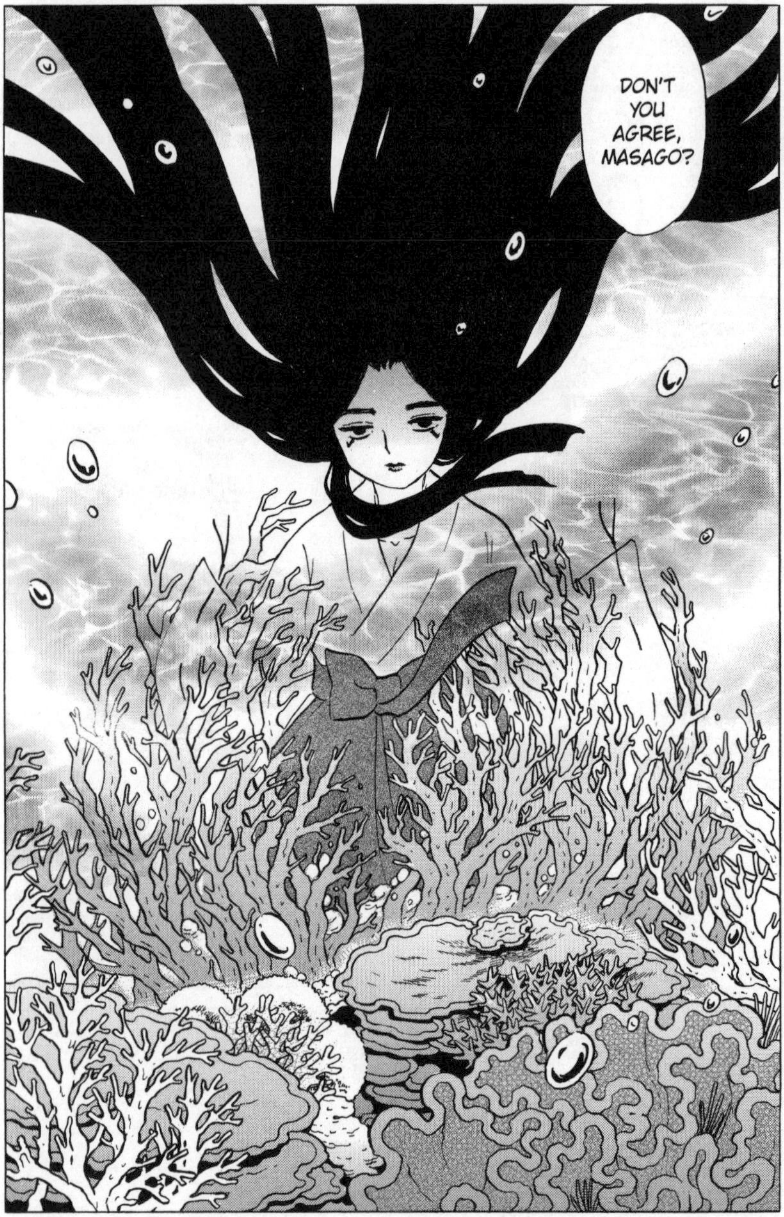
DON'T YOU AGREE, MASAGO?

Chapter 9:
The Undersea Shrine

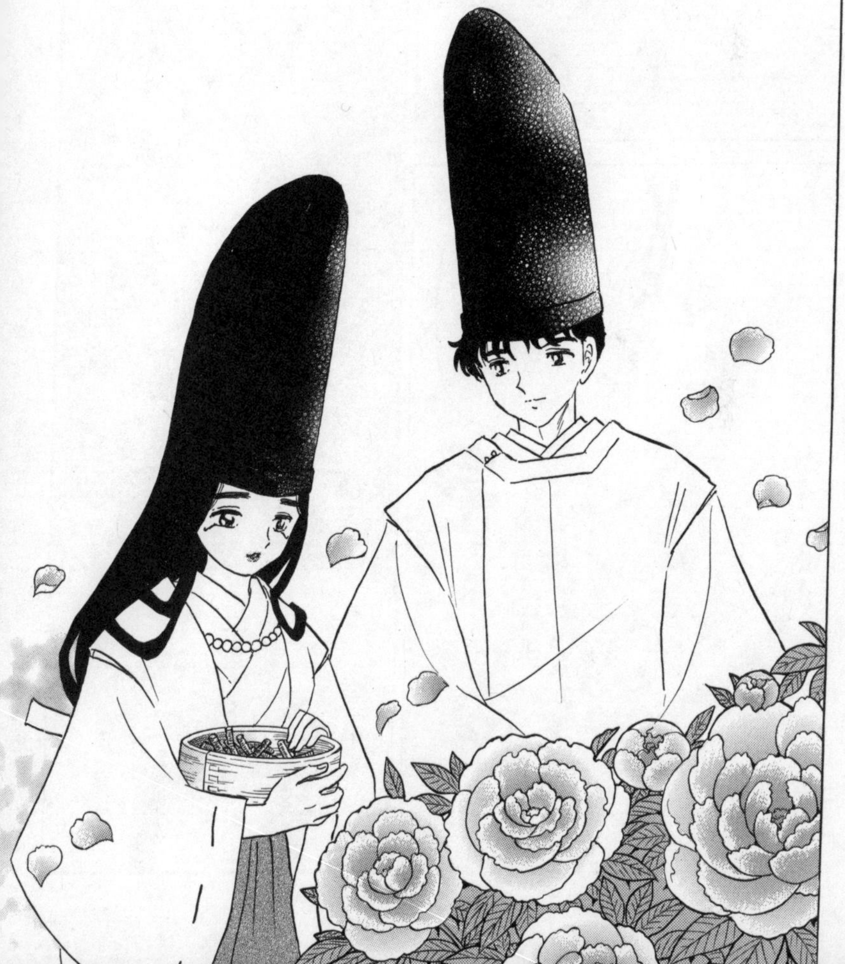

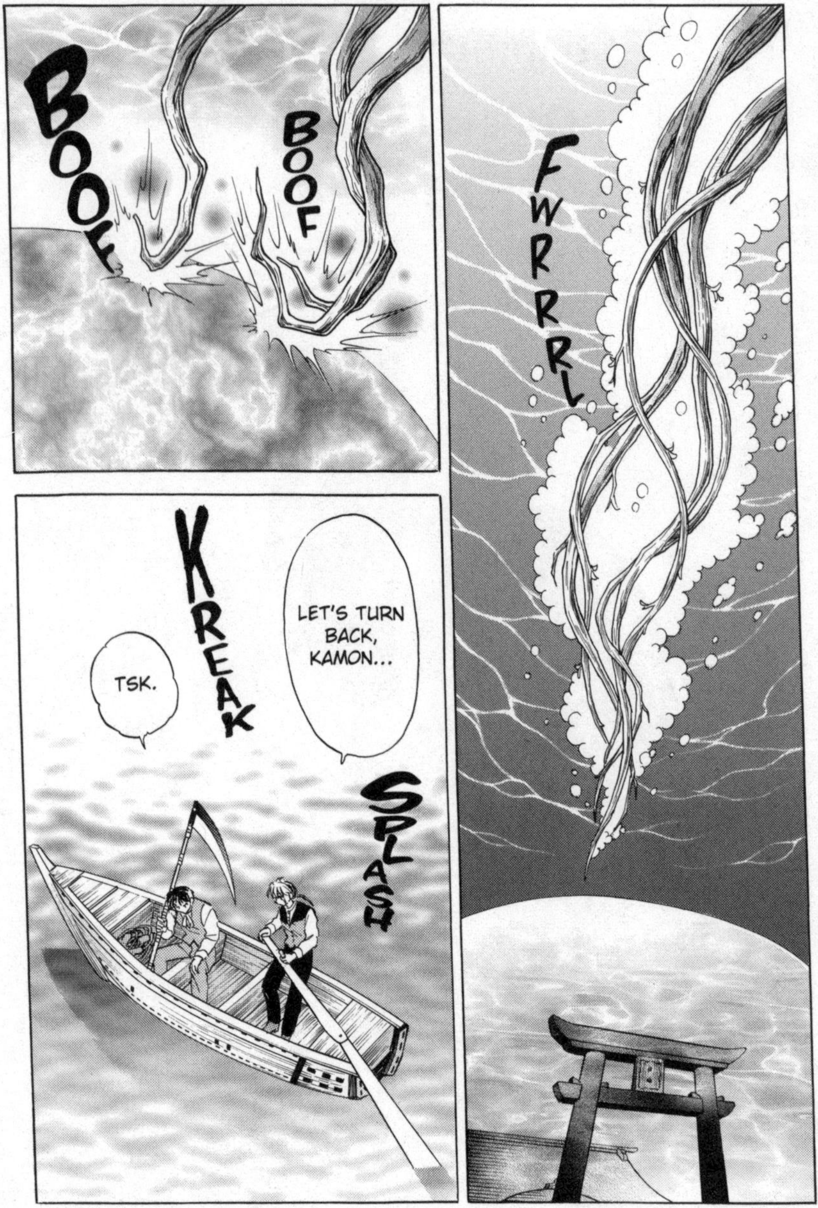
FWRRRL
BOOF
BOOF
KREAK
LET'S TURN BACK, KAMON...
TSK.
SPLASH

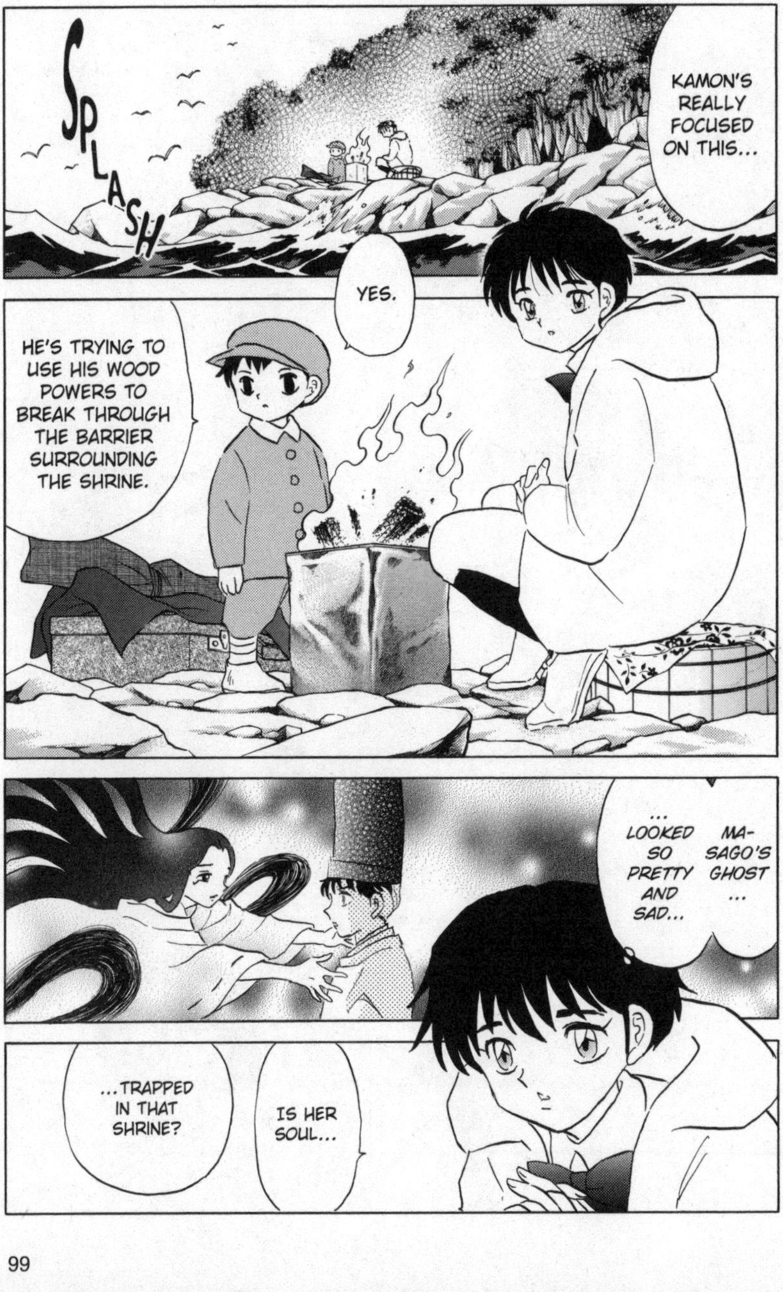
KAMON'S REALLY FOCUSED ON THIS...
SPLASH
YES.
HE'S TRYING TO USE HIS WOOD POWERS TO BREAK THROUGH THE BARRIER SURROUNDING THE SHRINE.
MA-SAGO'S GHOST ...
... LOOKED SO PRETTY AND SAD...
IS HER SOUL...
...TRAPPED IN THAT SHRINE?

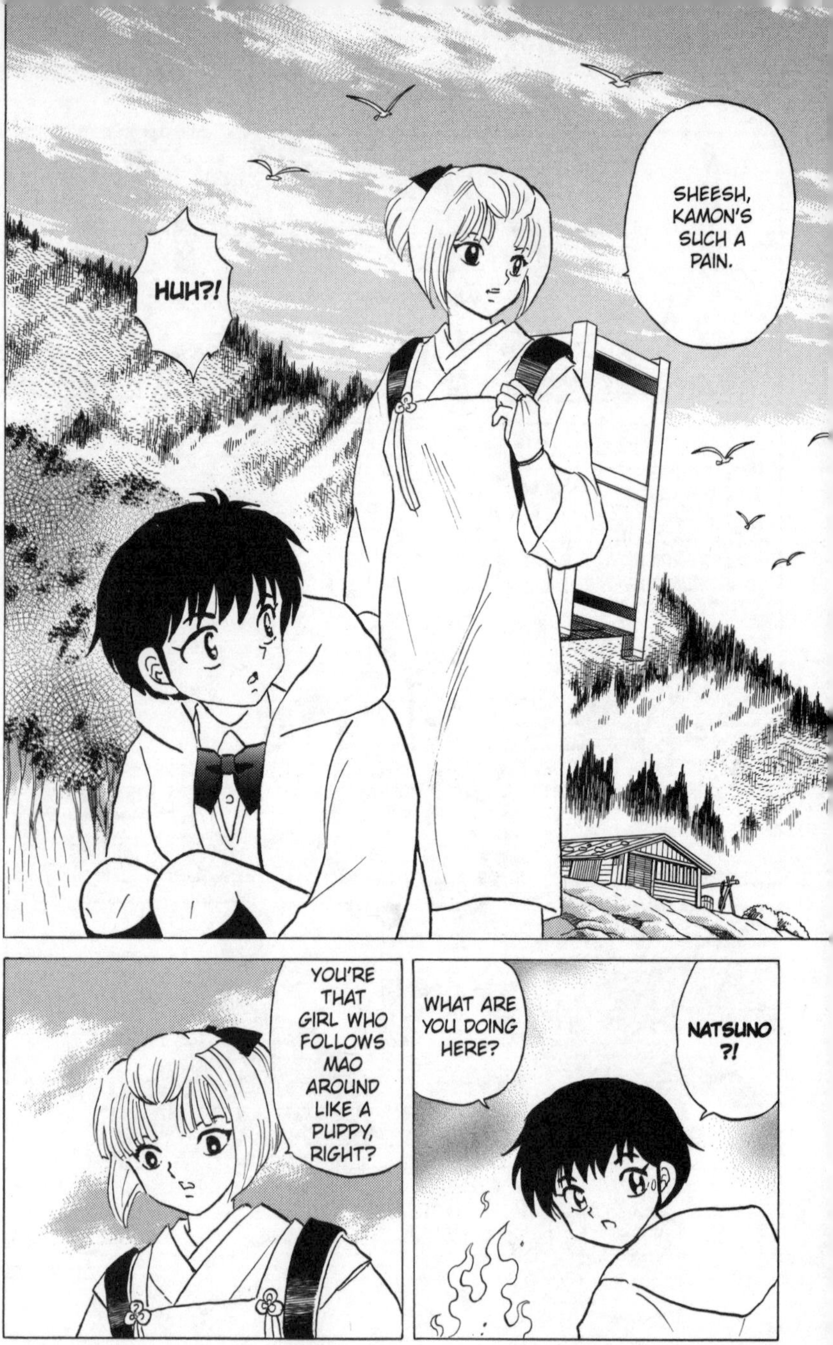
SHEESH, KAMON'S SUCH A PAIN.
HUH?!
NATSUNO ?!
WHAT ARE YOU DOING HERE?
YOU'RE THAT GIRL WHO FOLLOWS MAO AROUND LIKE A PUPPY, RIGHT?

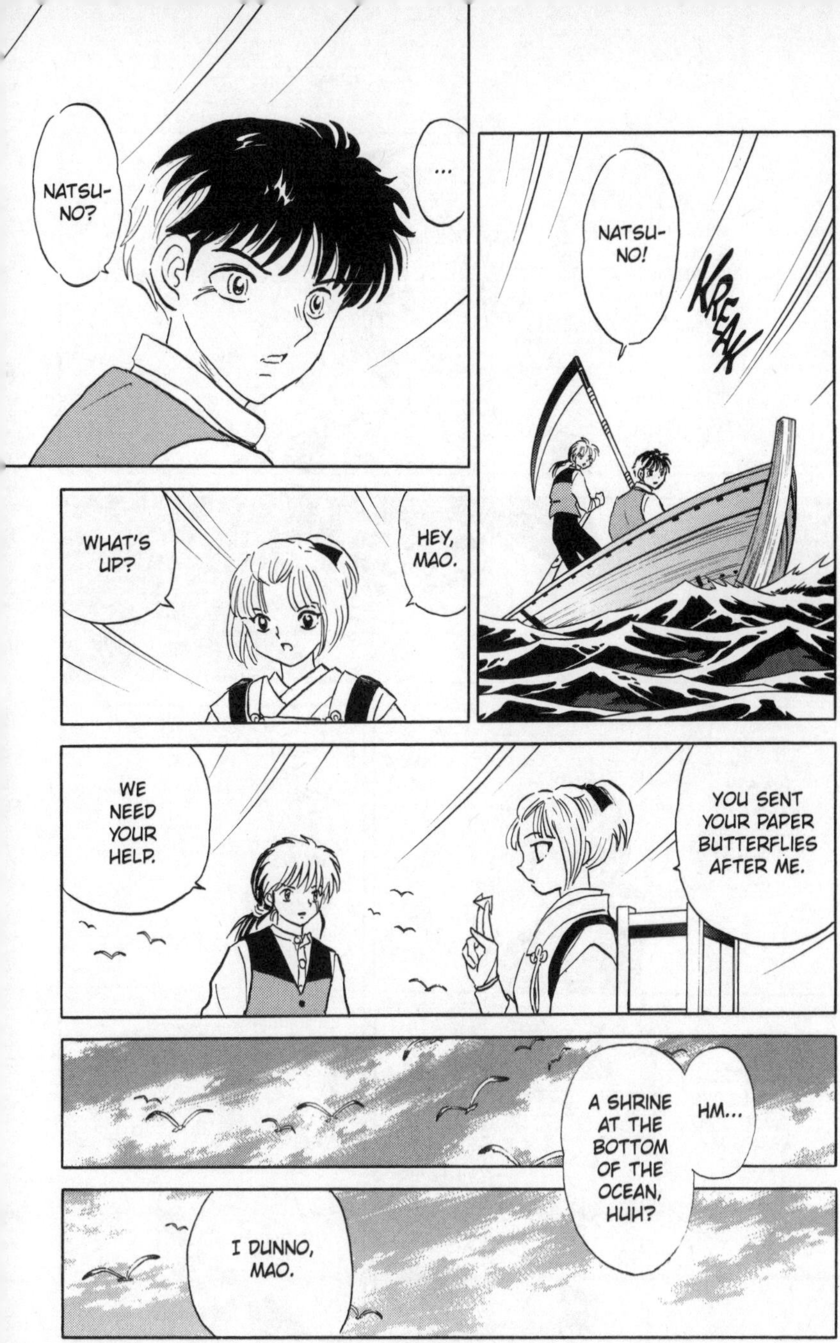
NATSU-NO!
KREAK
...
NATSU-NO?
HEY, MAO.
WHAT'S UP?
YOU SENT YOUR PAPER BUTTERFLIES AFTER ME.
WE NEED YOUR HELP.
HM...
A SHRINE AT THE BOTTOM OF THE OCEAN, HUH?
I DUNNO, MAO.

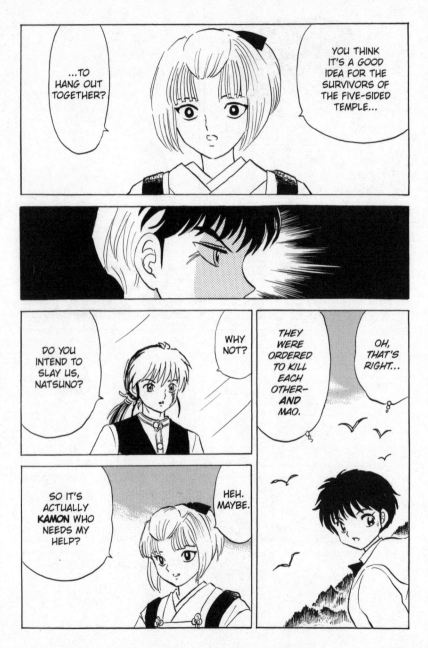

YOU THINK IT'S A GOOD IDEA FOR THE SURVIVORS OF THE FIVE-SIDED TEMPLE...
...TO HANG OUT TOGETHER?
OH, THAT'S RIGHT...
THEY WERE ORDERED TO KILL EACH OTHER— AND MAO.
WHY NOT?
DO YOU INTEND TO SLAY US, NATSUNO?
HEH. MAYBE.
SO IT'S ACTUALLY KAMON WHO NEEDS MY HELP?

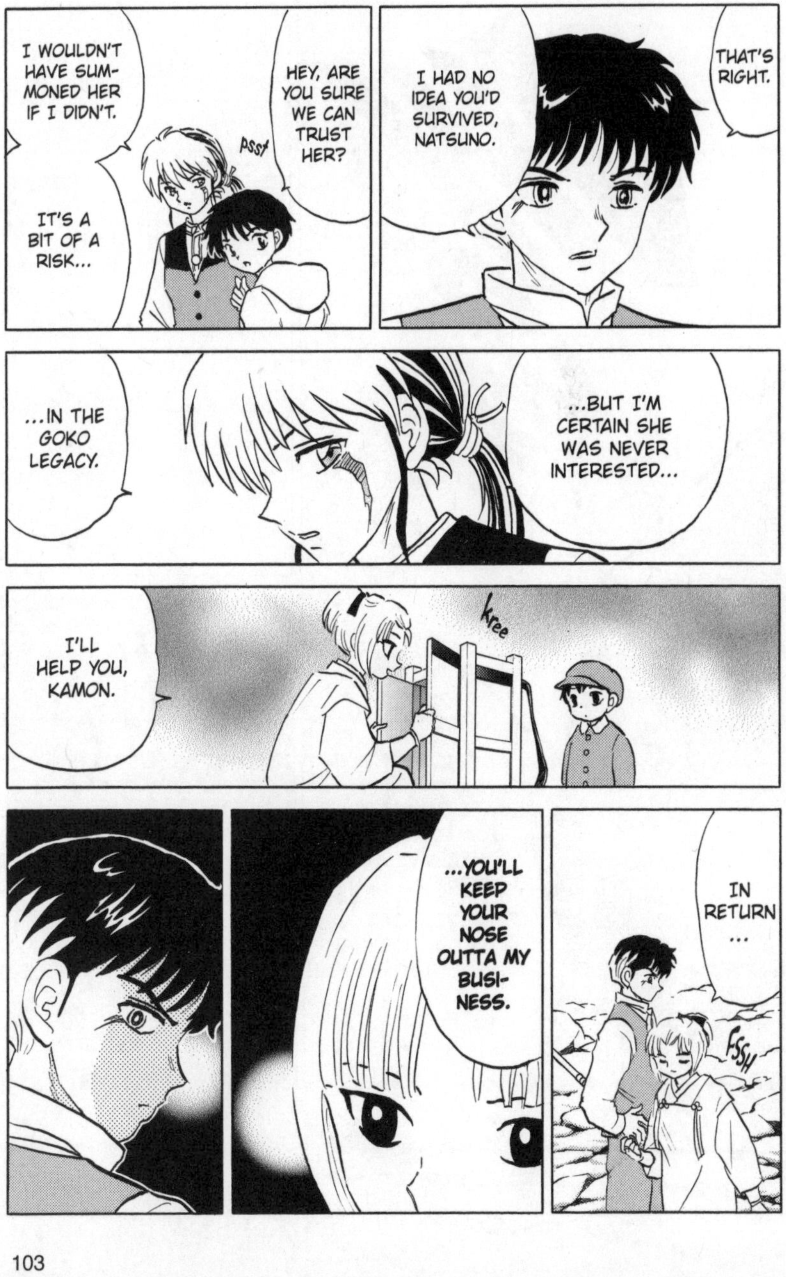
THAT'S RIGHT.
I HAD NO IDEA YOU'D SURVIVED, NATSUNO.
HEY, ARE YOU SURE WE CAN TRUST HER?
psst
I WOULDN'T HAVE SUMMONED HER IF I DIDN'T.
IT'S A BIT OF A RISK...
...BUT I'M CERTAIN SHE WAS NEVER INTERESTED...
...IN THE GOKO LEGACY.
kree
I'LL HELP YOU, KAMON.
IN RETURN ...
FSSH
...YOU'LL KEEP YOUR NOSE OUTTA MY BUSINESS.

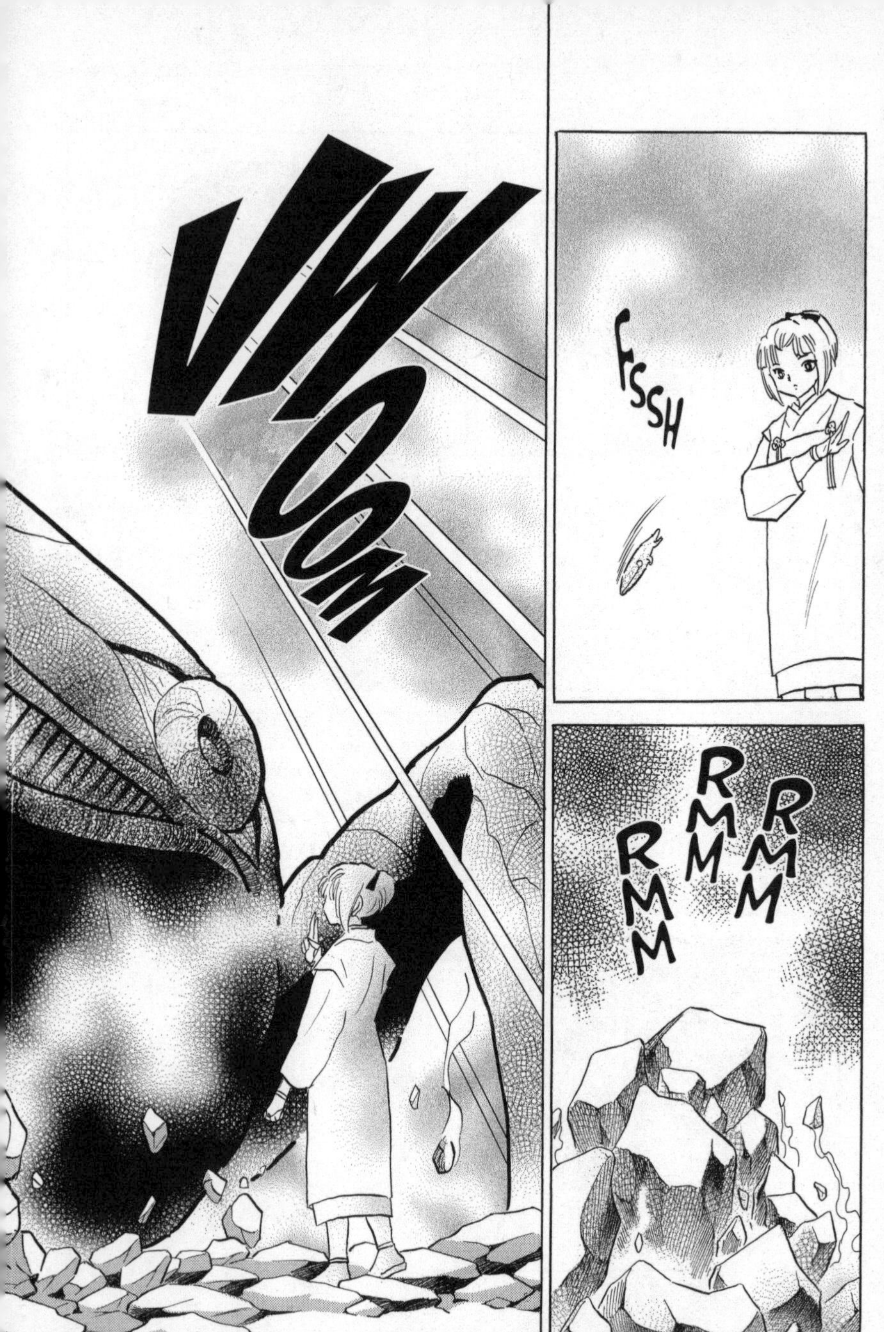
FSSH
RMM
RMM
RMM
VWOOM

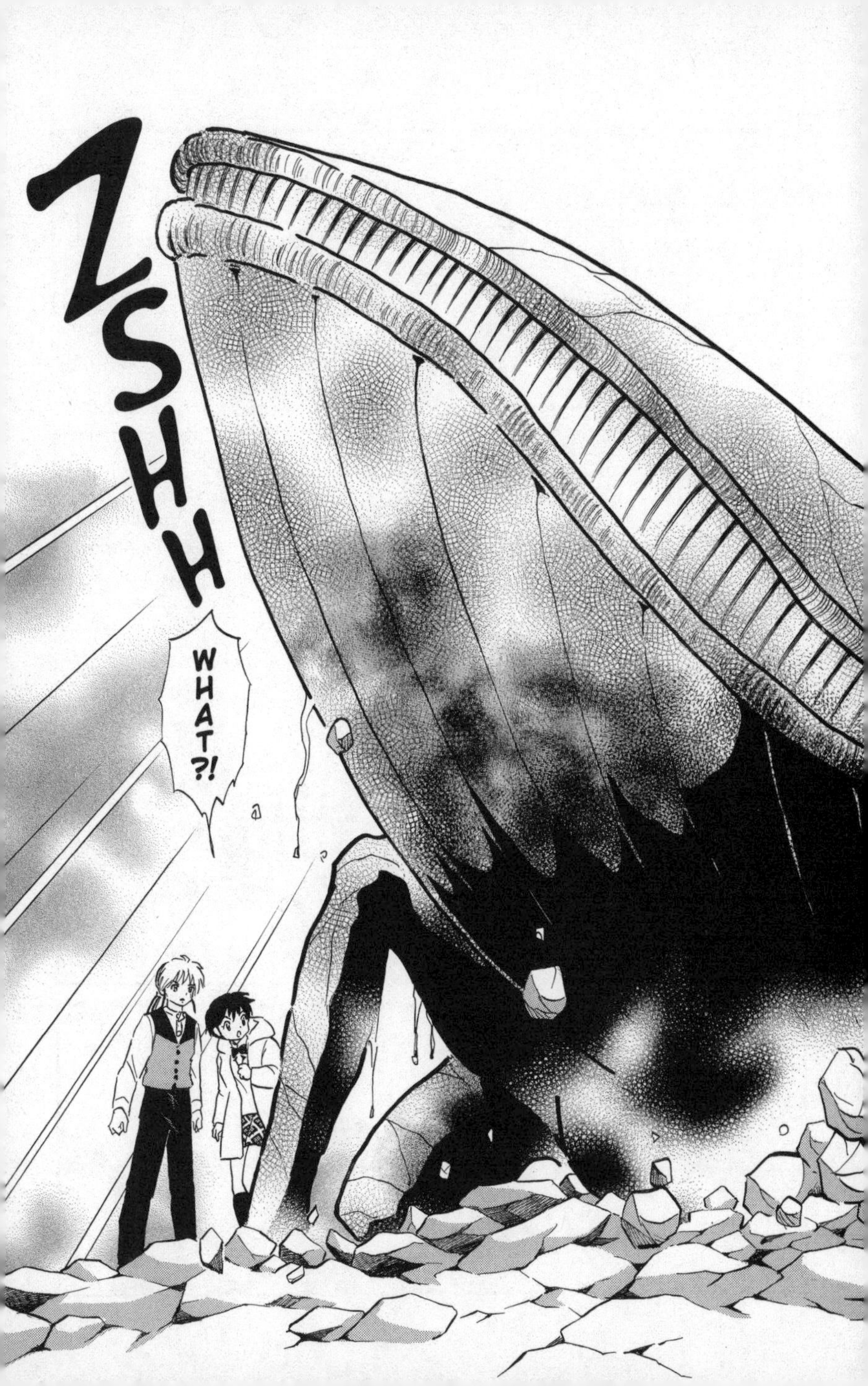
ZSHH
WHAT?!

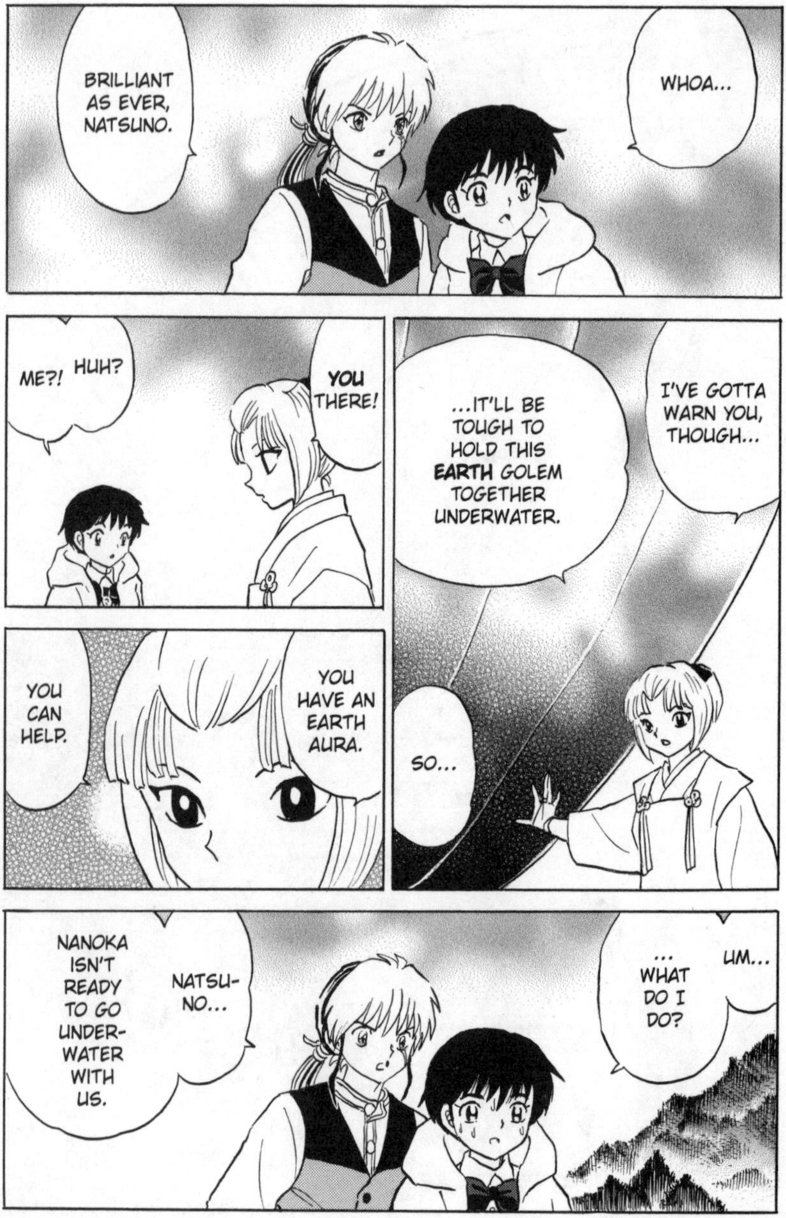
WHOA...
BRILLIANT AS EVER, NATSUNO.
I'VE GOTTA WARN YOU, THOUGH...
...IT'LL BE TOUGH TO HOLD THIS **EARTH** GOLEM TOGETHER UNDERWATER.
SO...
YOU THERE!
HUH?
ME?!
YOU HAVE AN EARTH AURA.
YOU CAN HELP.
UM...
...WHAT DO I DO?
NATSU-NO...
NANOKA ISN'T READY TO GO UNDER-WATER WITH US.

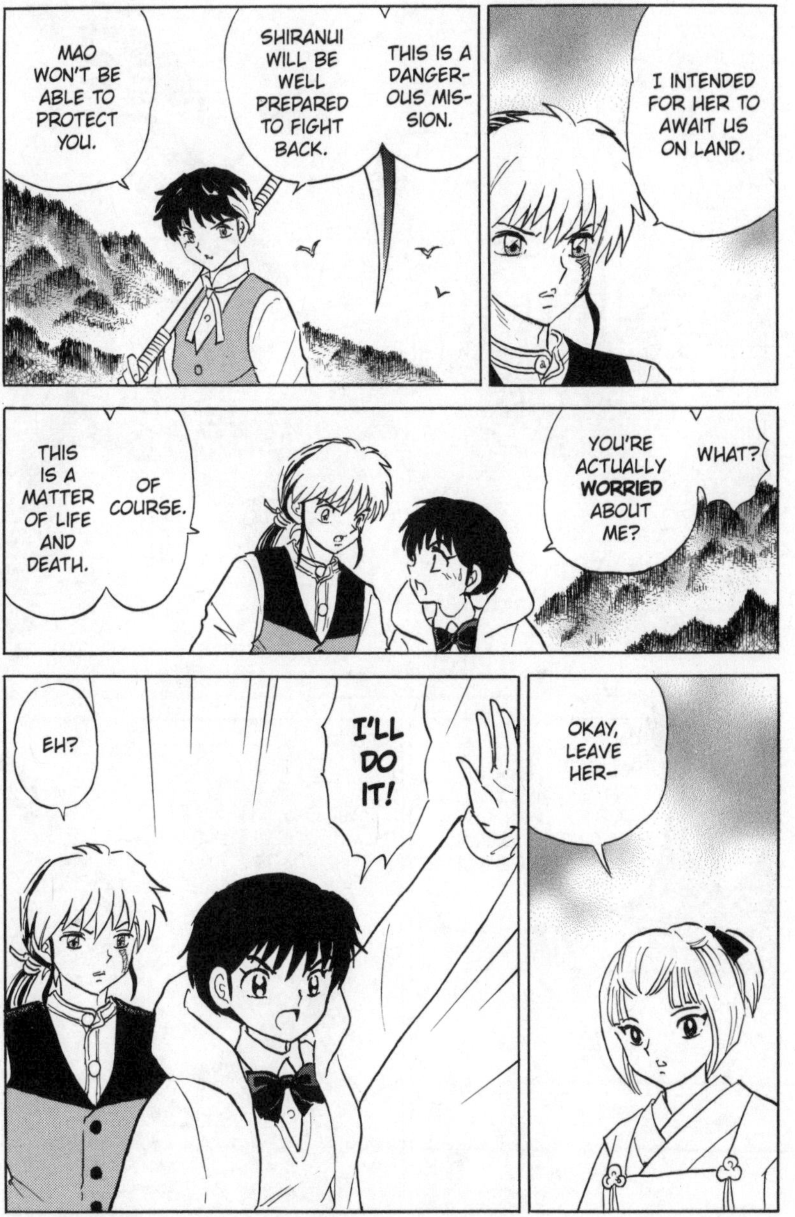
I INTENDED FOR HER TO AWAIT US ON LAND.
THIS IS A DANGEROUS MISSION.
SHIRANUI WILL BE WELL PREPARED TO FIGHT BACK.
MAO WON'T BE ABLE TO PROTECT YOU.
WHAT?
YOU'RE ACTUALLY **WORRIED** ABOUT ME?
OF COURSE.
THIS IS A MATTER OF LIFE AND DEATH.
OKAY, LEAVE HER–
I'LL DO IT!
EH?

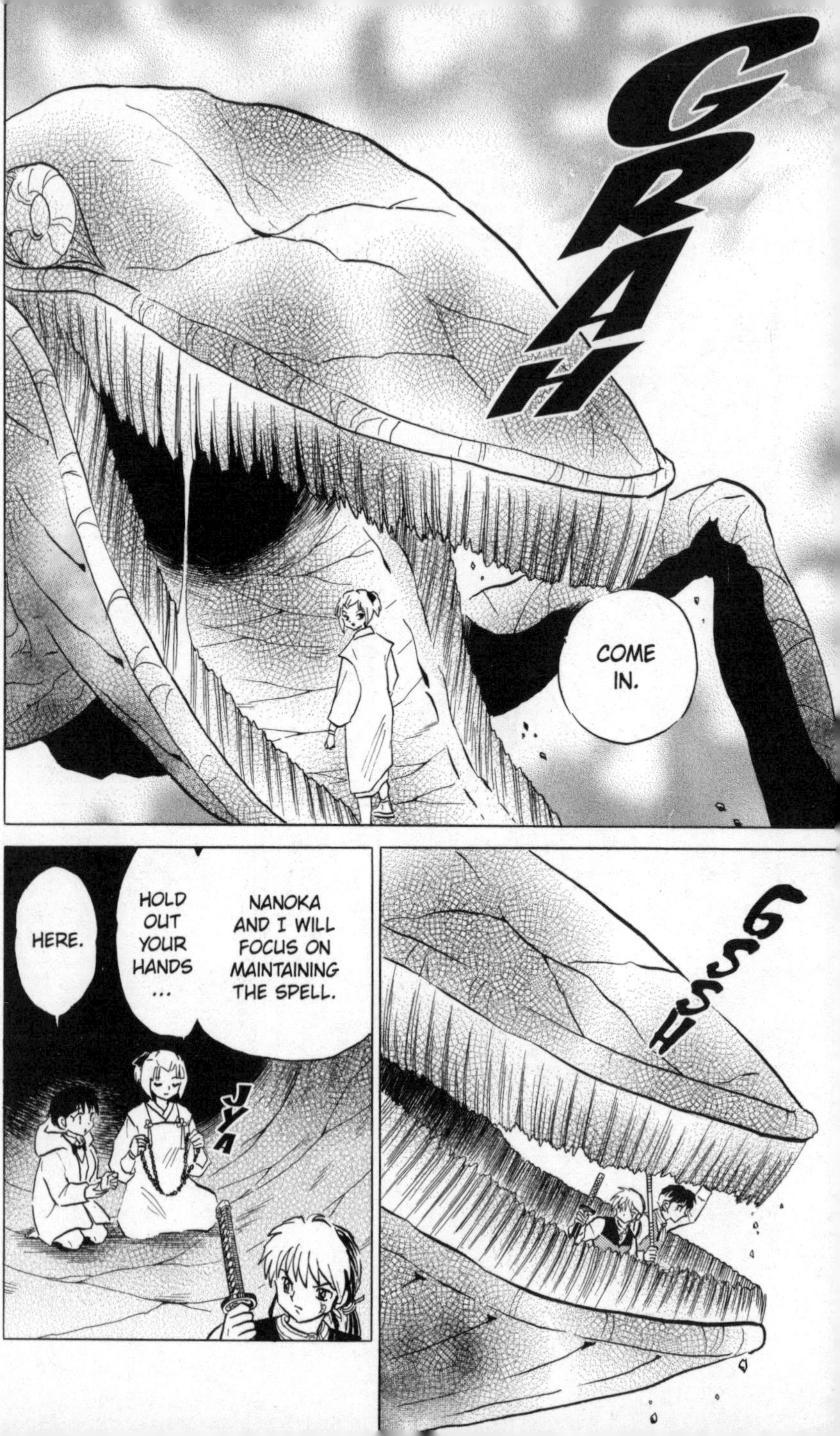
GRAH
COME IN.
GSSH
NANOKA AND I WILL FOCUS ON MAINTAINING THE SPELL.
HOLD OUT YOUR HANDS ...
HERE.
JYA

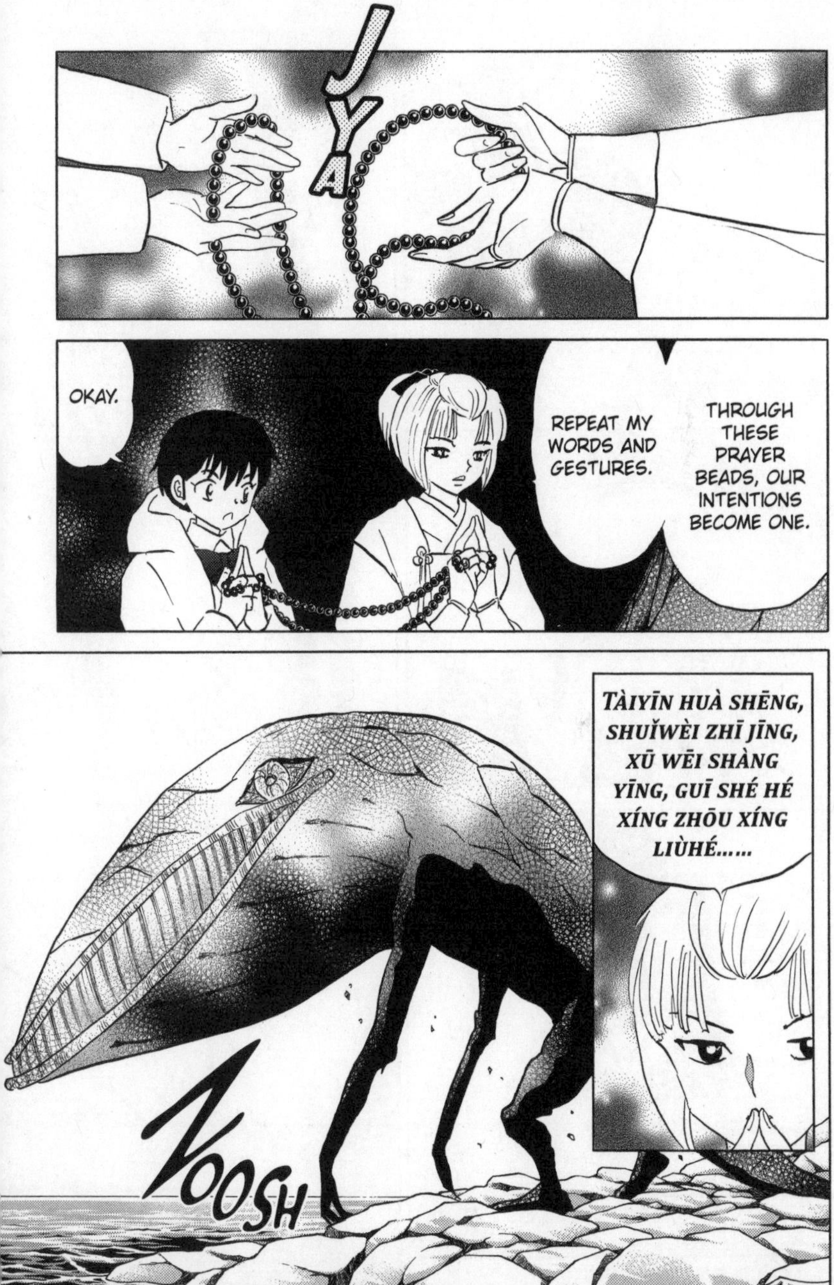
JYA
THROUGH THESE PRAYER BEADS, OUR INTENTIONS BECOME ONE.
REPEAT MY WORDS AND GESTURES.
OKAY.
TÀIYĪN HUÀ SHĒNG, SHUǏWÈI ZHĪ JĪNG, XŪ WĒI SHÀNG YĪNG, GUĪ SHÉ HÉ XÍNG ZHŌU XÍNG LIÙHÉ……
VOOSH

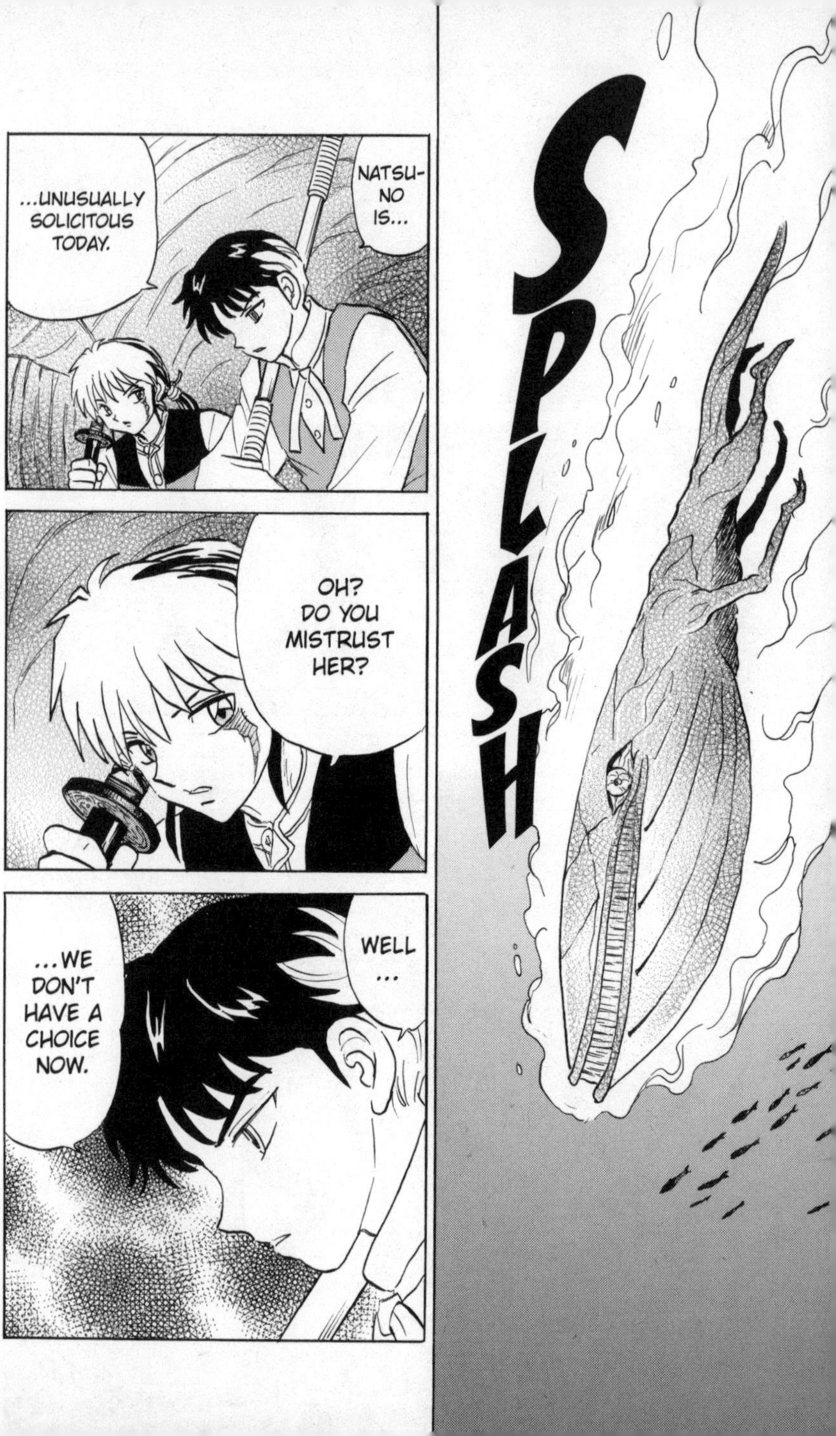
SPLASH
NATSU-NO IS...
...UNUSUALLY SOLICITOUS TODAY.
OH? DO YOU MISTRUST HER?
WELL...
...WE DON'T HAVE A CHOICE NOW.

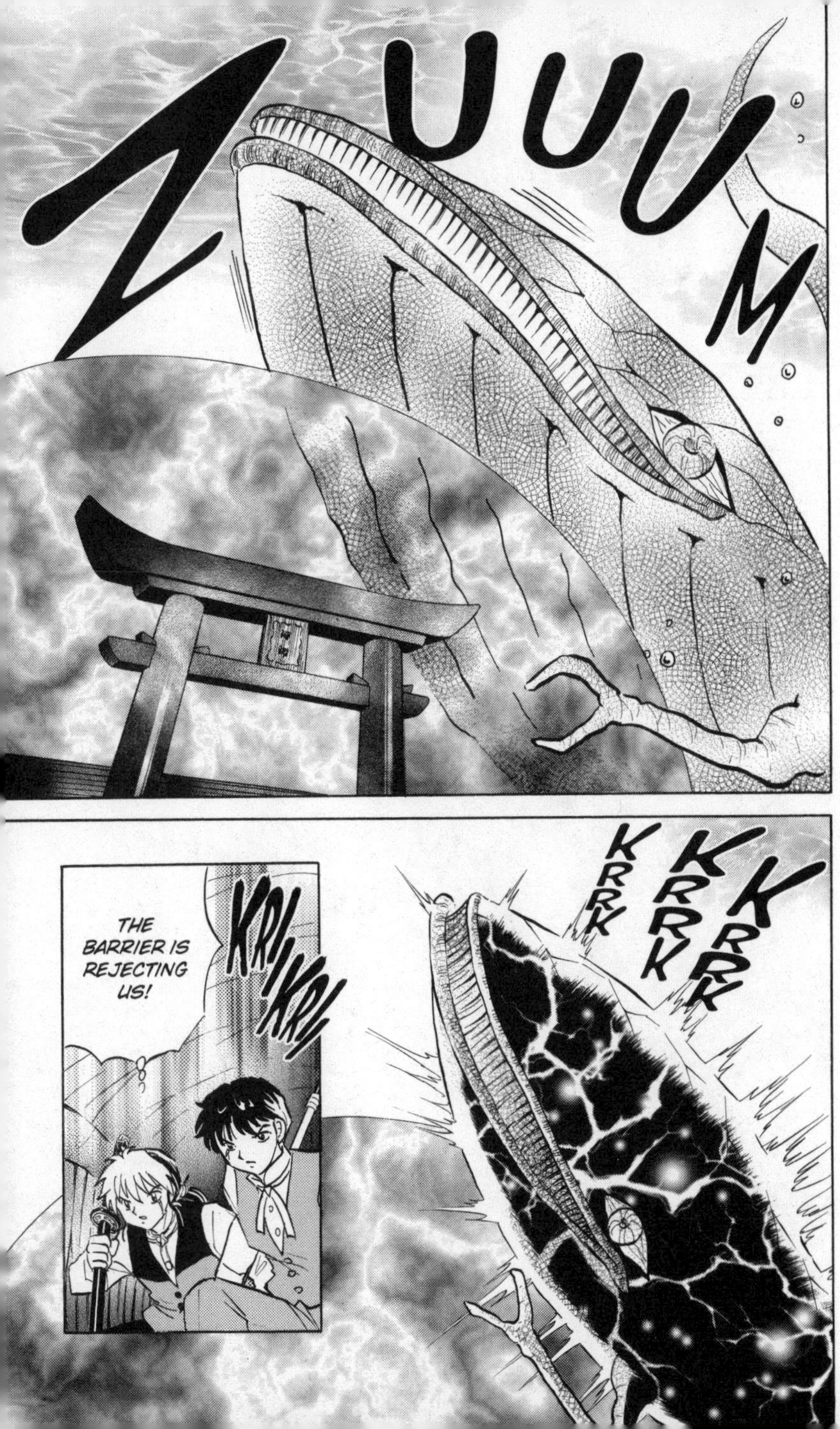
ZUUUM
KRRK
KRRK
KRRRK
THE BARRIER IS REJECTING US!
KRI KRI KRI

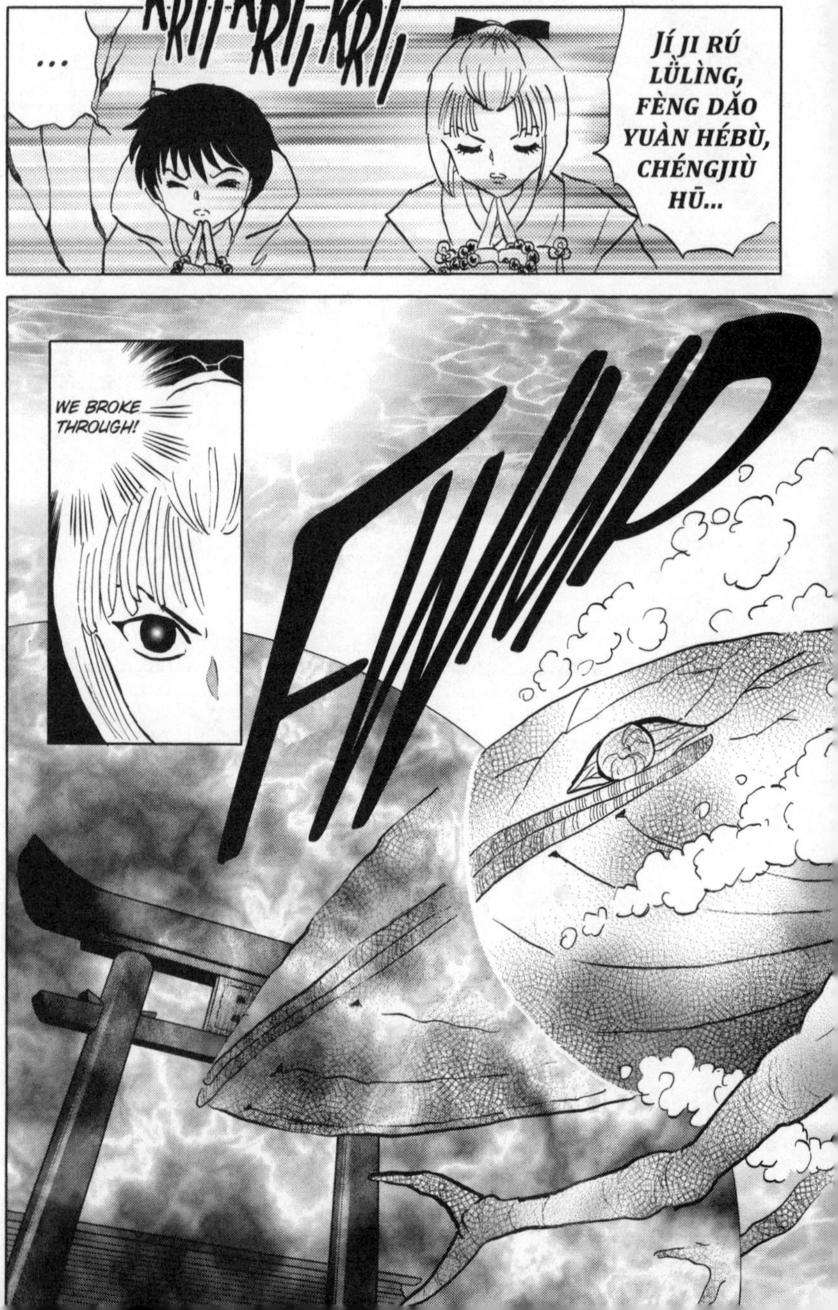
JÍ JI RÚ LǛLÌNG, FÈNG DǍO YUÀN HÉBÙ, CHÉNGJIÙ HŪ...
KRI KRI KRI
...
FWMP
WE BROKE THROUGH!

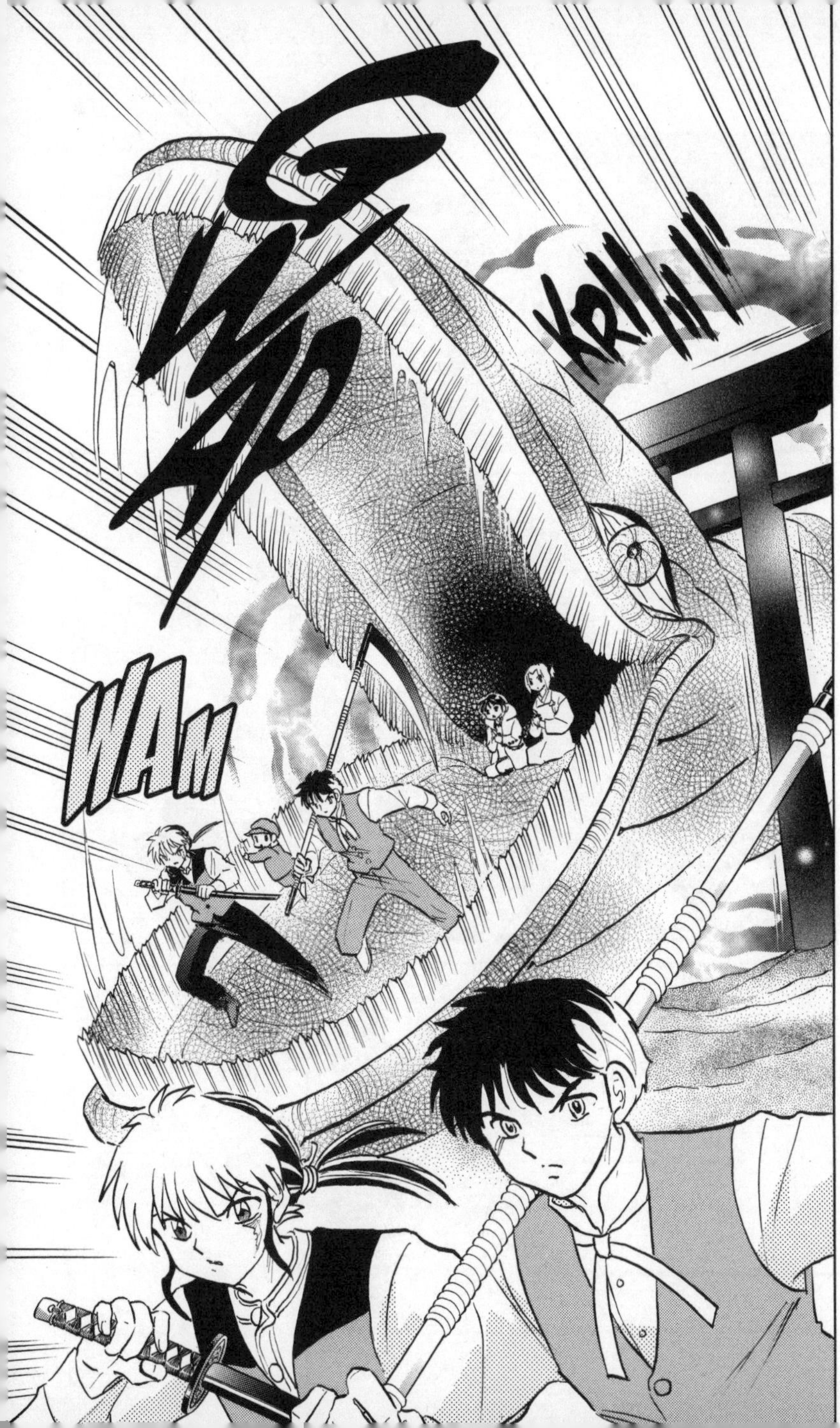
KRIIII
GWAP
WAM

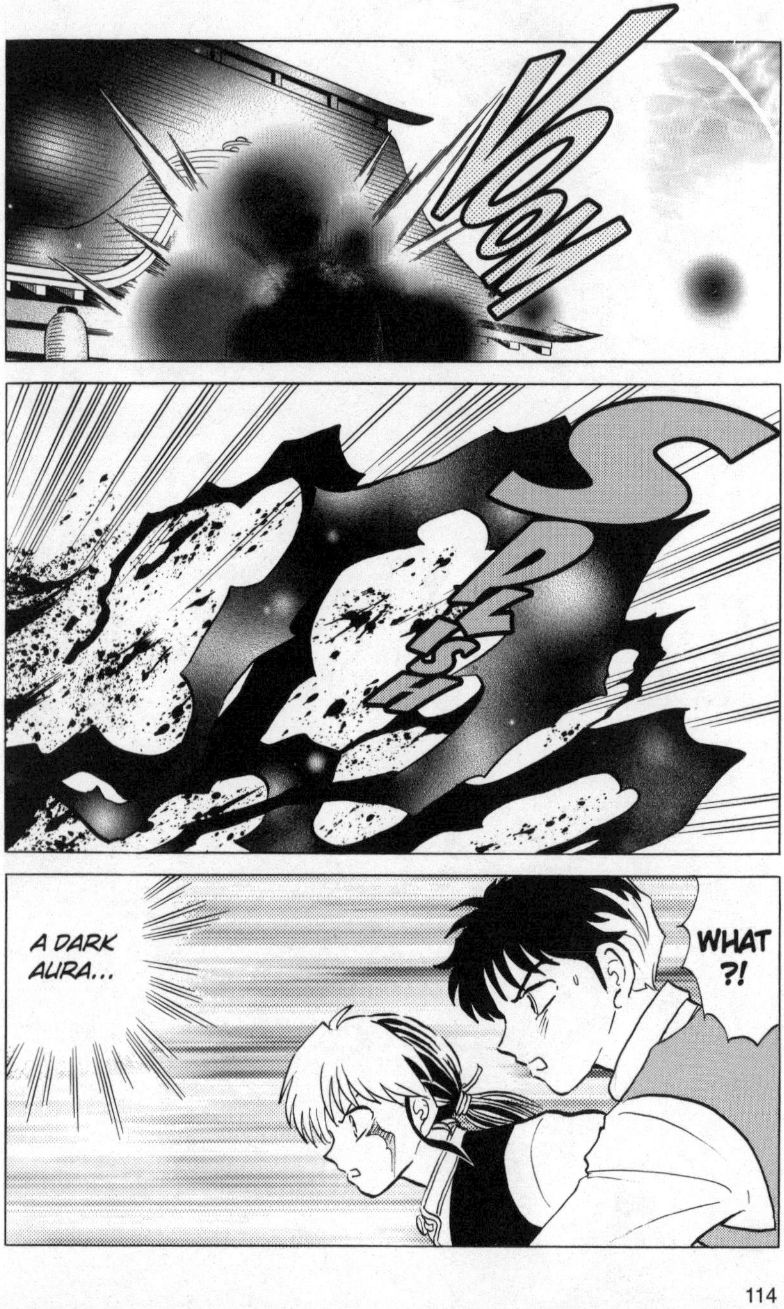
VOOM
SPLISH!
WHAT ?!
A DARK AURA...

Chapter 7:
Bound to the Wheel of Fate

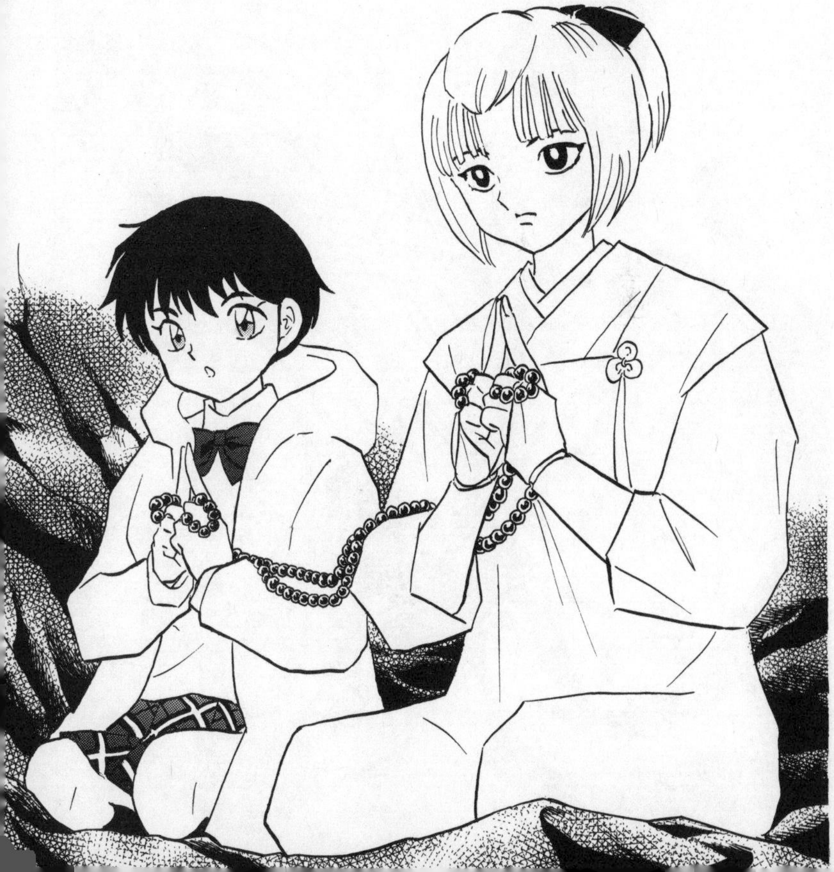

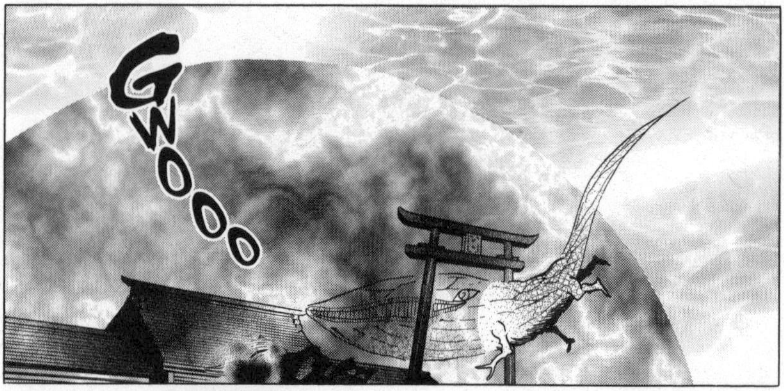
GWOOO

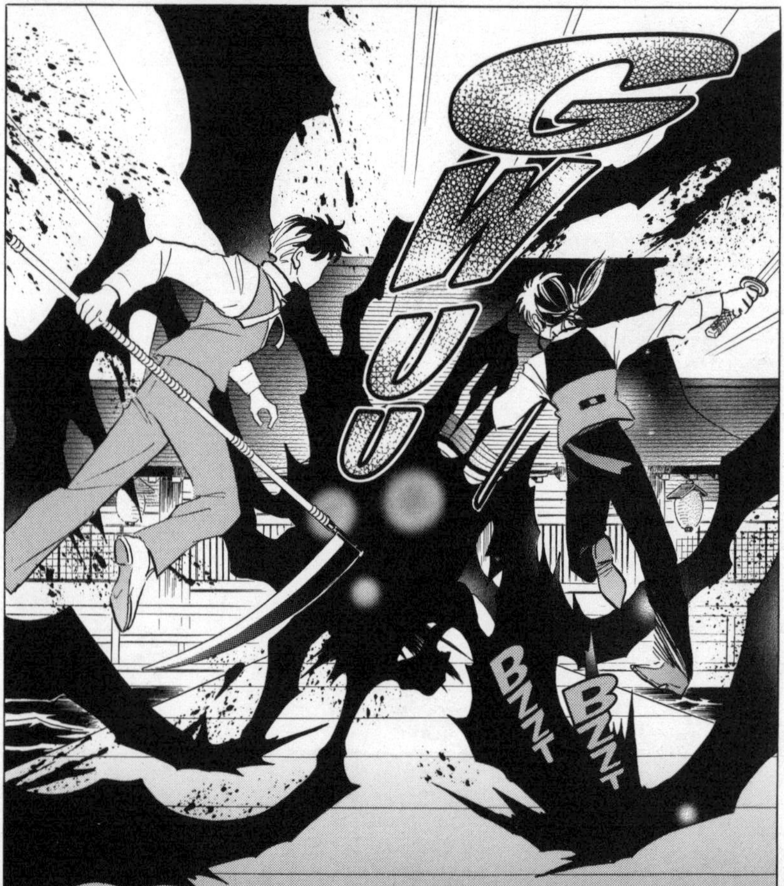
GWUUU
BZZZT
BZZZT

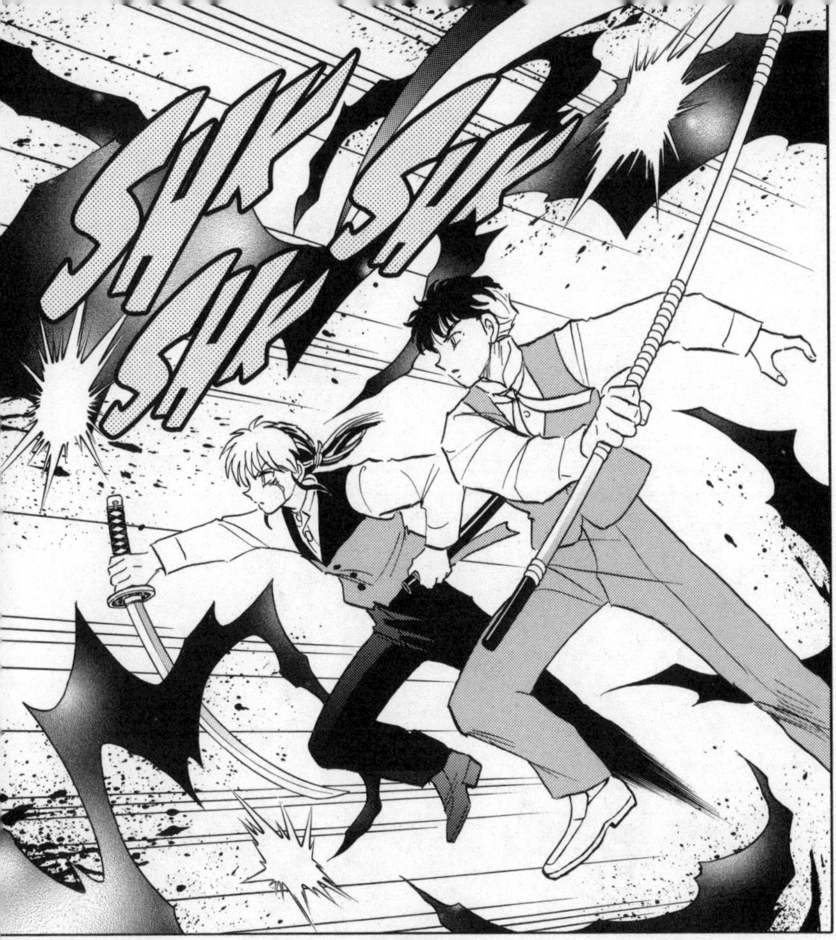
SHK SHK SHK

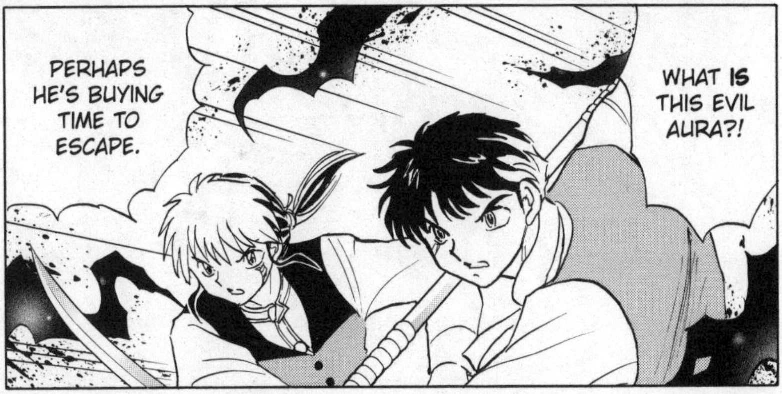
WHAT **IS** THIS EVIL AURA?!
PERHAPS HE'S BUYING TIME TO ESCAPE.

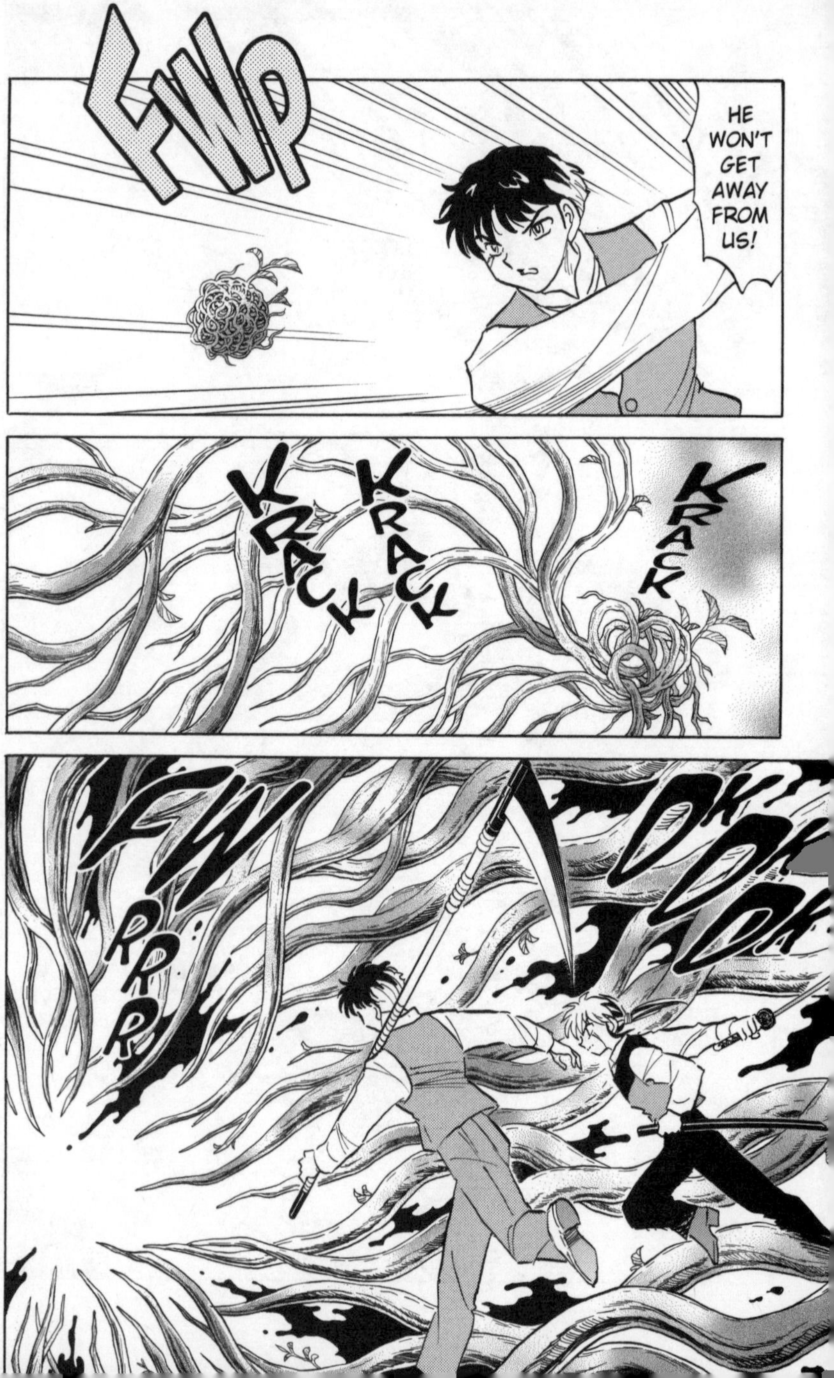
HE WON'T GET AWAY FROM US!
FWP
KRACK
KRACK
KRACK
DOK DOK DOK
FWRRRR

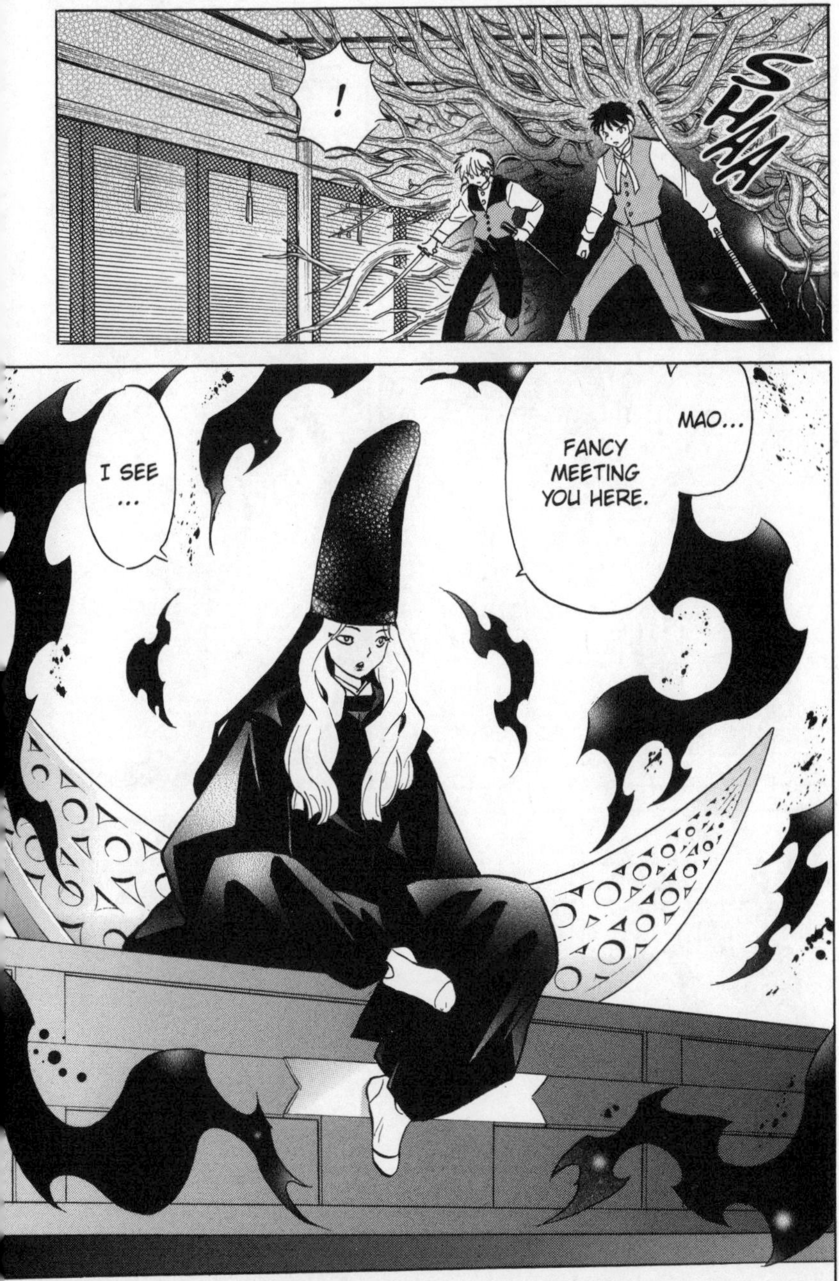
SHAA
!
MAO... FANCY MEETING YOU HERE.
I SEE ...

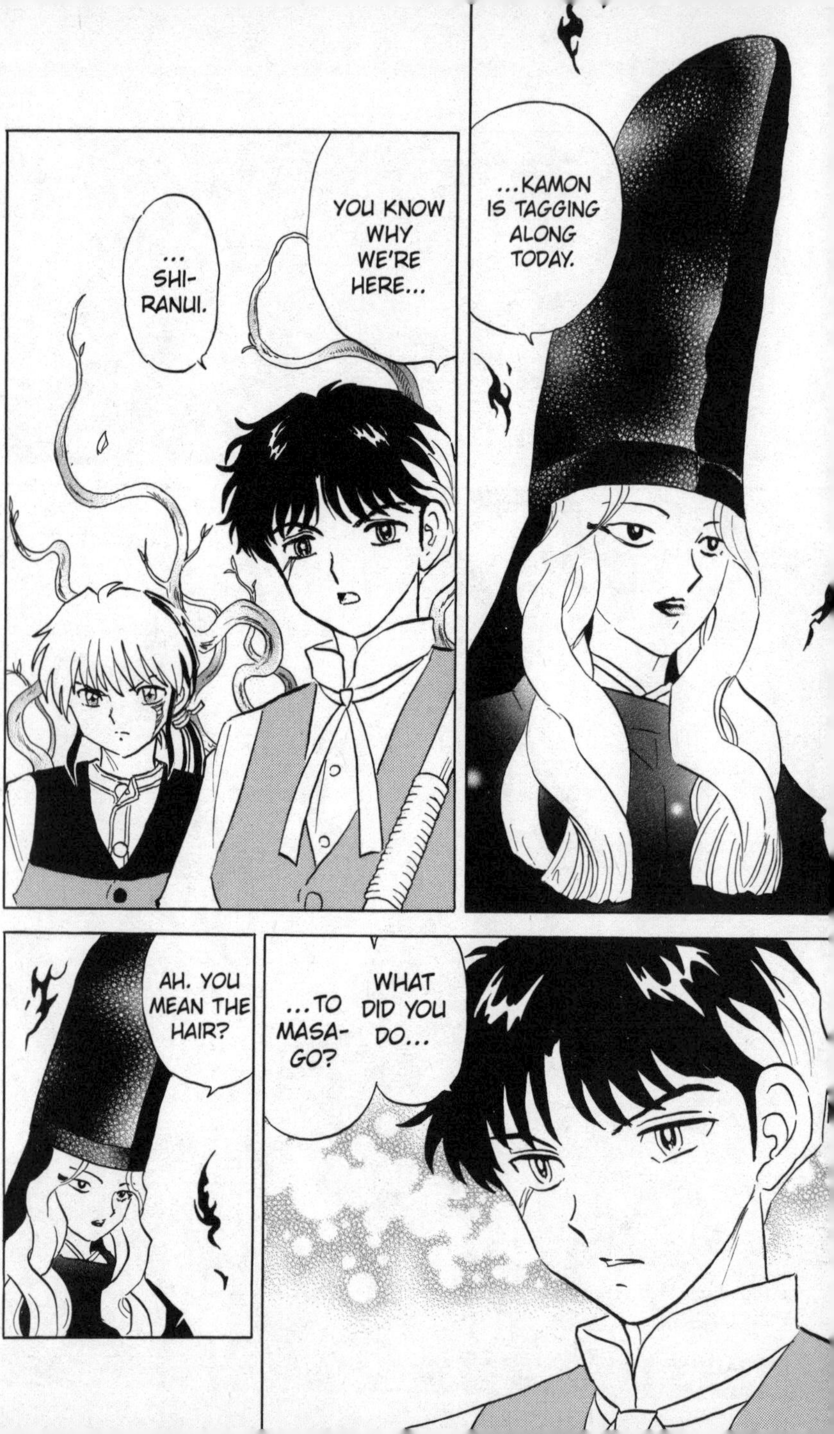
...KAMON IS TAGGING ALONG TODAY.
YOU KNOW WHY WE'RE HERE...
... SHI-RANUI.
WHAT DID YOU DO...
...TO MASA-GO?
AH. YOU MEAN THE HAIR?

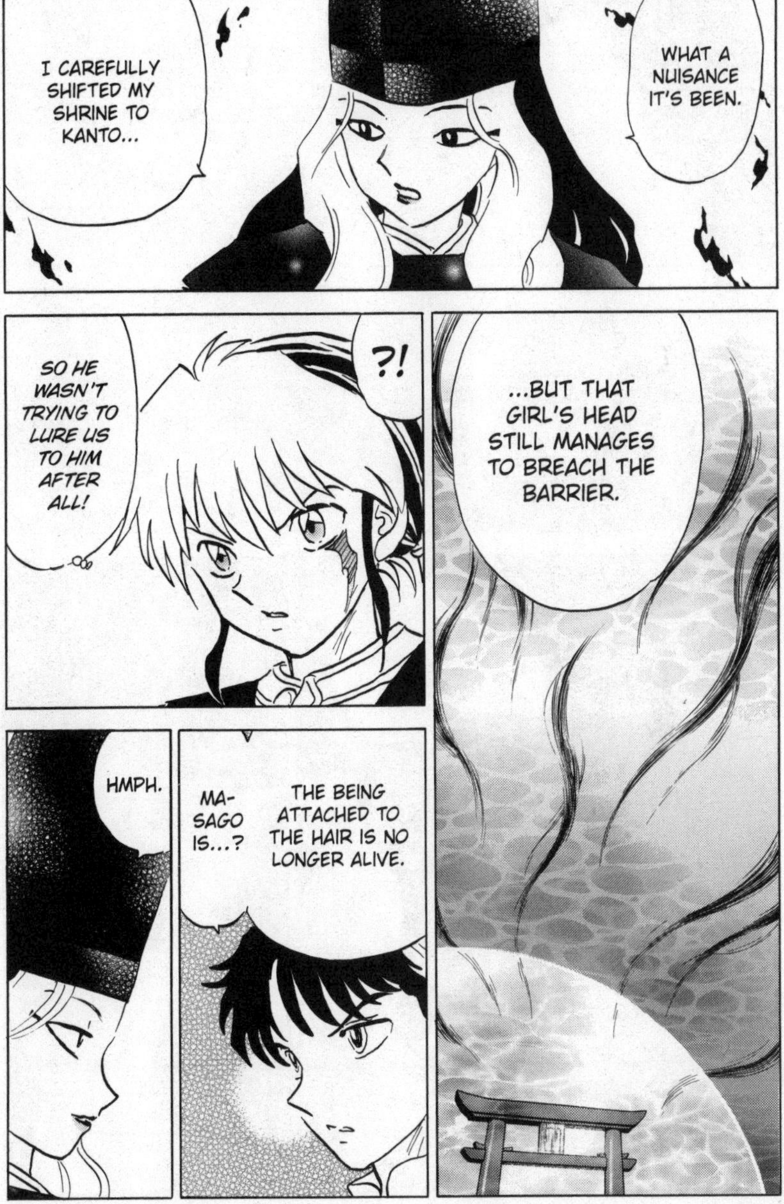
WHAT A NUISANCE IT'S BEEN.
I CAREFULLY SHIFTED MY SHRINE TO KANTO...
...BUT THAT GIRL'S HEAD STILL MANAGES TO BREACH THE BARRIER.
?!
SO HE WASN'T TRYING TO LURE US TO HIM AFTER ALL!
THE BEING ATTACHED TO THE HAIR IS NO LONGER ALIVE.
MA-SAGO IS...?
HMPH.

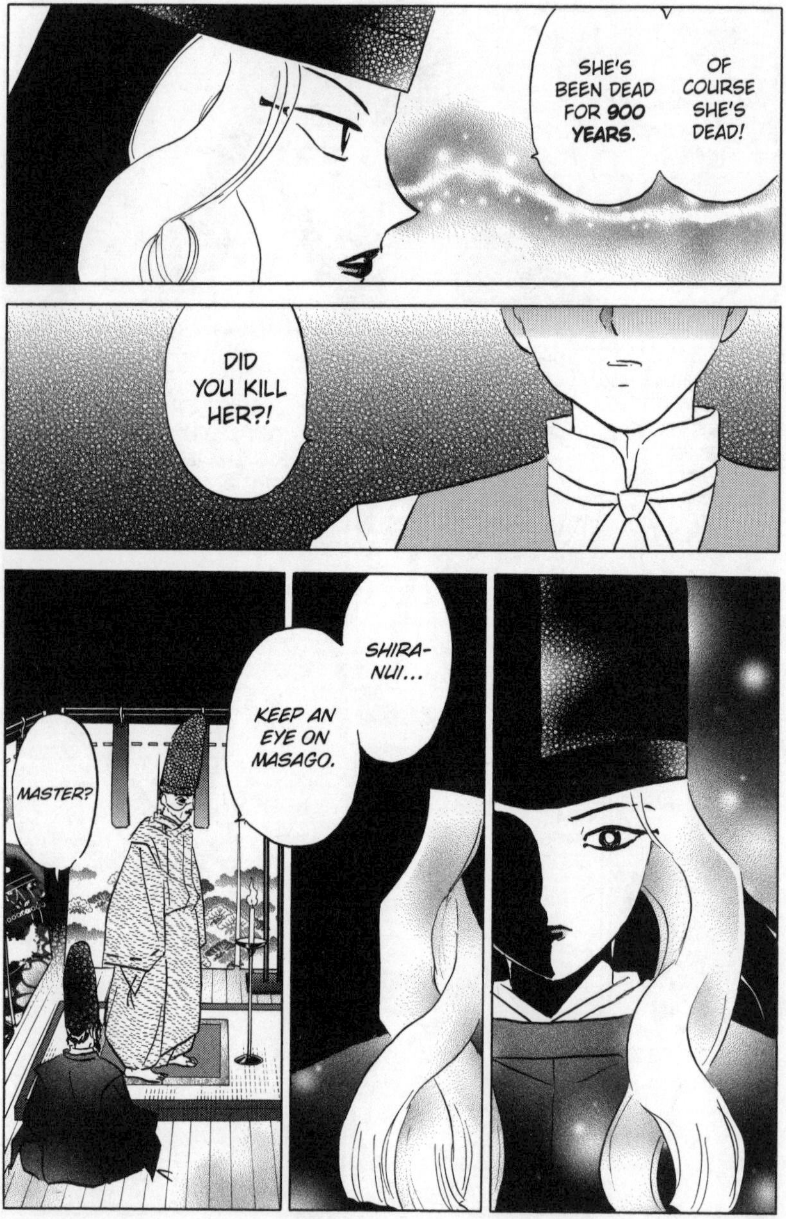
OF COURSE SHE'S DEAD!
SHE'S BEEN DEAD FOR 900 YEARS.
DID YOU KILL HER?!
SHIRA-NUI...
KEEP AN EYE ON MASAGO.
MASTER?

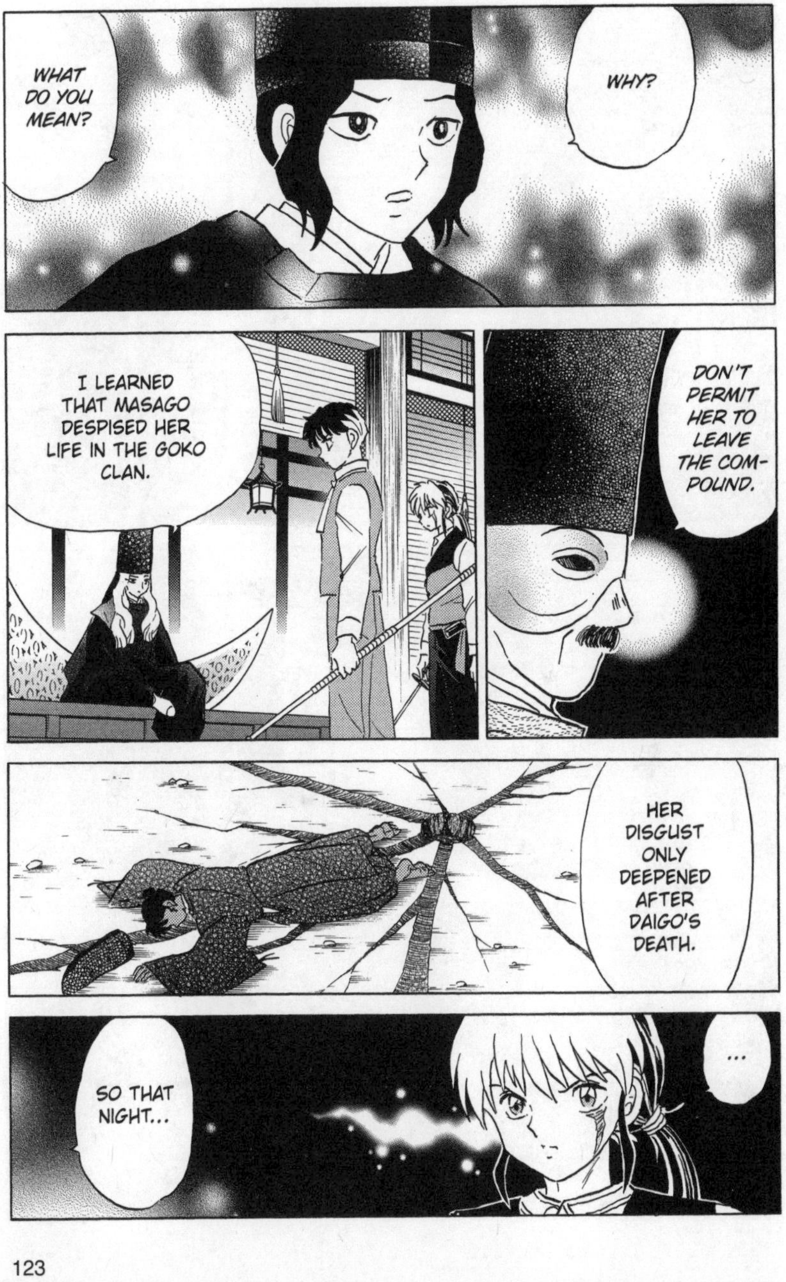
WHY?
WHAT DO YOU MEAN?
DON'T PERMIT HER TO LEAVE THE COM-POUND.
I LEARNED THAT MASAGO DESPISED HER LIFE IN THE GOKO CLAN.
HER DISGUST ONLY DEEPENED AFTER DAIGO'S DEATH.
...
SO THAT NIGHT...

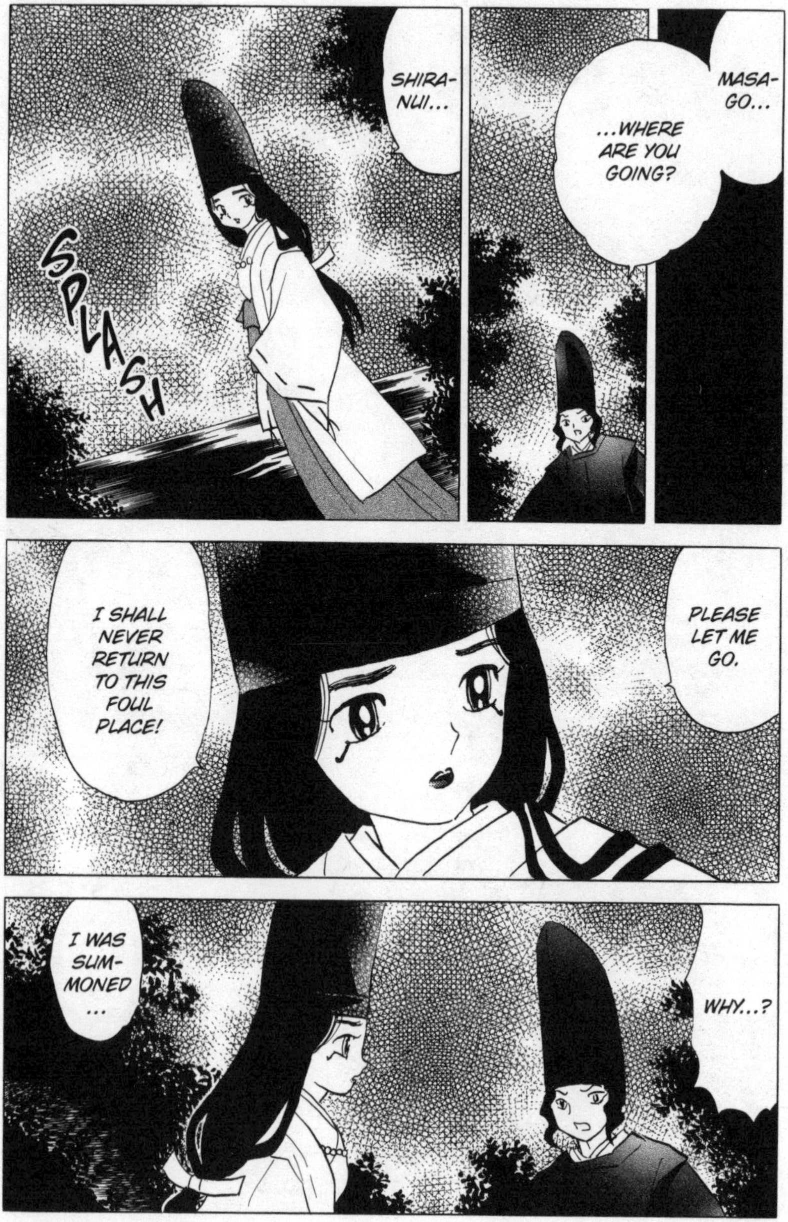
MASA-GO...
...WHERE ARE YOU GOING?
SHIRA-NUI...
SPLASH
PLEASE LET ME GO.
I SHALL NEVER RETURN TO THIS FOUL PLACE!
WHY...?
I WAS SUM-MONED ...

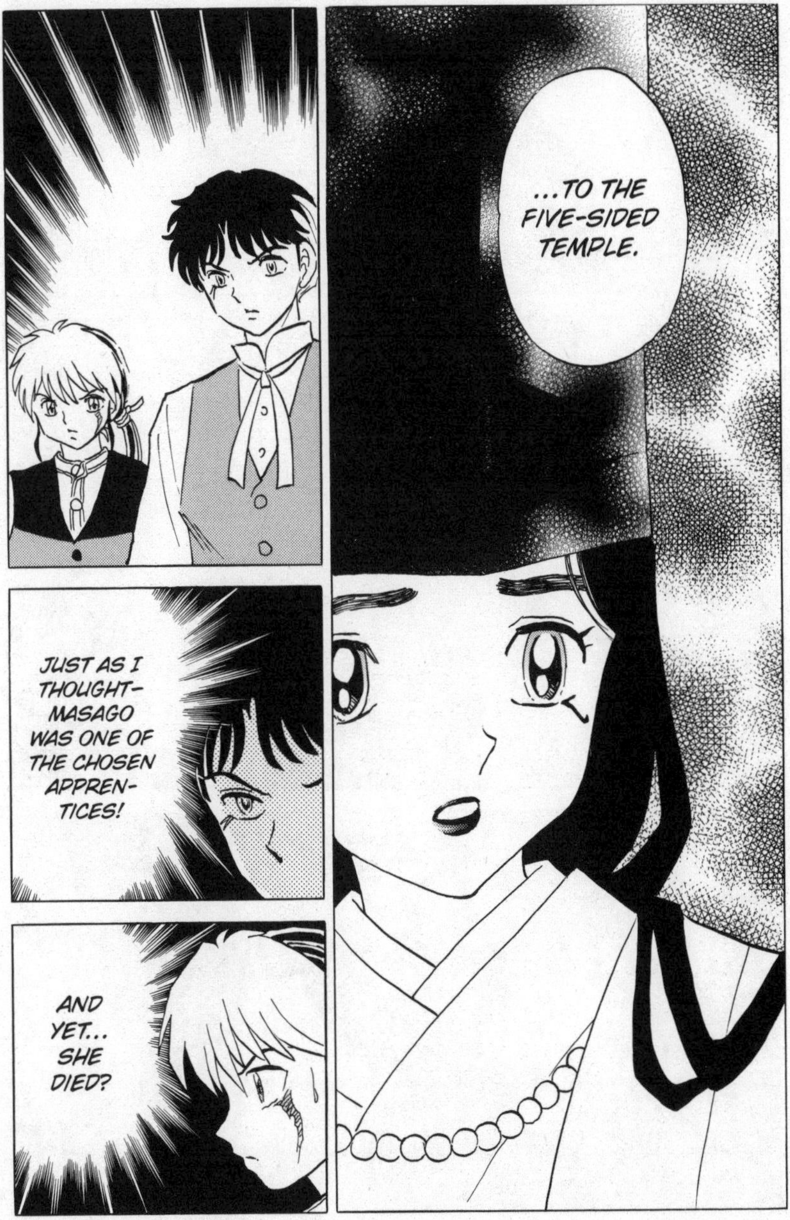
...TO THE FIVE-SIDED TEMPLE.
JUST AS I THOUGHT-MASAGO WAS ONE OF THE CHOSEN APPREN-TICES!
AND YET... SHE DIED?

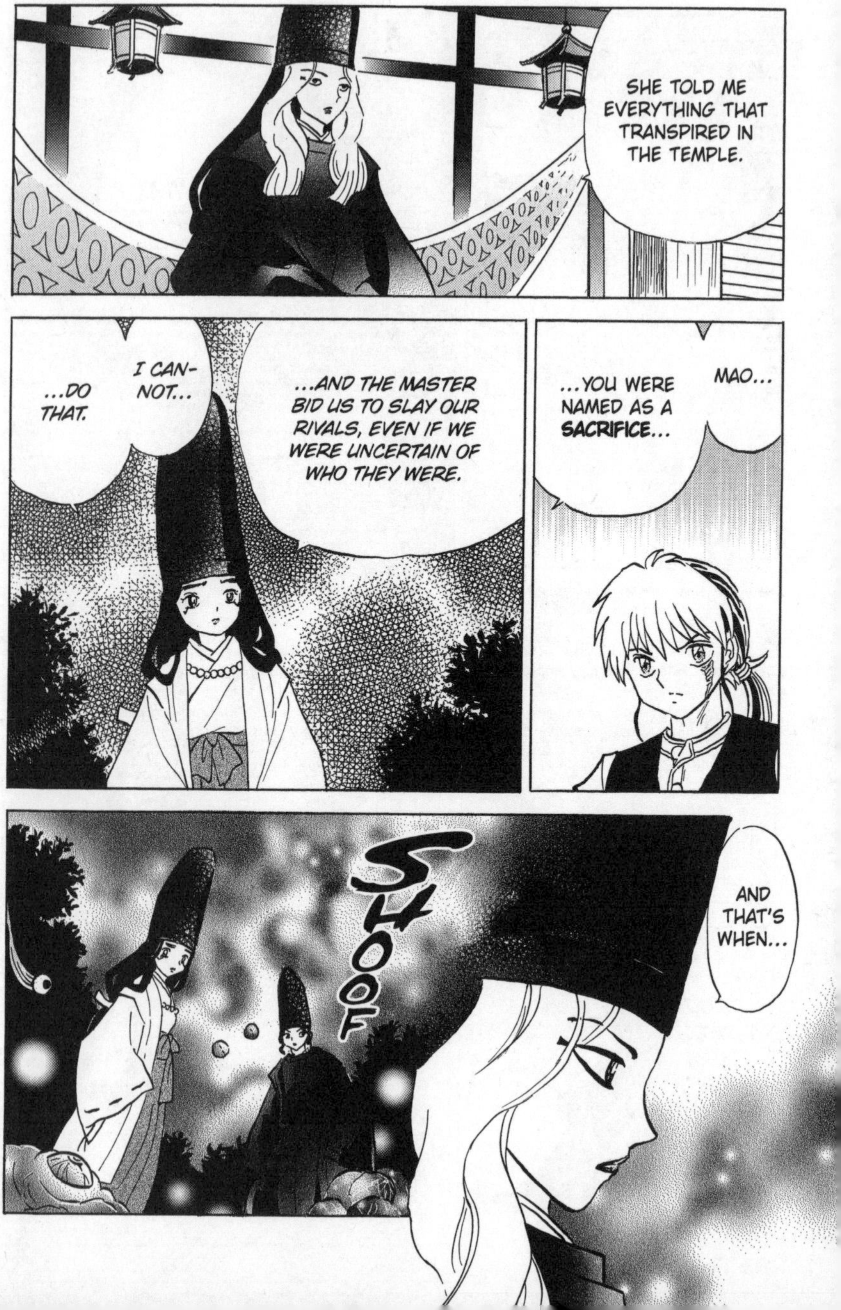
SHE TOLD ME EVERYTHING THAT TRANSPIRED IN THE TEMPLE.
MAO...
...YOU WERE NAMED AS A **SACRIFICE**...
...AND THE MASTER BID US TO SLAY OUR RIVALS, EVEN IF WE WERE UNCERTAIN OF WHO THEY WERE.
I CAN-NOT...
...DO THAT.
AND THAT'S WHEN...
SHOOOF

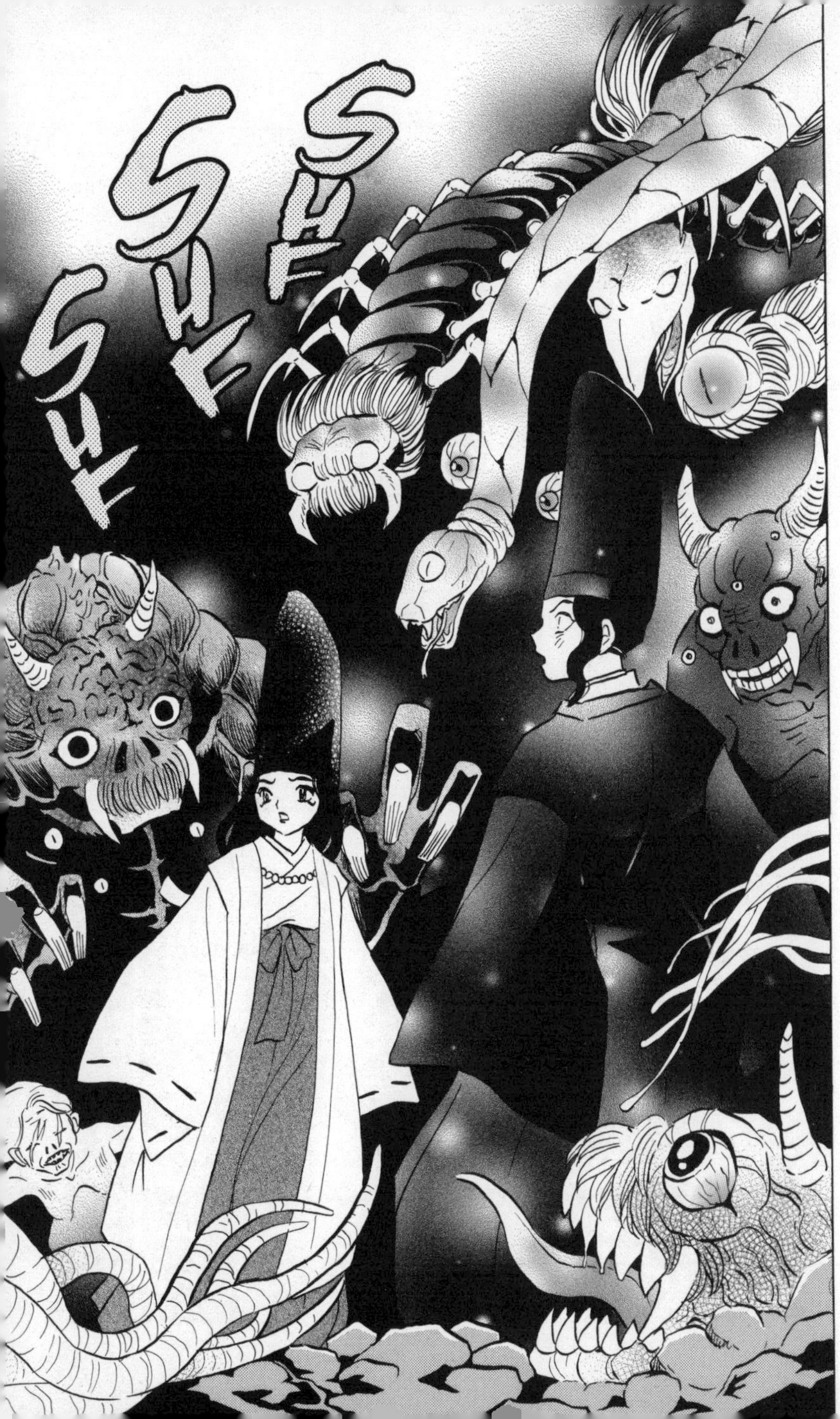
SHFF SHFF SHFF

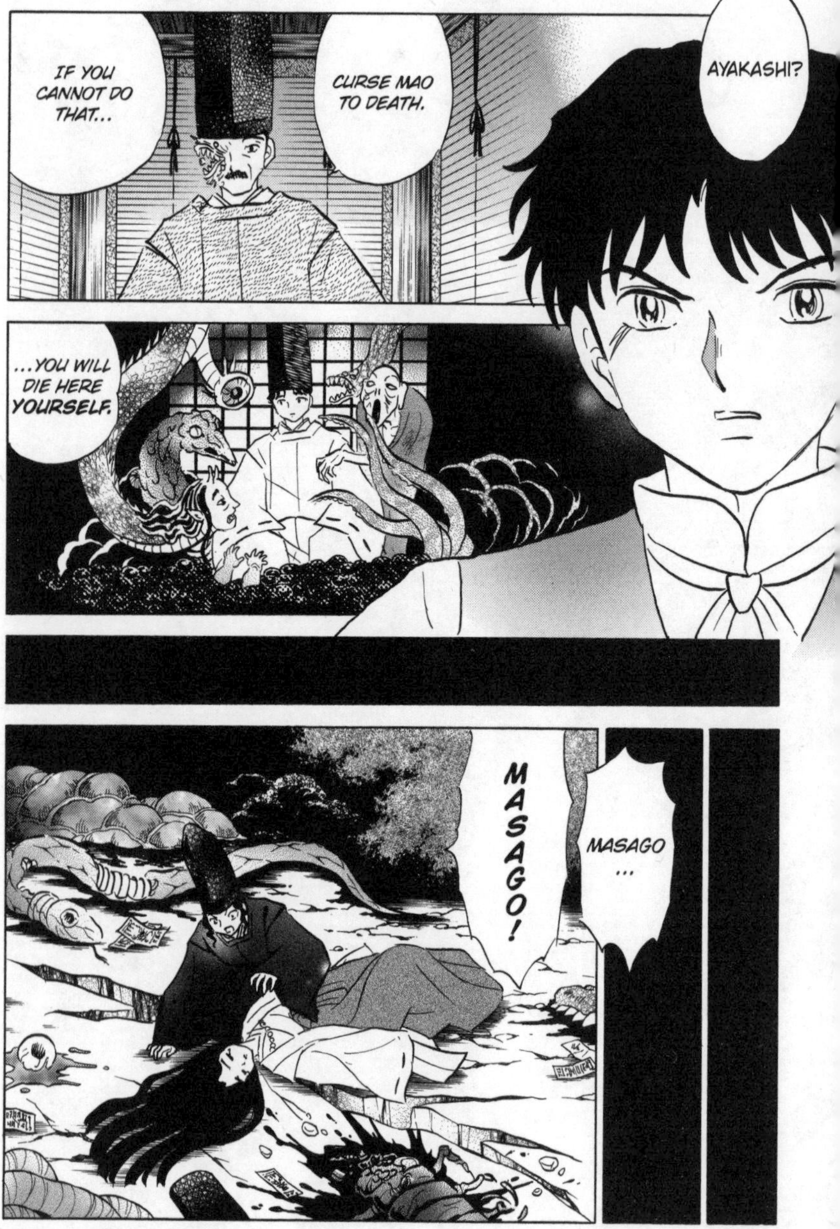
AYAKASHI?
CURSE MAO TO DEATH.
IF YOU CANNOT DO THAT...
...YOU WILL DIE HERE YOURSELF.
MASAGO ...
MASAGO!

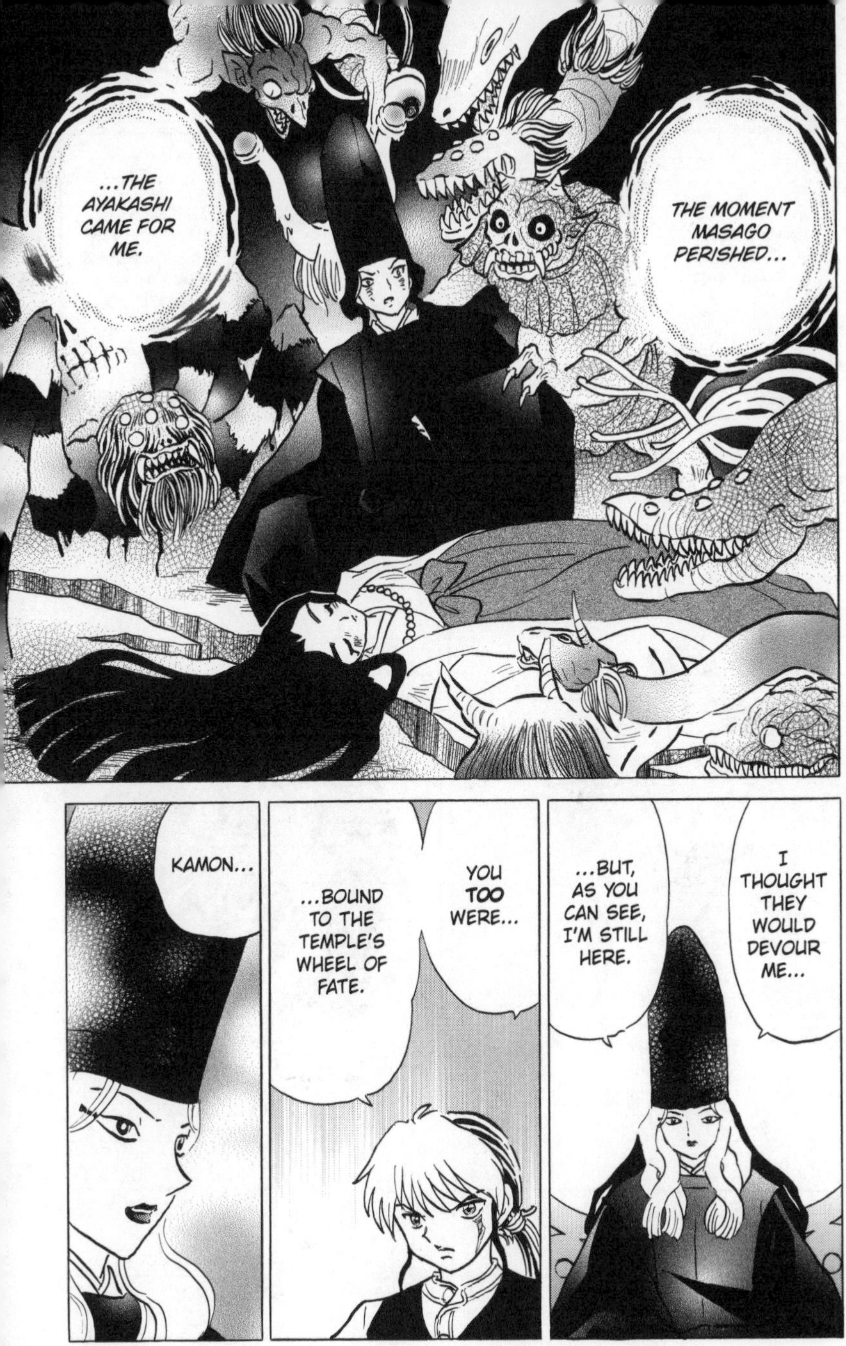
THE MOMENT MASAGO PERISHED...
...THE AYAKASHI CAME FOR ME.
I THOUGHT THEY WOULD DEVOUR ME...
...BUT, AS YOU CAN SEE, I'M STILL HERE.
YOU TOO WERE...
...BOUND TO THE TEMPLE'S WHEEL OF FATE.
KAMON...

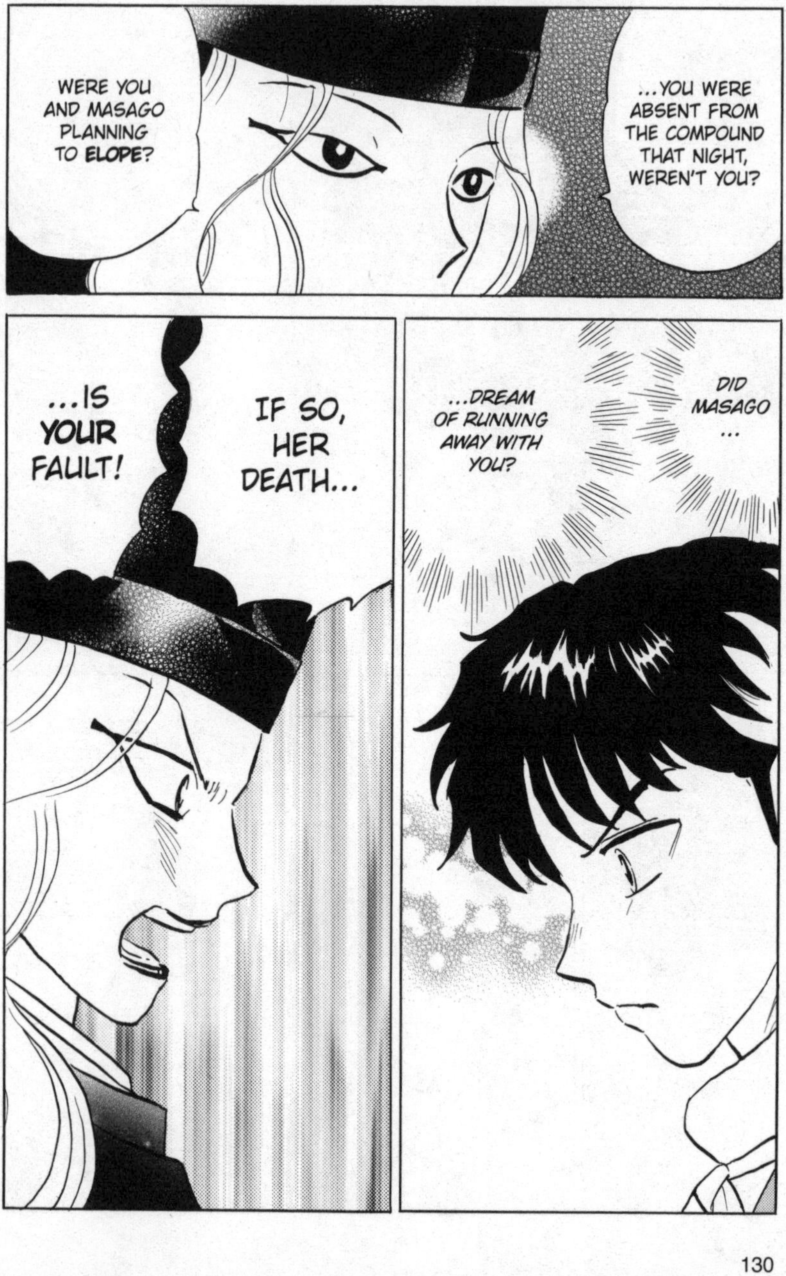
...YOU WERE ABSENT FROM THE COMPOUND THAT NIGHT, WEREN'T YOU?
WERE YOU AND MASAGO PLANNING TO **ELOPE**?
DID MASAGO...
...DREAM OF RUNNING AWAY WITH YOU?
IF SO, HER DEATH...
...IS **YOUR** FAULT!

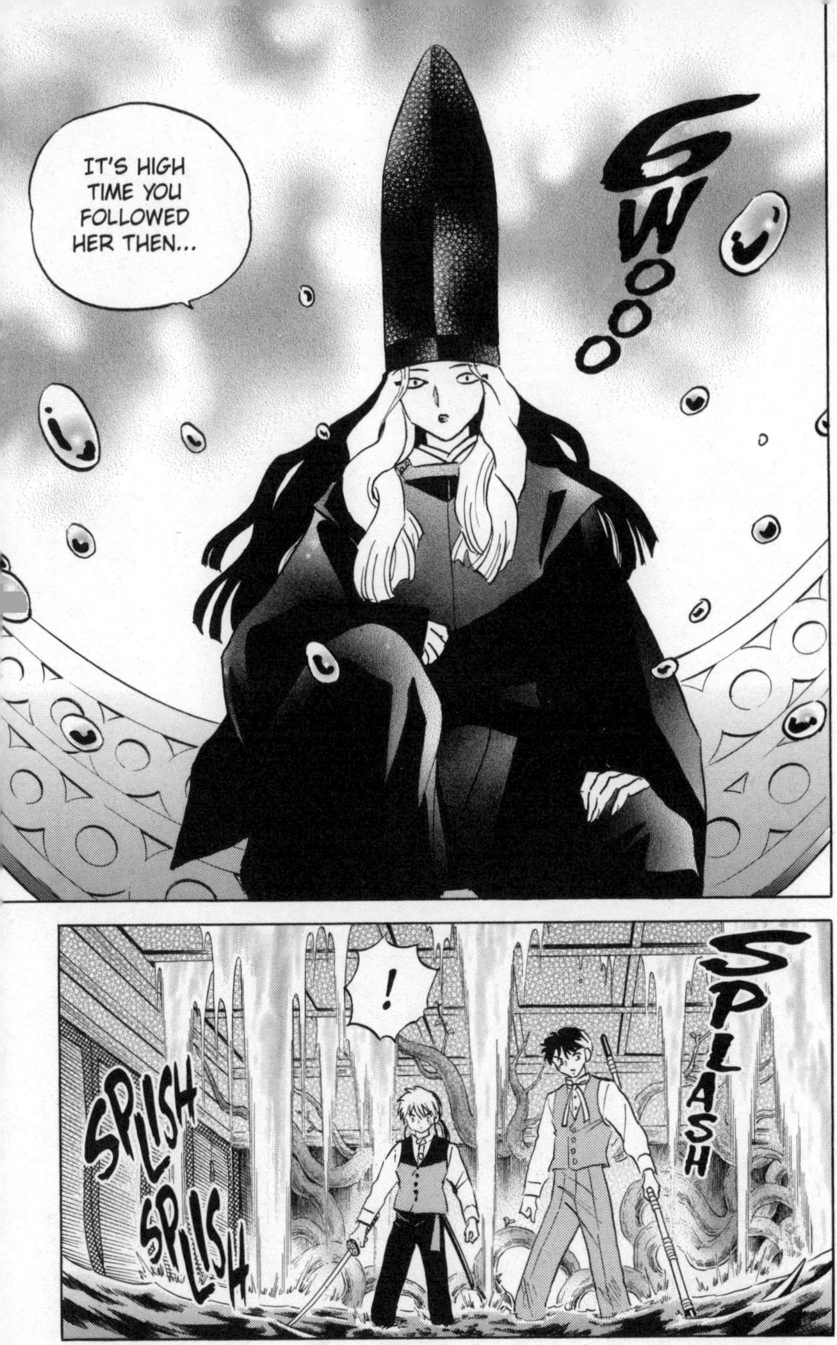
GWOOOO
IT'S HIGH TIME YOU FOLLOWED HER THEN...
SPLASH
!
SPLISH SPLISH

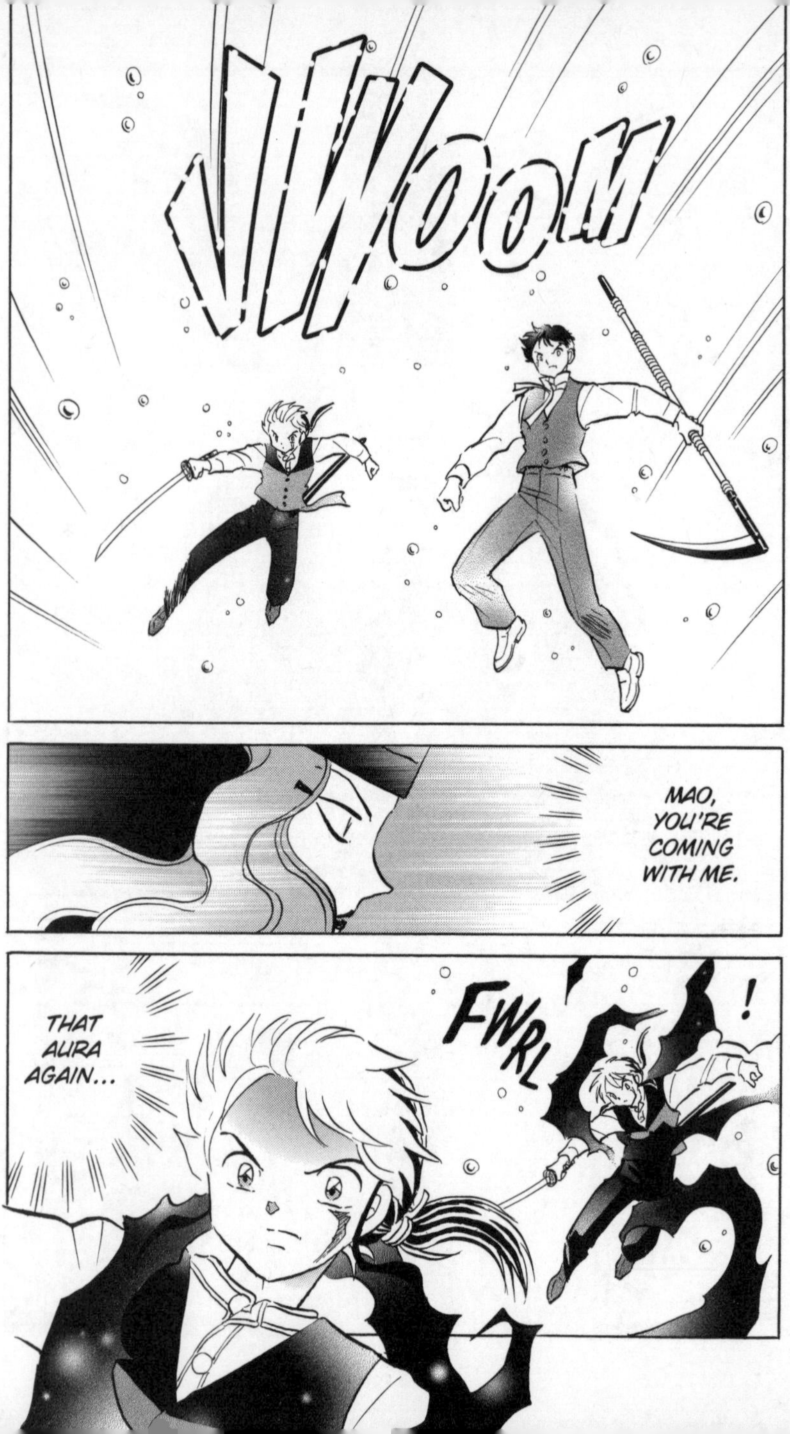
VWOOM
MAO, YOU'RE COMING WITH ME.
FWRL
!
THAT AURA AGAIN...

Chapter 8: Within the Evil Aura

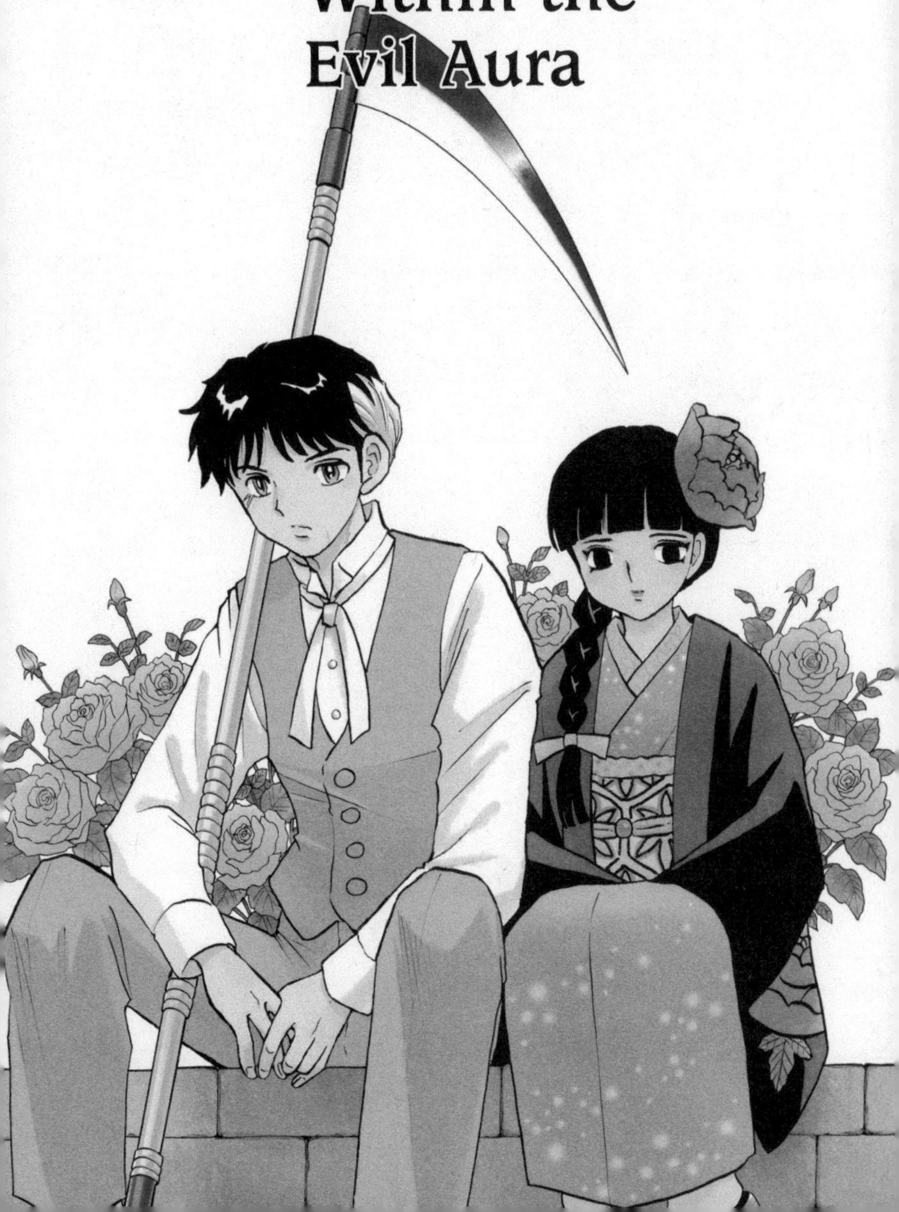

MAO

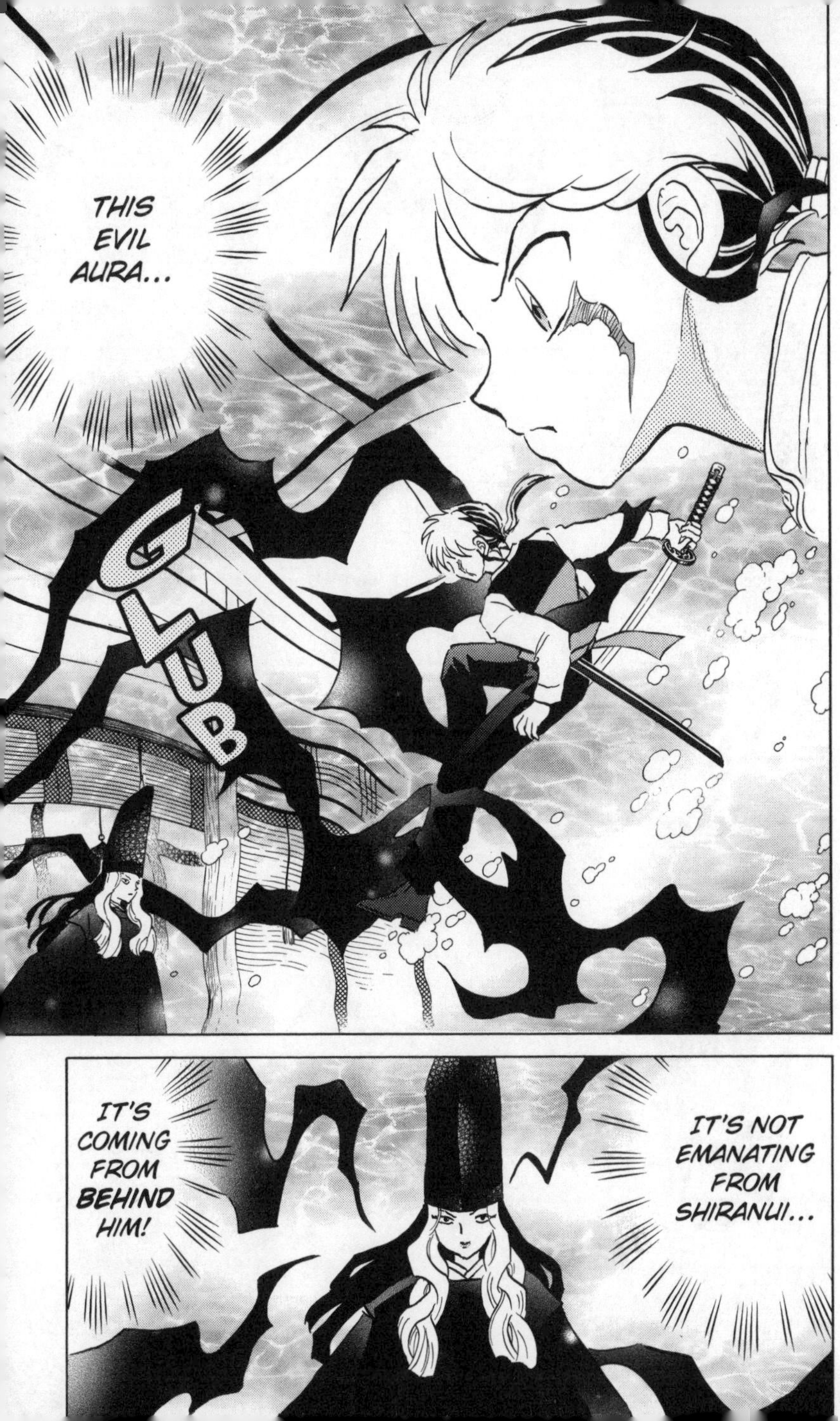
THIS EVIL AURA...
GLUB
IT'S NOT EMANATING FROM SHIRANUI...
IT'S COMING FROM BEHIND HIM!

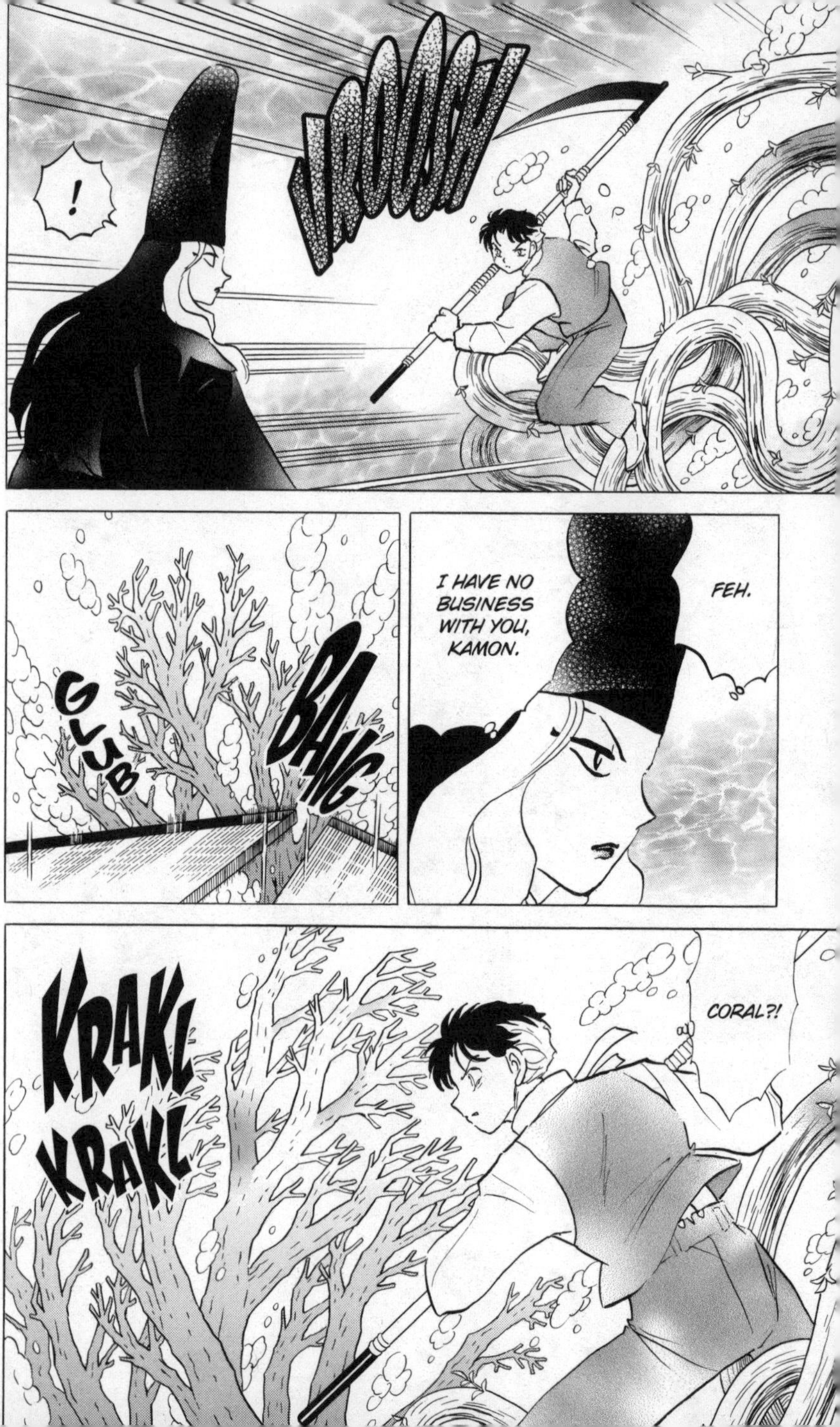
!
FEH.
I HAVE NO BUSINESS WITH YOU, KAMON.
BANG
GLUB
CORAL?!
KRAKL KRAKL

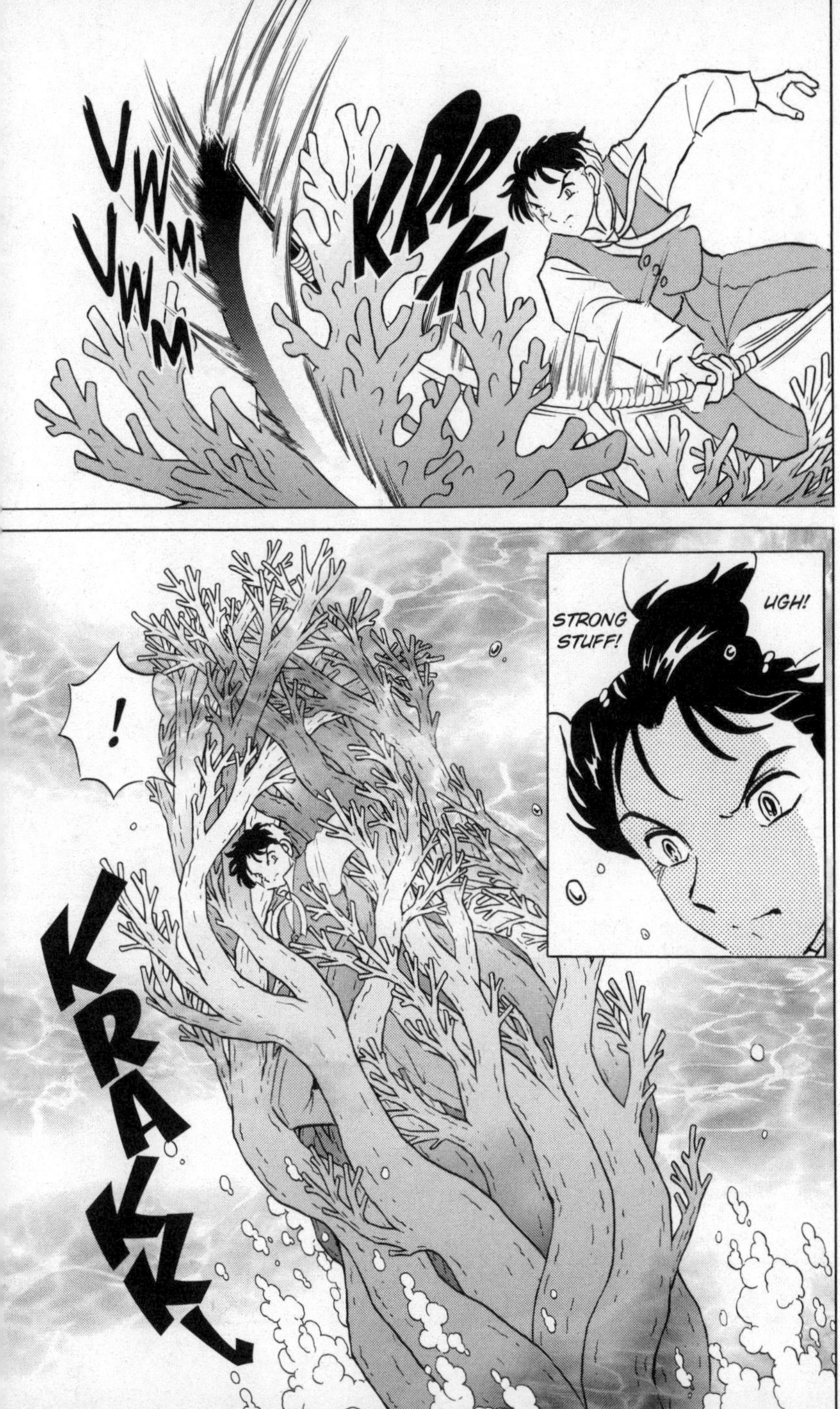
KRRK
VWM VWM
UGH!
STRONG STUFF!
!
KRAKKL

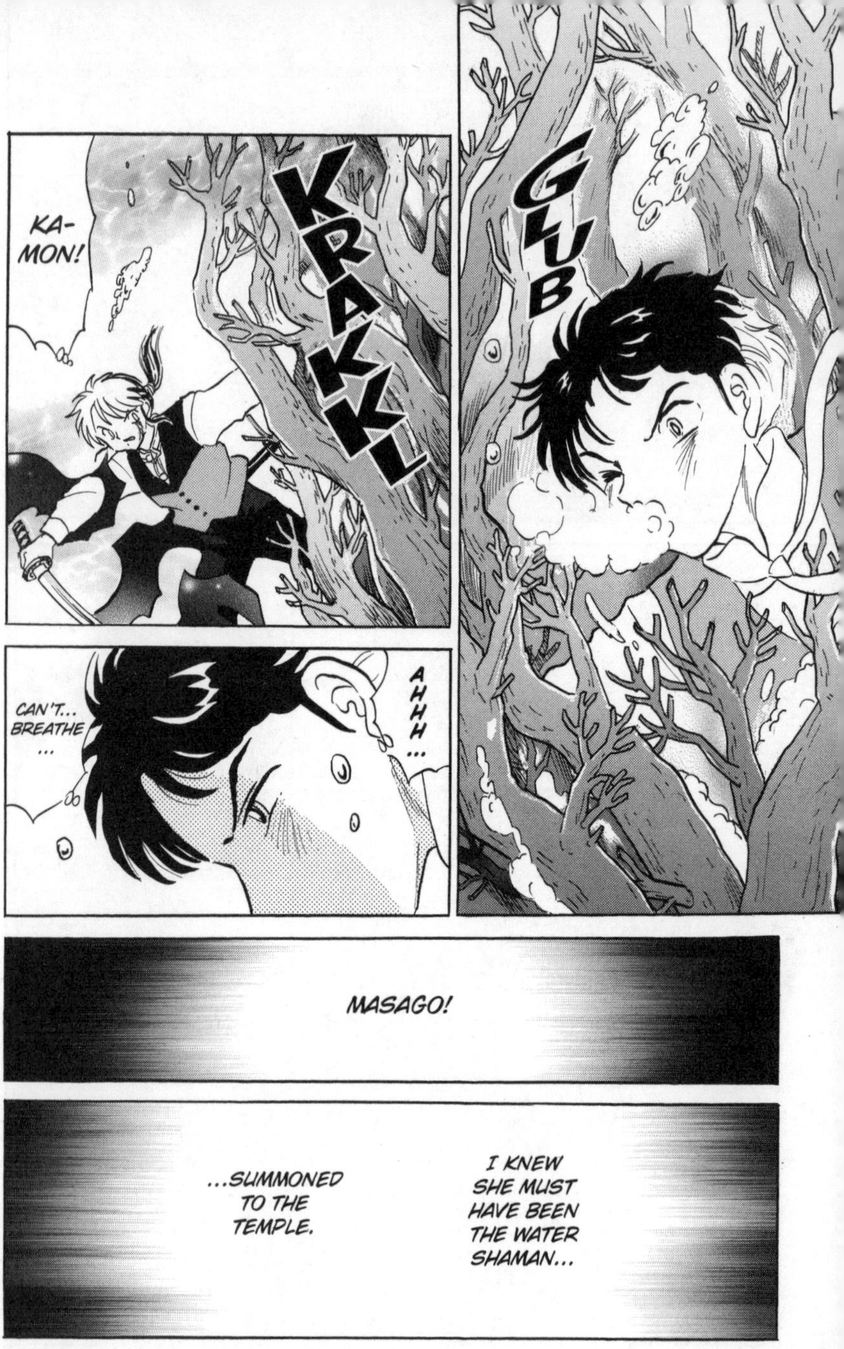
GLUB
KRAKKL
KA-MON!
AHHH...
CAN'T... BREATHE...
MASAGO!
I KNEW SHE MUST HAVE BEEN THE WATER SHAMAN...
...SUMMONED TO THE TEMPLE.

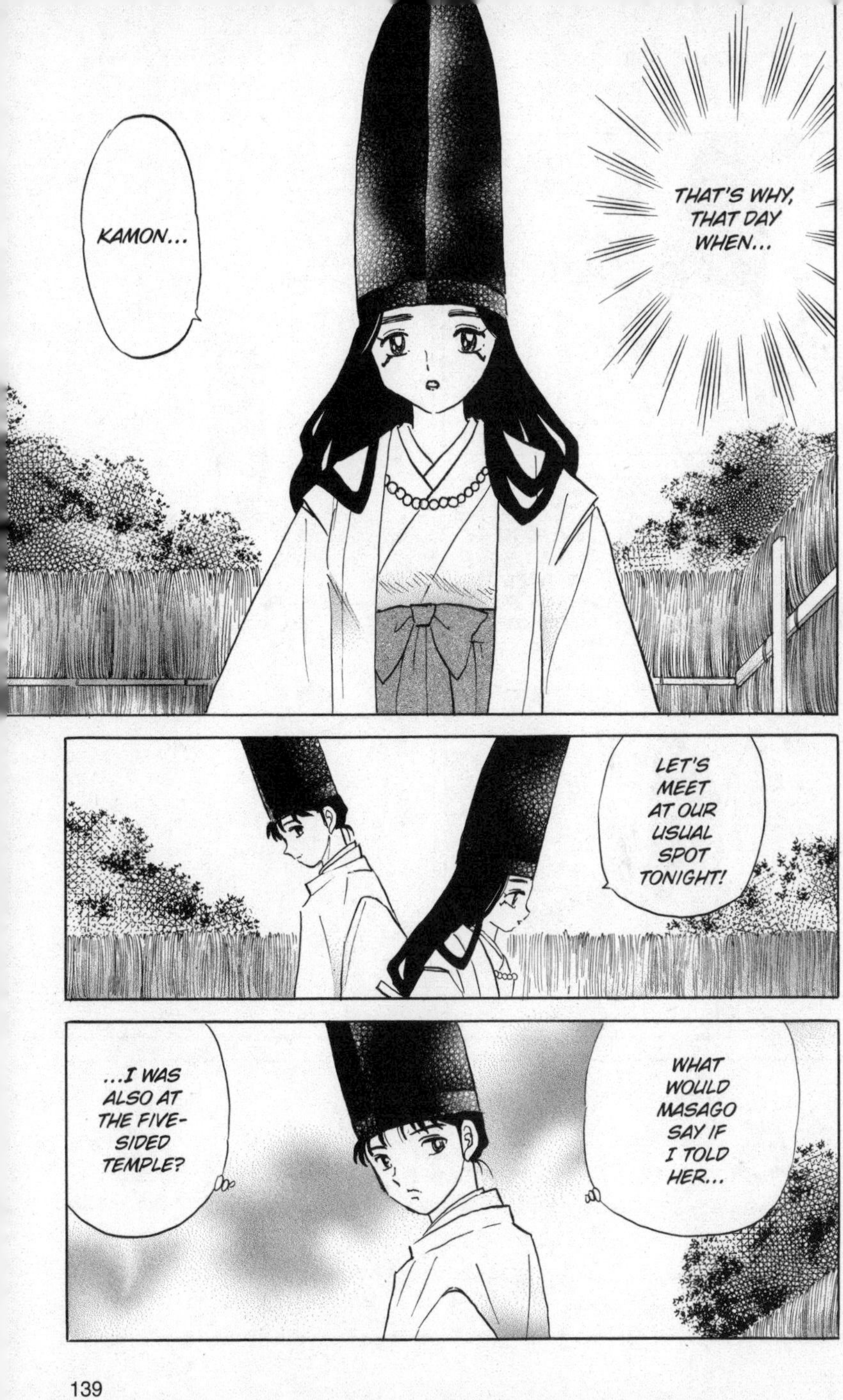
THAT'S WHY, THAT DAY WHEN...
KAMON...
LET'S MEET AT OUR USUAL SPOT TONIGHT!
WHAT WOULD MASAGO SAY IF I TOLD HER...
...I WAS ALSO AT THE FIVE-SIDED TEMPLE?

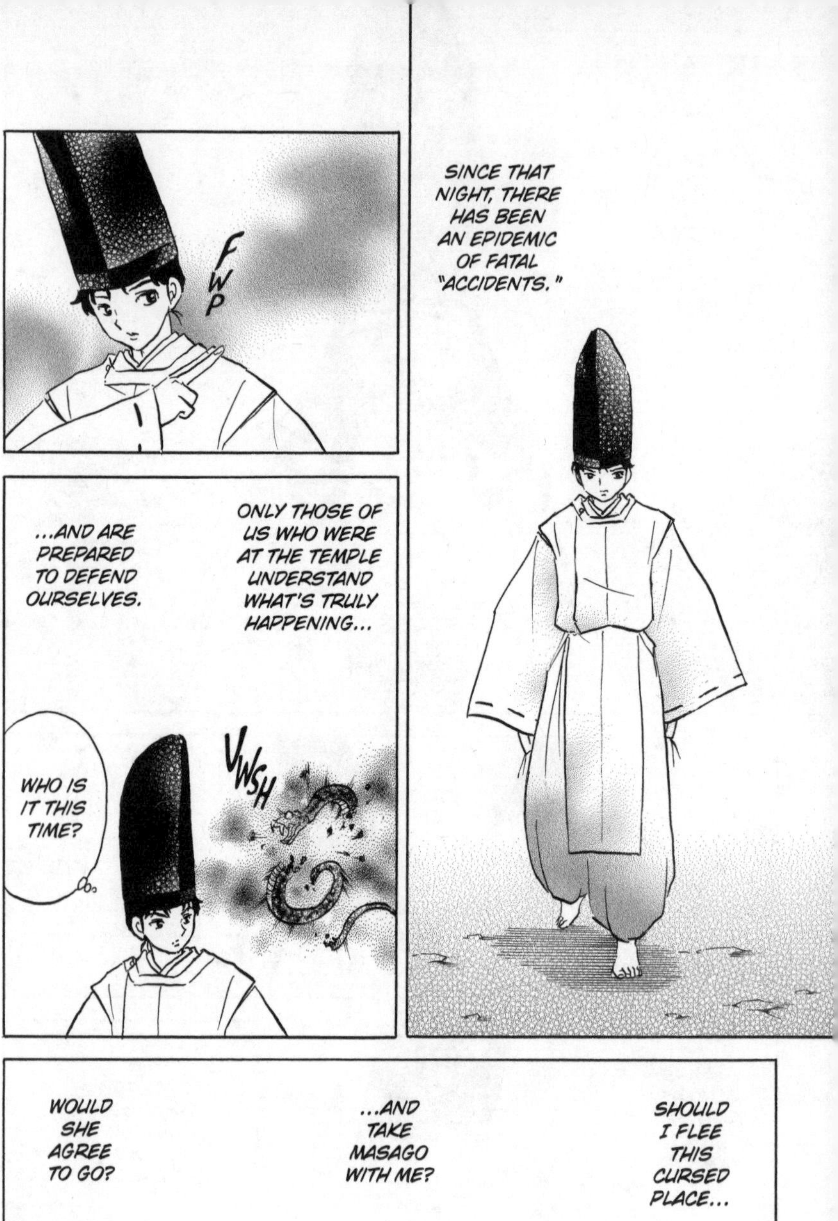
SINCE THAT NIGHT, THERE HAS BEEN AN EPIDEMIC OF FATAL "ACCIDENTS."
FWP
ONLY THOSE OF US WHO WERE AT THE TEMPLE UNDERSTAND WHAT'S TRULY HAPPENING...
...AND ARE PREPARED TO DEFEND OURSELVES.
VWSH
WHO IS IT THIS TIME?
SHOULD I FLEE THIS CURSED PLACE...
...AND TAKE MASAGO WITH ME?
WOULD SHE AGREE TO GO?

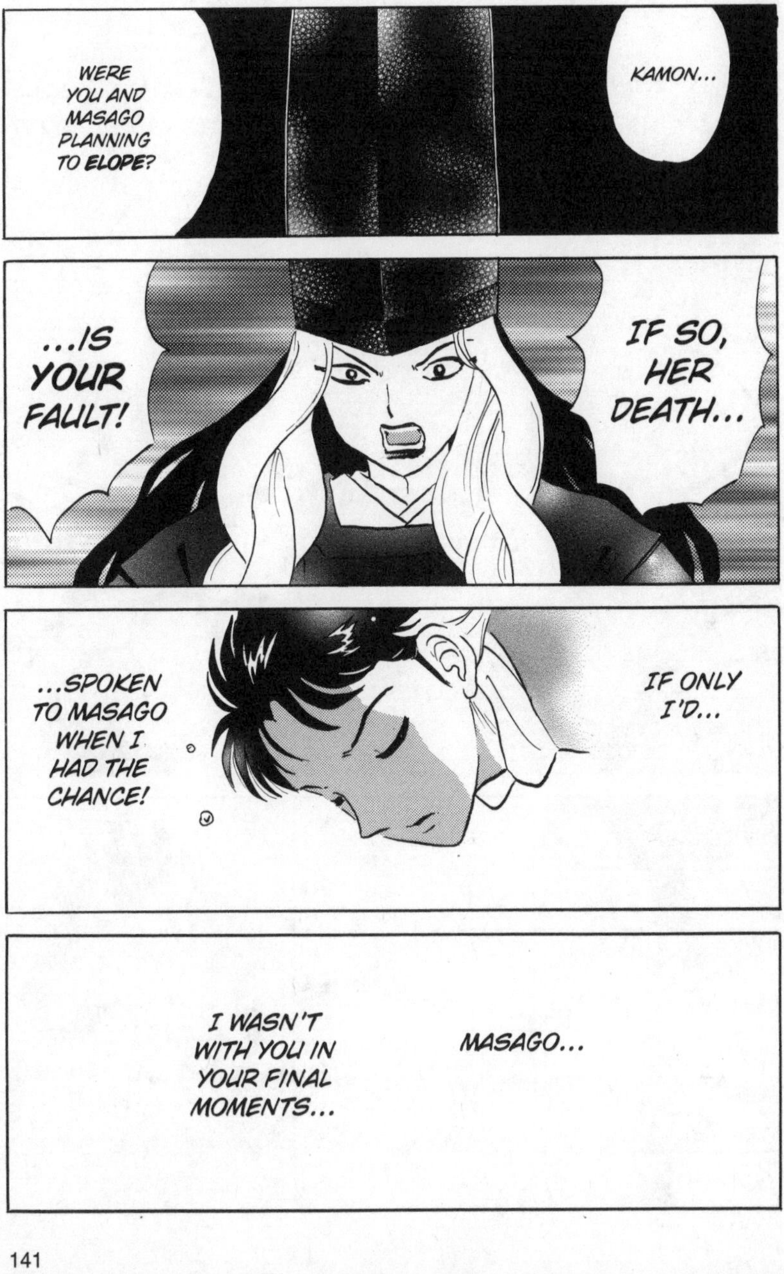
KAMON...
WERE YOU AND MASAGO PLANNING TO ELOPE?
IF SO, HER DEATH...
...IS YOUR FAULT!
IF ONLY I'D...
...SPOKEN TO MASAGO WHEN I HAD THE CHANCE!
MASAGO...
I WASN'T WITH YOU IN YOUR FINAL MOMENTS...

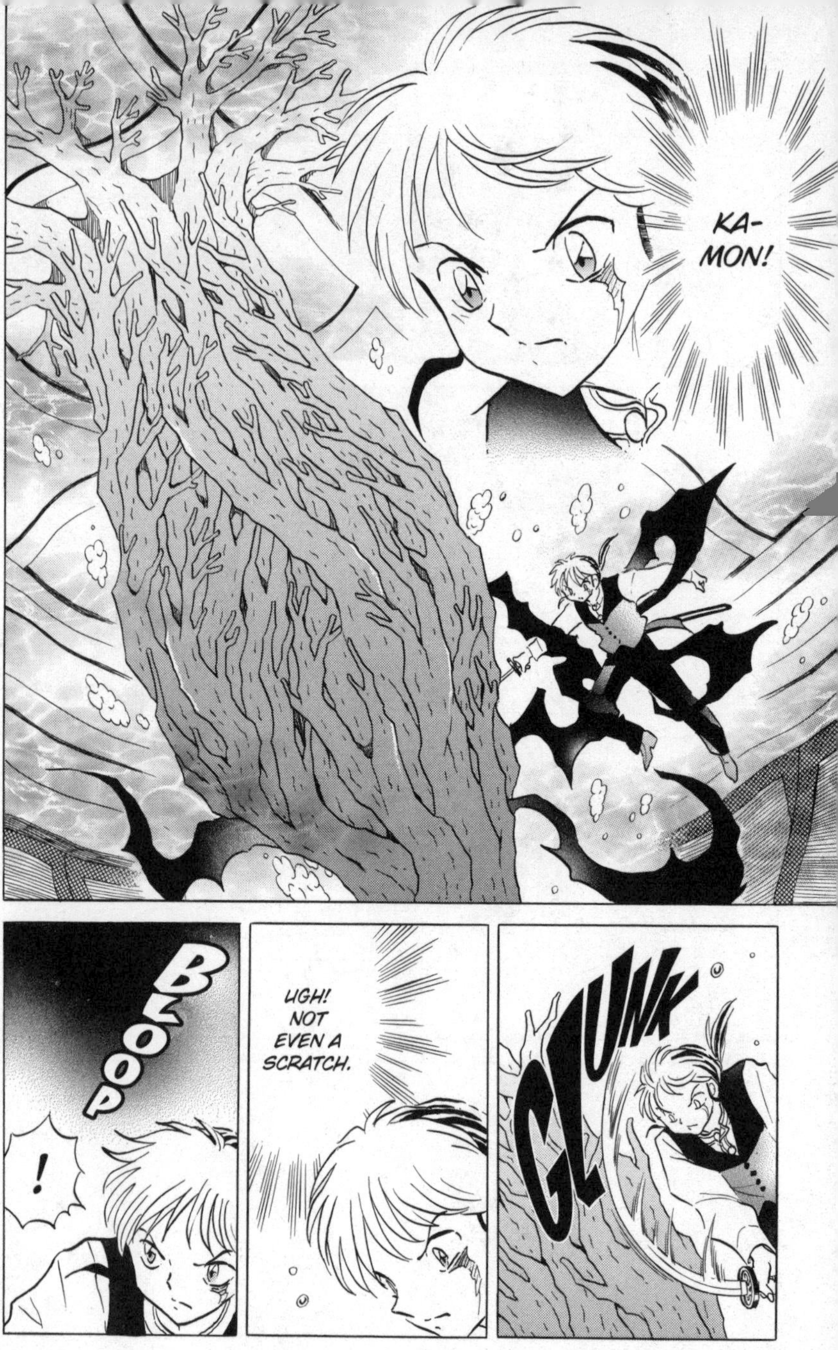
KA-MON!
GLUNK
UGH! NOT EVEN A SCRATCH.
BLOOP
!

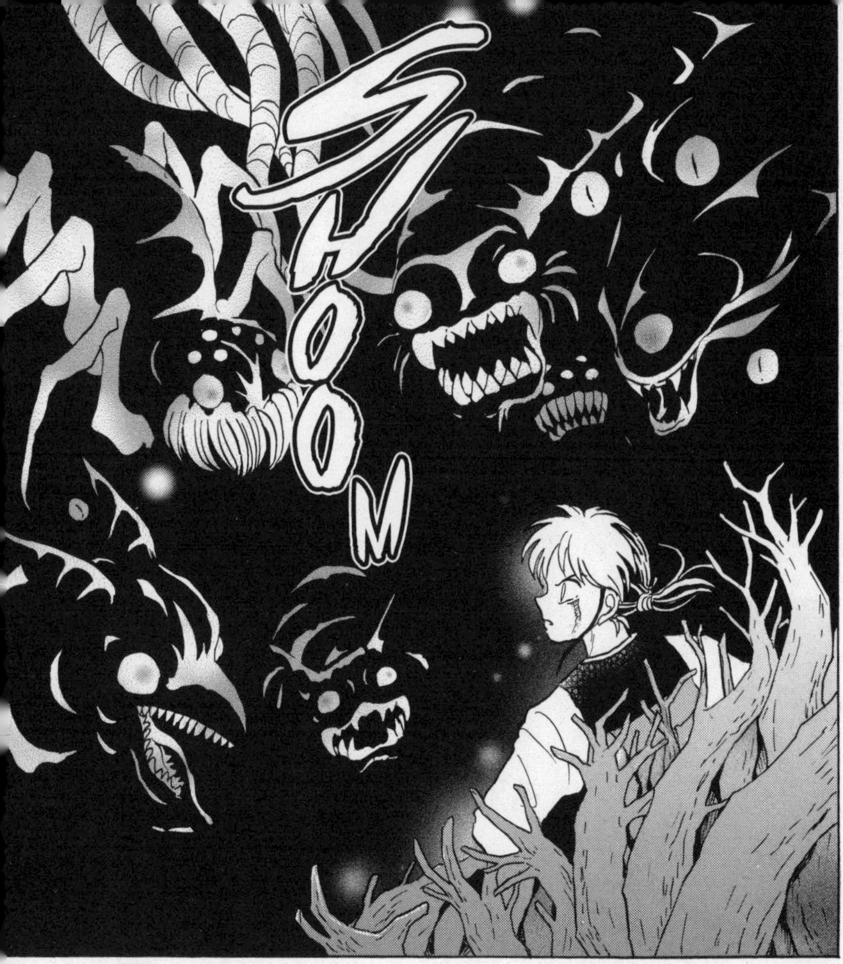
SHOOOM

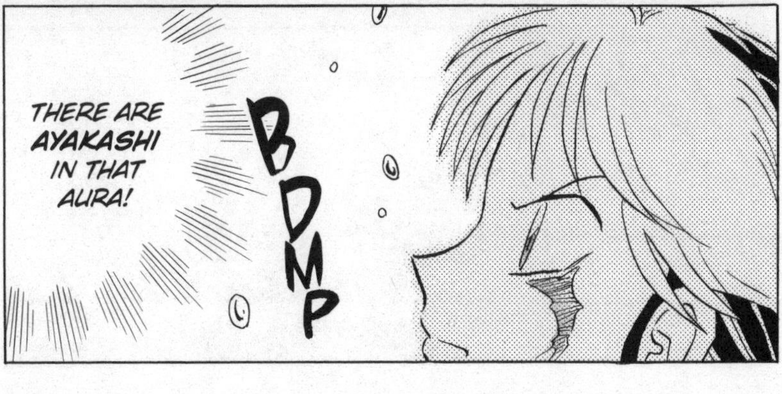
BDMP
THERE ARE AYAKASHI IN THAT AURA!

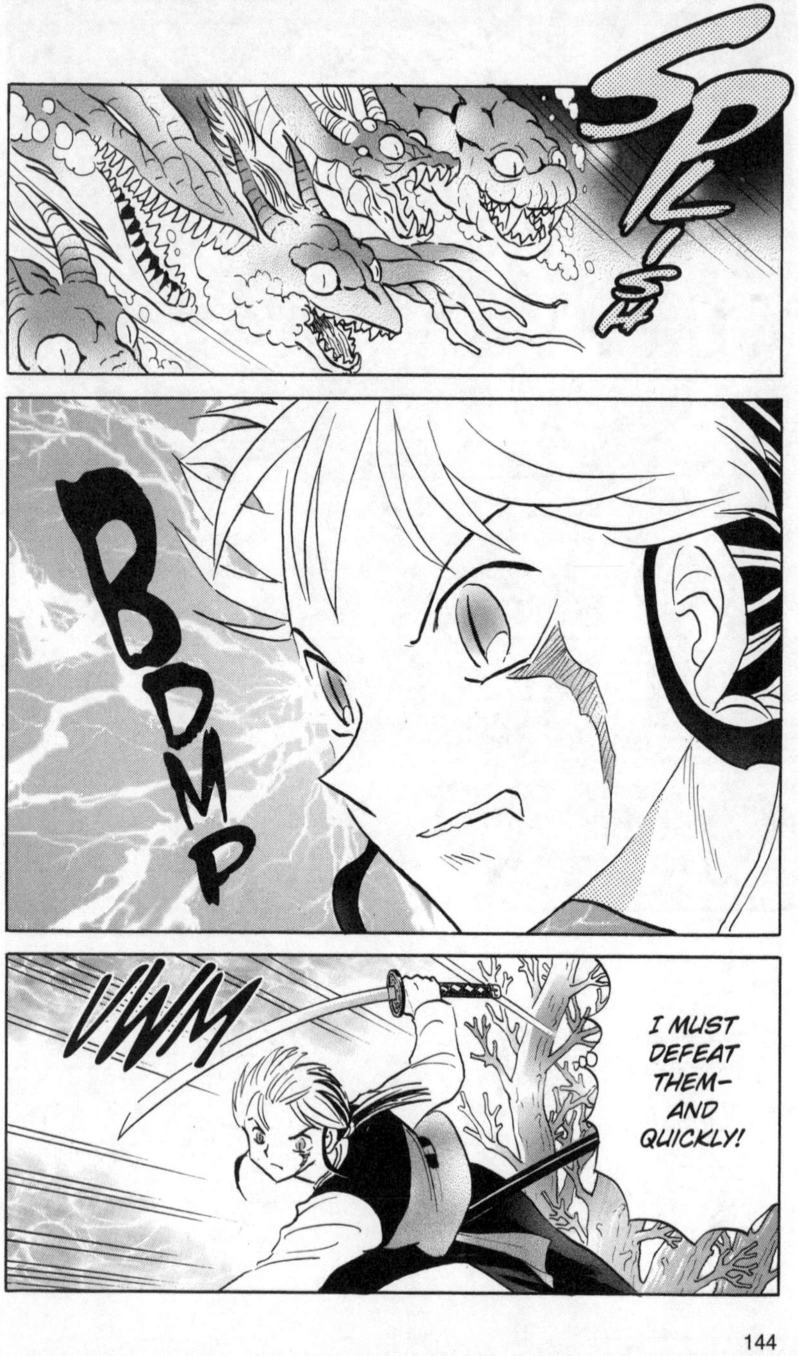
SPLSH
BDMP
I MUST DEFEAT THEM— AND QUICKLY!
VWM

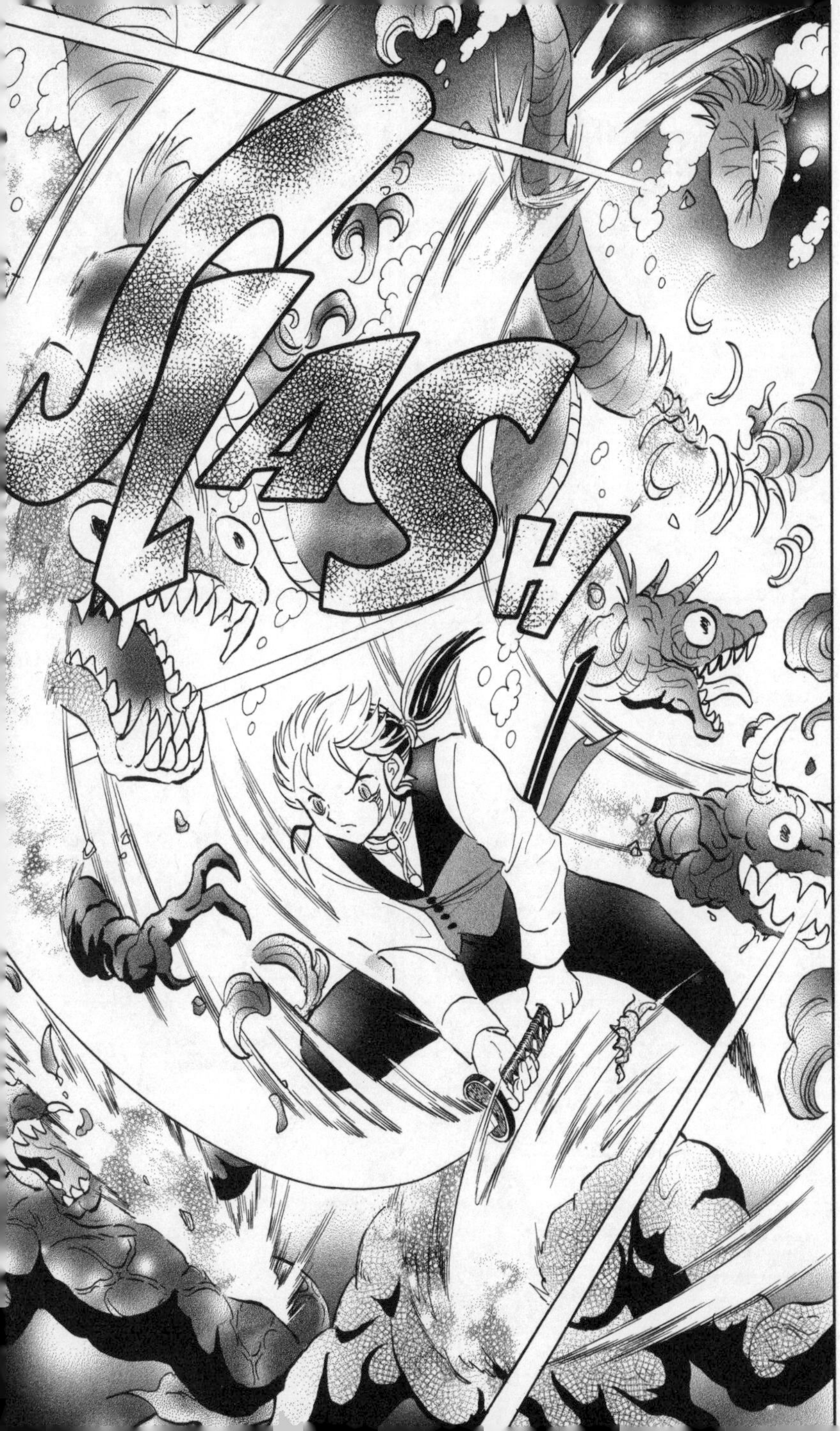
SLASH

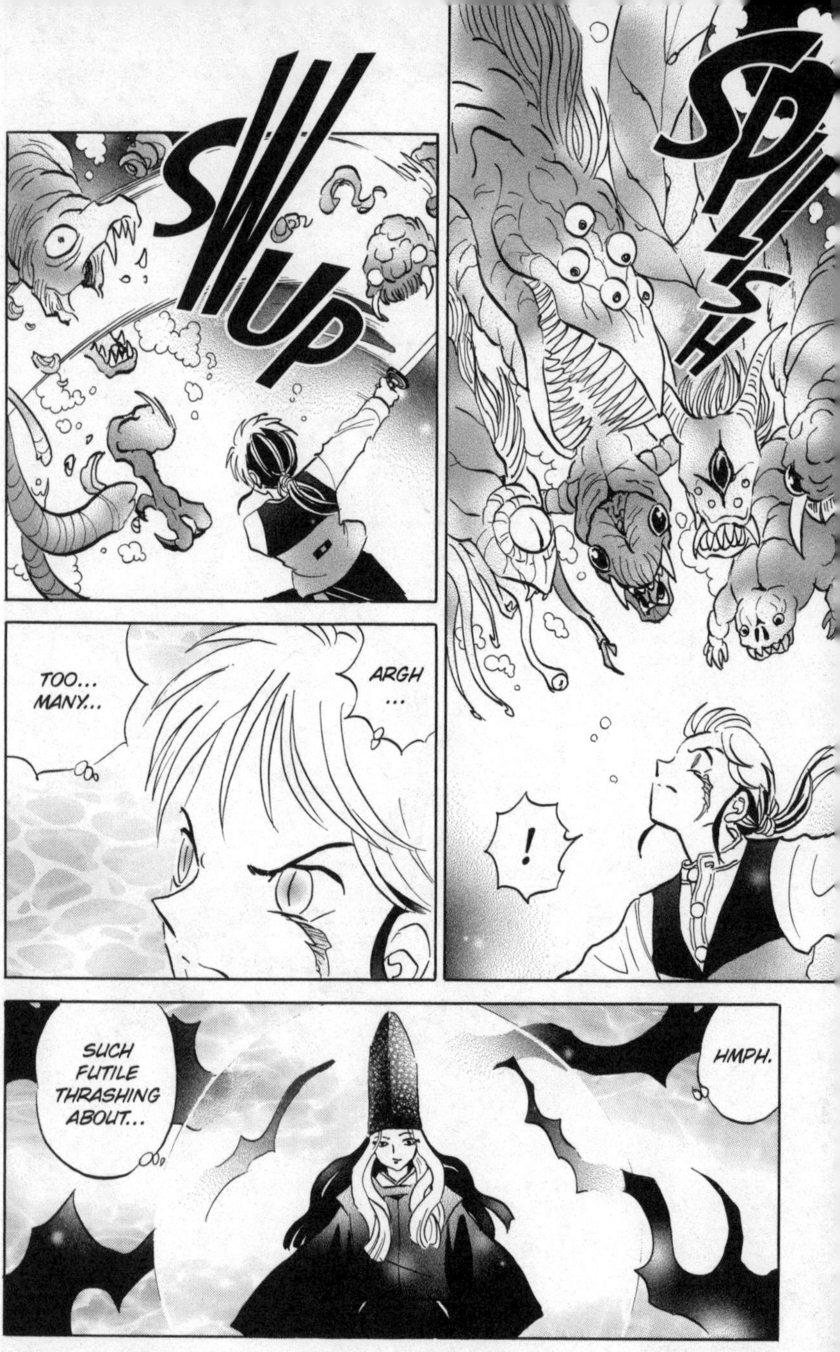
SPLISH
!
SWUP
ARGH ...
TOO... MANY...
HMPH.
SUCH FUTILE THRASHING ABOUT...

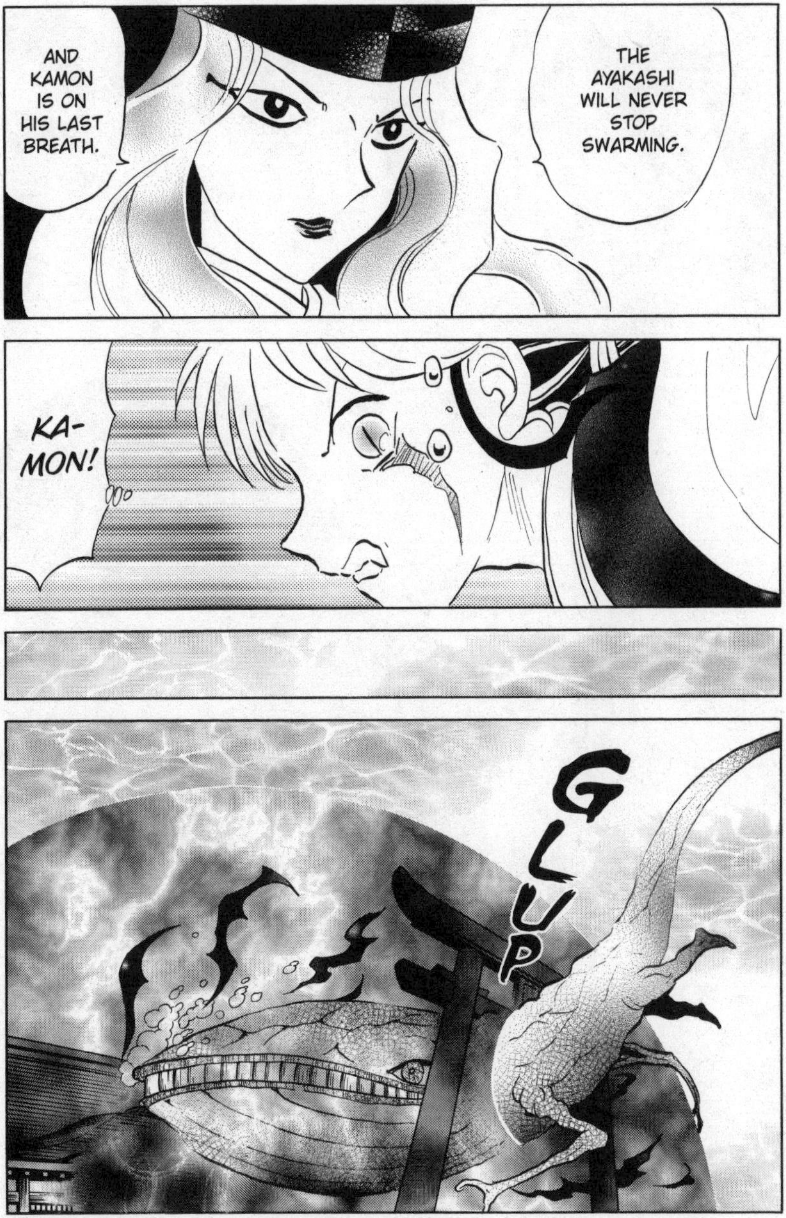
THE AYAKASHI WILL NEVER STOP SWARMING.
AND KAMON IS ON HIS LAST BREATH.
KA-MON!
GLUP

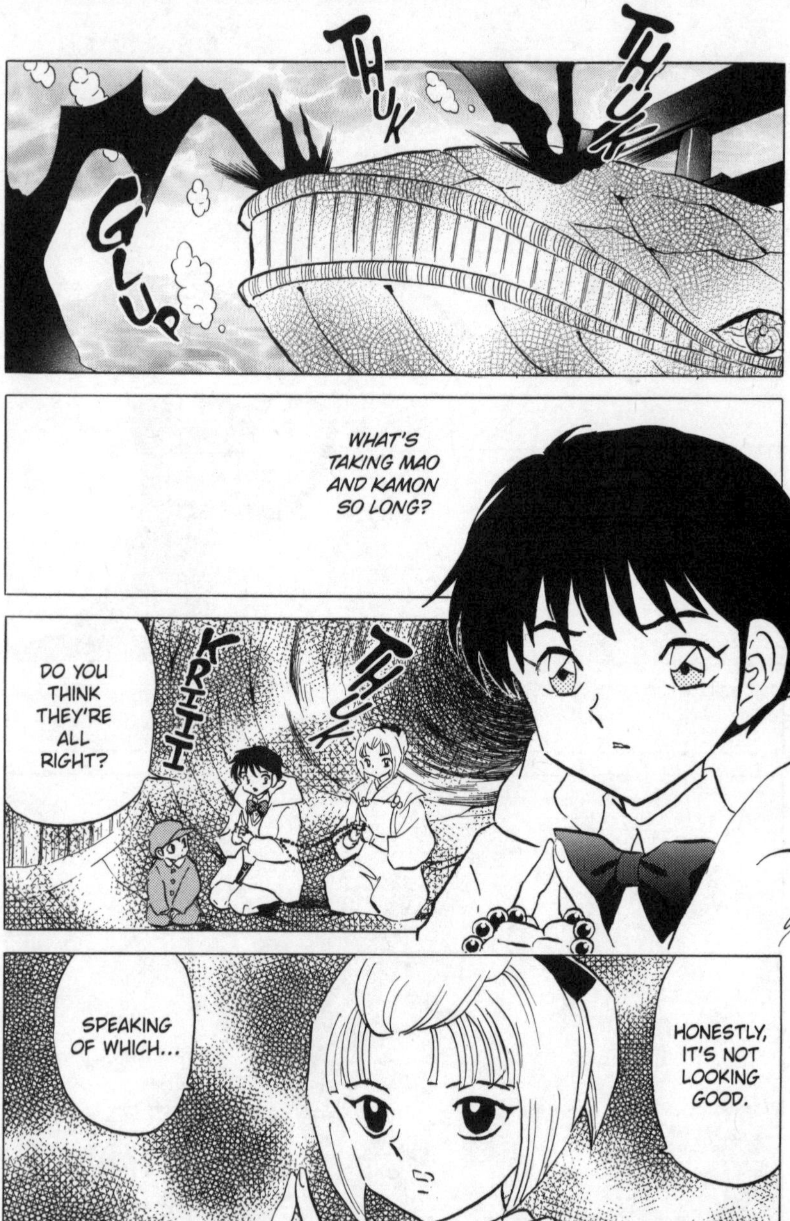
THUK
THUK
GLUP
WHAT'S TAKING MAO AND KAMON SO LONG?
THUK
KRIIII
DO YOU THINK THEY'RE ALL RIGHT?
HONESTLY, IT'S NOT LOOKING GOOD.
SPEAKING OF WHICH...

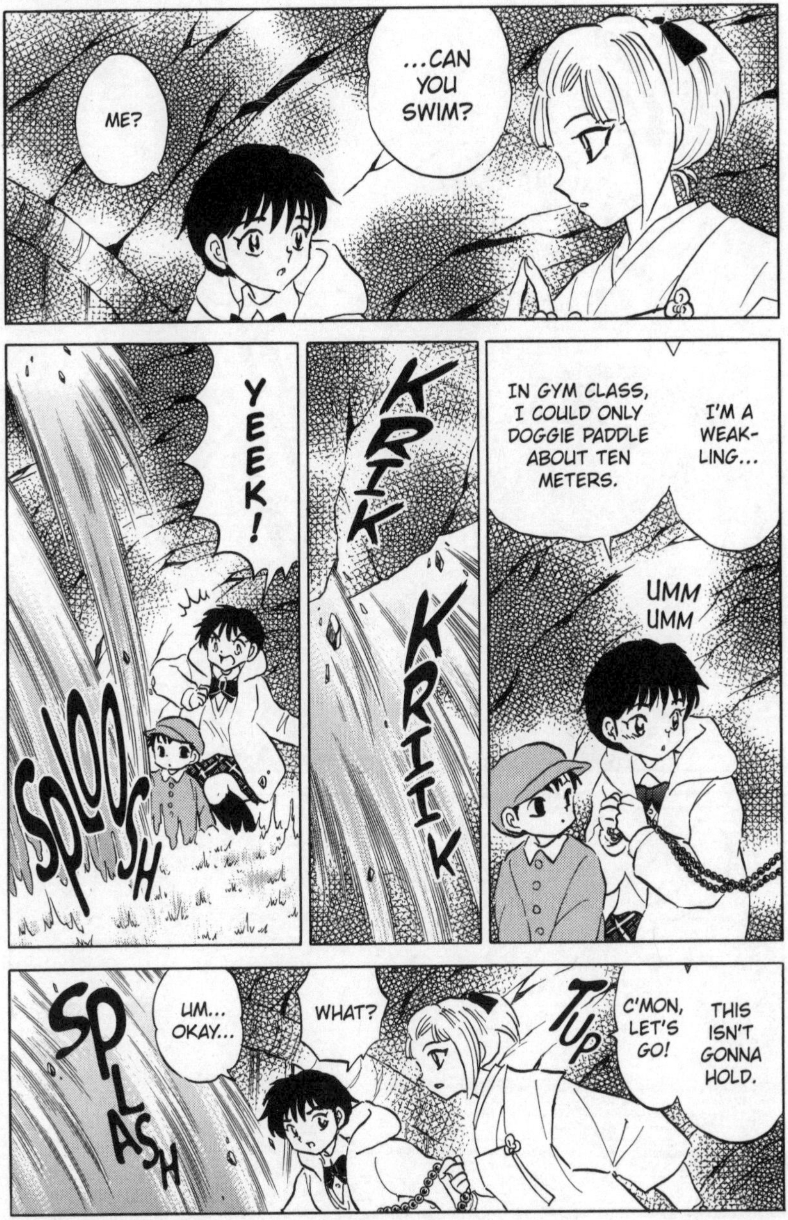
...CAN YOU SWIM?
ME?
I'M A WEAK-LING...
IN GYM CLASS, I COULD ONLY DOGGIE PADDLE ABOUT TEN METERS.
UMM UMM
KRIK
KRIIK
YEEK!
SPLOOSH
THIS ISN'T GONNA HOLD.
C'MON, LET'S GO!
TUP
WHAT?
UM... OKAY...
SPLASH

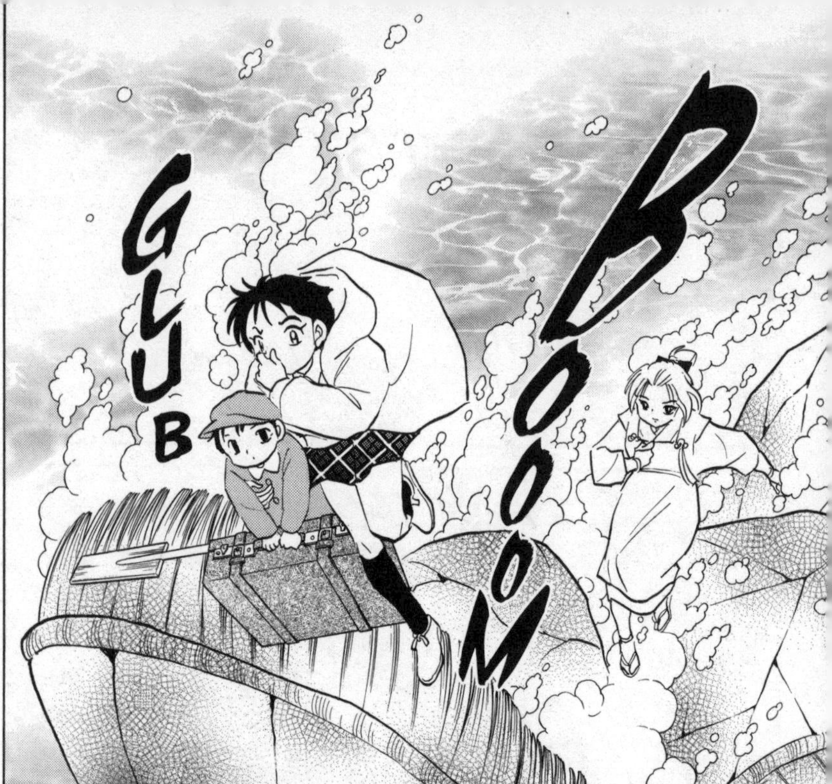
BOOOOOM
GLUB

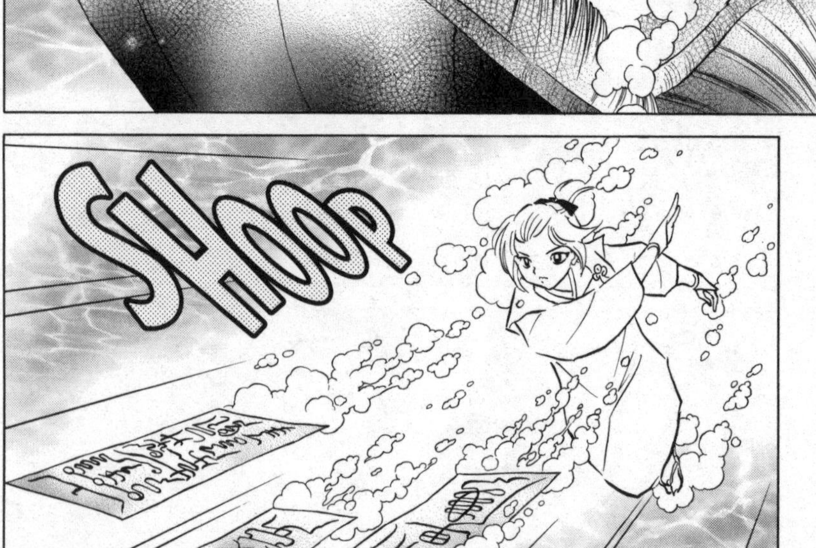
SHOOP

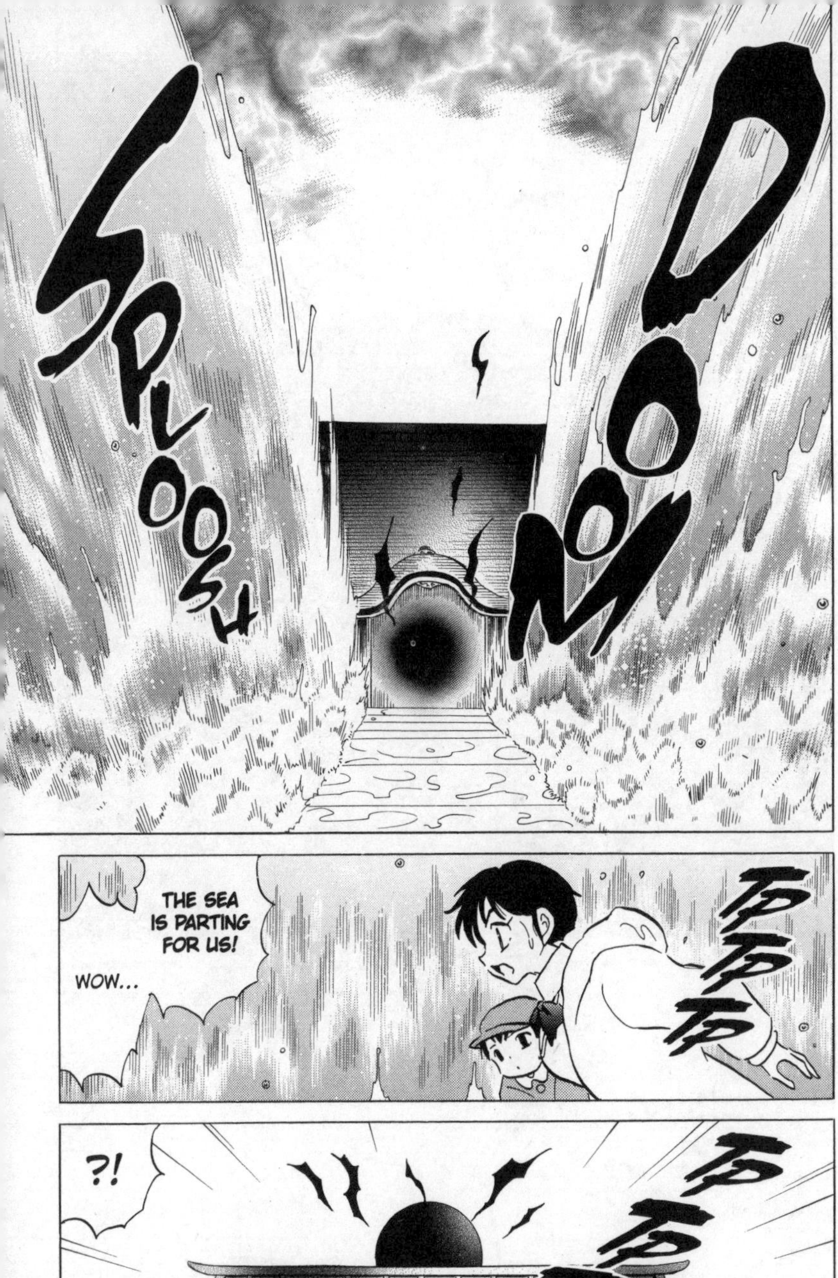
DOOM
SPLOOSH
TP TP TP TP
THE SEA IS PARTING FOR US!
WOW...
TP TP TP
?!

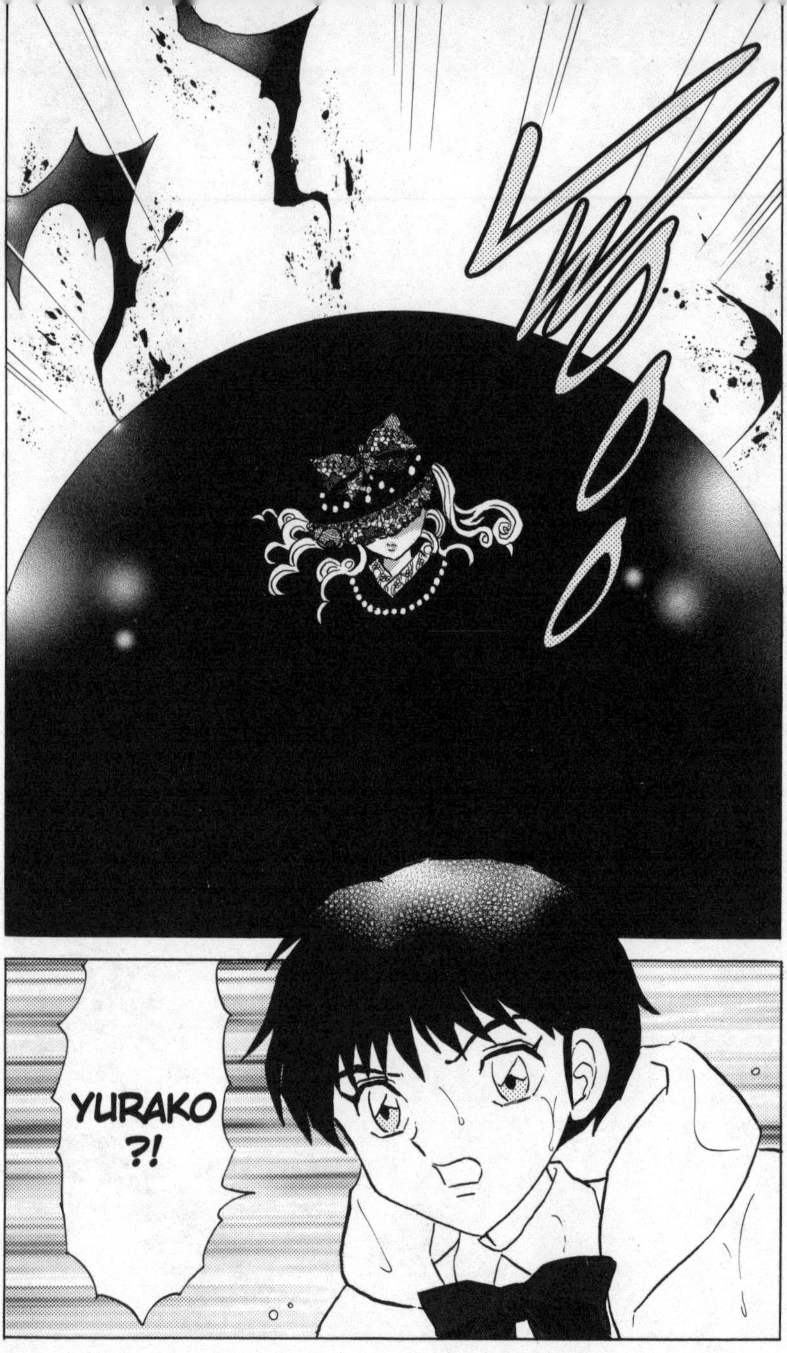
YURAKO ?!

Chapter 9: Protection

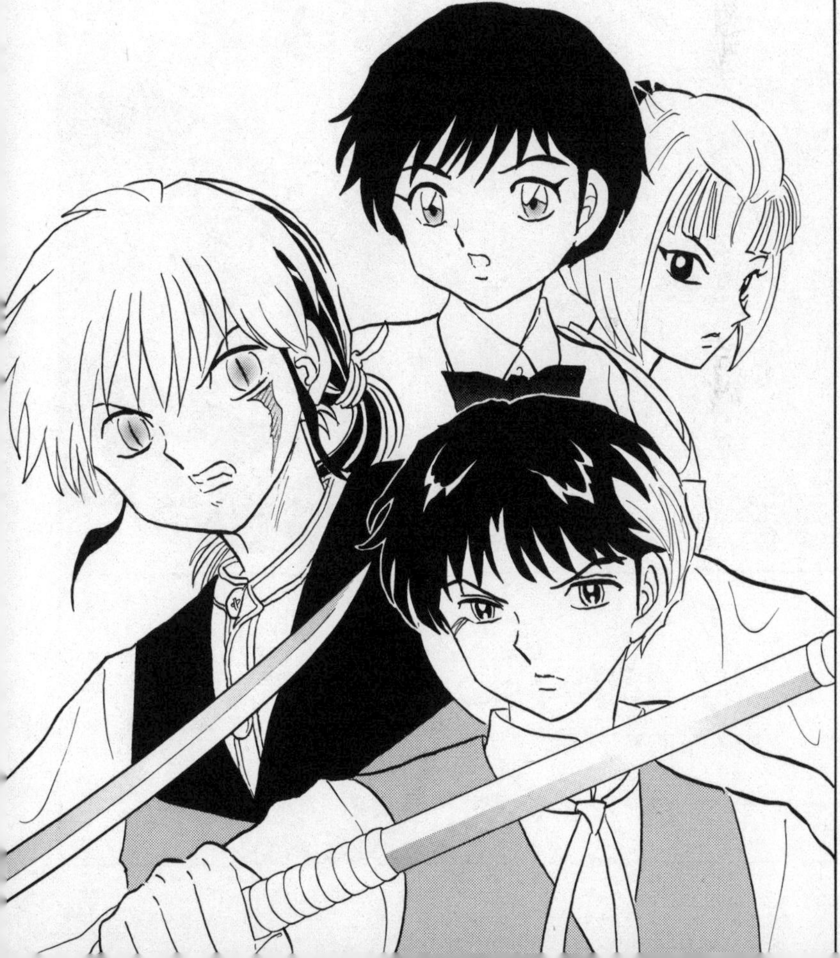

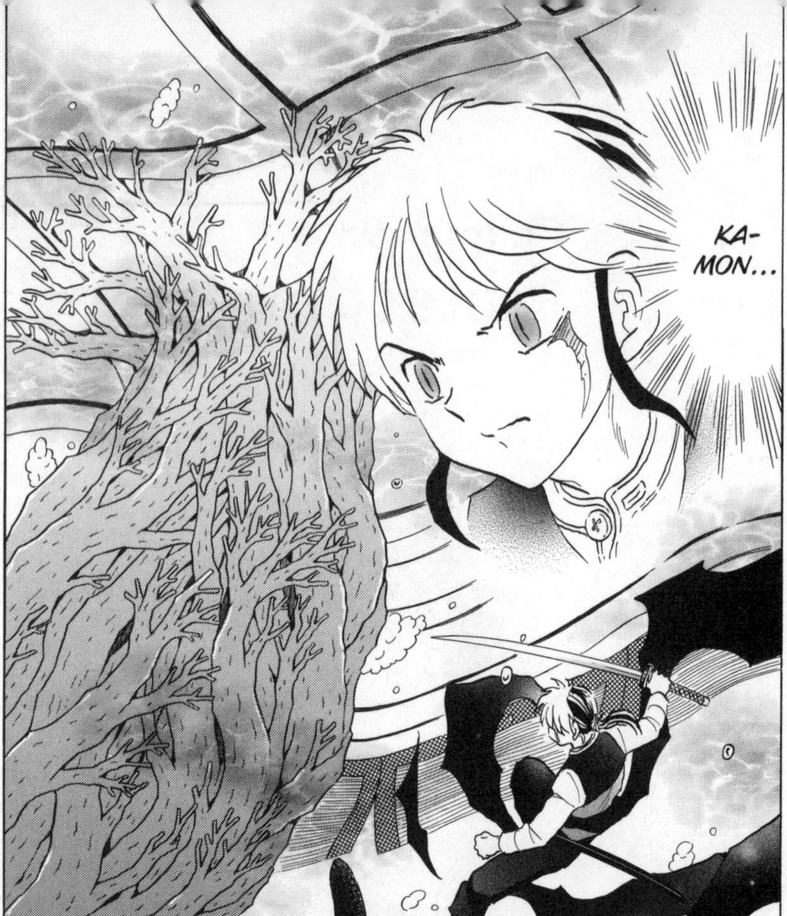
KA-
MON...

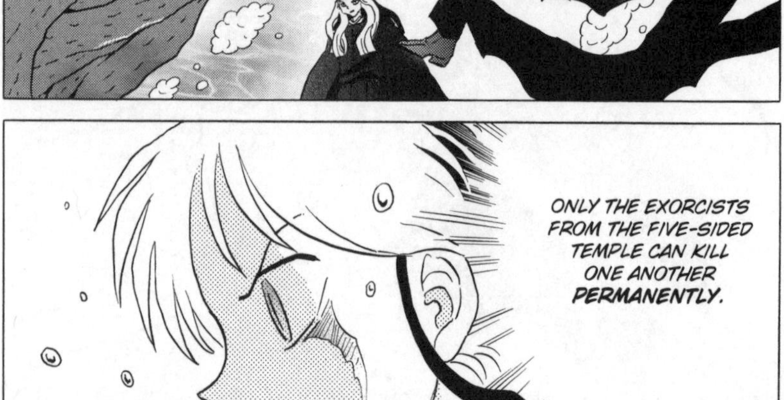
ONLY THE EXORCISTS FROM THE FIVE-SIDED TEMPLE CAN KILL ONE ANOTHER PERMANENTLY.

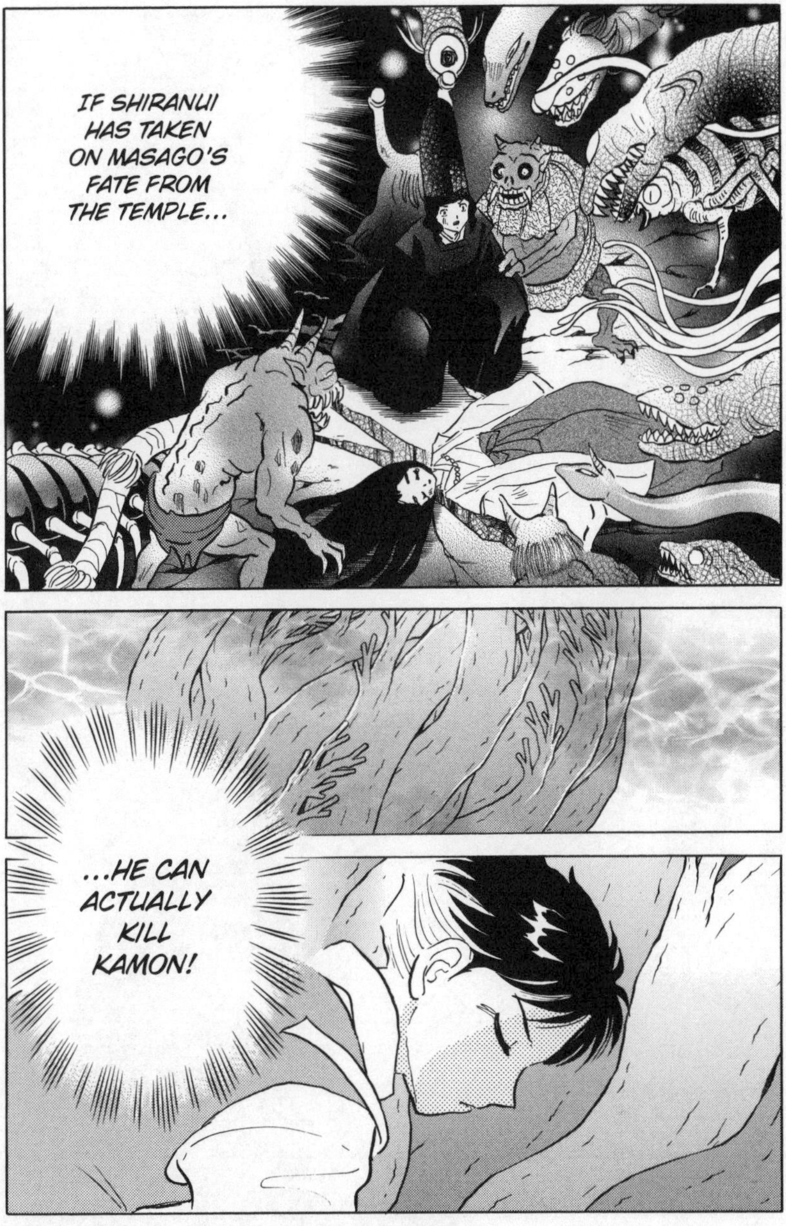
IF SHIRANUI HAS TAKEN ON MASAGO'S FATE FROM THE TEMPLE...
...HE CAN ACTUALLY KILL KAMON!

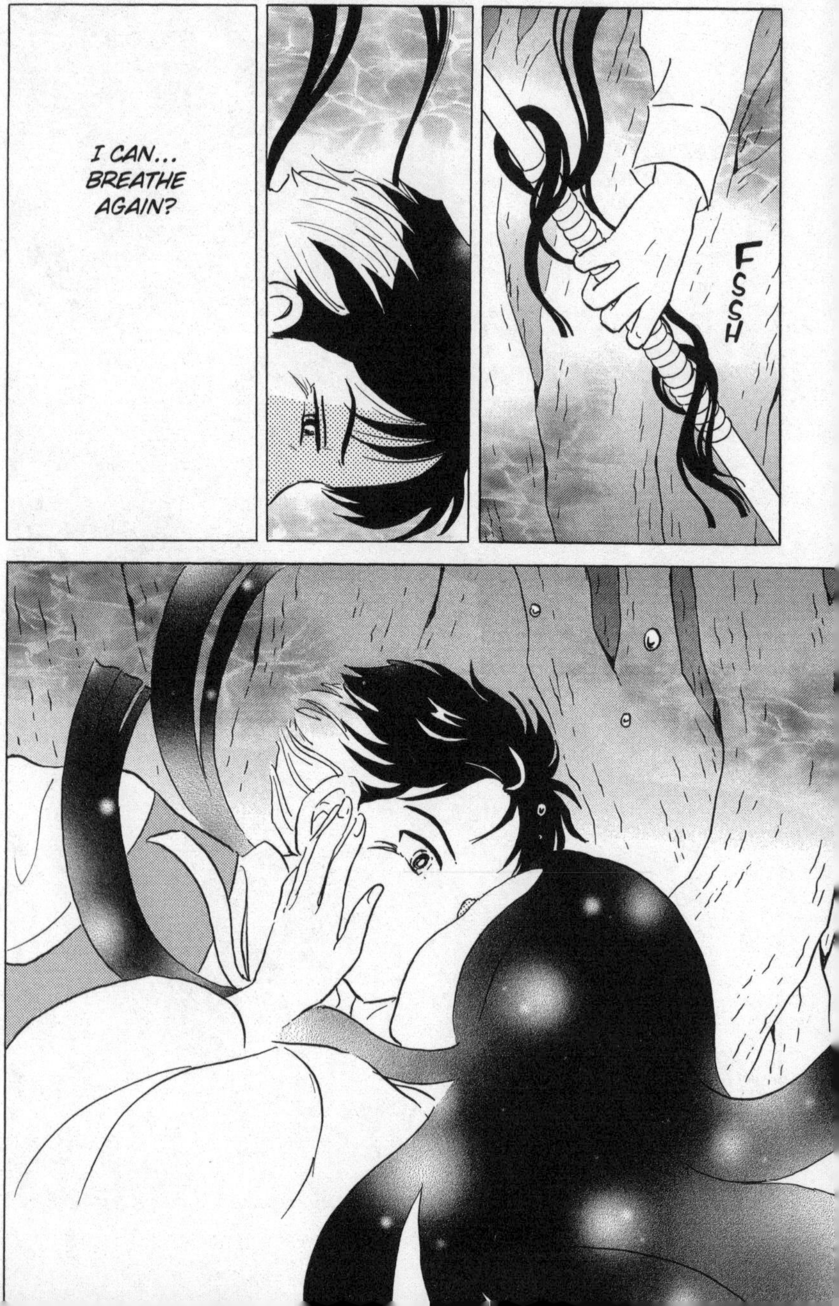
FSSH
I CAN... BREATHE AGAIN?

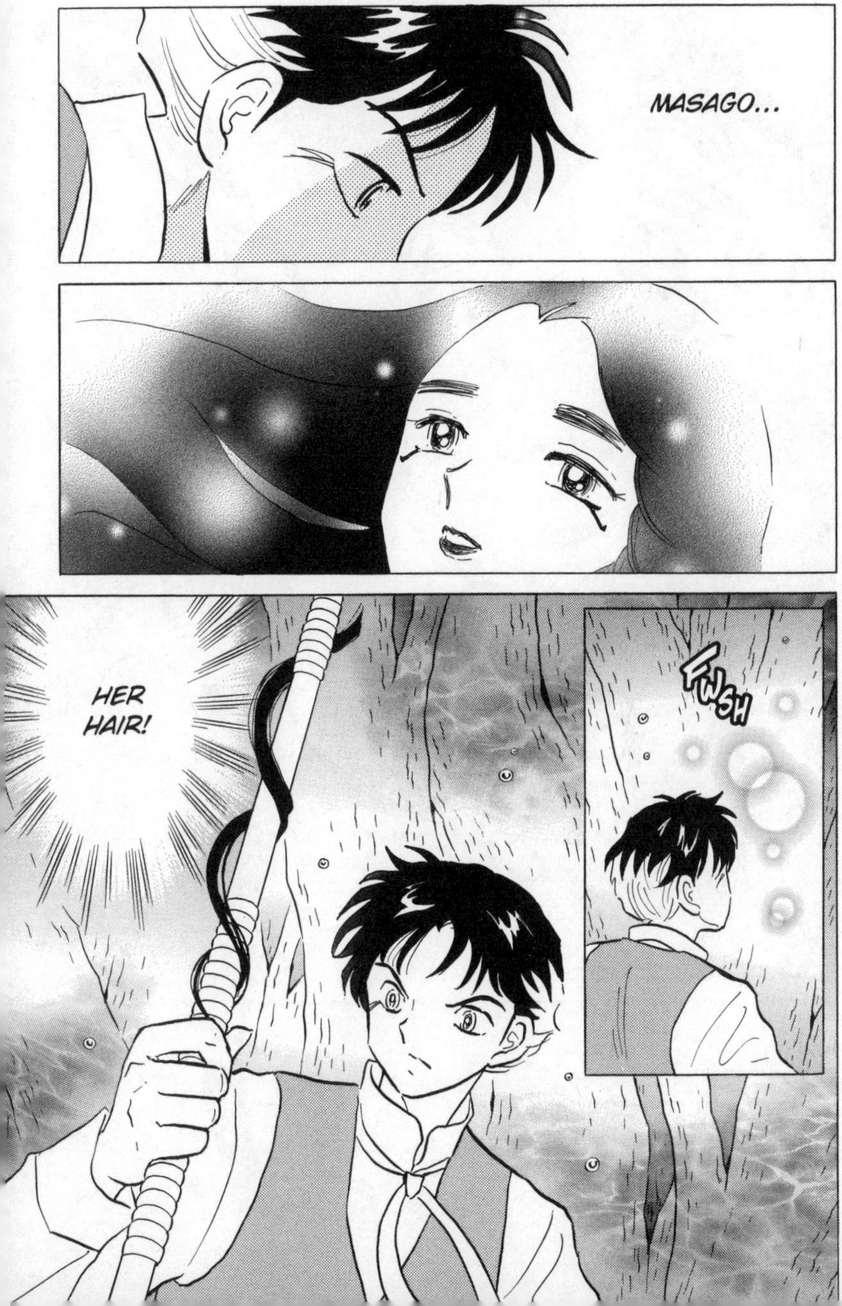
MASAGO...
FWSH
HER HAIR!

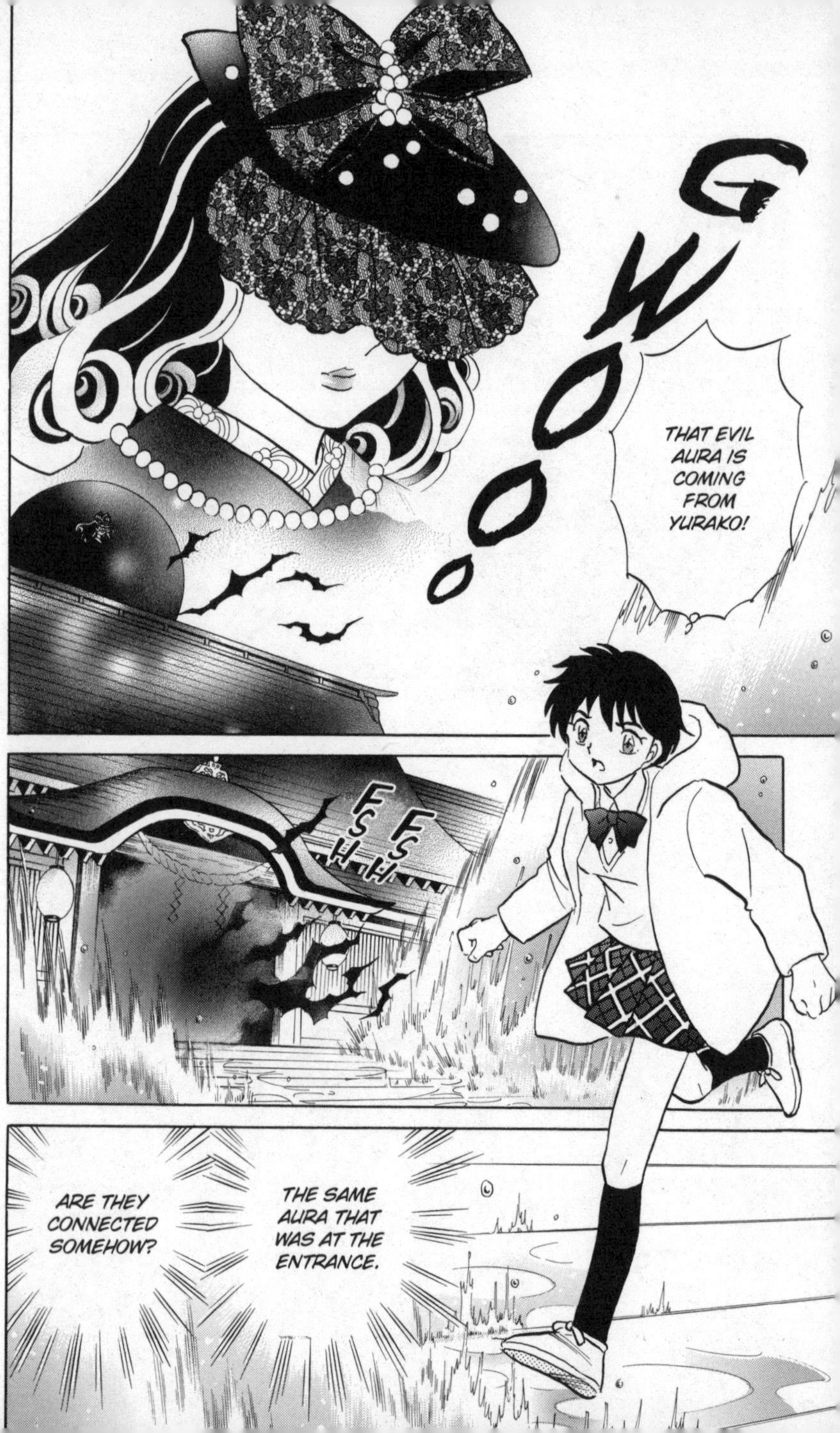
GWOOOO
THAT EVIL AURA IS COMING FROM YURAKO!
FSHH FSHH
THE SAME AURA THAT WAS AT THE ENTRANCE.
ARE THEY CONNECTED SOMEHOW?

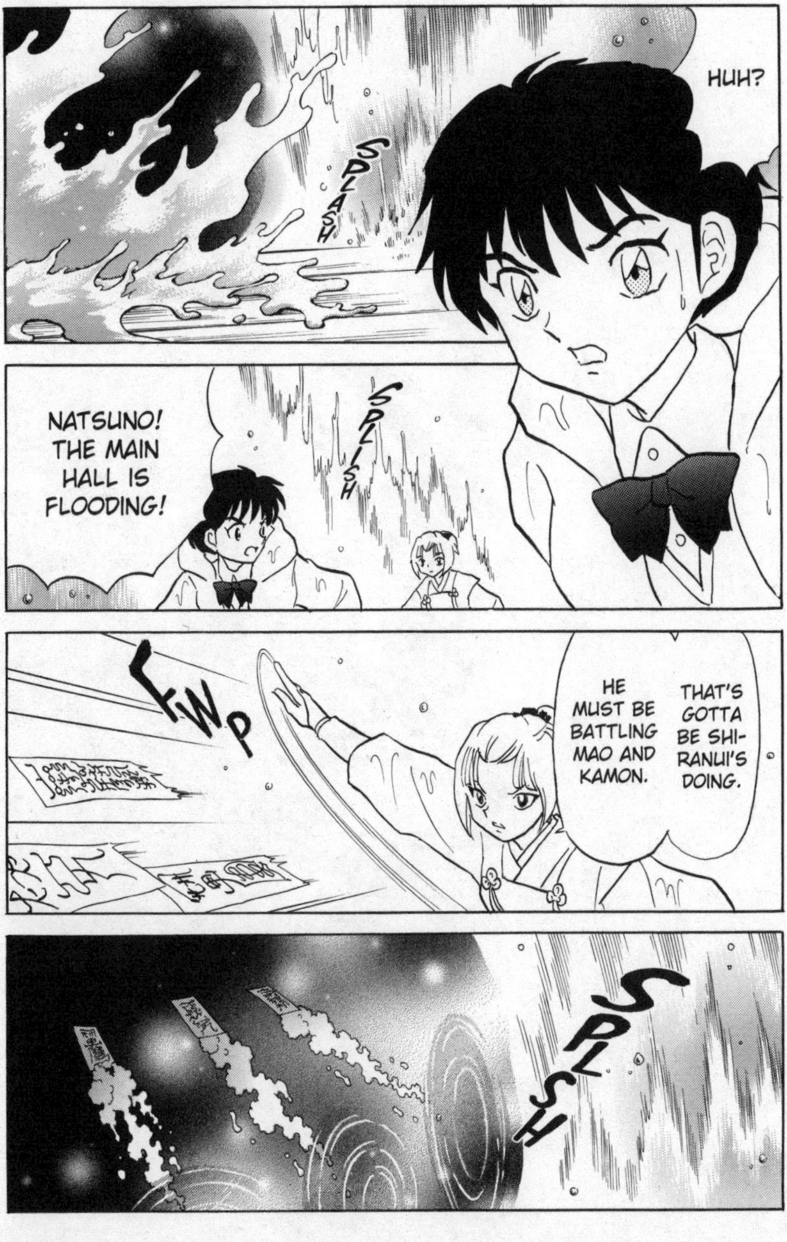
HUH?
SPLASH
SPLISH
NATSUNO! THE MAIN HALL IS FLOODING!
THAT'S GOTTA BE SHI-RANUI'S DOING.
HE MUST BE BATTLING MAO AND KAMON.
FWP
SPLISH

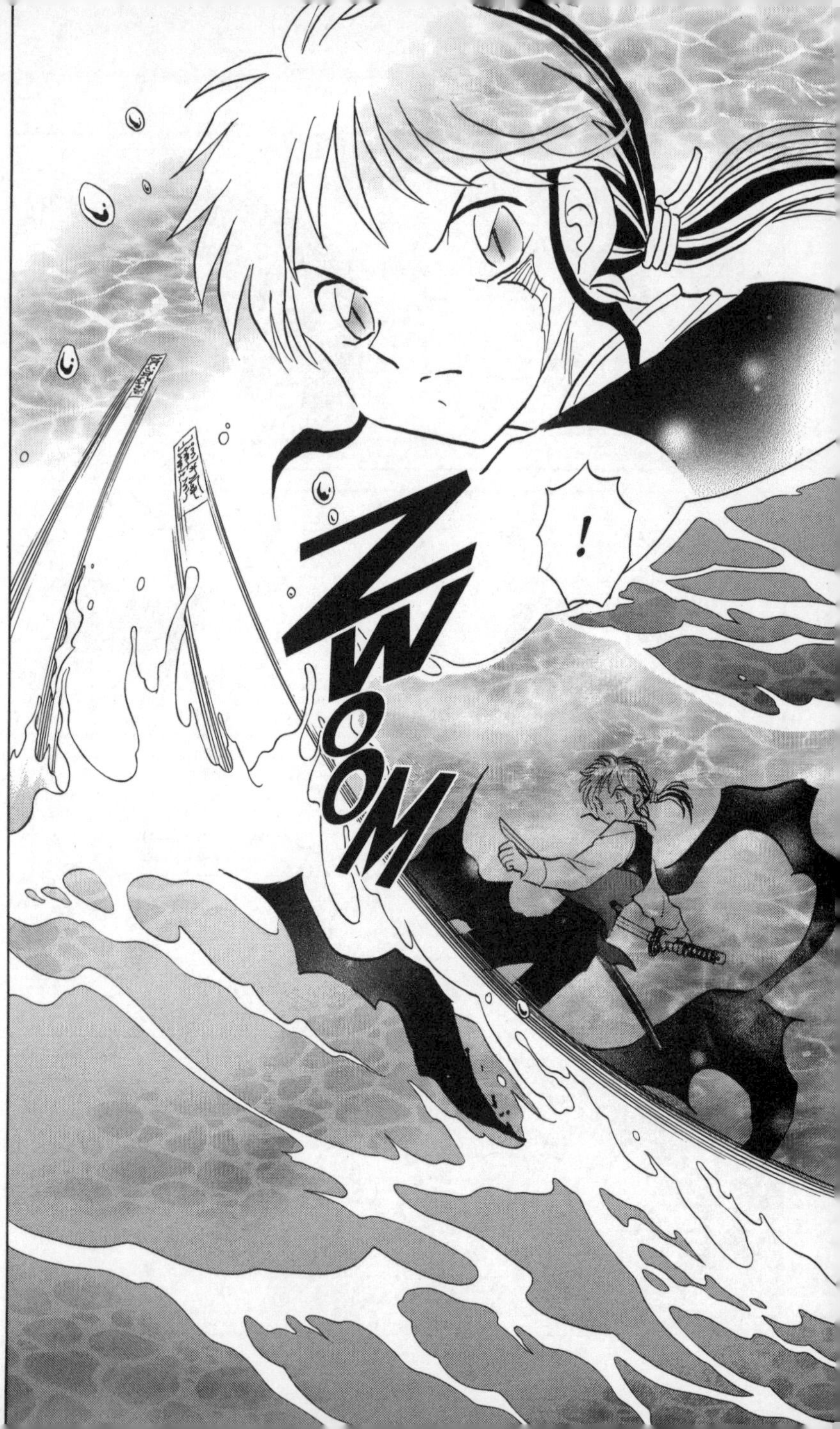
!
VWOOM

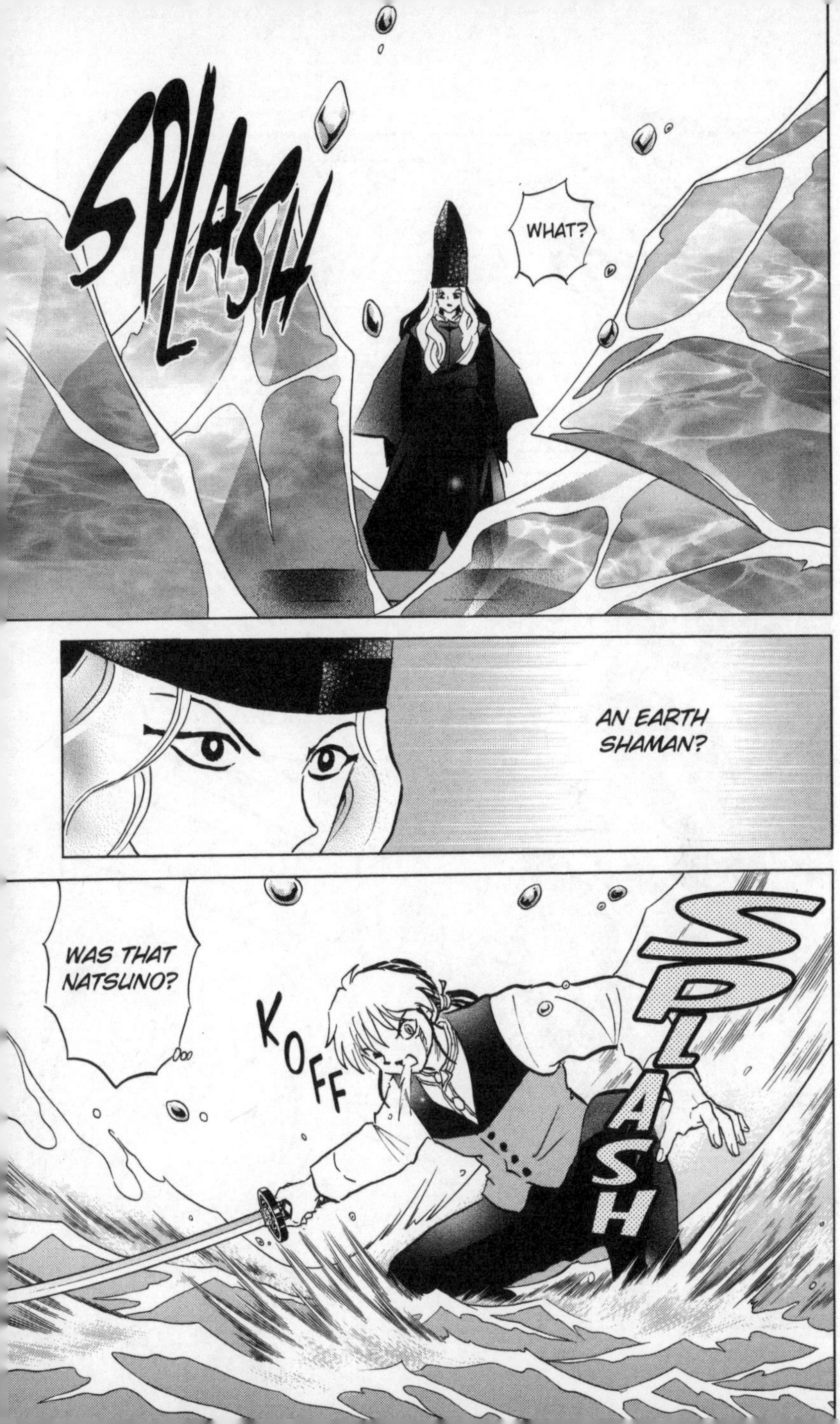
SPLASH
WHAT?
AN EARTH SHAMAN?
SPLASH
WAS THAT NATSUNO?
KOFF

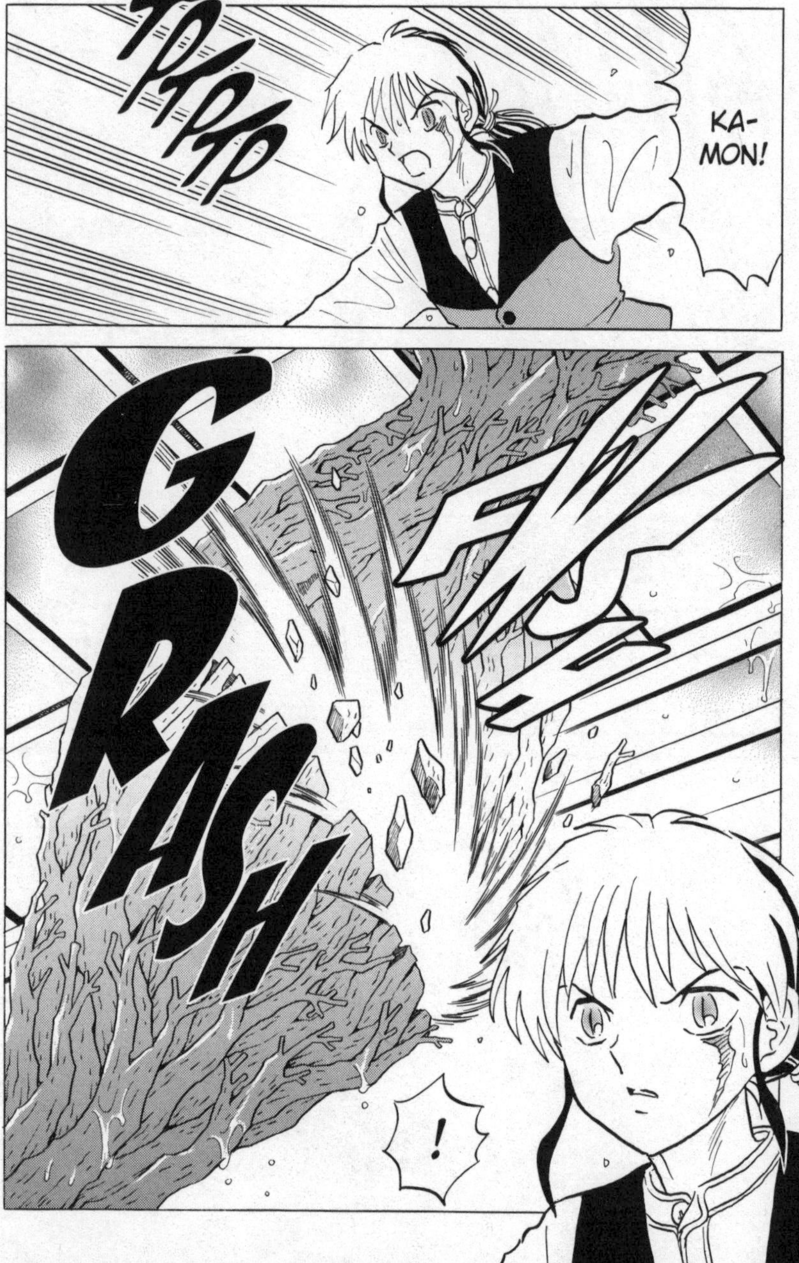
KA-
MON!
TPTPTP
CRASH
!

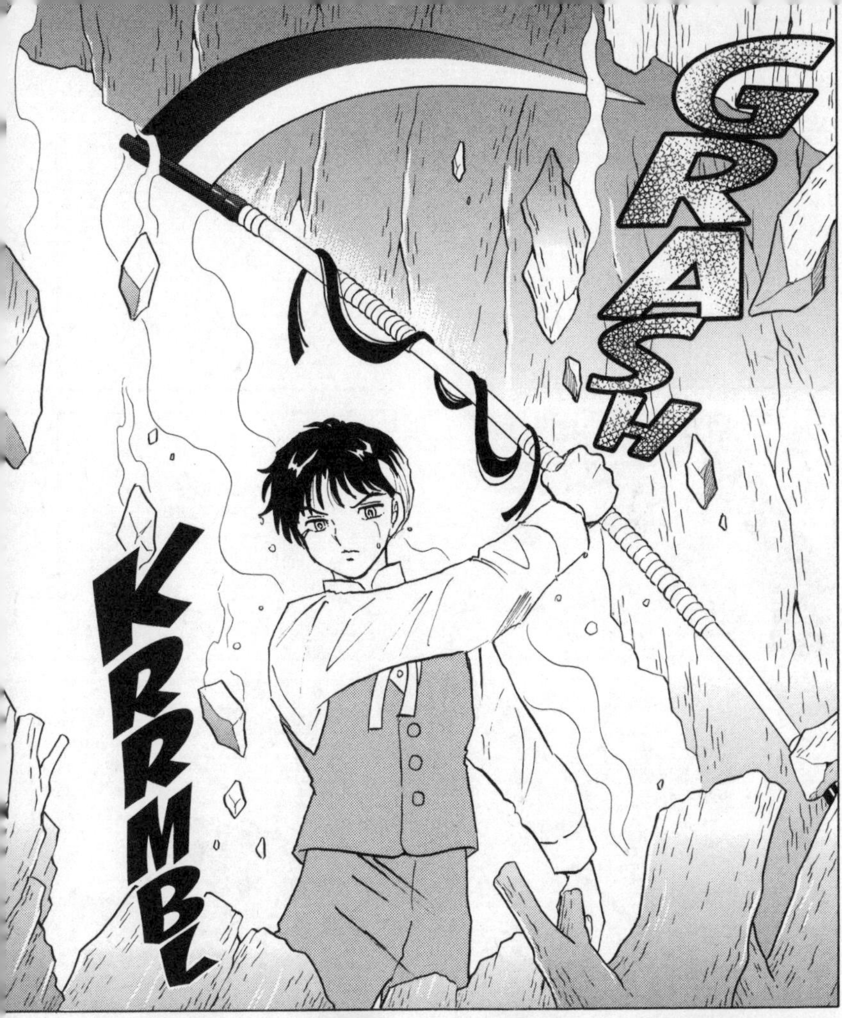
GRASH
KRRMBL

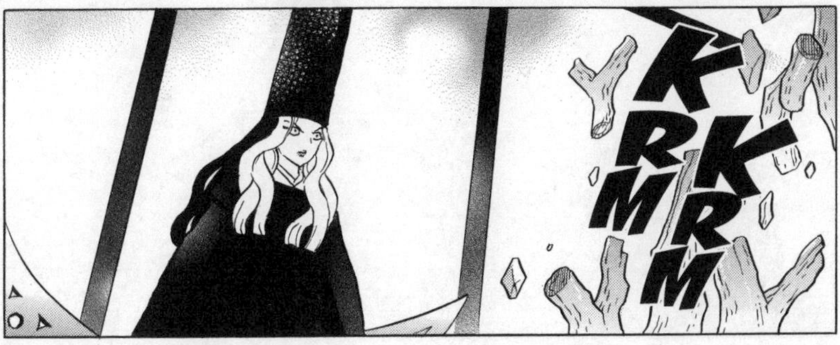
KRM
KRM

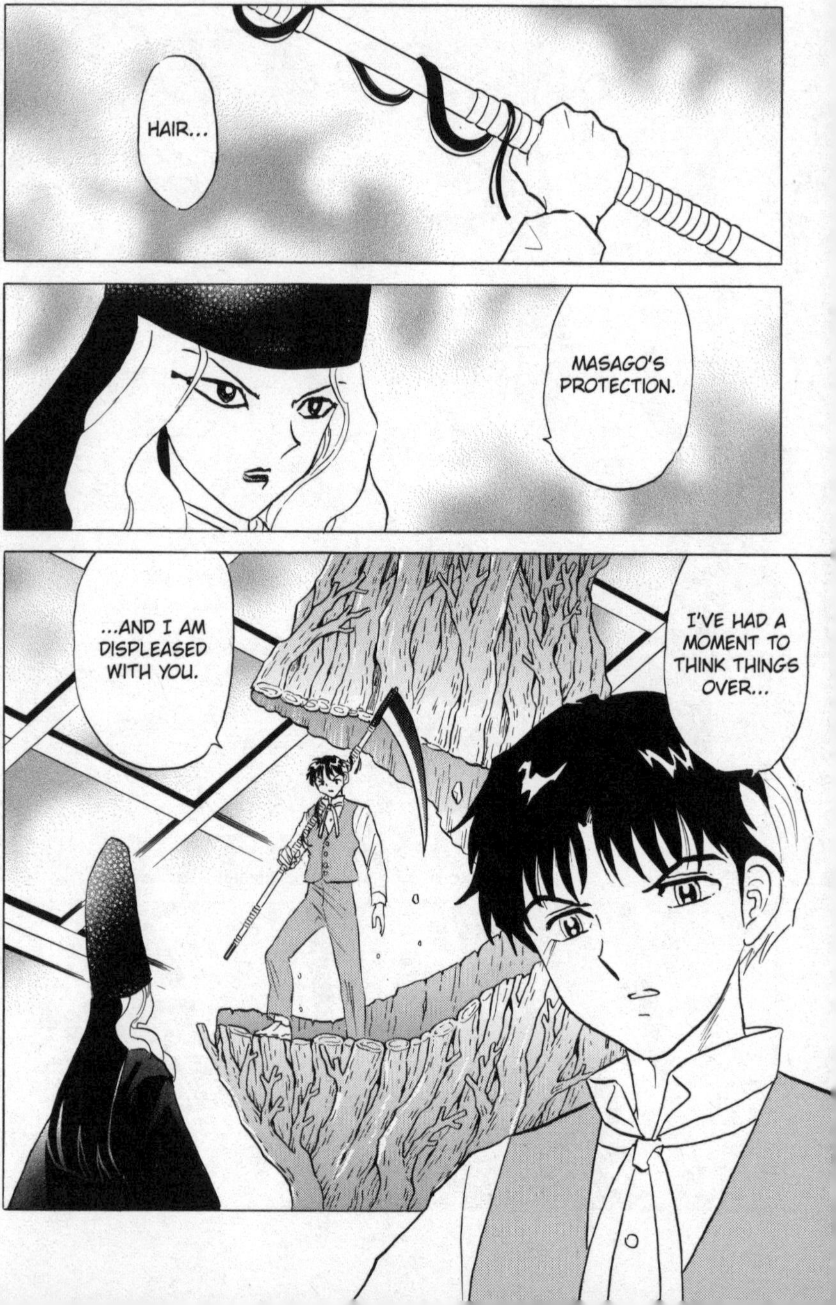
HAIR...
MASAGO'S PROTECTION.
I'VE HAD A MOMENT TO THINK THINGS OVER...
...AND I AM DISPLEASED WITH YOU.

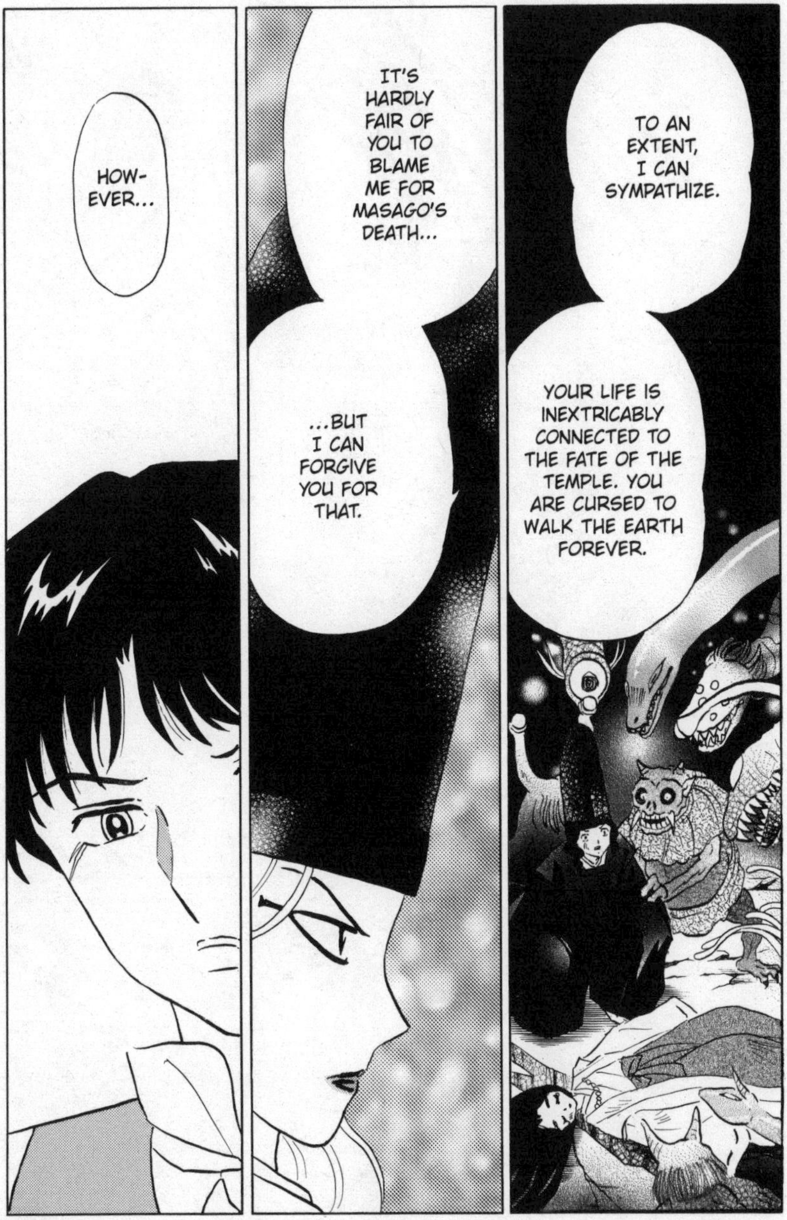
TO AN EXTENT, I CAN SYMPATHIZE.
YOUR LIFE IS INEXTRICABLY CONNECTED TO THE FATE OF THE TEMPLE. YOU ARE CURSED TO WALK THE EARTH FOREVER.
IT'S HARDLY FAIR OF YOU TO BLAME ME FOR MASAGO'S DEATH...
...BUT I CAN FORGIVE YOU FOR THAT.
HOW-EVER...

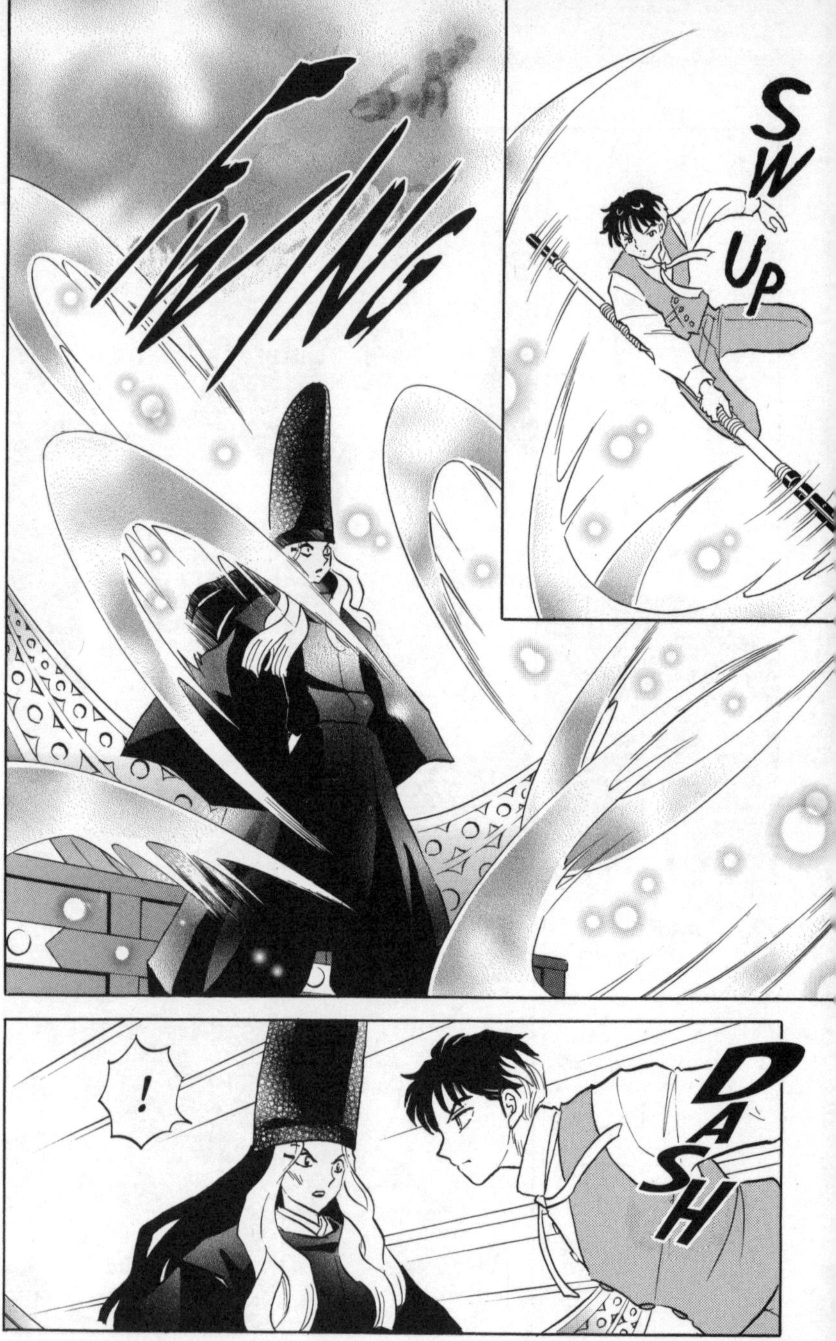
SWUP
FWING
DASH
!

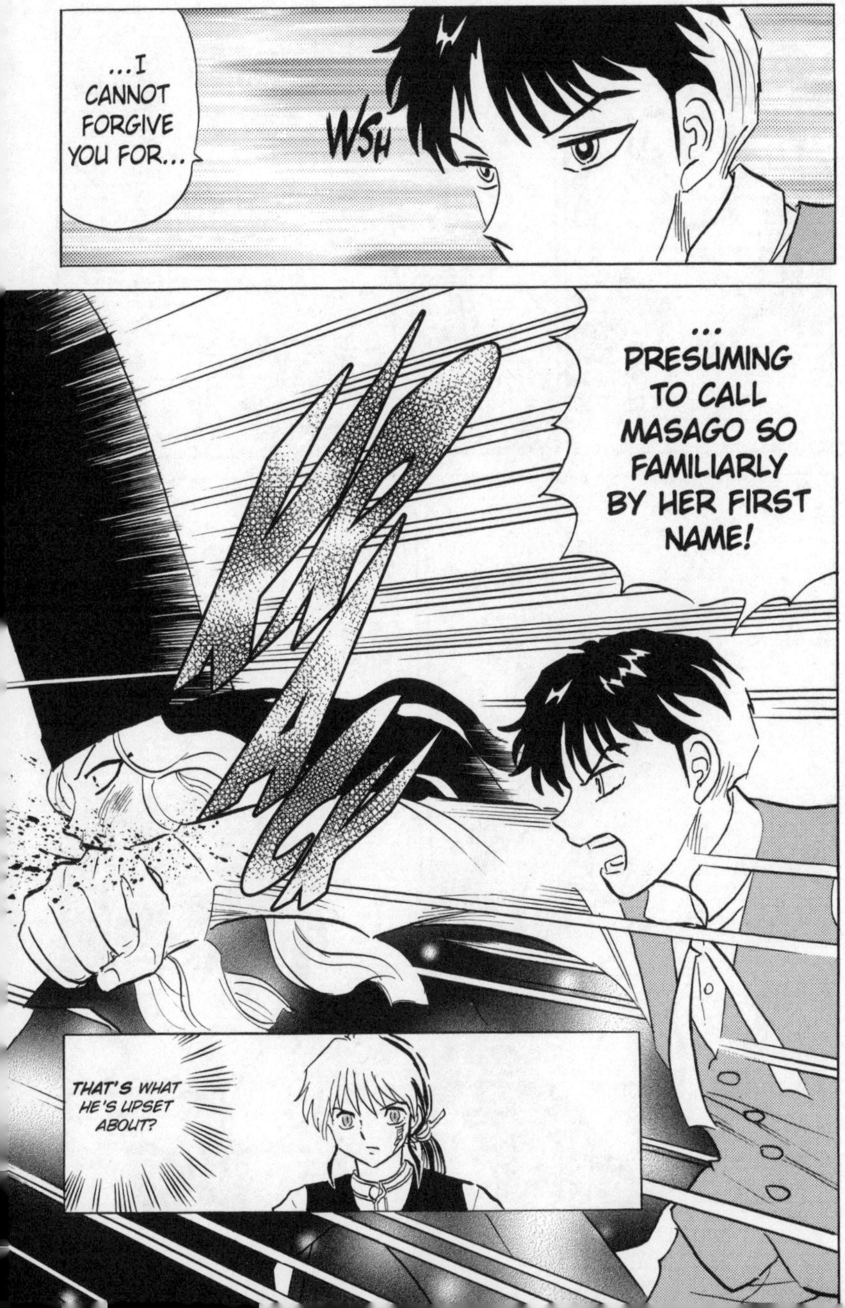
...I CANNOT FORGIVE YOU FOR...
WSH
... PRESUMING TO CALL MASAGO SO FAMILIARLY BY HER FIRST NAME!
THAT'S WHAT HE'S UPSET ABOUT?

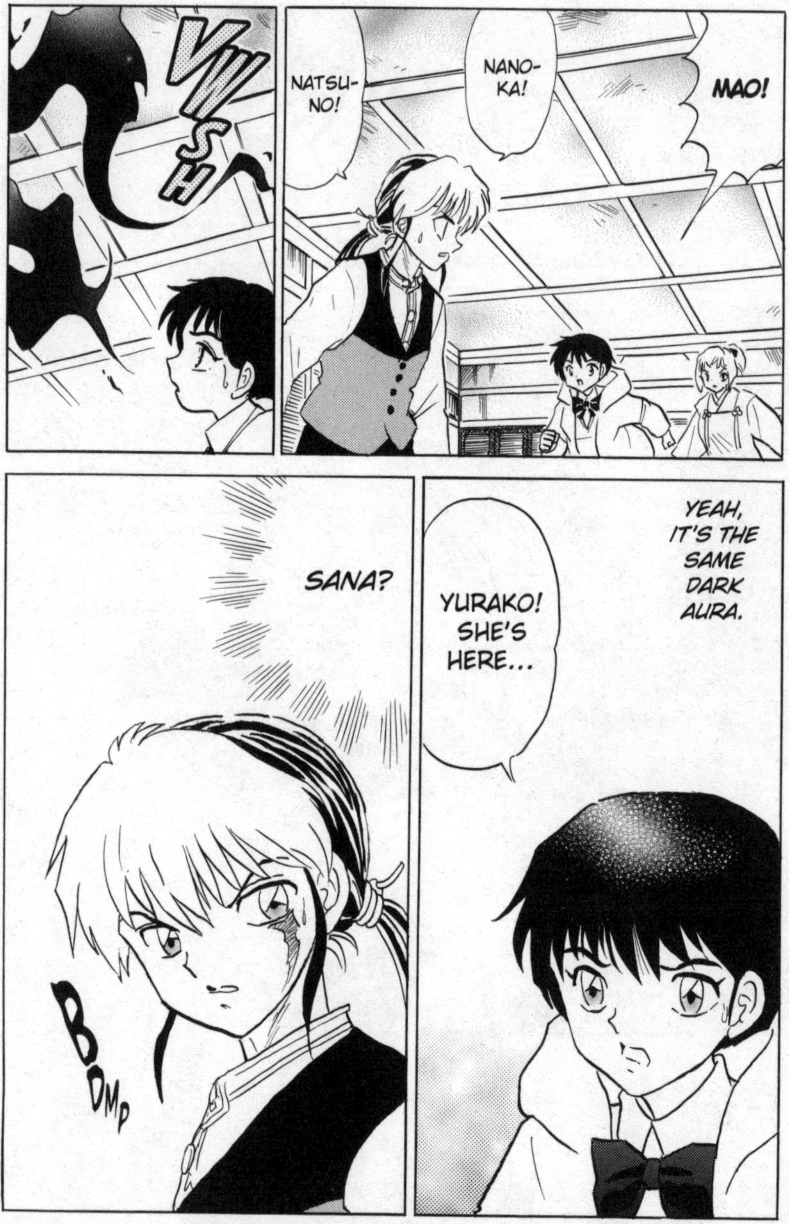
MAO!
NANO-KA!
NATSU-NO!
VWISH
YEAH, IT'S THE SAME DARK AURA.
YURAKO! SHE'S HERE...
SANA?
BOMP

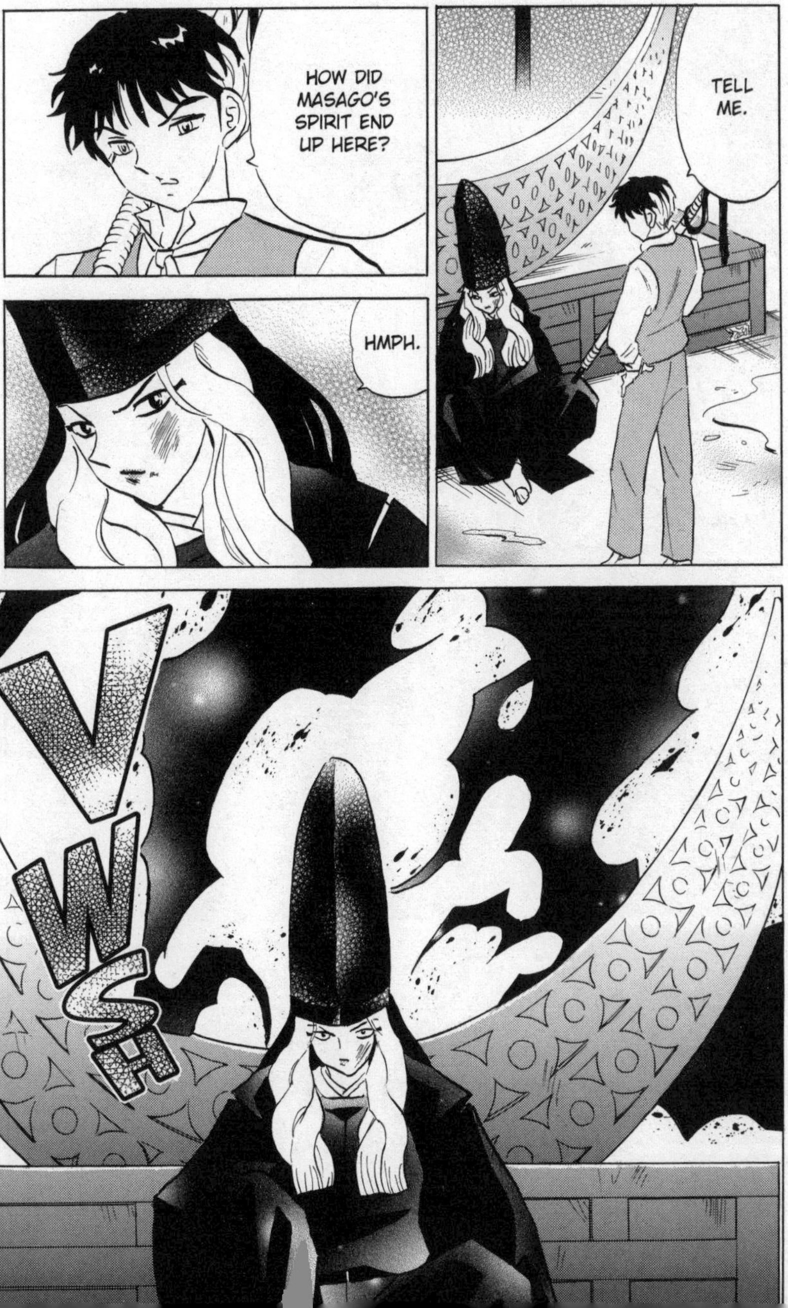
TELL ME.
HOW DID MASAGO'S SPIRIT END UP HERE?
HMPH.
VWSH

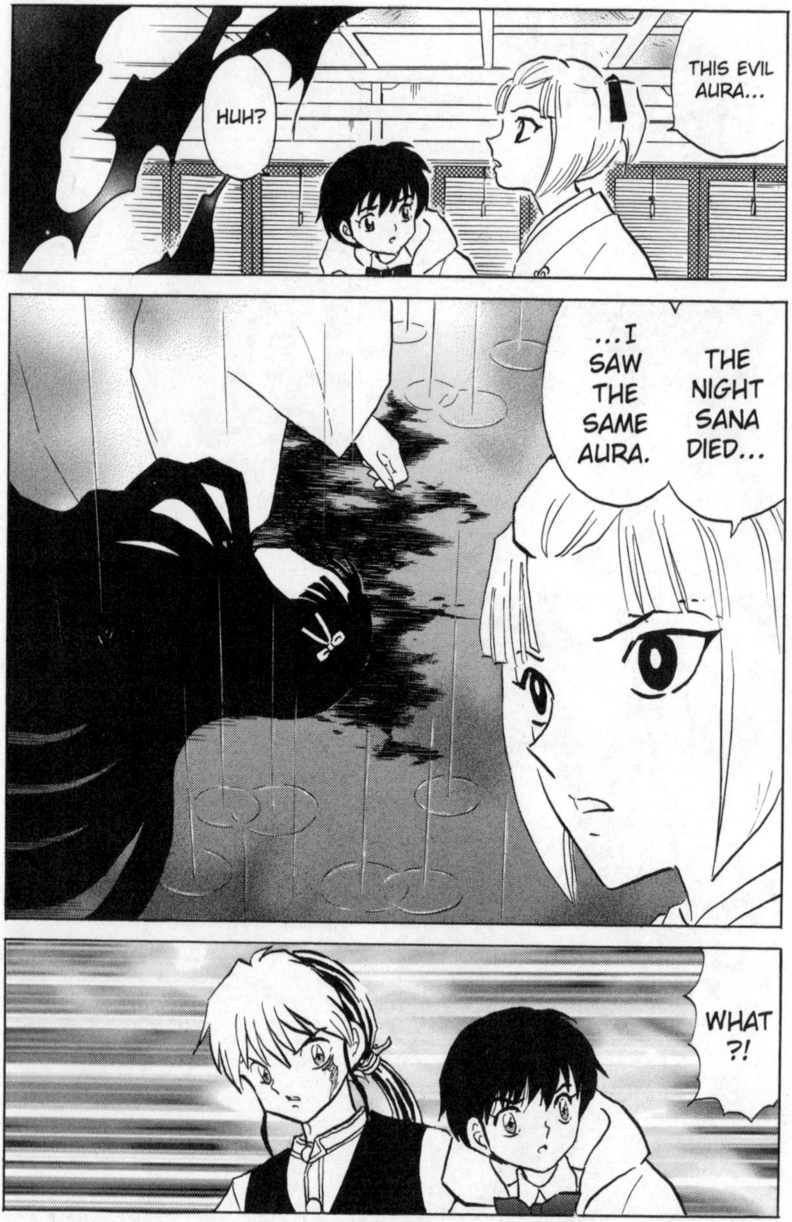

THIS EVIL AURA...
HUH?
THE NIGHT SANA DIED...
...I SAW THE SAME AURA.
WHAT?!

Chapter 10: The Undying Corpse

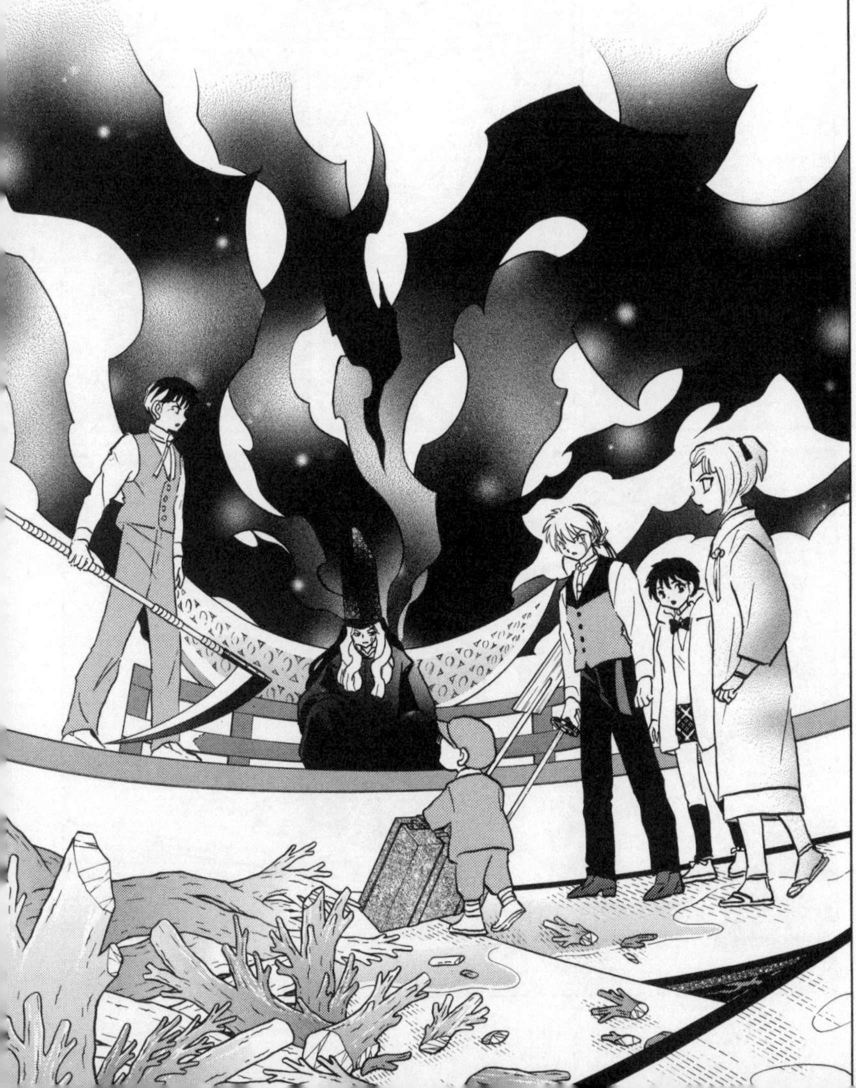

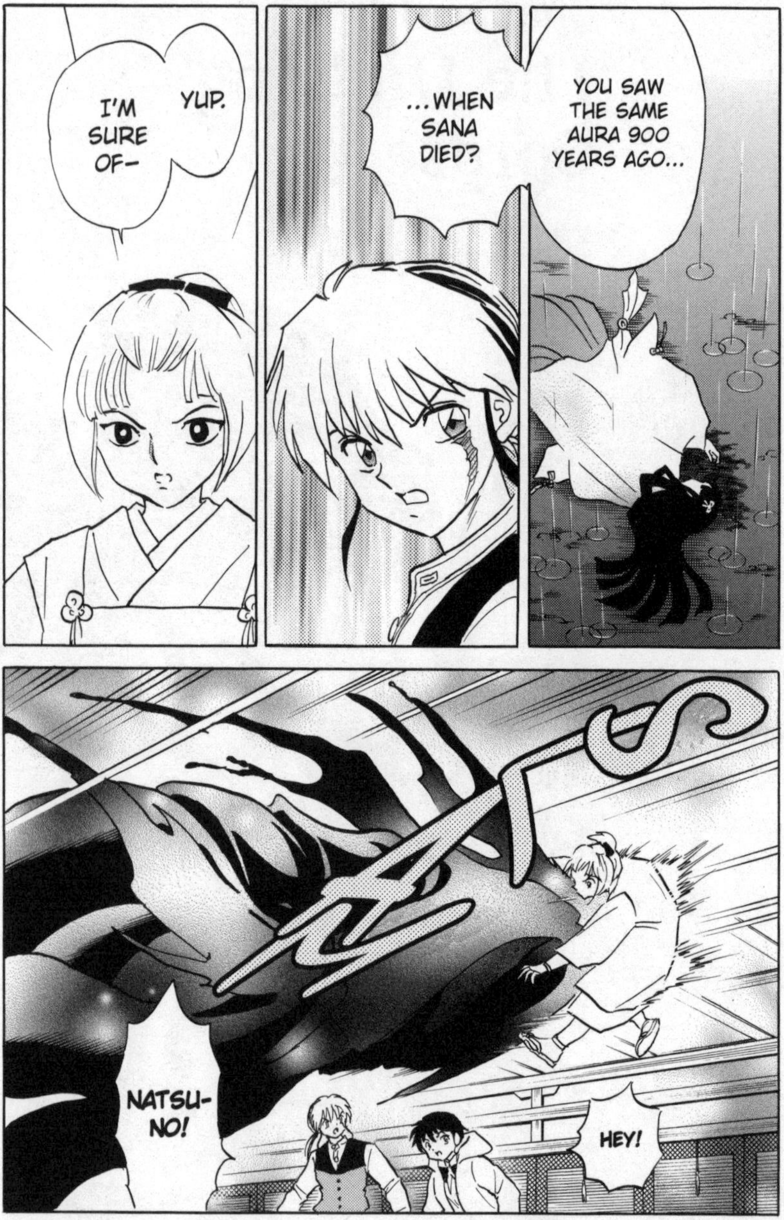
YOU SAW THE SAME AURA 900 YEARS AGO...
...WHEN SANA DIED?
YUP.
I'M SURE OF-
HEY!
NATSU-NO!

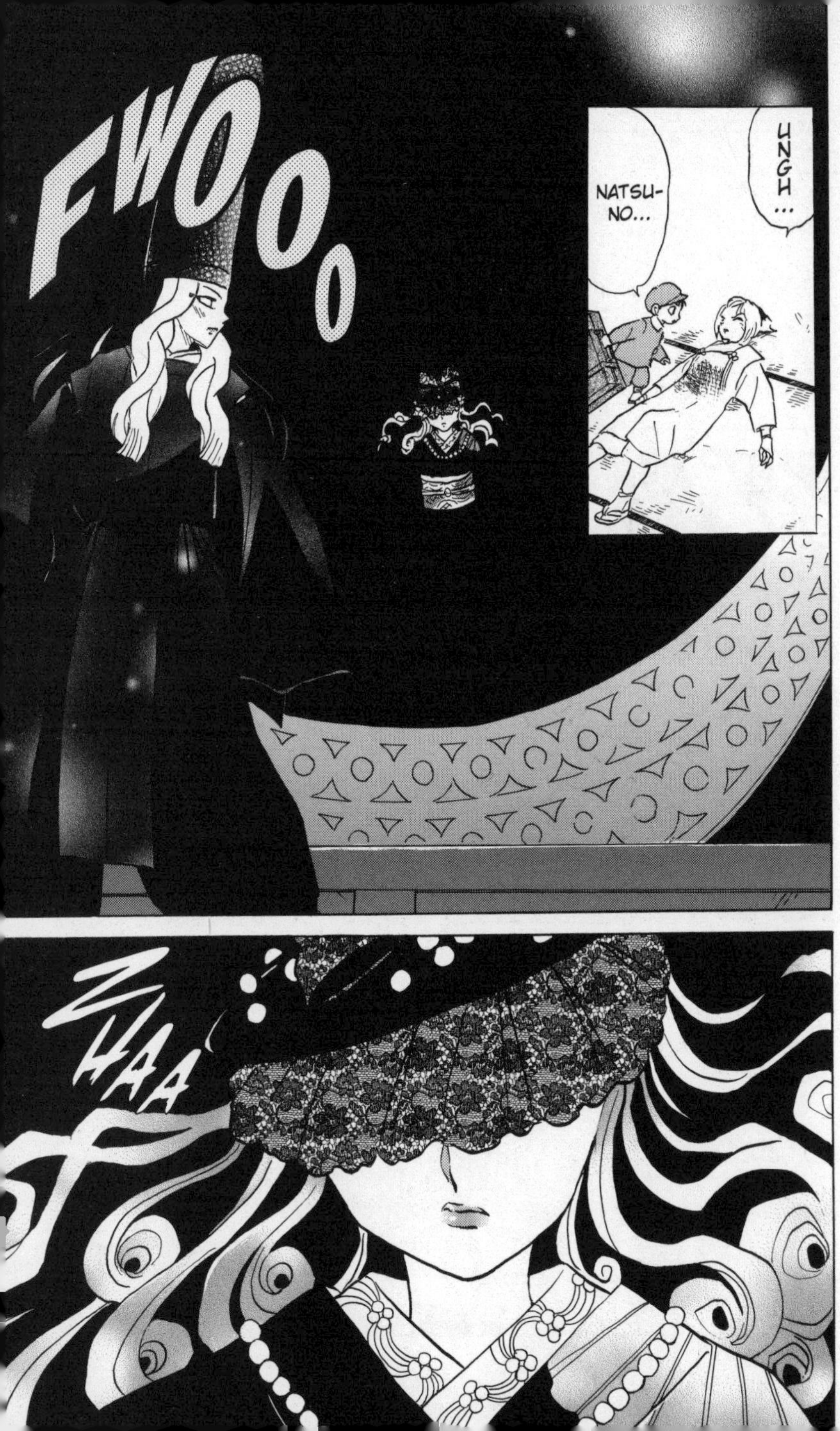
UNGH...
NATSU-NO...
FWOOOO
ZHAA

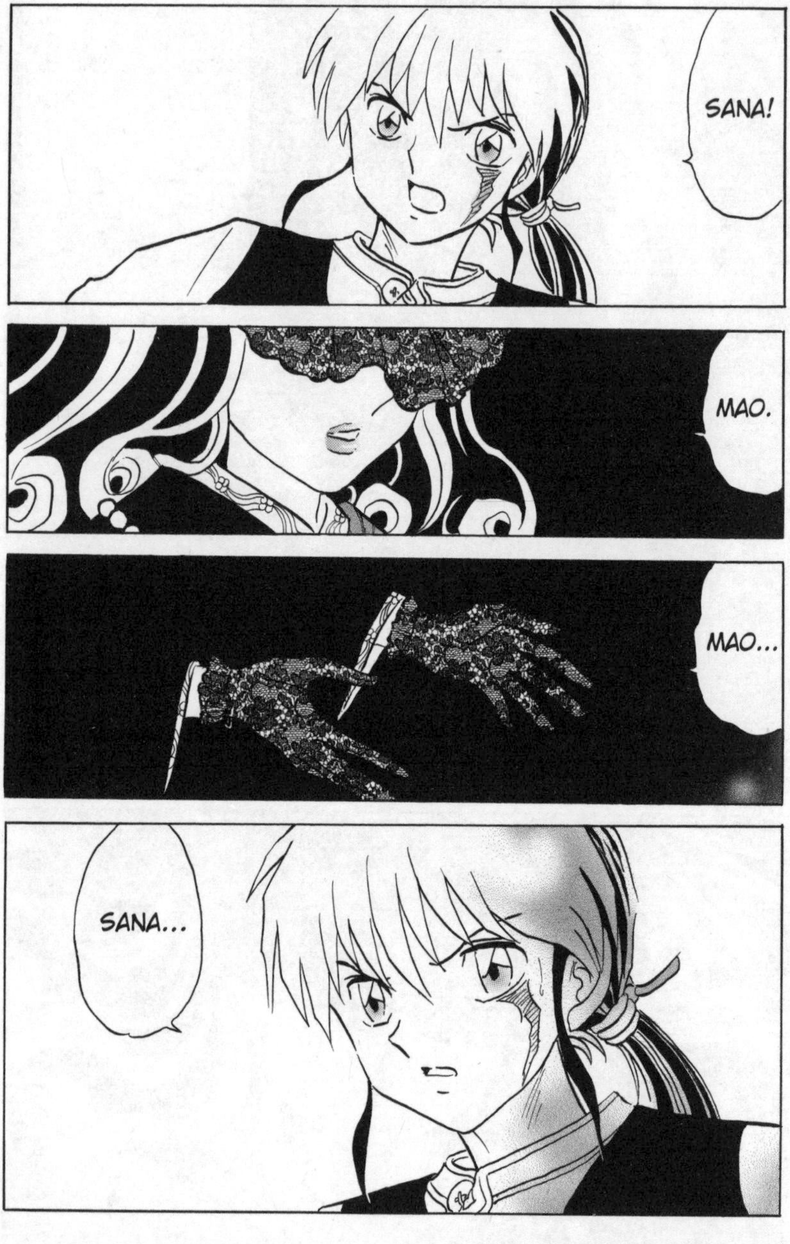
SANA!
MAO.
MAO...
SANA...

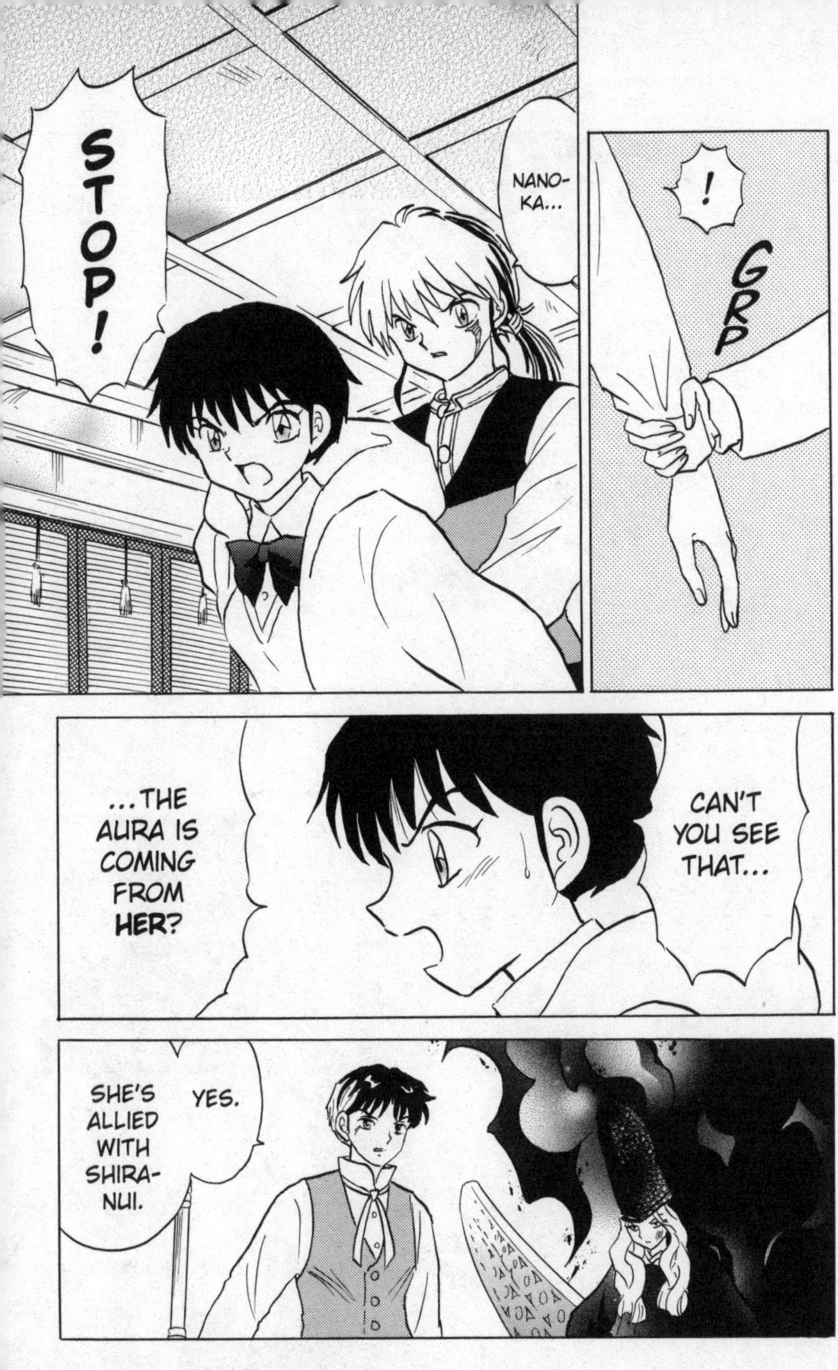
!
GRP
NANO-KA...
STOP!
CAN'T YOU SEE THAT...
...THE AURA IS COMING FROM HER?
YES.
SHE'S ALLIED WITH SHIRA-NUI.

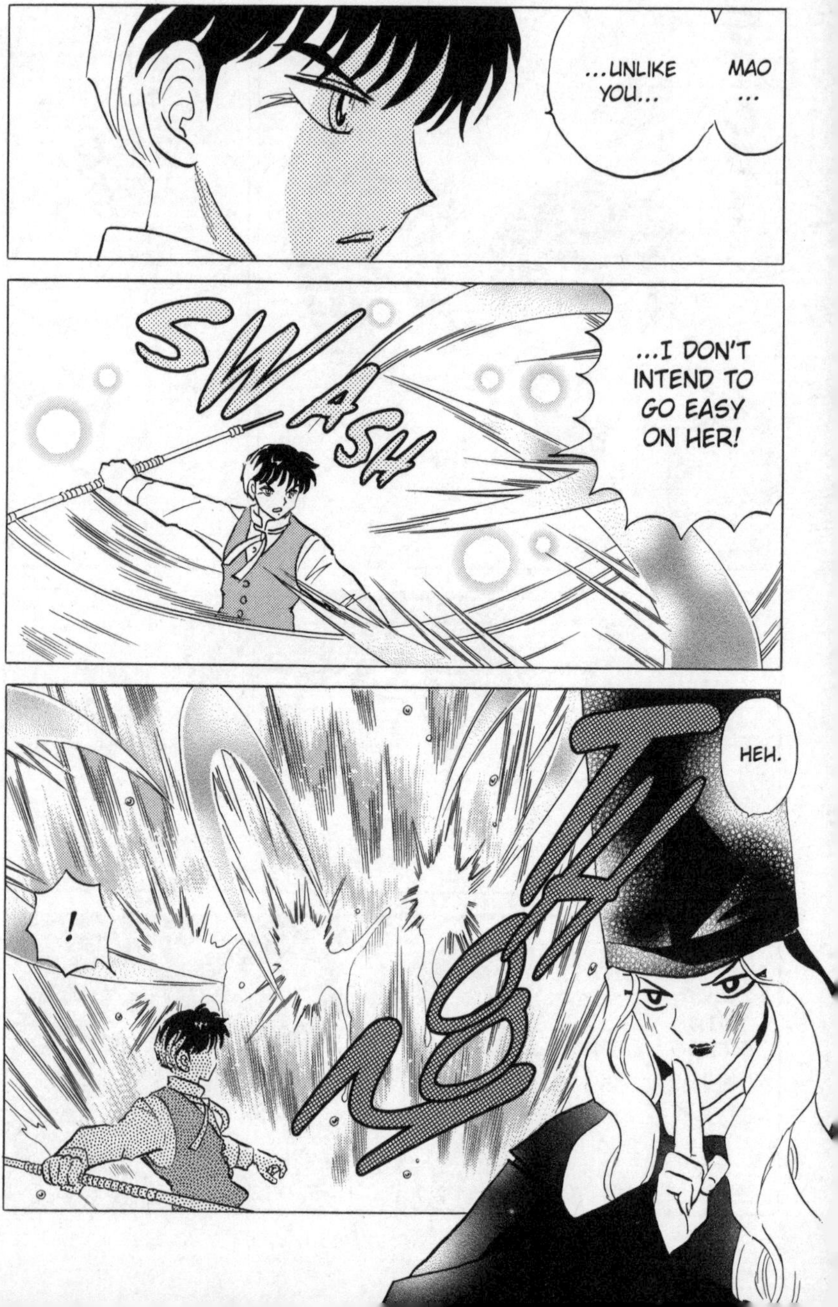
MAO ...
...UNLIKE YOU...
SWASH
...I DON'T INTEND TO GO EASY ON HER!
HEH.
THOOM
!

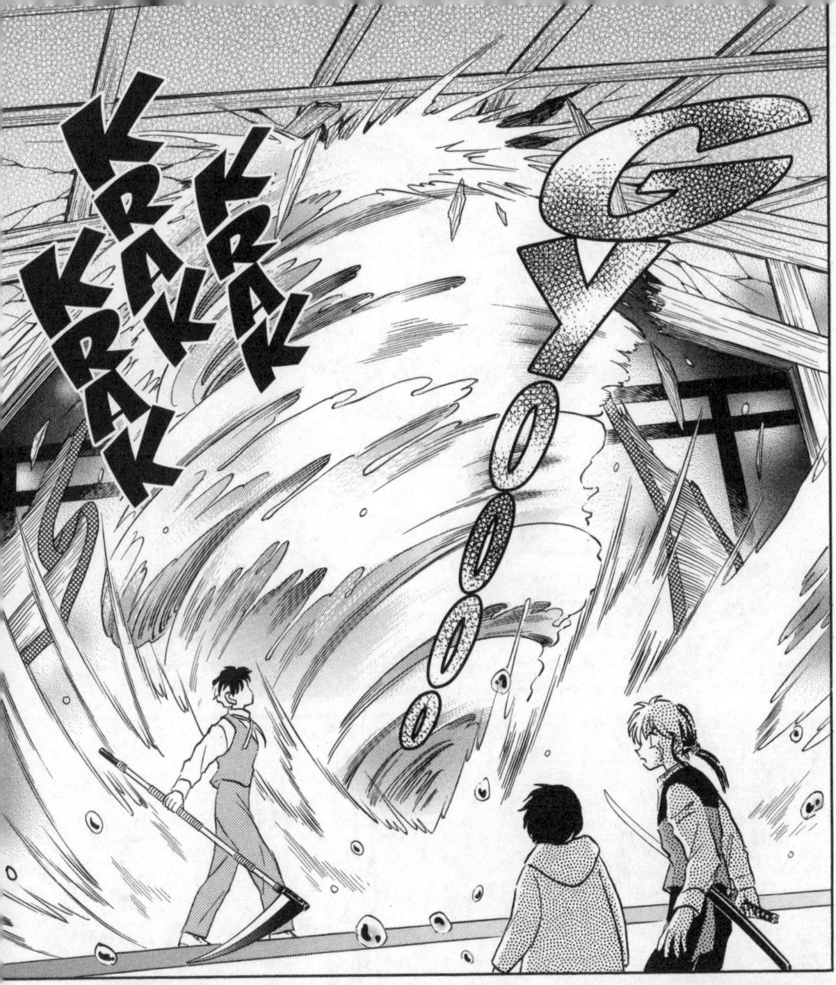
GYOOOOOOO
KRAKRAK
KRAKRAK

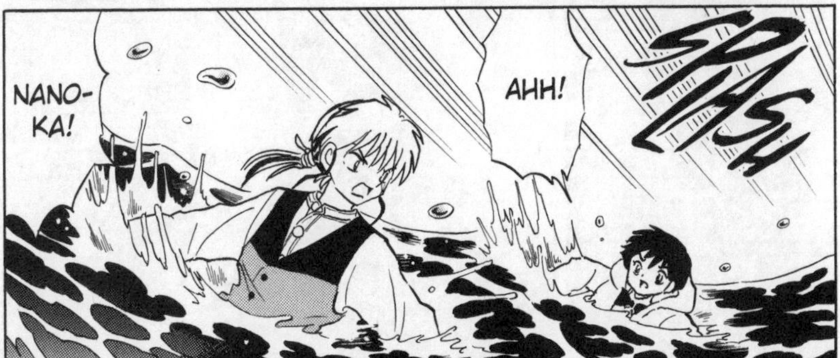
SPLASH
AHH!
NANO-
KA!

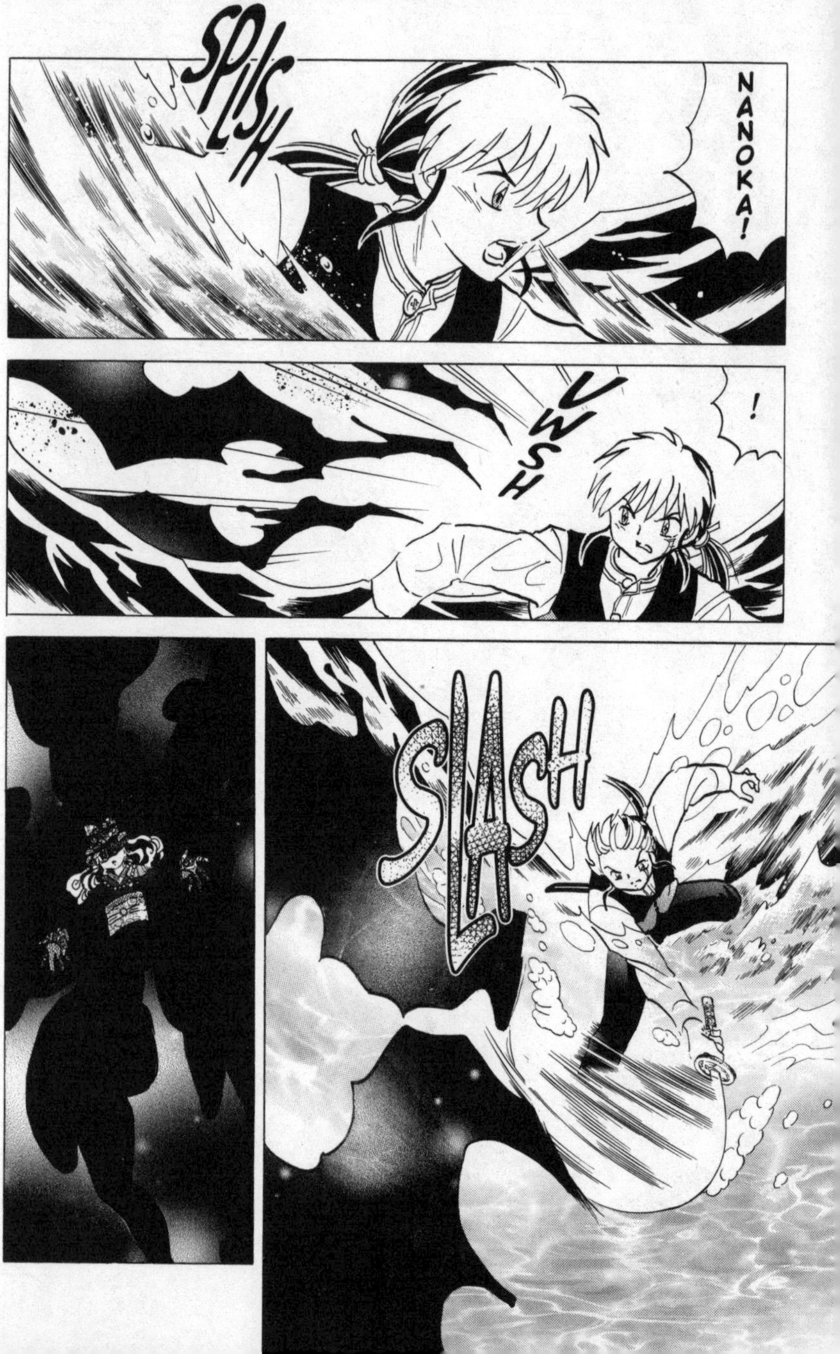
NANOKA!
SPLISH
!
VWSH
SLASH

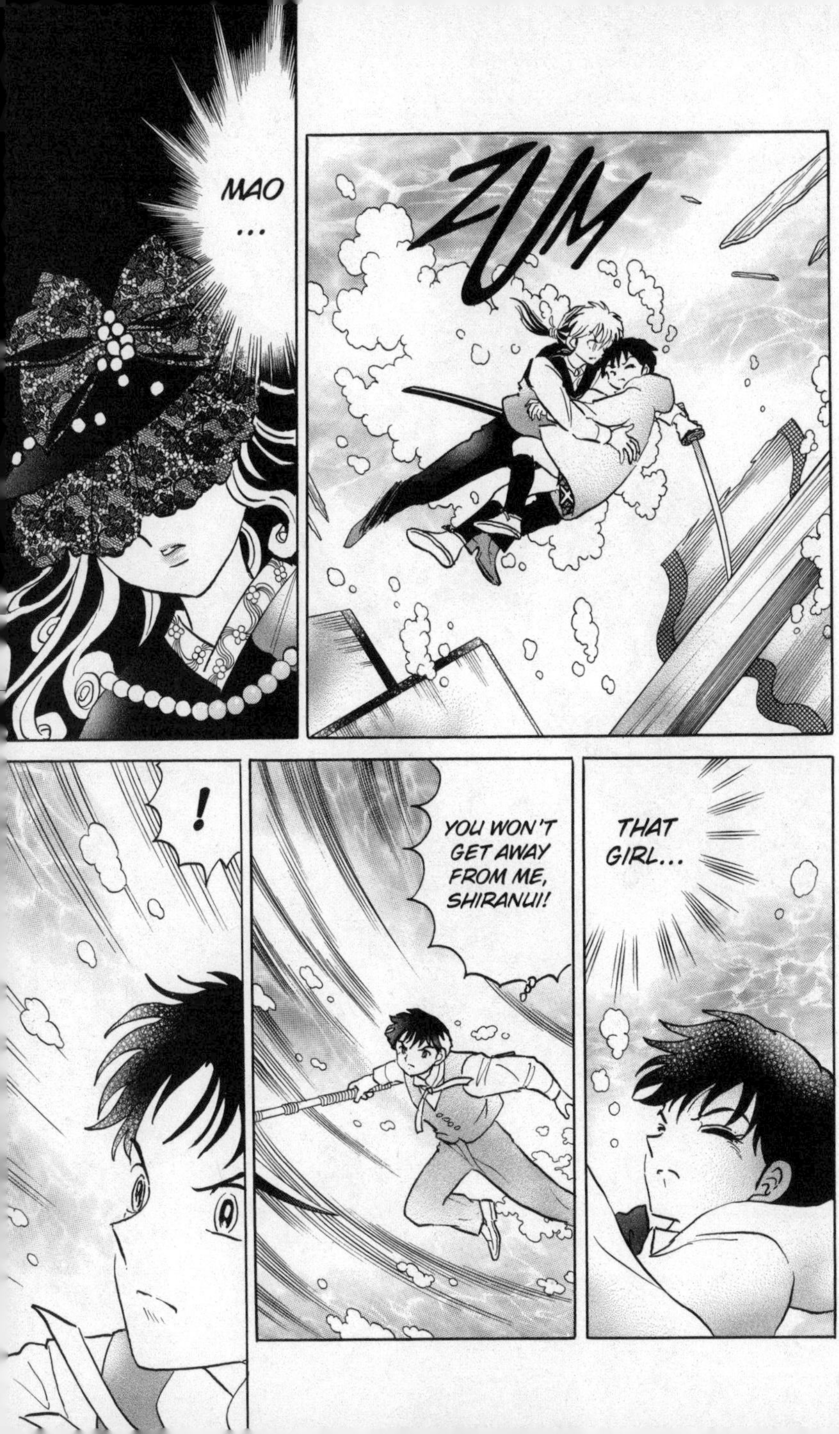
ZUM
MAO ...
THAT GIRL...
YOU WON'T GET AWAY FROM ME, SHIRANUI!
!

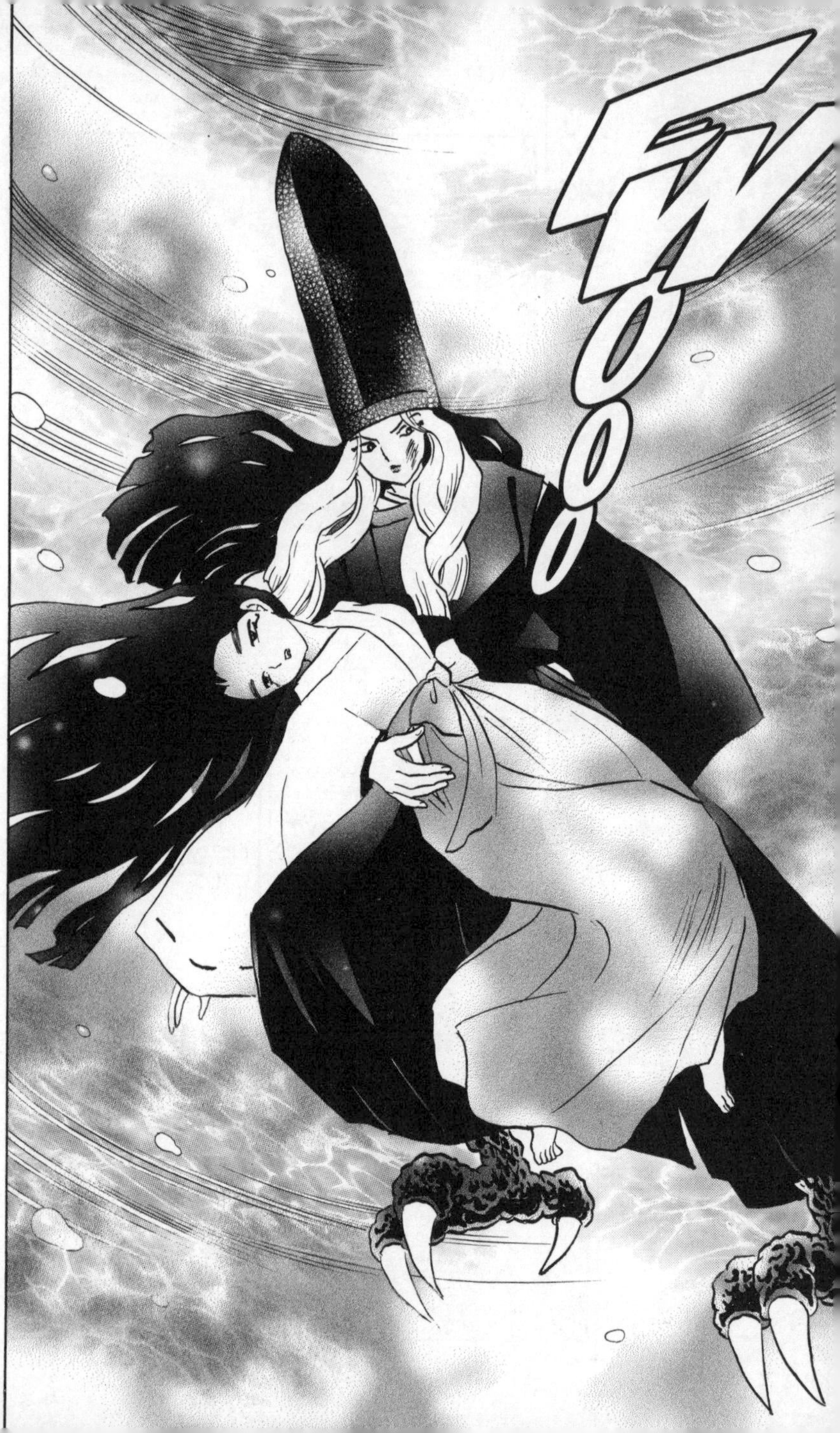
FWOOO

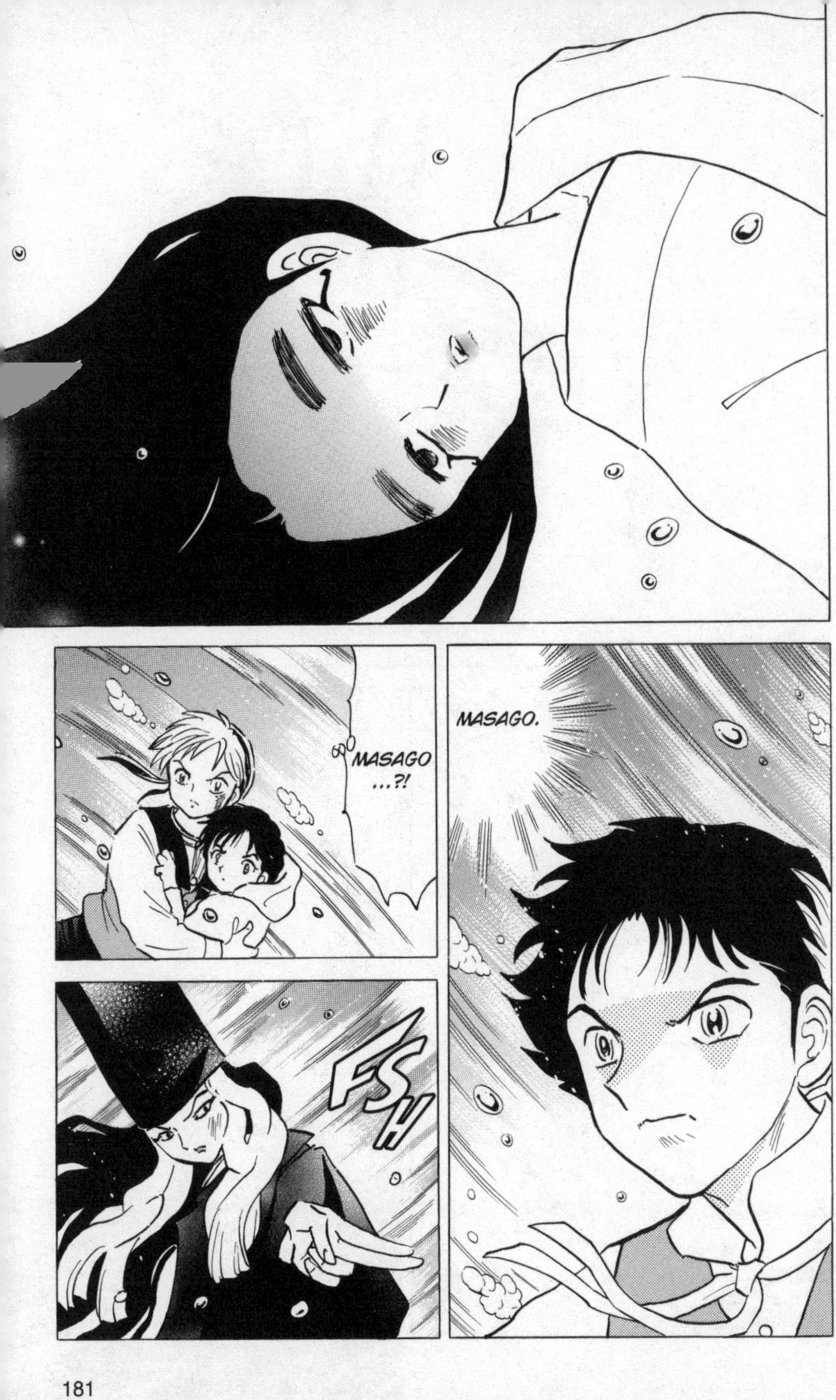
MASAGO.
MASAGO ...?!
FSH

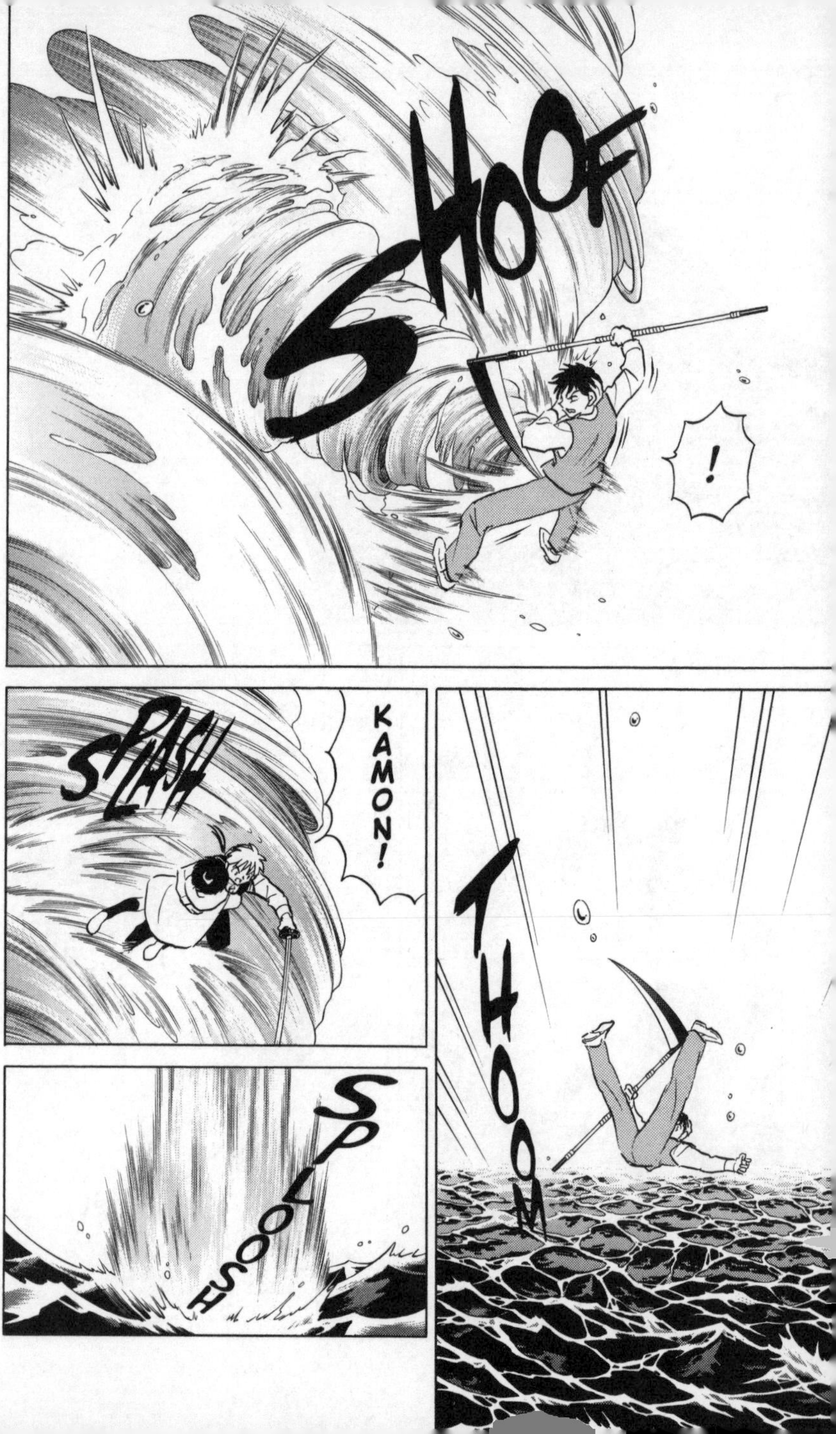
SHOOF
!
THOOM
KAMON!
SPLASH
SPLOOSH

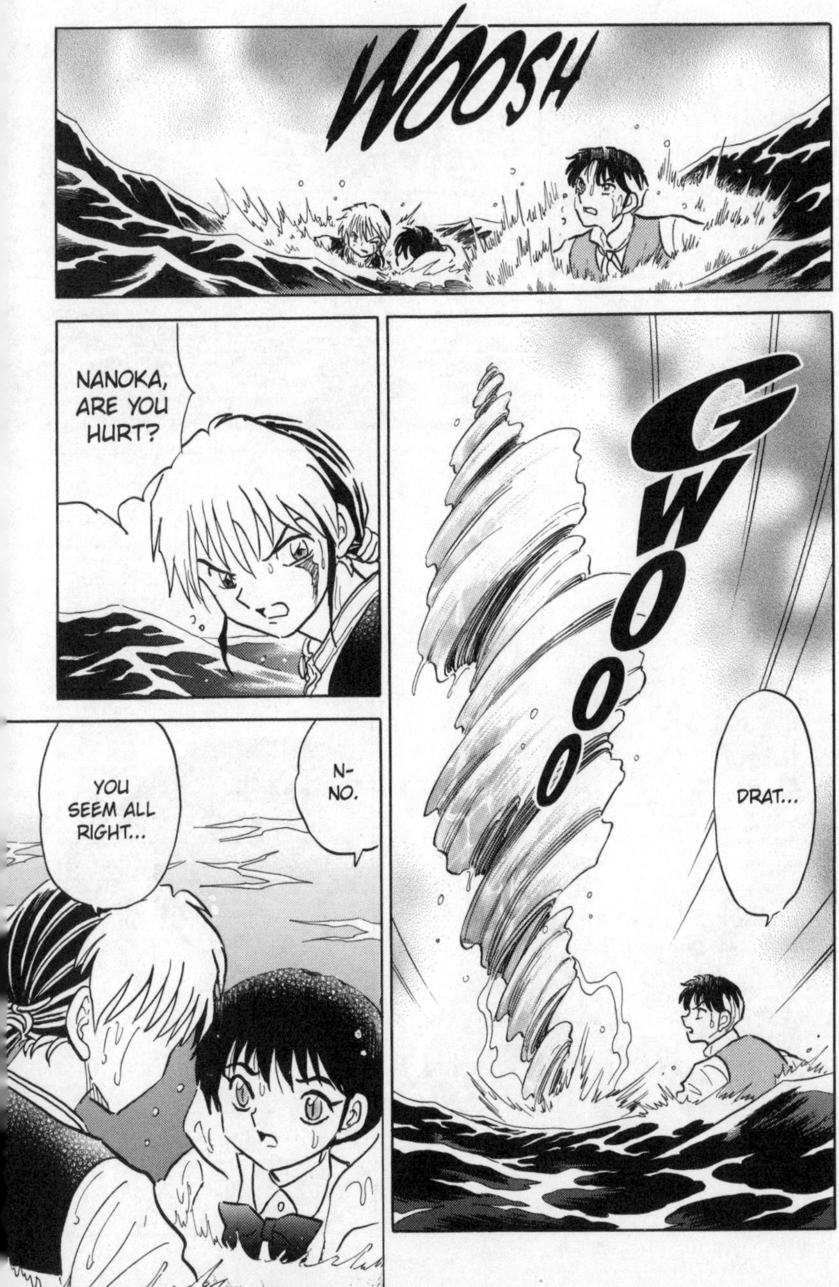
WOOSH
GWOOOO
DRAT...
NANOKA, ARE YOU HURT?
N- NO.
YOU SEEM ALL RIGHT...

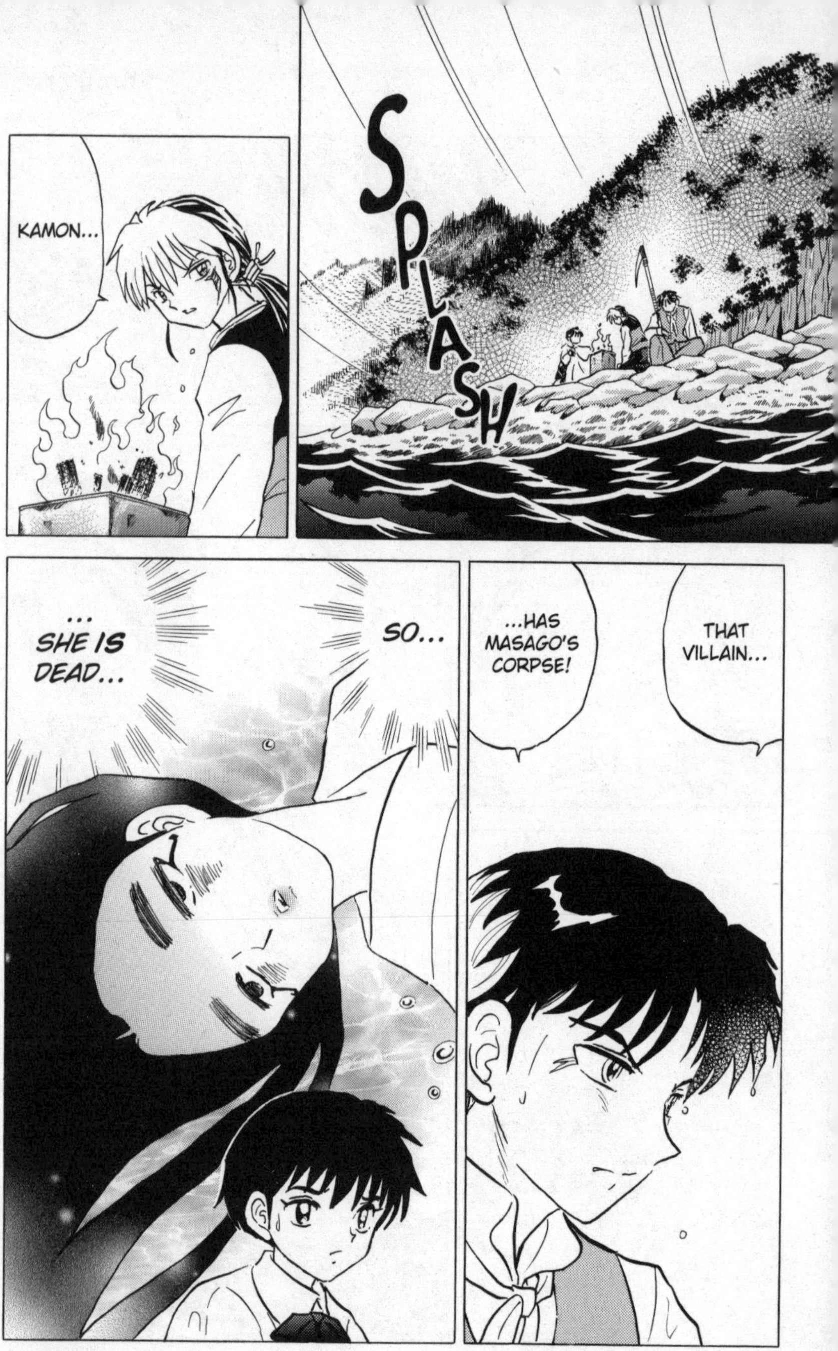
SPLASH
KAMON...
THAT VILLAIN...
...HAS MASAGO'S CORPSE!
SO...
...SHE IS DEAD...

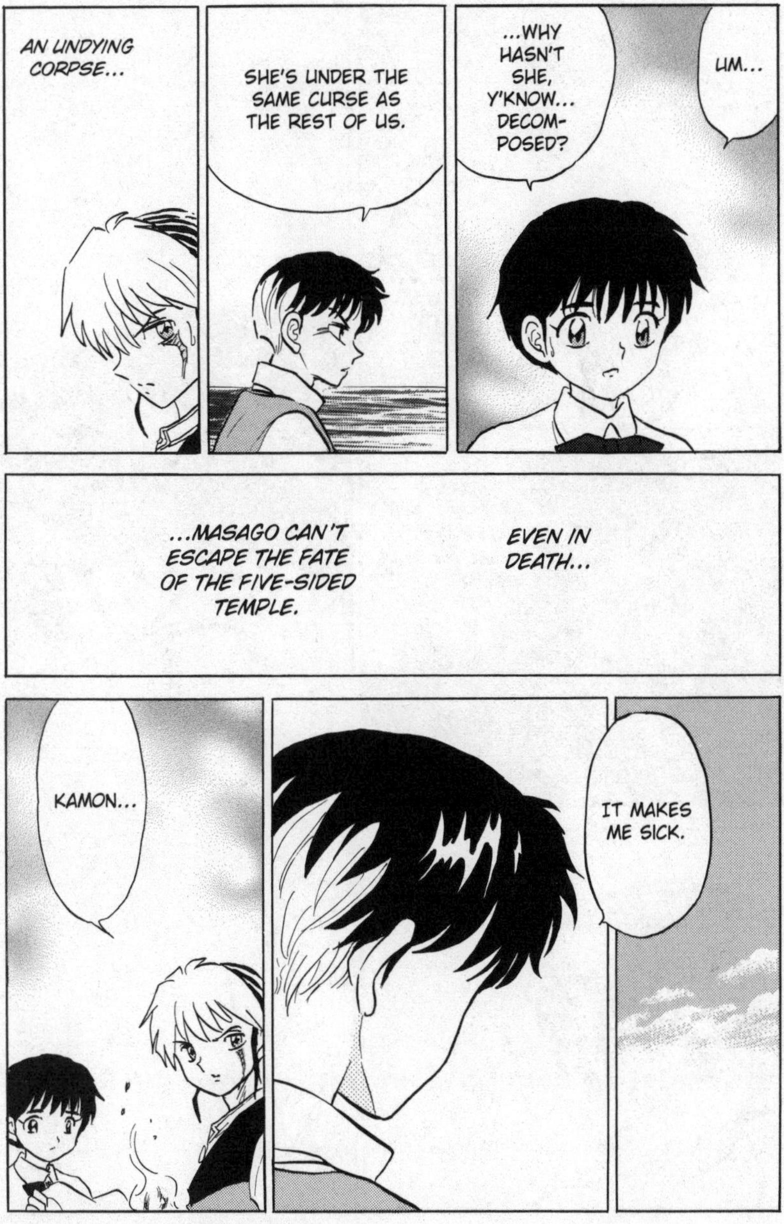
UM...
...WHY HASN'T SHE, Y'KNOW... DECOMPOSED?
SHE'S UNDER THE SAME CURSE AS THE REST OF US.
AN UNDYING CORPSE...
EVEN IN DEATH...
...MASAGO CAN'T ESCAPE THE FATE OF THE FIVE-SIDED TEMPLE.
IT MAKES ME SICK.
KAMON...

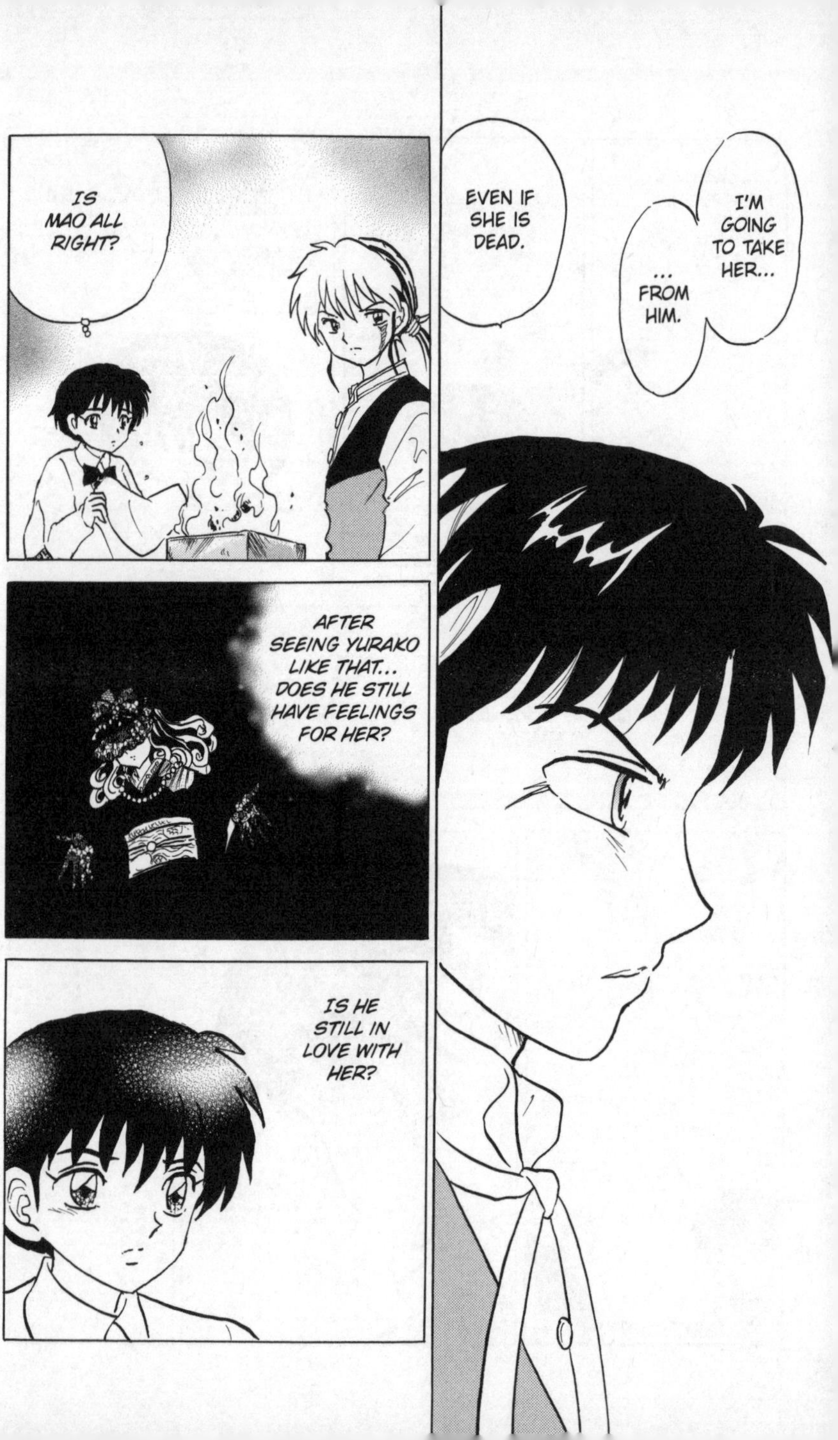
I'M GOING TO TAKE HER...
...FROM HIM.
EVEN IF SHE IS DEAD.
IS MAO ALL RIGHT?
AFTER SEEING YURAKO LIKE THAT... DOES HE STILL HAVE FEELINGS FOR HER?
IS HE STILL IN LOVE WITH HER?

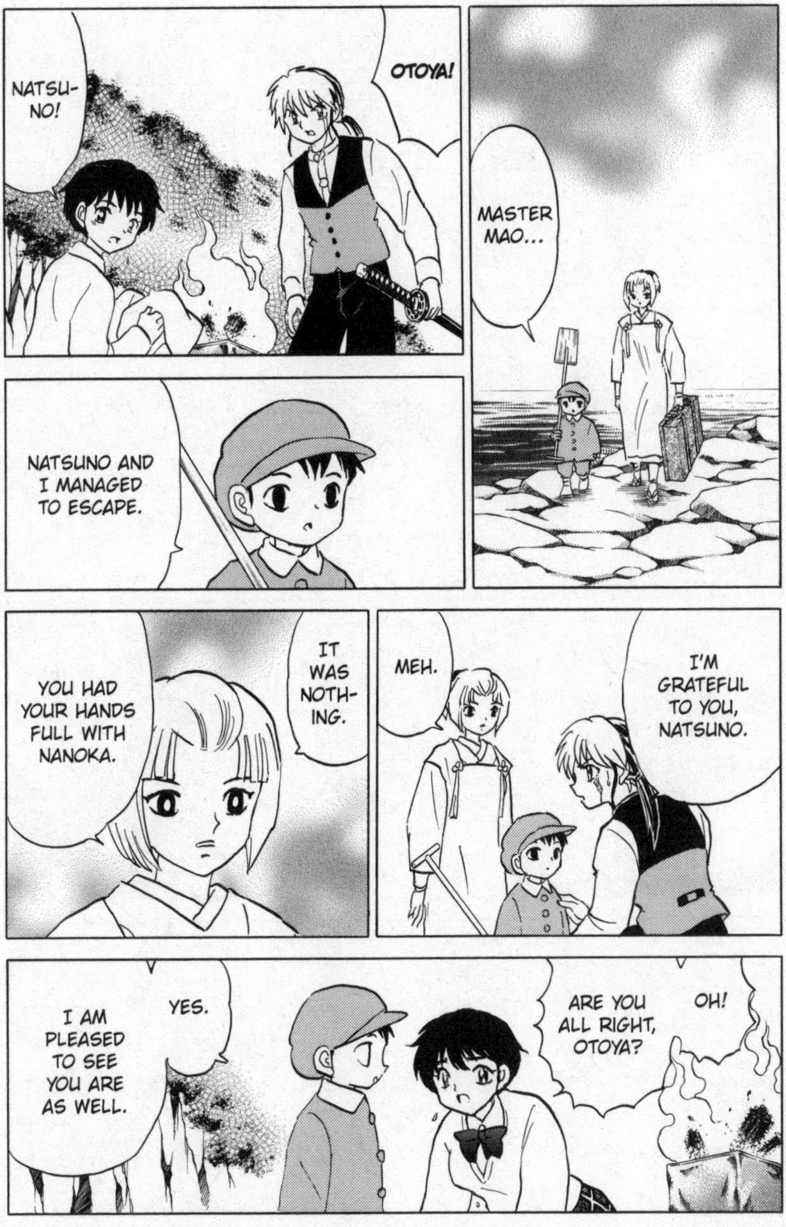
MASTER MAO...
OTOYA!
NATSU-NO!
NATSUNO AND I MANAGED TO ESCAPE.
I'M GRATEFUL TO YOU, NATSUNO.
MEH.
IT WAS NOTH-ING.
YOU HAD YOUR HANDS FULL WITH NANOKA.
OH!
ARE YOU ALL RIGHT, OTOYA?
YES.
I AM PLEASED TO SEE YOU ARE AS WELL.

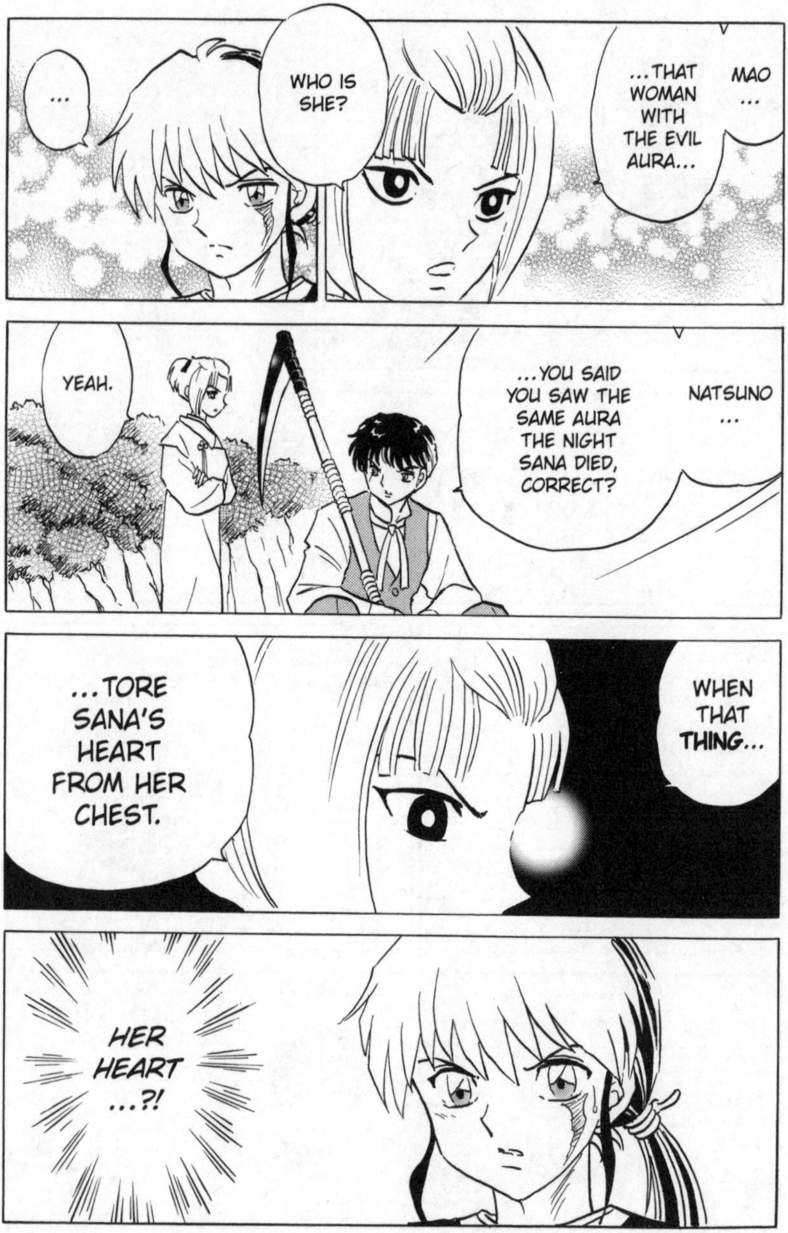
MAO ...
...THAT WOMAN WITH THE EVIL AURA...
WHO IS SHE?
...
NATSUNO ...
...YOU SAID YOU SAW THE SAME AURA THE NIGHT SANA DIED, CORRECT?
YEAH.
WHEN THAT THING...
...TORE SANA'S HEART FROM HER CHEST.
HER HEART ...?!

TO BE CONTINUED...

MAO

Rumiko Takahashi

The spotlight on Rumiko Takahashi's career began in 1978 when she won an honorable mention in Shogakukan's prestigious New Comic Artist Contest for *Those Selfish Aliens*. Later that same year, her boy-meets-alien comedy series, *Urusei Yatsura*, was serialized in *Weekly Shonen Sunday*. This phenomenally successful manga series was adapted into anime format and spawned a TV series and half a dozen theatrical-release movies, all incredibly popular in their own right. Takahashi followed up the success of her debut series with one blockbuster hit after another—*Maison Ikkoku* ran from 1980 to 1987, *Ranma ½* from 1987 to 1996, and *Inuyasha* from 1996 to 2008. Other notable works include *Mermaid Saga*, *Rumic Theater*, and *One-Pound Gospel*.

Takahashi was inducted into the Will Eisner Comic Awards Hall of Fame in 2018. She won the prestigious Shogakukan Manga Award twice in her career, once for *Urusei Yatsura* in 1981 and the second time for *Inuyasha* in 2002. A majority of the Takahashi canon has been adapted into other media such as anime, live-action TV series, and film. Takahashi's manga, as well as the other formats her work has been adapted into, have continued to delight generations of fans around the world. Distinguished by her wonderfully endearing characters, Takahashi's work adeptly incorporates a wide variety of elements such as comedy, romance, fantasy, and martial arts. While her series are difficult to pin down into one simple genre, the signature style she has created has come to be known as the "Rumic World." Rumiko Takahashi is an artist who truly represents the very best from the world of manga.

MAO
VOLUME 7
Shonen Sunday Edition

STORY AND ART BY
RUMIKO TAKAHASHI

MAO Vol. 7
by Rumiko TAKAHASHI

Original Japanese edition published by SHOGAKUKAN.
English translation rights in the United States of America, Canada, the United Kingdom, Ireland, Australia, and New Zealand arranged with SHOGAKUKAN.

Original Cover Design: Chie SATO + Bay Bridge Studio

Translation/Junko Goda
English Adaptation/Shaenon K. Garrity
Touch-Up Art & Lettering/James Gaubatz
Cover & Interior Design/Yukiko Whitley
Editor/Annette Roman

Printed in the U.S.A.

Published by VIZ Media, LLC
P.O. Box 77010
San Francisco, CA 94107

10 9 8 7 6 5 4 3 2 1
First printing, September 2022

ratings.viz.com RATED T+ OLDER TEEN

PARENTAL ADVISORY
MAO is rated T+ for Older Teen and is recommended for ages 16 and up. This volume contains fantasy violence.

VIZ MEDIA
viz.com

SHONEN SUNDAY
shonensunday.com

Coming in Volume 8...

As Mao and company begin to uncover Yurako's true identity, another mystery lands on their doorstep. Who or what is causing members of the Kagami family to commit shocking acts of violence? Unfortunately, our friends soon discover the truth in the old saying "No good deed goes unpunished." Then, when a puppet master gains control of Mao, no one is safe. Plus, Mao and Nanoka go on...a date?!

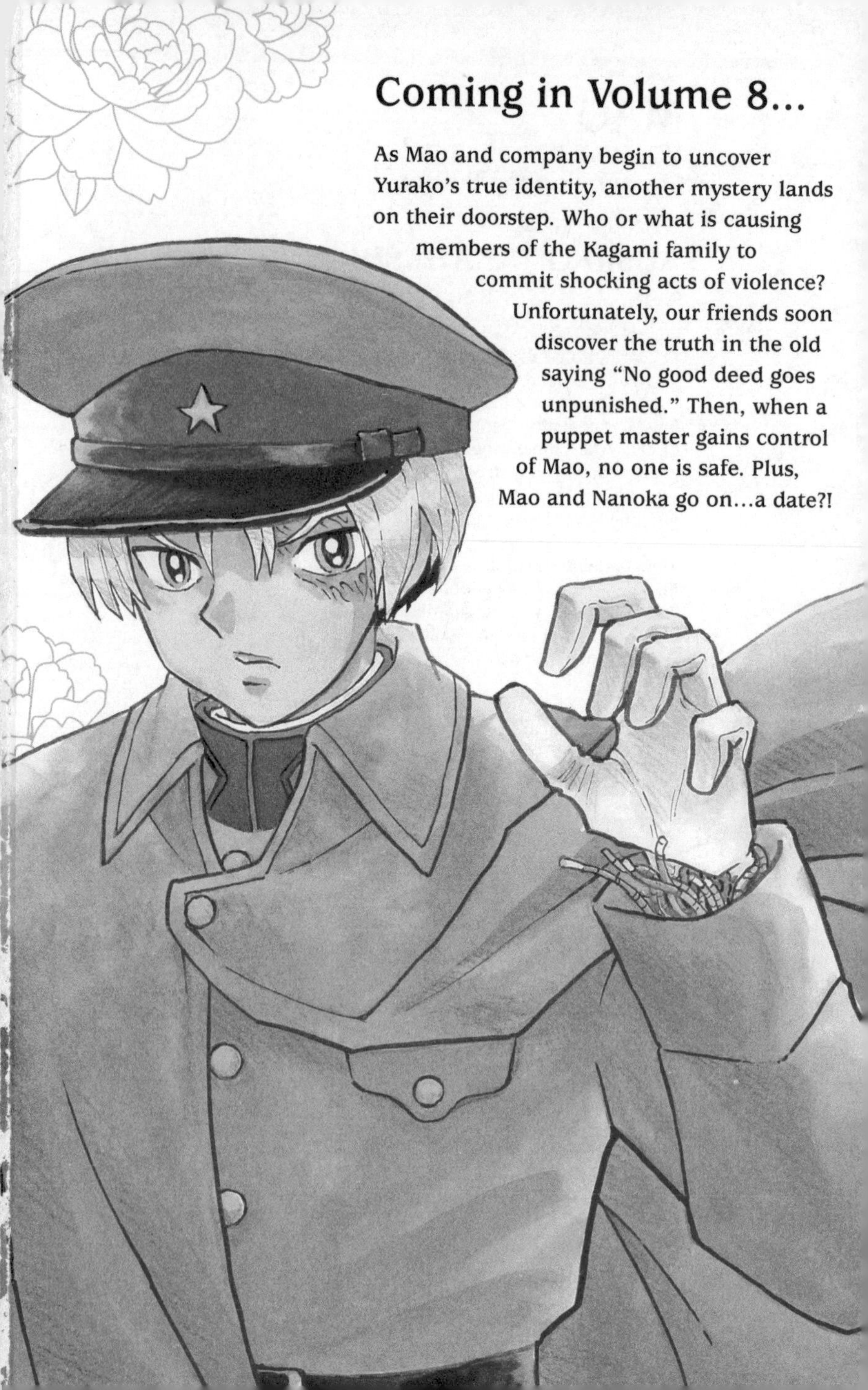